D1357017

Modern Architecture and the Lifeworld

Essays in Honor of Kenneth Frampton

ІКОРАБЛЬ НА МЕЛИ

Modern Architecture and the Lifeworld

Essays in Honor of Kenneth Frampton

Edited by Karla Cavarra Britton and Robert McCarter

Frontispiece: Kenneth Frampton, *The Unfinished Modern Project in Homage to it and Habermas*, collage, 1991.
(For identification of images within the collage see p. 315.)

First published in the United Kingdom in 2020
by Thames & Hudson Ltd, 181A High Holborn,
London WC1V 7QX

First published in the United States of America in 2020
by Thames & Hudson Inc., 500 Fifth Avenue, New York,
New York 10110

Designed by gradedesign.com

British Library Cataloguing-in-Publication Data
A catalogue record for this book is available from
the British Library

Library of Congress Control Number 2020933622

ISBN 978-0-500-34363-0

Printed and bound in Malaysia

Contents

Introduction
Karla Cavarra Britton and Robert McCarter 8

PART I

The Social, Cultural, and Ecological Nature of Architecture 18

Kenneth Frampton's Idea of the "Critical"
Mary McLeod 20

World Architecture and Critical Practice
Wang Shu 43

Site-Specificity, Skilled Labor, and Culture: Architectural Principles in the Age of Climate Change
Wilfried Wang 53

That Pesky Paradisiacal Instinct ...
Harry Francis Mallgrave 65

Paradoxes of Progress
Joan Ockman 80

Engaging the Lifeworld in Architectural Design: Phenomenology and Hermeneutics
Alberto Pérez-Gómez 94

PART II

Histories and Pedagogies of Architecture 103

Kenneth Frampton's Elusive Constructivism
Jean-Louis Cohen 106

Editing History: The Bauhaus at MoMA, 1938
Barry Bergdoll 120

Frampton and Japan
Ken Tadashi Oshima 137

Dialectics of Utopia/Utopian Dialectics
Anthony Vidler 153

Kenneth Frampton: Apropos Housing and Cities
Richard Plunz 162

Proportion and Harmony: Mathematics and Music in Architecture
Juhani Pallasmaa 171

Mannerism Matters
Robert Maxwell 187

The Birth of Architecture from the Spirit of Conversation
Kurt W. Forster 197

On Robert Venturi's *Complexity and Contradiction in Architecture*
Rafael Moneo 208

A Time of Heroics: Paul Rudolph and Yale, 1958–1965
Robert A.M. Stern with Leopoldo Villardi 228

PART III

Operational Criticism, Landform, and Tectonic Presence 248

On Kenneth Frampton
Steven Holl 250

An Englishman in New York
Wiel Arets 258

From the Field: Critical Regionalism and Tectonic Culture Applied
Brad Cloepfil 265

Architectural Osmosis
Yvonne Farrell and Shelley McNamara 278

Public Natures: A Roundtable Discussion
Kenneth Frampton, Marion Weiss, Michael A. Manfredi
with Justin Fowler 288

Architecture and Nature: A Recurring State of Mind
Emilio Ambasz 300

Value and the Metaphor of Phenomenology in the "Visual Schemes" of Kenneth Frampton
Ashley Simone 308

From the Archives of Kenneth Frampton
Brigitte Shim and Howard Sutcliffe 327

Picture Credits 342

Acknowledgments 343

Biography of Kenneth Frampton 344

Biographies of Contributors 345

Index 347

Introduction

Karla Cavarra Britton and Robert McCarter

> It is necessary to recognize the limits of architecture as a *métier*; above all perhaps the fact that however much advanced techno-scientific methods may be employed in its realization, it is no more an applied science than it is a form of fine art. Despite the ubiquitous triumph of technological modernization, the practice of architecture is still to be more properly regarded as a craft, one which, at its full range, is dedicated to the significant formulation of the human environment. In this respect, it is always as much an ontological presence and an embodiment of societal value in spatial terms as it is an abstract or symbolic *representation*. Hence, it is doubtful whether it can ever be appropriately rendered as "fine art writ large." Unlike literature, music, painting and sculpture, or even theatre, photography and film, architecture cannot legitimately aspire to any kind of cultural autonomy since it is too intimately involved with the processes of everyday life and with that which Jürgen Habermas characterized as the unfinished modern project; in a word with that which Marshall Berman has since identified as the *pastoral* or caring mode as opposed to the *counter-pastoral* of the negative avant-garde.[1]
>
> Kenneth Frampton, *Labour, Work and Architecture* (2002)

To offer a collection of essays in gratitude to a respected scholar, teacher, and practitioner is in this day already a small act of resistance. The sense of recognized indebtedness and intellectual lineage that such a *Festschrift*, or sustained celebratory writing, betrays is immediately at odds with the momentary character of contemporary public discourse. And yet, such an act of opposition also becomes all the more appropriate, given the lifetime of accumulated work by way of which Kenneth Frampton has sought to deepen our thinking about and commitment to the act of building as a matter of decisive cultural significance that cannot be reduced to the transitory. As such, our ambitions as editors in assembling this volume reach beyond the merely honorific. We have attempted instead to trace a terrain of discourse and debate which has not only been inhabited by Frampton in the generous spirit of his own work, but also which defines many of the challenges, both existential and professional, that architects will necessarily continue to confront in the future. By mapping debates related to Frampton's work, this volume is intended to be as much prospective as retrospective—an invitation to further writing and critique inspired by his example.

By way of beginning, it will be constructive to specify how the title for this volume was chosen. The term "lifeworld" (or *Lebenswelt*) should be addressed both in its broader sense and in what it implies for Frampton's own critical stance. It has been part of philosophical discourse at least since Edmund Husserl's phenomenological work of the 1930s, denoting what may be thought of as the pre-critical "world as we find it" (to allude to Ludwig Wittgenstein's phrase), a world that is experienced *together* by a community or culture as a given. It was extended by Jürgen Habermas to include the communicative background of practices, ideas, and attitudes that inform our interaction with the world around us. The fertility of the term for Frampton stems from this overlap of semantic meanings. As Frampton makes clear, "Architecture as opposed to any other art form is irredeemably mixed up with the life-world," and in this respect it is as much a context for culture and life as it is a cultural expression.[2] So the relationship of building to architecture, and of architecture to culture, has provided Frampton with a broad framework for his advocacy, indicated by such key words as critical, resistance, ideology, ethical, and tectonic—a lexicon of terms which he maintains even with a sometimes intuitive and open relationship to their multiple significations. Paul Goldberger has observed that Frampton writes, based on a radical premise for a theorist of modern architecture, that "buildings are real things ... He believes that the way in which buildings are built—the materials architects use and the way in which they choose to put them together—can be a complete, even profound expression of an architectural idea."[3] Or as Frampton has remarked about himself, "If there is a virtue to my writing it is that I write with the mind of an architect."[4]

Frampton approaches the question of architecture as an integral part of the lifeworld from diverse angles. In the opening to *Modern Architecture: A Critical History*, for example, he argues that, "the history of modern architecture is as much about consciousness and polemical intent as it is about buildings themselves."[5] His focus on the lifeworld's relationship to architecture is recorded through changing patterns, from the history of the Modern Movement, to the attention he gives to structure and materials, to his more recent understandings of contemporary urbanism and landscape. As Frampton has continued to explore ideas of the contemporary in "world architecture," the focus on the lifeworld has increasingly turned towards the megalopolis and above all to the issue of what he has called "environmental education," not only as this concerns the profession, but also in relation to the way this affects society as a whole.[6] Two of the principal dimensions of Frampton's relationship to architecture are accounted for in his theoretical formulation that "the *tectonic* and the *spatial* are complementary and equally pertinent to the inflected articulation of *macro* and *micro* space on which the socio-cultural potential of architecture so evidently depends."[7]

Frampton's concern for the world as we inhabit it owes a debt to his reading of Hannah Arendt's *The Human Condition* (1958), an encounter from which he has said, "I will never really recover—the way she influenced my total attitude to architecture and to life in general."[8] She provided him with concepts to stimulate his own thought and a horizon against which to set his own work. Although Arendt does not speak directly of architecture, she gives an account of how "human activities"—and by implication all aspects of built production and construction—may be understood throughout Western history. In particular, her distinction between labor, work, and action provided a foundation for Frampton's thought and his perception of the difference between building as an activity grounded in the biological process of the human body, and architecture as a process corresponding to the unnaturalness of human existence.[9] This distinction has been a perspective against which to set his themes and thought in all aspects of his production—from publications and editorial work to urban ideas and teaching. The implications of these ideas have made it integral to the ways in which Frampton has questioned the use of contemporary patterns of land settlement, and his observations have, in the end, often sounded in his public reflections, as if he is an ethical observer, commentator, and critic for the profession. In this respect Frampton has made clear that "the socio-ecological implications of our current patterns of land settlement" and the relevance of design to landscape have greater critical consequence than architecture on its own.[10]

In anticipation of Kenneth Frampton's ninetieth birthday in November 2020, twenty-seven architects, historians, and theorists from around the world responded

1 Kenneth Frampton, holding his *Studies in Tectonic Culture*, September 2019. Photograph by Jeff Bickert.

to our invitation to write in tribute to the breadth and influence of his oeuvre. As the Ware Professor of Architecture at Columbia University's Graduate School of Architecture, Planning, and Preservation (where he has taught since 1972), Frampton has exerted a global influence on both the theory and the practice of architecture. This book is representative of his contributions as a writer, architect, editor, and teacher and his impact on ideas and projects across continents and geographies—and the range of authors is indicative of this influence, from colleagues to ideological adversaries to former students. In the essays, historians have, for instance, linked his writing and teaching to a nuanced understanding of the transitional schools and movements in design in the twentieth century, including the Bauhaus, the Russian avant-garde, modern social housing, and Japanese modernism. Others have aligned him with some of the most prominent leaders in twentieth-century architectural thought, and to theorists and critics who are central to architectural education. Members of the exclusive fraternity of Pritzker Prize Laureates such as Portuguese master Álvaro Siza, the Spanish Rafael Moneo, Wang Shu from China, and Yvonne Farrell and Shelley McNamara from Ireland have sent contributions. European historians of Frampton's generation have underscored his pivotal place within a long tradition of architectural writing and thought by offering their own prototypical essays. And a new generation of architects and urbanists from Canada, Holland, and the United States have contributed their reflections about the impact of his work as a teacher and mentor and his influence on their contemporary practices in architecture, landscape, and urban design in countries as far reaching as Peru, Russia, Italy, and China.

Cumulatively, this book reveals the ways in which Frampton himself observes and talks about architecture, by reflecting back the issues he has made central to the discipline over the last five decades: from early work for cover designs as technical editor for *Architectural Design*, to in-depth early investigations into new fields of research in Russia and Japan, to his advocacy of large-scale urban landform design. His deep appreciation for the *working reality* of the architect's life, combined with the actual and poetic act of construction and materials, and his pursuant energy and belief in what architecture can teach us about our human condition, have made him for many a model of the architect–scholar. His writing and teaching have given a generation of architects a framework and a language for understanding the relationship between the political, ecological, and economic dimensions of their practice and the wider world, while articulating a vision for the profession as socially responsible, environmentally grounded, and culturally engaged.

As the essays illustrate, the innumerable professional connections that Frampton has made around the globe are a testament to the intensity of his personal relationships with colleagues, students, and friends. Rather than the disengaged observations of an outsider to practice, Frampton's criticism comes from his deep and nuanced understanding of the discipline, of the nature of the life and work of the contemporary architect, and of the larger historical and cultural contexts in which the architect operates, making his insights at once both pertinent and penetrating. This is indicated by the brief, yet telling contribution that Portuguese architect Álvaro Siza wrote for this volume:

> In space and time a lifelong traveler.
> Eyes, ears and voice that find, receive, understand and send—open to the sharing.

Aware of Frampton's stature in the field, the Canadian Centre for Architecture now holds his papers in its archives, which will undoubtedly contribute over time to a fuller understanding of his ideas and the various polemical debates in which he has been an active voice. In addition, his extensive library has since 2016 been the "Kenneth Frampton Architectural Book Collection" at the Department of Architecture at the University of Hong Kong, documenting his attentiveness to the international architectural publications of the twentieth century, especially those journals published in Italy, Spain, Japan, and England. Between his time as a young architect and editor of *Architectural Design* in the 1960s in England, and the abundant awards, lectures, and publications still well underway at the time of writing, he has been the author of numerous books (including the world's most widely employed university text on the history of modern architecture) and countless scholarly essays, and has been responsible for exhibitions and projects which he has often designed in great detail. His support of other writers is evidenced in the countless introductions he has offered to various architectural works by other authors (a rare architectural book, it has been said, is one without an introduction by Kenneth Frampton). The influence of his writing on other fields, too, remains strikingly apparent.

Yet the concept with which Frampton is most associated is that of "critical regionalism," which he himself described in a 2013 lecture at SCI-Arc (Southern California Institute of Architecture) as something of "a corner into which I have painted myself." The term was first advanced, as Frampton is quick to note, by Alexander Tzonis and Liane Lefaivre in their 1981 essay, "The Grid and the Pathway." Frampton describes his own gravitation toward it as a response to his realization that the liberative modern project in which he had been schooled had lost its point of reference at Columbia's Graduate School of Architecture in the 1980s. This shift was encapsulated by the 1980 Venice Biennale, from whose organizing committee Frampton resigned upon learning of its "anti-modernist" orientation. In response, he began to develop concepts that would become the core of his Critical Regionalism, such as marginal practice, local building practices, the bounded nature of architecture, the importance of site inflection, and the centrality of tactility and the corporeal.

It is difficult to fully comprehend the enormous impact of Frampton's resulting essay of 1983, "Towards a Critical Regionalism: Six Points for an Architecture of

Resistance," a statement of opposition to the prevailing patterns of contemporary practice that many scholars consider his masterwork.[11] The text, which has been frequently revised and reprinted in various incarnations, is at heart a set of principles for a way of navigating architectural process. It is a statement (or manifesto) that chronicles Frampton's continuous dialogue between the world and culture. Certainly among the most intensely debated of his writings, this statement has impacted the thinking and practice of theorists and practitioners in the fields of literature, the arts, sociology, and anthropology, as well as discussions of architecture, on almost every continent. It has challenged understandings about the relationship between architecture and scenography, whose implications many architects are still working to comprehend. Significantly, it reflects the influence of a second seminal writing for Frampton (in addition to Arendt's *Human Condition*): Paul Ricœur's 1965 essay on "Universal Civilization and National Cultures." The essay outlines how technology-based universal civilization must be mediated by its hybridization with local culture and tradition—the intellectual foundation upon which the regionalist impulse is grounded.

Various critics have challenged the idea of "critical regionalism," often in relation to a concern that it ultimately represents a form of postcolonialism—what Jane Jacobs called "a revisionary form of imperialist nostalgia that defines the colonized as always engaged in conscious work against the 'core.'"[12] Yet Frampton's global interest in the local practice of architecture has also put him in the position of championing architects whose work had been relatively less well known in European and North American circles—one thinks, for example, of the numerous works by contemporary designers in South Asia, Africa, and Latin America which he has celebrated in his lectures and writings over the last decades. And within this volume, several authors speak of the influence of Frampton's defense of the specificity of site with reference to their own work, such as the Chinese Wang Shu or the Irish team of Yvonne Farrell and Shelley McNamara. (Moreover, the continuing influence and fecundity of the concept are exhibited by the recently published volume *Critical Regionalism Revisited.*[13]) Frampton's preoccupation with the points outlined within Critical Regionalism is nevertheless present, and continuously reworked, deeply intertwined with all his work including his analysis of urban forms. It was from these observations that he developed his historical and comparative analysis of countless building projects and urban plans. His work took into account not only the siting of buildings, their relationship to topography, and their immediate environments, but the possibility for transforming urban territories into landscapes. Thus Frampton developed through the points of Critical Regionalism an understanding that included both the scale of a building's immediate environment (as well as that of urban ensembles) and large terrains (with the scope and scale of territories). As he himself defined the series of topics: "These themes vary from practical strategies to be applied within the limitations of our epoch to wider critical forays that can only be exercised and thus fulfilled in a much longer term."[14]

Following "Towards a Critical Regionalism" of 1983, Frampton's most important critical contribution to the understanding of the practice of modern architecture and its place in the larger history of the discipline was his *Studies in Tectonic Culture: The Poetics of Construction in Nineteenth and Twentieth Century Architecture* of 1995 (**1**). Developed from the Francis Craig Cullivan Lecture given at Rice University in 1986, and first introduced in the essay "Rappel à l'Ordre: The Case for the Tectonic" of 1990, the concept of tectonic culture has rightly been understood as introducing an "other" or alternate history of architecture, one based not on the formal concerns of the art historian, but on the poetics of construction and the matters of making with which architecture as a métier is inextricably intertwined in its practice in the lifeworld. Returning architecture to its ancient roots in the poetics of construction, and in the revelation and cladding of structure, Frampton examined the rise of the concept of the tectonic and its complement, the stereotomic, at the dawn of the Enlightenment. He then traced its path through the work of Frank Lloyd Wright, Auguste Perret, Mies van der Rohe, Louis Kahn, Jørn Utzon, and Carlo Scarpa. It is intriguing to note that Frampton's initial development of the concept of tectonic culture took place from 1986 to 1990, directly following the emergence of Critical Regionalism. He has recently remarked that in the late 1980s he came to realize that Critical Regionalism was "too fragile" alone to foster and sustain a resistance to scenographic post-modernism, and that the concept of tectonic culture offered a stronger and deeper grounding in the history of the discipline as a métier.[15] This is surely one of the primary reasons that "tectonic culture" has proven to be so influential on contemporary architectural practices.

Although Le Corbusier remains a touchstone for much of Frampton's reflection ("we will never quite finish with the labyrinthine scope of his production"[16]), Frampton has also been a seminal influence in expanding our horizons of the true scope and meaning of modernism (**2**). Most recently, Frampton's *L'altro Movimento Moderno* (to be published in English as *The Other Modern Movement*) focused on eighteen architects who, although not among the most prominent figureheads of the Modern Movement, nevertheless expanded and developed it according to its widest cultural and experiential potential which can now be seen as a counterpoint to today's aestheticization of form—figures such as Rudolf Schindler, Erich Mendelsohn, Eileen Gray, or Willem Dudok, to name only four.[17] Moreover, Frampton has studiously—and liberally—leveraged his awareness of the authentic breadth of modern architectural production on behalf of his students, frequently pointing them toward illuminating explorations of their own in this wider tradition. This fruitful lineage between mentor and student is among the most substantial legacies to which this volume bears witness.

2 Le Corbusier holds Modulor figure to horizon in Chandigarh, India, 1951.

3 Antoine Bourdelle, "La méditation d'Apollon et les Muses," study for the frieze on Auguste Perret's Théâtre des Champs Elysées, Paris, 1913.

What Frampton has taught us through his attentiveness to the built environment and its cultural and socio-economic meaning is that by talking about one thing, you are almost always talking about something much more. For him, architecture is always a means for expanding horizons, and engaging with a larger world: modern architecture is as much a social and political expression as it is an aesthetic statement. As a result of this conviction, he has used architecture to examine the underlying complexity of many contemporary issues: neoliberalism; the place of labor in a late-capitalist society; cultural identity in an era of mass and placeless society; democratic values and the hope for their resurgence in the wake of the collapse of the Soviet Union; and the remaking of cities through new models of urbanism around the world. In the course of examining such a wide range of topics, Frampton betrays at times a certain resignation to the degradation not only of the natural and urban environments, but of human society itself. He often quotes a remark attributed to the British politician Margaret Thatcher: "There is no alternative," seeing in this lack of choices a kind of disaster. Yet he remains committed to a modicum of hope located in the possibility of small political units, city-states, and local democracies. These are, as he has said in numerous public lectures, "the one hope that we have." Moreover, he finds in many works of modern and contemporary architecture a "secular spirituality" that continues to ground the humanistic values to which he is so attached: he has pointed to the work of Japanese master Tadao Andō, to the mysticism of Luis Barragán, or to the Miesian links to the work of the theologian Guarino Guarini, or even to the concern for the sacred and profane in the late work of Le Corbusier.

Frampton recalls that when he left his native Britain in 1966 to take up a position at Princeton University, he experienced for the first time the undifferentiated urbanized region of the Boston–Washington corridor from the air, when taking a helicopter from Kennedy Airport. "I'd never seen so much electrical power—this is in the mid '60s—or gasoline burning before my eyes as in one of those sublime panoramas that you are never likely to forget." Roughly coinciding with his first encounter with Hannah Arendt's book, this incident sealed his attachment to New York, and to the urban environment in which his thinking, and response, to architecture would mature. It was there that he assumed the role, to quote his Columbia colleague Edward Said, of a "public intellectual:"

> ... an individual with a specific public role in society that cannot be reduced to simply being a faceless professional, a competent member of a class just going about her/his business ... an individual endowed with a faculty for representing, embodying, articulating a message, a view, an attitude, a philosophy or opinion to, as well as for, a public. And this role has an edge to it, and cannot be played without a sense of being someone whose place it is publicly to raise embarrassing questions, to confront orthodoxy and dogma (rather than to produce them). ... The intellectual does so based on universal principles: that all human beings are entitled to expect decent standards of behavior concerning freedom and justice from worldly powers or nations, and that deliberate or inadvertent violations of these standards need to be testified and fought against courageously.[18]

Indicative of the complexity of his approach to such a role, Frampton has pointed to the "dialogical habit of mind," which is exemplified in Le Corbusier's embrace of the opposing forces of light and shadow personified by Apollo and Medusa (**3**).[19] In one of Frampton's most carefully worked texts, the conclusion of his Introduction to *Studies in Tectonic Culture*, he summarizes the intellectual stance that he had staked out in all his writings:

> In the last analysis, everything turns as much on exactly *how* something is realized as on an overt manifestation of its form. This is not to deny spatial ingenuity but rather to heighten its character through its precise realization. Thus the presencing of a work is inseparable from the manner of its foundation in the ground and ascendancy of its structure through the interplay of support, span, seam and joint—the rhythm of its revetment in the modulation of its fenestration. Situated at the interface of culture and nature, building is as much about the ground as it is about built form. Close to agriculture, its task is to modify the earth's surface in such a way as to take care of it, as in Heidegger's concept of *Gelassenheit* or letting be. Hence the notion of "building the site," in Mario Botta's memorable phrase, is of greater import than the creation of free-standing objects, and in this regard building is as much about the topos as it is about technique. Furthermore, despite the privatization of modern society, architecture, as opposed to building, tends to favor the space of public appearance rather than the privacy of the

domus. At the same time, it is as much about place-making and the passage of time as it is about space and form. Light, water, wind, and weathering, these are the agents by which it is consummated. Inasmuch as its continuity transcends mortality, building provides the basis for life and culture. In this sense, it is neither high art nor high technology. To the extent that it defies time, it is anachronistic by definition. Durations and durability are its ultimate values. In the last analysis it has nothing to do with immediacy and everything to do with the unsayable. What was it Luis Barragán said? "All architecture which does not express serenity fails in its spiritual mission." The task of our time is to combine vitality with calm.[20]

1 Kenneth Frampton, "Introduction: On the Predicament of Architecture at the Turn of the Century," *Labour, Work and Architecture: Collected Essays on Architecture and Design* (London: Phaidon, 2002), 8.
2 Kenneth Frampton, "Seven Points for the Millennium: An Untimely Manifesto" (keynote address given at the Twentieth Congress of the UIA, Beijing, 1999), *The Journal of Architecture*, 5 (Spring 2000): 23.
3 Paul Goldberger, "Bricks and Mortar," review of *Studies in Tectonic Culture* by Kenneth Frampton, *New York Times* (March 10, 1996), https://www.nytimes.com/1996/03/10/books/bricks-and-mortar.html (accessed December 20, 2019).
4 Biennale Architettura 2018: Kenneth Frampton Golden Lion Achievement, https://www.youtube.com/watch?v=HadCPq7er9g (accessed December 20, 2019).
5 Kenneth Frampton, *Modern Architecture: A Critical History*, rev. edition (London: Thames & Hudson, 1985), 9.
6 Frampton, "Seven Points for the Millennium: An Untimely Manifesto."
7 Ibid.
8 Kenneth Frampton, "Megaform as Urban Landscape," Senior Loeb Scholar Lecture, Graduate School of Design, Harvard University, October 23, 2017, gsd.harvard.edu/event/kenneth-frampton/ (accessed December 9, 2019).
9 See Hannah Arendt, *The Human Condition* (Chicago: The University of Chicago Press, 1958), 7. Drawing a distinction between labor and work, Arendt argued that labor is human activity directed at meeting biological necessities for the preservation of the species. Whereas work, on the other hand, may be distinguished from labor, and comprises a process, which is not intended for consumption.
10 Ibid.
11 Kenneth Frampton, "Towards a Critical Regionalism: Six Points for an Architecture of Resistance," in *The Anti-Aesthetic: Essays on Postmodern Culture*, ed. Hal Foster (Port Townsend, WA: Bay Press, 1983).
12 Jane Jacobs, *Edge of Empire: Postcolonialism and the City* (London: Routledge, 1996), 14–15. Quoted in Keith Eggener, "Placing Resistance: A Critique of Critical Regionalism," *Journal of Architectural Education*, 55/4 (May 2002): 234.
13 Tom Avermaete and Lea-Catherine Szacka, eds., *Critical Regionalism Revisited*, OASE 103 (August 2019).
14 Frampton, "Seven Points for the Millennium: An Untimely Manifesto."
15 Kenneth Frampton, in conversation with the editors on January 16, 2020.
16 Kenneth Frampton, *Le Corbusier* (London: Thames & Hudson, 2001), 6.
17 Kenneth Frampton, *L'altro Movimento Moderno*, ed. Ludovica Molo (Mendrisio: Mendrisio Press, 2015; published in English as *The Other Modern Movement*, ed. Ashley Simone, New Haven, CT, and London: Yale University Press, 2020).
18 Edward Said, *Representations of the Intellectual* (New York: Vintage Press, 1994), 11–12.
19 Frampton, *Le Corbusier*, 7.
20 Kenneth Frampton, *Studies in Tectonic Culture: The Poetics of Construction in Nineteenth and Twentieth Century Architecture*, ed. John Cava (Cambridge: MIT Press, 1995), 27.

PART I

The Social, Cultural, and Ecological Nature of Architecture

The essays in this first section frame the intellectual background, key ideas, and debates of Kenneth Frampton's work, and thereby help to establish the themes for the rest of the book. Most importantly, these essays collectively insist on the breadth of fields that have influenced Frampton's writing, including the Frankfurt School; modern philosophical hermeneutics; and the environmental crisis. As Joan Ockman writes in her essay, Frampton was among the first and most consistent architectural critics to speak out against the building industry's abusive environmental practices. Two foundational essays in particular provide the groundwork for much of the book: Mary McLeod's dynamic reading of Frampton's intellectual formation and impact; and Wang Shu's argument for the importance of Frampton's understanding of the critical in relation to world architectural practice.

McLeod's essay provides a valuable analysis of Frampton's formation as a theorist and writer and the evolution of his intellectual vocation; she takes up his role within many of the key debates in the field of architectural theory over the last thirty years. While addressing the importance of the word "critical" in Frampton's usage, McLeod provides the essential details of Frampton's training and formation, including his origins in post-war England; his time as a designer with Douglas Stephen and Partners; the early circle of influence on his thinking, such as James Stirling; the design layouts by Gae Aulenti and his tenure as an editor for *Architectural Design*; and his encounter with the work of Hannah Arendt. McLeod identifies those writers to whom Frampton was drawn—Ricœur, Arendt, and Habermas in particular—and relates his use of the word "critical" to Walter Benjamin and the Frankfurt School. She places Frampton within a field of theoretical discourse while positioning his thought in juxtaposition to some of the most notable historians of the twentieth century such as Sigfried Giedion and Manfredo Tafuri.

The architect Wang Shu, from Hangzhou, China, also addresses the theme of the critical, in this case in relation to the urban crisis facing cities in the twenty-first century. In his discussion of the impact of Frampton's thinking on contemporary "world architecture," Wang points to his personal experience of the explosive urban development that has happened within Chinese cities, noting by way of example that Hanghzou has expanded by a factor of twenty in just thirty years. As Frampton has written, Wang's work (carried out in partnership with Lu Wenyu at the Amateur Architecture Studio) has come into being in "categorical opposition to the recent, rapacious development that has engulfed large tracts of the Chinese continent."[1]

Wilfried Wang extends these arguments by addressing the need to implement urban and architectural designs appropriate to the age of climate change. Frampton's writing is latent within Wang's own concerns for the ways in which global climate change has transformed conventional "lifeworlds." In particular, Wang raises the issue of the process of autonomization; the bureaucratization of technology; and the de-skilling of society. He points to how the real-estate building industry and ivory-tower academia "pursue autonomous goals, unrelated to issues of sustainability."

Harry Mallgrave, too, expands on the immediate crisis attending the built environment, discussing irresponsible land use; the deterioration of historic fabric; and the loss of regional traditions and identities. He brings together many of the themes that are discussed throughout this volume, including the intensely progressive dimension of architecture and its deep interrelationship with the earth, especially the cultivation of the land, and the idea of the garden. Mallgrave does this by addressing the concept of "paradise," distinguishing it from the "more troublesome word" of "utopia." For Mallgrave the idea of paradise is focused upon the personal or inner yearning for happiness. And so he asks the question: how do new models in the humanistic and biological sciences inform design? Tapping into Dalibor Vesely's desire for a "poetic mythos," he identifies the ways mood now infuses our every environmental niche.

Joan Ockman's essay, "Paradoxes of Progress," further deepens the theme of architecture and the environmental calamity, through her retelling of Hermann Hesse's parable "The City," written in 1910. Ockman reads the parable in light of the current era, which has seized upon the label "Anthropocene" to describe the connection between human and natural history. Using the photographer Lu Guang's graphic images of the steel-producing region of Hebei Province in China and vistas of Inner Mongolia's pockmarked pasture land, Ockman offers a commentary on the twenty-first century in the light of Hesse's fable.

Enlarging the terrain of architecture's reach still further, Alberto Pérez-Gómez calls our attention to Frampton's rigorous critical stance and its roots in the discourse of hermeneutics. He notes that the physical environment, cities and their architecture matter in ways that would have been hard to acknowledge in earlier phases of modernity. He reflects on the lifeworld through contemporary enactive cognitive science with a focus on how the environment is a constitutive part of animal and human consciousness. "It is not simply a matter of aesthetic preference or ornament," he argues. "The human condition as such is at stake, and this involves much more than physical survival, comfort, hygiene, and ecological sustainability; it requires the preservation of linguistic differences and with it, true cultural diversity, gestures, and habits. It requires spaces for human communication with affective qualities, challenging and yet respectful of habitual action."

1 Kenneth Frampton, "Kenneth Frampton on the Work of Wang Shu and Lu Wenyu," *ArchDaily* (March 23, 2017), https://www.archdaily.com/867419/kenneth-frampton-on-the-work-of-wang-shu-and-lu-wenyu (accessed December 9, 2019).

Kenneth Frampton's Idea of the "Critical"

Mary McLeod

Kenneth Frampton is arguably the most influential architectural historian since Sigfried Giedion (**4**, **18**). His book *Modern Architecture: A Critical History* has been released in four editions and translated into thirteen languages since it was published in 1980 (**6**), and his 1983 essay "Towards a Critical Regionalism: Six Points for an Architecture of Resistance" may have been translated into even more.[1] And despite serious criticism about the essay's contradictions and limitations, including Frampton's own subsequent reservations about it,[2] it has probably had more impact on architects than any single essay published in the past fifty years, perhaps because of its ambiguities and contradictions: architects and firms such as John and Patricia Patkau and Brigitte Shim and Howard Sutcliffe in Canada; Yvonne Farrell and Shelley McNamara of Grafton Architects and Sheila O'Donnell and John Tuomey in Ireland; Wang Jun-Yang and Rocco Yim in China; and Marina

Towards a Critical Regionalism:
Six Points for an Architecture of Resistance

KENNETH FRAMPTON

The phenomenon of universalization, while being an advancement of mankind, at the same time constitutes a sort of subtle destruction, not only of traditional cultures, which might not be an irreparable wrong, but also of what I shall call for the time being the creative nucleus of great cultures, that nucleus on the basis of which we interpret life, what I shall call in advance the ethical and mythical nucleus of mankind. The conflict springs up from there. We have the feeling that this single world civilization at the same time exerts a sort of attrition or wearing away at the expense of the cultural resources which have made the great civilizations of the past. This threat is expressed, among other disturbing effects, by the spreading before our eyes of a mediocre civilization which is the absurd counterpart of what I was just calling elementary culture. Everywhere throughout the world, one finds the same bad movie, the same slot machines, the same plastic or aluminum atrocities, the same twisting of language by propaganda, etc. It seems as if mankind, by approaching en masse *a basic consumer culture, were also stopped* en masse *at a subcultural level. Thus we come to the crucial problem confronting nations just rising from underdevelopment. In order to get on to the road toward modernization, is it necessary to jettison the old cultural past which has been the* raison d'être *of a nation?... Whence the paradox: on the one hand, it has to root itself in the soil of its past, forge a national spirit, and unfurl this spiritual and cultural revindication before the colonialist's personality. But in order to take part in modern civilization, it is necessary at the same time to take part in scientific, technical, and political rationality, something which very often requires the pure and simple abandon of a whole cultural past. It is a fact: every culture cannot sustain and absorb the shock of modern civilization. There is the paradox: how to become modern and to return to sources; how to revive an old, dormant civilization and take part in universal civilization.*[1]

—Paul Ricoeur, *History and Truth*

16

4 Kenneth Frampton teaching at Princeton University, *c.* 1970.

5 Kenneth Frampton, "Towards a Critical Regionalism: Six Points for an Architecture of Resistance," published in *The Anti-Aesthetic: Essays in Postmodern Culture*, ed. Hal Foster (Port Townsend, WA: Bay Press, 1983).

6 Covers of the four editions of Kenneth Frampton's *Modern Architecture: A Critical History* (London: Thames & Hudson), left to right: 1980, 1985, 1992, 2007.

Tabassum (7) in Bangladesh have all cited it as inspiration. The list could run much longer. While the writings of other architectural historians, such as Reyner Banham and Manfredo Tafuri, may have had a greater impact on scholars, Frampton's writings—a mixture of history, criticism, and analysis—have inspired architects, especially those practicing outside of the United States (in places where the notion of "regionalism" or "locale" may have more resonance and meaning than in the States). Frampton's importance to architects might be compared to that of Vincent Scully, who gave credibility and support in the 1970s and 1980s to Louis Kahn, Robert Venturi, and the so-called "Grays"[3]—and thus helped validate the rise of postmodern architecture in the United States. Or, if one looks to Europe, one might compare him to Paolo Portoghesi and Charles Jencks, who likewise supported the emergence of postmodernism during this period. However, Frampton's own influence on architects has been much broader and over a much longer period of time than that of those historians: it is genuinely global in its reach and has lasted more than fifty years. In describing his own role in architecture, Frampton modestly prefers the word "writer" to "historian," "theorist," or "critic."[4] But this choice of words might also reflect his refusal to draw sharp distinctions between these categories.[5] He freely admits to being engaged in "operative criticism," the practice that Tafuri had so severely condemned in *Theories and History of Architecture* in 1968.[6]

Born in 1930 in Woking, Surrey, England, Frampton initially considered a career in agriculture and then opted for architecture, studying first at the Guildford School of Art and then in London at the Architectural Association (AA), where his teachers included Arthur Korn, Maxwell Fry and Jane Drew, and Alison and Peter Smithson. After graduating and working briefly at Chamberlin, Powell and Bon, he spent two years in the British army (which he describes now as a complete waste of time), followed by one highly productive year working in Israel for the modern architect Dov Karmi.[7] Returning to Britain in 1959, he spent a brief period at Middlesex County Council, and then from 1961 to 1965 was employed at Douglas

7 Marina Tabassum, Bait Ur Rouf Mosque, Dhaka, 2012. Kenneth Frampton invited Tabassum to give the ninth annual Kenneth Frampton Endowed Lecture at the Graduate School of Architecture and Urban Planning at Columbia University, September 2019.

Stephen and Partners in London, where in 1962 he designed the housing complex Corringham (13–15 Craven Hill Gardens) in Bayswater, a project indebted both to Le Corbusier and to Soviet designers of the 1920s (**8–9**). During this period, Frampton was also influenced by James Stirling's early architecture, especially his Leicester Engineering Building (which he considers a kind of synthesis of Alvar Aalto and Constructivism). In addition, while at Stephen's office, Frampton wrote and co-edited his first book, *British Buildings 1955–65*, and served, from 1962 to 1965, as technical editor of *Architectural Design* (*AD*). Inspired by Ernesto Rogers's journal *Casabella continuità* and Gae Aulenti's graphic design, he sought to give *AD* greater visual clarity and a more European outlook, producing several notable issues on those he considered "local" architects working in a specific European cultural context, such as one devoted to Angelo Mangiarotti and Bruno Morassutti, and Gino Valle, the latter practicing almost exclusively in Udine (**10**).[8] Later he would claim Valle as a "critical regionalist" and then as a representative of "tectonic culture," but at this earlier stage the word "critical" was absent from his writings.[9] In 1966, Frampton left England for the United States to accept a teaching position at Princeton University, where he remained until moving to Columbia University in 1972. For American architecture students in the late 1960s and 1970s, he was probably best known for his 1968 article "The Humanist versus the Utilitarian Ideal," an analysis of Hannes Meyer's and Le Corbusier's entries for the 1927 League of Nations competition. In that opposition, he sided not surprisingly with the humanist

8 Kenneth Frampton (project architect), Douglas Stephen and Partners, Corringham housing complex (13–15 Craven Hill Gardens), Bayswater, London, 1962–64.

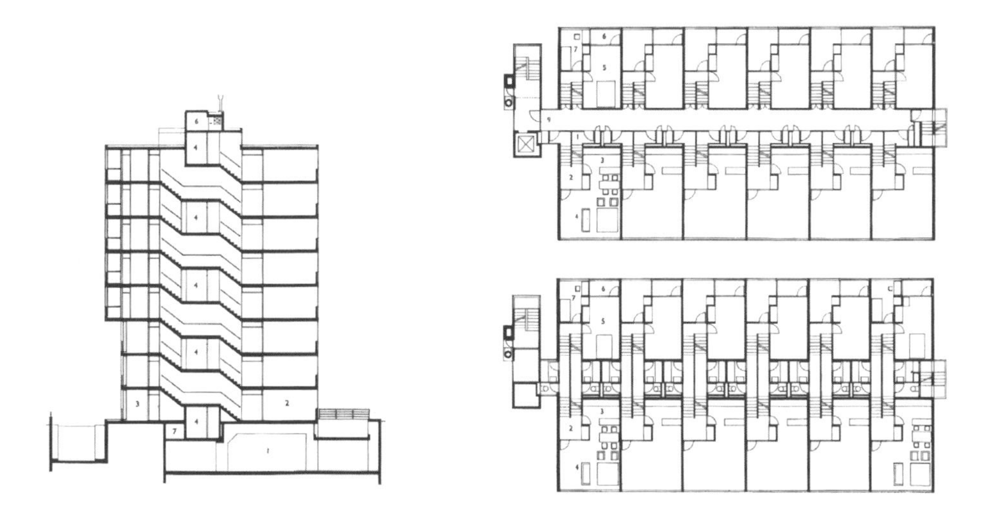

9 Kenneth Frampton, Douglas Stephen and Partners, section and plans of Corringham. Note the split section (with living room on the lower level, bedrooms on the upper level) influenced by Soviet housing designs of the 1920s.

10 Cover of an issue of *Architectural Design* (March 1964) devoted to the work of Mangiarotti and Morassuti and Gino Valle. Kenneth Frampton would later claim Valle's work as an example of "critical regionalism."

Le Corbusier, concluding the essay by declaring that Le Corbusier's project offered the possibility of both unifying and differentiating people in a moment of mass society.[10] (Here, he cited Hannah Arendt, who remains to this day a touchstone for his thought.) It was this essay that led Robin Middleton, then the technical editor of *AD* and an acquisitions editor of Thames & Hudson, to ask him to write a new survey of modern architecture.

During this period, Frampton was not especially political (he describes himself as "politically naive") or engaged with political theory other than Arendt's *The Human Condition*, which he read first in 1965 at the recommendation of Sam Stephens, a kind of polymath who taught architecture history in a "wildly sporadic fashion" at the AA.[11] However, as mentioned above, in the early 1960s Frampton was already interested in Constructivism; its fascination for him, though, was more aesthetic than political, having been sparked by Camilla Gray's pioneering book of 1962, *The Great Experiment: Russian Art 1863–1922*. It would not be until 1968 that his political and aesthetic interests would begin to conjoin—and it was in that same year that he began writing about Constructivist architecture, a subject largely missing from both Giedion's and Banham's surveys of modern architecture. By that time, Frampton was also a Fellow at the New York-based Institute for Architecture and Urban Studies (IAUS), and in 1972, he would become one of the founding editors of its journal, *Oppositions*. Also in 1972, he began teaching studio and history at Columbia University, where he continues to teach today. Shortly thereafter, he designed his first and only realized building complex in the United States, Marcus Garvey Park Village in Brownsville, Brooklyn, sponsored by IAUS (**11–12**). It was during his early years in the United States that Frampton began first to use the word "critical" to characterize his own writing and teaching.

Today, we take the word "critical" almost for granted as a term to describe both certain tendencies or ambitions in writing architectural history and certain kinds of architecture. Its usage has become almost ubiquitous, and it seems to serve as a trope indicating both analytical rigor and "leftist" political sympathies. In the past seventeen years or so, the word "critical" may have become better known in architecture circles for its countercurrent, the "post-critical," promoted by Robert Somol, Sarah Whiting, and Michael Speaks. Around 2002, these three then-young rebels reacted against certain poststructuralist currents in architecture, such as Derridean deconstruction and Lacanian analysis—that is, the arcane discourse that had dominated the journal *Assemblage* and so much of architectural theory in East Coast schools in the United States since the mid-1980s. In their view, theory had become removed from the new parameters of practice—namely digital technology and parametric design; and just as important, it denied the sensual experience of architecture.[12] Parenthetically, this use of the word "post-critical" in architecture is quite distinct (even if it overlaps in its appreciation of the sensual) from the much earlier philosophical position taken by Michael Polanyi or William Poteat, first articulated by Polanyi in the 1950s. These two thinkers sought a more encompassing form of knowledge, one that would go beyond traditional logic to embrace a personal knowledge of sense experience; in this regard their position shared much with that of Maurice Merleau-Ponty and indeed many of the figures whom Frampton himself admires, such as Arendt (despite political differences).[13]

What is usually less recognized by architectural historians, theorists, and practitioners (whether pro- or post-critical) is how deeply indebted they are to Frampton for the term "critical" in architecture—and how distinct his own position is from that which Somol, Whiting, and Speaks were rejecting (although undoubtedly, he would have some difficulties with their stance too). In 1980, Frampton was one of the first, if not the first, to use "critical" in the title of an English-language book on architecture (even though it should be stressed that he was by no means the first in architecture to be concerned with this issue: he was preceded by the more explicitly Marxist studies of the Venice School).[14] The word also appears in the titles of an issue of an *AD* profile that Frampton edited in 1982, *Modern Architecture and the Critical Present*, and of his influential 1983 essay "Towards a Critical Regionalism" (**13, 5**). He employed it in his teaching as well—in his seminar "Comparative Critical

11 Kenneth Frampton, Marcus Garvey Park Village, Brownsville, Brooklyn, New York, 1973–76. Rendering by Craig Hodgetts showing a view of a cul-de-sac to the street. The low-rise, high-density housing project was the only realized work resulting from a collaboration of the Institute for Architecture and Urban Studies and the Urban Development Corporation.

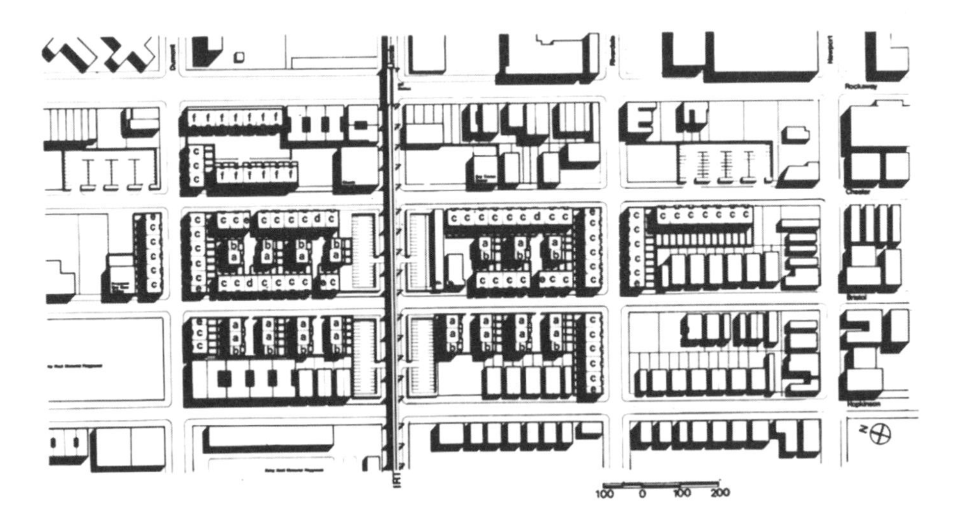

12 Kenneth Frampton, site plan of Marcus Garvey Park Village, 1973–76.

Analysis of Built Form," which he taught at Princeton University, beginning in the late 1960s, and then at Columbia University intermittently for almost fifty years. This pedagogical approach is encapsulated in his recent book *A Genealogy of Modern Architecture: Comparative Critical Analysis of Built Form* (2015), which provides an eloquent synopsis of many of the concerns that have shaped Frampton's teaching over the years.[15]

But *what* specifically does Frampton mean by "critical"? Although he gives us a few hints as to its meaning, it is not something he has ever discussed at length. One might say the word is almost synecdochical for him, in that it stands for a larger set of social concerns and agendas, including his commitment to leftist politics, which he has only occasionally articulated at length.[16]

The word "critical" has a long history, one that derives from the Greek word *kritikos*, meaning "judgment" or "discernment." Its modern usage derives from Immanuel Kant's three *Critiques*, especially the *Critique of Pure Reason*, in which he attempts to examine the limits of validity of a faculty, type, or body of knowledge through reflection; and then from Karl Marx's critique of political economy in *Capital*, in which critique is seen as kind of ideological dismantling, revealing the contradictions within capital itself. In general, this has meant that the word is associated with a certain kind of critical self-reflexivity (an examination that goes beyond intention or popular reception) and, in the case of Marxist theorists, a belief that such critical examination can contribute to social and political transformation. But Frampton's source, more specifically, like that for many others of his (and the following) generation, is the Frankfurt School, the group of scholars who worked at the Institute for Social Research in the 1930s, including Theodor Adorno, Max Horkheimer, and Herbert Marcuse, as well as those thinkers closely affiliated with it, such as Walter Benjamin. These scholars attempted to extend Marxism's ideological critique to the cultural sphere and to examine how mass culture had changed art's production and reception—and thus possibilities for radical social transformation. Critical Theory was intended to produce a kind of knowledge—one grounded in the historical context of both the object of study and that of the researcher—that was both elucidating and emancipatory. Thus, in contrast to positivist knowledge (which envisions natural science as a model of all cognition), this knowledge was seen as a form of action or praxis, and thus a means for social betterment. This objective, too, is fundamental to Frampton's own work.

Frampton was among the first in the English-speaking architectural world to read and reflect upon the Frankfurt School and, specifically, Benjamin's writings. His introduction to his first edition of *Modern Architecture: A Critical History* begins with a quote from Benjamin's "Theses on the Philosophy of History" (1940):

> A Klee painting named *Angelus Novus* [**14**] shows an angel looking as though he is about to move away from something he is in fixedly contemplating. His eyes

13 Cover of *Modern Architecture and the Critical Present*, *Architectural Design* Profile (London: Academy Editions, 1982). This publication, edited by Frampton, includes his critical commentary on current architecture, in addition to reviews of *Modern Architecture* by eminent architectural historians and critics.

> are staring, his mouth is open, his wings are spread. This is how one pictures the angel of history. His face is turned towards the past. Where we perceive a chain of events, he sees one single catastrophe which keeps piling wreckage upon wreckage and hurls it in front of his feet. The angel would like to stay, awaken the dead, and make whole what has been smashed. But a storm is blowing from Paradise: it has got caught in its wings with such violence that the angel can no longer close them. This storm irresistibly propels him into the future to which his back is turned, while the pile of debris before him grows skyward. This storm is what we call progress.

Later in that introduction Frampton states that he was influenced by a Marxist interpretation of history, and refers to his "affinity with the critical theory of the Frankfurt School," adding that it made him "acutely aware of the dark side of the Enlightenment."[17]

His interest in Benjamin and the Frankfurt School, however, precedes by more than a decade the publication of *Modern Architecture*. In fact, he had already decided on the subtitle of the book in 1970, when he agreed to write the Thames & Hudson survey, and in 1972, he used the same passage from "Theses on the

Philosophy of History" that opens *Modern Architecture* as an epigraph for his essay "Industrialization and the Crises in Architecture." This essay was published in the first issue of *Oppositions* and, later, he would characterize it "as a somewhat naïve attempt to adopt a Benjaminian approach to historical phenomena."[18]

How did Frampton discover Benjamin and, more generally, leftist politics? Perhaps, not coincidentally, his seminal essay on Pierre Chareau's Maison de Verre appeared in the same 1969 issue of *Perspecta*, Yale's student-produced magazine, as Benjamin's synopsis of his Arcades Project, "Paris: Capital of the Nineteenth Century."[19] In some regards, this meticulously designed issue—the embossed cover of which evokes the rubber floor tiles of the Maison de Verre—encapsulates both sides of Frampton's thought: his deep concern for architecture's formal and structural qualities and his social and political investigations, which sought to establish the links between politics, social conditions, and form. But more importantly, the 1960s were a moment of intense political engagement for many in the United States: first, the civil rights movement, followed by the increasingly intense protests against the Vietnam War, and then the women's liberation movement. Frampton has said that, paradoxically, it was going to the States that "radicalized" him. He explains his conversion by quoting a comment that the English architect Michael Glickman once made to him: "You have to understand, in England the claws are hidden but in the States they are visible."[20] In other words, the brutality and pervasive power of capitalism and the military–industrial state were blatantly visible in the States. Like others at Princeton's School of Architecture, he was involved in the university strike in May 1970 after the Kent State massacre.

Frampton's interest in Benjamin was undoubtedly sparked by his long-standing admiration of Arendt (still very much apparent in his 2015 *Genealogy of Modern Architecture*). Arendt edited and wrote the introduction to *Illuminations*, the first collection in English of Benjamin's writings. The book came out in 1968, and included Benjamin's best-known essay, "The Work of Art in the Age of Mechanical Reproduction," as well as his "Theses on the Philosophy of History." These two essays might be seen as embodying the two sides of Frampton's interest in Benjamin during this period: on the one hand, his almost utopian faith in technology's potential to improve human life and his deep commitment to mass housing, which parallels in some ways Benjamin's position in the first essay; and, on the other hand, his increasing pessimism about society's capacity to use technology judiciously and to sustain an authentic and meaningful culture in the face of ever-sweeping modernization, even as one accepts its inevitability. One thinks here of Paul Klee's angel being blown forward, even as he looks to the past, in Benjamin's "Theses."

An additional influence on Frampton in the late 1960s was Frankfurt School philosopher Herbert Marcuse. Alan Colquhoun, who taught with Frampton at Princeton in the 1960s, had given him his copy of *Eros and Civilization*, first published in 1955 and reissued in 1966.[21] In this book, which was seminal to

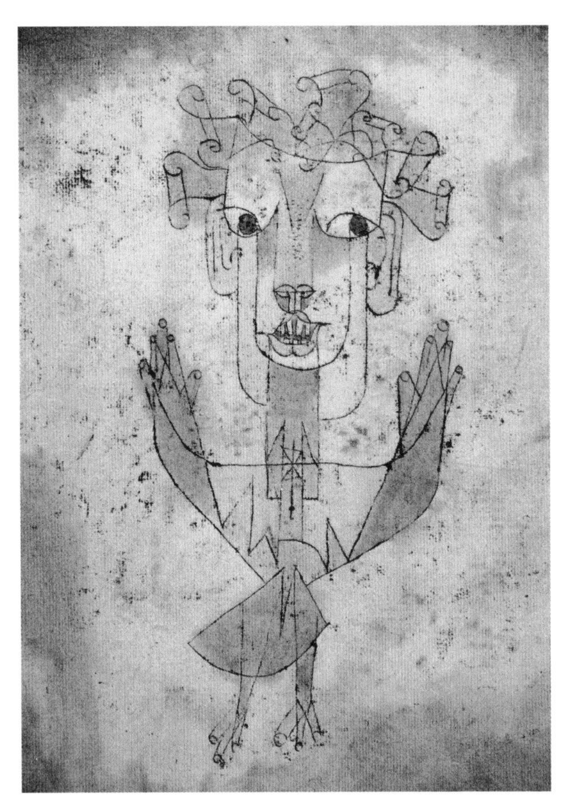

14 Paul Klee, *Angelus Novus*, monoprint, 1920. Walter Benjamin bought this oil-transfer drawing in 1921 and he hung it in every apartment in which he lived.

the emergence of the New Left and a political strain of American counterculture, Marcuse focused not on class struggle but rather on the repression of eros, which he saw as a product of contemporary industrial relations, namely the alienated labor of "advanced industrial society." Marcuse called for a non-repressive civilization founded on non-alienated libidinal work, a goal reminiscent of that of the nineteenth-century French utopian socialist Charles Fourier. These themes resonated with Frampton's own growing concern for craft, an attention to detail—what I might call "care"—and for the sensuous aspects of architecture; or, put another way, his refusal to "separate the reality of work from the pleasure of life," as he so succinctly stated in his 1976 essay "The Volvo Case."[22] The role that Marcuse—and more generally the Frankfurt School—played in the evolution of Frampton's own thinking is most evident in the postscript to his 1983 essay on Arendt, "The Status of Man and the Status of His Objects." Here, he mentions two issues that he felt Arendt, who was not a Marxist, had either suppressed or suspended in her conclusion to *The Human Condition*: "First, the problematic cultural status of play and

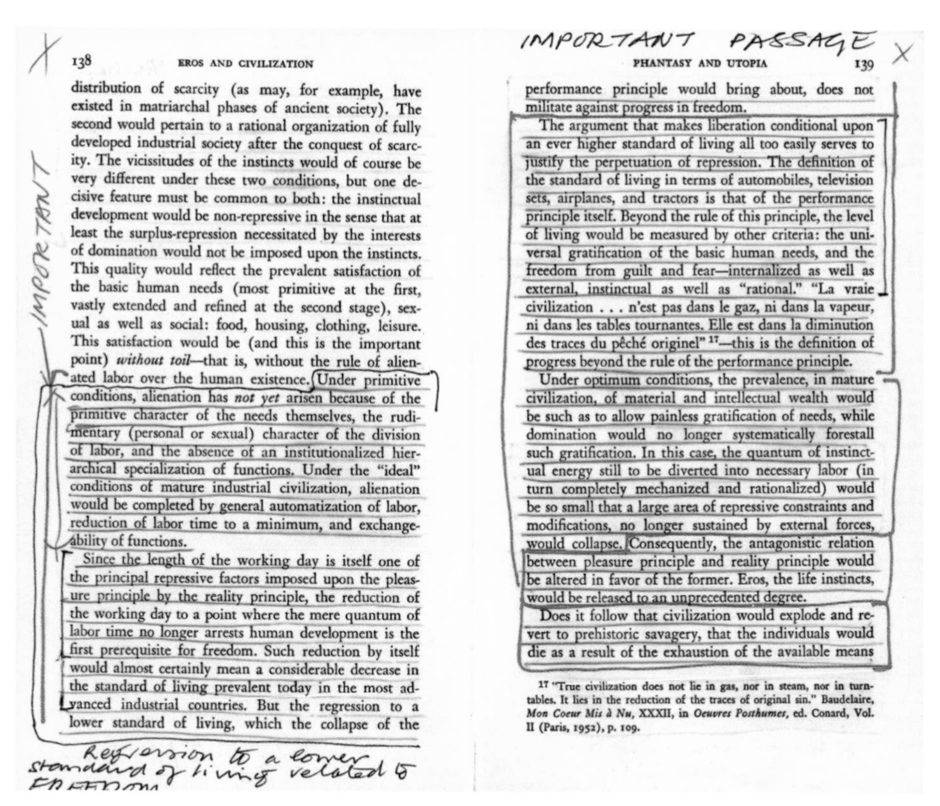

138 EROS AND CIVILIZATION

distribution of scarcity (as may, for example, have existed in matriarchal phases of ancient society). The second would pertain to a rational organization of fully developed industrial society after the conquest of scarcity. The vicissitudes of the instincts would of course be very different under these two conditions, but one decisive feature must be common to both: the instinctual development would be non-repressive in the sense that at least the surplus-repression necessitated by the interests of domination would not be imposed upon the instincts. This quality would reflect the prevalent satisfaction of the basic human needs (most primitive at the first, vastly extended and refined at the second stage), sexual as well as social: food, housing, clothing, leisure. This satisfaction would be (and this is the important point) *without toil*—that is, without the rule of alienated labor over the human existence. Under primitive conditions, alienation has *not yet* arisen because of the primitive character of the needs themselves, the rudimentary (personal or sexual) character of the division of labor, and the absence of an institutionalized hierarchical specialization of functions. Under the "ideal" conditions of mature industrial civilization, alienation would be completed by general automatization of labor, reduction of labor time to a minimum, and exchangeability of functions.

Since the length of the working day is itself one of the principal repressive factors imposed upon the pleasure principle by the reality principle, the reduction of the working day to a point where the mere quantum of labor time no longer arrests human development is the first prerequisite for freedom. Such reduction by itself would almost certainly mean a considerable decrease in the standard of living prevalent today in the most advanced industrial countries. But the regression to a lower standard of living, which the collapse of the

PHANTASY AND UTOPIA 139

performance principle would bring about, does not militate against progress in freedom.

The argument that makes liberation conditional upon an ever higher standard of living all too easily serves to justify the perpetuation of repression. The definition of the standard of living in terms of automobiles, television sets, airplanes, and tractors is that of the performance principle itself. Beyond the rule of this principle, the level of living would be measured by other criteria: the universal gratification of the basic human needs, and the freedom from guilt and fear—internalized as well as external, instinctual as well as "rational." "La vraie civilization . . . n'est pas dans le gaz, ni dans la vapeur, ni dans les tables tournantes. Elle est dans la diminution des traces du pêché originel"[17]—this is the definition of progress beyond the rule of the performance principle.

Under optimum conditions, the prevalence, in mature civilization, of material and intellectual wealth would be such as to allow painless gratification of needs, while domination would no longer systematically forestall such gratification. In this case, the quantum of instinctual energy still to be diverted into necessary labor (in turn completely mechanized and rationalized) would be so small that a large area of repressive constraints and modifications, no longer sustained by external forces, would collapse. Consequently, the antagonistic relation between pleasure principle and reality principle would be altered in favor of the former. Eros, the life instincts, would be released to an unprecedented degree.

Does it follow that civilization would explode and revert to prehistoric savagery, that the individuals would die as a result of the exhaustion of the available means

[17] "True civilization does not lie in gas, nor in steam, nor in turntables. It lies in the reduction of the traces of original sin." Baudelaire, *Mon Coeur Mis à Nu*, XXXII, in *Oeuvres Posthumes*, ed. Conard, Vol. II (Paris, 1952), p. 109.

15 Two pages from Kenneth Frampton's copy of Herbert Marcuse's *Eros and Civilization* (New York: Vintage, 1962), which was given to him by Alan Colquhoun. Frampton uses the last paragraph on page 138 from Marcuse's chapter "Phantasy and Utopia" as an epigraph for his 1969 essay "The City of Dialectic," published in *Architectural Design* (October 1969).

pleasure in a future labouring society after its hypothetical liberation from the compulsion of consumption (Marcuse) and, second, the remote and critical possibility for mediating the autonomous rationality of science and technique through the effective reconstitution of … an effective political realm (Habermas)."[23] Frampton's copy of *Eros and Civilization* is so well-worn and marked up that its cover and Colquhoun's inscription have long since disappeared (**15**).

Thus, it is these two authors—Benjamin and Marcuse—who introduced Frampton in the late 1960s to the Frankfurt School and what came to be known as Critical Theory. They would soon be followed by Jürgen Habermas, whose *Towards a Rational Society* was translated into English in 1970, and Adorno, whose *Minima Moralia* (1951) was translated into English in 1974.[24] Alessandra Latour, an Italian graduate student and teacher in urban design at Columbia (and then a committed Marxist), gave Frampton a copy of Adorno's book, and he opened his 1983 essay on Arendt with a quotation from it, one that again encapsulates the mixture of despair and messianic hope that has characterized so much of his own writing since the late

1960s.[25] Until the 1980s, very little by Adorno or Horkheimer had been translated into English, and Frampton readily admits that he never read cover-to-cover the one book that seems to correspond most with his own disdain of commodification and mass culture, Adorno and Horkheimer's *Dialectic of the Enlightenment*, which had been translated into English in 1972. Adorno's *Aesthetic Philosophy* was not translated until 1984.[26]

Two more thinkers, however—individuals with whom Frampton had direct personal contact—are crucial to understanding his interest in Marxist cultural theory, and, especially, in its potential application to architecture. The first is Tomás Maldonado, the Argentine concrete painter, industrial designer, and theorist, who succeeded Max Bill as Rector at the Hochschule für Gestaltung in Ulm and who was also a visiting professor at Princeton in the late 1960s.[27] Frampton had already met Maldonado at Ulm in 1963, when he visited Germany as technical editor of *AD*;[28] at that time he also first encountered a second individual, the Swiss-French Marxist Claude Schnaidt, who also taught at Ulm and who would write the first monograph on Hannes Meyer, a book that Frampton has long admired.[29] Frampton discussed both writers in his 1974 essay, "Apropos Ulm: Curriculum and Critical Theory," in *Oppositions* 3, which was his first published use of the word "critical" in a title. In Ulm, he explained, he found a model for raising "critical consciousness of the role of design in contemporary society."[30] (Maldonado had used "critical" in the subtitle of the 1972 English translation of *La Speranza Progettuale*, which was titled *Design, Nature, and Revolution: Toward a Critical Ecology*.) It should be noted, though, that Frampton's use of "critical" here has little to do with the Frankfurt School but rather with a more general commitment to a Marxist position that unites theory and action. In fact, Maldonado specifically cites Antonio Gramsci for his theory of "praxiology" or "theory of practice"—a "model of action oriented toward overcoming the dichotomy between theory and practice."[31] One of the most telling quotes in *Modern Architecture: A Critical History* is from Schnaidt's essay "Architecture and Political Commitment" of 1967. It is worth repeating in full, as it so eloquently summarizes the critical position that underlies Frampton's own text:

> In the days when the pioneers of modern architecture were [still] young, they thought like William Morris that architecture should be an "art of the people for the people." Instead of pandering to the tastes of the privileged few, they wanted to satisfy the requirements of the community. They wanted to build dwellings, matched to human needs, to erect a Cité Radieuse. But they had reckoned without the commercial instincts of the bourgeoisie who lost no time in arrogating their theories to themselves and pressing them into service for the purposes of money-making. Utility quickly became synonymous with profitability. Anti-academic forms became the new décor of the ruling classes. The rational dwelling was transformed into the minimum dwelling, the Cité Radieuse into the urban

> conglomeration and austerity of line into poverty of form. The architects of the trade unions, co-operatives, and social municipalities were enlisted in the service of the whisky distillers, detergent manufacturers, the bankers, and the Vatican. Modern architecture, which wanted to play its part in the liberation of mankind by creating a new environment to live in, was transformed into a giant enterprise for the degradation of the human habitat.[32]

With this statement, Schnaidt, and thus Frampton, was insisting upon the need to recognize the extent that modern architecture, despite its progressive intentions, had been shaped by the dictates of profit and capitalism; but also implicit in this passage, and perhaps even more clearly in Frampton's conclusion to the book, is the desire to propose something more than *Existenzminimum*—a commitment to a richer, more fulfilling world. And here, we have again the particular synthesis that underlies so much of Frampton's thought and what might be seen as the goal of his critical perspective: an architectural modernity that is not reduced to rational instrumentality and minimum dwelling, but rather offers a liberatory vision that enriches habitation and community life while still embracing technological progress. In other words, it is an architectural vision very much compatible with Marcuse's broader cultural argument in *Eros and Civilization*.

Frampton's discontent with architecture's commodification and environmental degradation was further fueled by the rise of postmodern architecture and its increasing emphasis on scenographic effects in design. This is very apparent by 1982–83, the year of his *AD* issue *Modern Architecture and the Critical Present* and the publication of "Towards a Critical Regionalism" in Hal Foster's anthology *The Anti-Aesthetic*. The anthology also included Habermas's sweeping indictment of postmodern thought, prompted by the Venice Architecture Biennale of 1980, and in part the motivation for Frampton's own essay (he was originally on the organizing committee of the Biennale but soon resigned once he recognized the direction that Portoghesi's exhibition would take). The intense debate among architects and social thinkers of the period arising from discussions about postmodernism had intensified Frampton's awareness not only of the failures and limits of the Modern Movement's embrace of technology and social transformation but also of the increasing complicity of contemporary architecture with the forces of capitalism. In other words, he used his citations of members of the Frankfurt School and Marxists such as Schnaidt and Maldonado to criticize both modern and postmodern architecture, if increasingly with a critical lens directed at the latter. But it might also be said, as Fredric Jameson later so brilliantly explicated in *The Seeds of Time* (1994), that Frampton's "arrière-garde" critique was itself participating in the celebration of pluralism and difference so typical of both postmodernism and late capitalism (that is, a post-Fordist economy that can customize its products for local markets), even as it sought to retain some vestige of utopian hope in its proposal of an "architecture of resistance."[33] One might say that he hoped to fashion a progressive strategy out of the materials of tradition and nostalgia (as well as a more considered use of technology) that would stand, even if metonymically, against the commodification rampant in late capitalism.[34] Frampton continued to share with Marcuse a belief in art as a reminder of an alternative world, even as he acknowledged its incapacity to effect large-scale change, at least without the presence of larger political, social, and cultural movements.

As important as the Frankfurt School was to Frampton, his understanding of what a critical position might entail can also be seen as linked to another tradition, perhaps not consciously on his part, one that has been very much part of his thought since the early 1970s. Habermas, in his 1968 book *Knowledge and Human Interests*, distinguished between critical political and social theory, notably that of the Frankfurt School, and "self-reflective" cultural theory. He equated the latter with hermeneutics, a theory concerned with the meaning of human texts and symbolic expressions, one that effaces the boundary between factual and symbolic understanding.[35] While Habermas acknowledged the "conservative" side of hermeneutics—that it is inherently concerned with existing meanings and cultural tradition rather than with new possibilities, and thus social transformation—he argued that it offers a necessary critique of positivism in its insistence on individual life experience which must then be adapted to general categories. Although literary critical theory is now associated with numerous other tendencies, including Derridean deconstruction, post-colonial theory, identity politics, gender studies, and even environmental analyses, this other—earlier—meaning of cultural theory that Habermas articulated seems to reflect Frampton's own concerns for meaning and cultural expression (even if they have evolved over the years to include some of the approaches just mentioned). This is perhaps never so apparent as in his oft-cited and influential essay of 1983, "Towards a Critical Regionalism," which opens with a long quotation from Paul Ricœur's 1961 essay "Universal Civilization and National Cultures." Ricœur, who is known for uniting phenomenology and hermeneutics and for extending hermeneutic investigation beyond the literary sphere, presciently posed the recurring quandary of developing nations (but one that affects all cultures): "There is the paradox: how to become modern and to return to sources: how to revive an old, dormant civilization" —which he referred to earlier as "a cultural past"—"and take part in universal civilization."[36] Frampton was introduced to Ricœur's work by the phenomenologist Dalibor Vesely, who had opted not to review Frampton's *Modern Architecture* in the 1982 publication of *AD*.[37]

Embracing Ricœur's paradox—that is, between modernity and tradition or between universal civilization and regional cultures—Frampton proposed in his influential 1983 essay a strategy of arrière-garde action, a kind of holding operation, salvaging the cultural meaning of architecture against the onslaught of an ever-pervasive instrumental rationality. The variety of sources in this essay is itself telling: not only his beloved Arendt, but also Marcuse, Benjamin, and Heidegger—in brief, both the Frankfurt School and phenomenology. In the essay, Frampton tries to find a means of practice that would unite his Marxist sympathies and deep commitment to an egalitarian society with his phenomenological or experiential concerns emphasizing place, light, and tactility—in short, the sensual dimensions of architecture (in fact, the very qualities that the post-critical crowd found missing in so much poststructuralist critical theory). While Frampton's effort to unite these two seemingly contradictory perspectives may be unique among architectural critics and historians—and distinct from Tafuri's, let alone those of his IAUS colleagues—his struggle for such a synthesis was not so rare among philosophers, whether Marxists such as Marcuse and Henri Lefebvre, or existentialists and phenomenologists, such as Jean-Paul Sartre and the younger Merleau-Ponty, who attempted to reconcile their philosophical ideas with their political commitment to a classless society (even if they would later part ways about the necessity of proletarian revolution). Tafuri himself admits in his largely positive review of Frampton's *Modern Architecture: A Critical History* that such a reconciliation between these two seemingly disparate positions is possible, although Frampton himself has never tried systematically to do so in his writing.[38] Only later would he read seriously Merleau-Ponty's *Phenomenology of Perception*, a source that he cites in *A Genealogy of Modern Architecture*, where it would seem that the phenomenological strain in his thinking dominates.

In "Towards a Critical Regionalism," one senses, perhaps more than in any of his other writings to date, the importance of the word "critical" for Frampton. He believed it was essential to distinguish his vision of regionalism from conservative appeals to nostalgia and tradition, and even from its lingering associations with *Blut und Boden*—a position he states forcefully in his third point.[39] Nonetheless, one wonders at times if his commitment to political critique is undermined or mitigated by his reveries about architecture's experiential qualities. Can the qualities that he so deeply values in architecture—such as tactility and the articulation of structure—really serve as modes of resistance, as a kind of arrière-garde holding operation? Is it possible to reconcile his belief in technology as a democratic and liberating tool that can improve living conditions for all classes, especially the most impoverished, with his rejection of mass culture and technology's pervasive presence in American society, which he associates with mindless gratification and environmental degradation (television, highways, and air conditioning, etc.)? And given the proliferation of images and the homogenizing effects of ever-increasing globalization, is it possible to accept his elevation of structure over surface effects, or his emphasis on place and urban identity, especially in contexts that seem to defy any kind of regional or even topographical specificity? Like Lefebvre, who is not a central figure for Frampton but who also drew from both Marxism and phenomenology, Frampton seems to be searching for a logic (and, in his case, an aesthetic vision) that would embrace the paradoxes of two seemingly disparate worldviews in his search for reservoirs of resistance against the onslaught of "commodity culture" and the "imperatives of production." And in a manner somewhat

16 Alvar Aalto, Säynätsalo Town Hall, Säynätsalo, Finland, 1949–51.

reminiscent of Benjamin, he relies on a series of quotations and fragments, rather than one unified argument, to make his points.[40] But whether one accepts his synthesis or not, or even fully embraces his aesthetic vision, what undoubtedly makes his position so appealing to so many architects is his belief that critique should not be purely negative—that is, it should not only serve to elucidate the shortcomings and contradictions of the status quo but also take the risk of proposing alternatives that might offer, however modestly, the promise of a richer, more fulfilling existence.

If over the years, Frampton has increasingly recognized the limits of architecture's own transformative powers given the hegemony of global capital, he sees proposing positive examples of architecture as a "strategy of *sidestepping*—sidestepping a tendency toward closure that seems to constrain the living present in such a way that you sometimes feel you can't do anything."[41] Although these models reflect an increasing concern for experiential qualities and what he calls the "poetics" of construction and structure, one thing has remained constant, as he recently stated: his "commitment to the socialist aspect of the modern project."[42] Here, his position seems closer to that of both Habermas and Gramsci, who emphasize culture's potential as a constructive force countering prevailing ideologies, than to that of Tafuri and Adorno, who seem to accept a darker, more totalizing view of capitalism's power.[43] In fact, one might argue that where Frampton departs from Tafuri is not so much as an operative critic—for Frampton's models or preferences are not part of a seamless teleological narrative in the sense of Giedion or Bruno Zevi, two of Tafuri's "operative" historians—but rather in his willingness to propose strategies for architecture that might

17 Jørn Utzon, Bagsvaerd Church, Copenhagen, Denmark, 1968–76.

offer something more than the zero-sum game of market forces. To avoid closure, he seeks to present, as he has explained, a "wide variety of work" (**16, 17**).[44]

But the gap between Tafuri and Frampton might not be quite as great as it first appears. At the conclusion of *Architecture and Utopia*, and after a relentless account of modern architecture's "useless" utopianism and its serial failures to generate radical social change, Tafuri offers a glimmer of hope to architects: they might work in public offices as "technicians," that is, organizers of building activities and planners of process, a role involving the dissolution of traditional disciplinary boundaries.[45] Frampton's hope, though, resides within architecture itself. He is still willing to see the generative—and positive—qualities of form and experience in order to create a space for architectural practice that resists the most blatant forces of commodification.

Frampton is acutely aware of the difficulties of his own belief in the transformative values of both architecture and criticism, and in a 2001 interview with Gevork Hartoonian, he specifically addresses Tafuri's rejection of "operative history":

> I was recently re-reading the didactic introduction, wherein he [Tafuri] writes: "Doing away with outdated myths, one certainly does not see on the architectural horizon any ray of an alternative, of a technology 'of the working class'." I am aware that the Marxist "hard line," then as now, thinks of my writing as operative criticism, as permitting the survival of anachronistic hopes of design as a liberative agent, which Tafuri dismissed as regressive. However, he also concedes that under present circumstances one is "left to navigate in empty space, in

18 Kenneth Frampton, New York, 2010.

> which anything can happen but nothing is decisive"—which sums up, I suppose, basically what I think about my position.[46]

In the last essay of Frampton's book *Labour, Work and Architecture*, "Minimal Moralia: Reflections on Recent Swiss German Production" (1997), a rather sharp assessment of some recent trends in Swiss architecture, he states in a beautiful passage what navigating—and writing—in this "empty space" means to him:

> One can only hope that others will be able to sustain their early capacity or, alternatively, to reveal an untapped potential for the pursuit of the art of architecture in all its anachronistic fullness. One perhaps needs to add that one does not indulge in critique for the sake of a gratuitous negativity, but rather to spur the critical sensibility, to sharpen the debate, to overcome, as far as this is feasible, the debilitating dictates of fashion, and above all to guard against the ever-present threat, in a mediatic age, of sliding into an intellectual somnambulance where everything seems to appear to be for the aestheticized best in the best of all commodified worlds.[47]

1 Kenneth Frampton, *Modern Architecture: A Critical History* (London: Thames & Hudson, 1980; New York and Toronto: Oxford University Press, 1980); and Kenneth Frampton, "Towards a Critical Regionalism: Six Points for an Architecture of Resistance," in *The Anti-Aesthetic: Essays on Postmodern Culture*, ed. Hal Foster (Port Townsend, WA: Bay Press, 1983), 16–30. Subsequent editions of *Modern Architecture* were published by Thames & Hudson in 1985, 1992, and 2007. Frampton has recently

completed the manuscript of a fifth edition, which increases the book's geographical range. *Modern Architecture* has been translated into Chinese, Dutch, French, Estonian, German, Greek, Hungarian, Italian, Japanese, Portuguese, Russian, Serbian-Croatian, and Spanish.

2 See especially, Kenneth Frampton, "Place-Form and Cultural Identity," in *Design After Modernism: Beyond the Object*, ed. John Thackara (New York: Thames & Hudson, 1988), 51–66; and Kenneth Frampton, "Critical Regionalism Revisited," in *Critical Regionalism: The Pomona Proceedings*, ed. Spyros Amourgis (Pomona, CA: College of Environmental Design, California State Polytechnic University, 1991), 34–39. In "Place-Form and Cultural Identity" Frampton expresses reservations about the suffix "-ism" in his use of the word "regionalism" because of its links with style. Prior to the version of "Critical Regionalism" that appeared in the Foster anthology, Frampton wrote in 1982 "Prospects for a Critical Regionalism," which appeared in *Perspecta: The Yale Architectual Journal*, 20 (1983): 177–95, and in 1987 he wrote another essay, "Ten Points on an Architecture of Regionalism: A Provisional Polemic," published in *Center 3: New Regionalism* (Austin: Center for American Architecture and Design, 1987), 20–27. Although this essay does not have the word "critical" in the title, it concludes with a plea for a "critical basis from which to evolve a contemporary architecture of resistance."

3 The "Grays" was a term used in the 1970s to characterize a group of architects, including Allan Greenberg, Aldo Guirgola, Charles Moore, Robert A.M. Stern, and Robert Venturi, who were seen as more "inclusive" in their approach to design (for example, making references to vernacular forms and tradition) than the so-called "Whites" or the group of architects known as the "New York Five," who were influenced by Le Corbusier's villas of the 1920s.

4 Kenneth Frampton, preface to *Labour, Work and Architecture: Collected Essays on Architecture and Design* (London and New York: Phaidon Press, 2002), 6; see also unpublished interview of Kenneth Frampton by Daniel Talesnik, "The Role of an Architectural Historian," October 22, 2013, in "Seven Interviews between October 2011 and October 2013," 50 pp. typed manuscript, p. 46. These interviews will be published in 2020 by Columbia Books on Architecture and the City, distributed by Columbia University Press.

5 I am indebted to Cesare Birignani, who read an earlier version of this paper, for this observation.

6 Frampton, preface to *Labour, Work and Architecture*, 7; Manfredo Tafuri, *Theories and History of Modern Architecture*, trans. Giorgio Verrecchia (New York: Icon Editions/Harper & Row, 1980), ch. 4. In this book, first published in Italian in 1968, Tafuri defined "operative criticism" as "an analysis of architecture (or the arts in general) that, instead of an abstract survey, has in its objective the planning of a precise poetical tendency, anticipated in its structures and derived from historical analyses programmatically distorted and finalised" (p. 141).

7 Conversation with Kenneth Frampton, May 21, 2018; he also talked about this period in an interview with Talesnik, June 26, 2012; Talesnik, "The Role of an Architectural Historian," 16–17.

8 Kenneth Frampton, ed., *Italy / The Work of Mangiarotti & Morassuti & Gino Valle, Architectural Design*, 34/3 (March 1964).

9 At *AD*, he also published Constant's New Babylon and the work of Yona Friedman. See Constant Nieuwenhuys, "New Babylon: An Urbanism of the Future," *Architectural Design*, 34/6 (June 1964): 304–5; Yona Friedman, "Ports on Channel Bridge," *Architectural Design*, 33 (April 1963): 158–59; and Friedman, "Towards a Mobile Architecture," *Architectural Design*, 33 (November 1963): 509–10.

10 Kenneth Frampton, "The Humanist versus the Utilitarian Ideal," *Architectural Design*, 38/3 (March 1968): 134–36, repr. in Frampton, *Labour, Work and Architecture*, 109–19. In a 2003 interview with Stan Allen and Hal Foster, Frampton explained his preference for Le Corbusier over Meyer in a query about Michael Hays's more positive valuation of Meyer. "Your question makes me think again of the limits of any particular historical moment. Is it unfair to suggest that the critical rigor upheld by Hays and possibly by Tafuri, in their defense of the anticompositional and the antihumanist, is still a form of waiting, as it were, for the revolutionary moment when a radical transformation might occur and a new acceptance of the fact that this is hardly likely to happen, that this option might not be available any more. Then the question arises: which is the more realist of the two positions? It's not that I'm against what Hannes Meyer represented, but on a broader historical front, I have to ask which position is the more operatively critical." Stan Allen and Hal Foster, "A Conversation with Kenneth Frampton," *October*, 106 (Autumn 2003): 56.

11 Frampton, conversation with the author, May 21, 2018.

12 See especially, Robert Somol and Sarah Whiting, "Notes around the Doppler Effect and Other Moods of Modernism," *Perspecta*, 33, *Mining Autonomy* (2002): 72–77; and Michael Speaks, "Design Intelligence and the New Economy," *Architectural Record*, 190/1 (January 2002): 72–79.

13 Michael Polyani, *Personal Knowledge: Towards a Post-Critical Philosophy* (Chicago: University of Chicago Press, 1958); William H. Poteat, *Polyanian Meditations: In Search of a Post-Critical Logic* (Durham, NC: Duke University Press, 1985).

14 Here, especially, it is important to acknowledge Tafuri's *Theories and History of Architecture* of 1968, which explored in depth issues of historiography and criticism drawing heavily from the Frankfurt School, especially the writings of Walter Benjamin. Tafuri quoted at length Giulio Carlo Argan's *La crisi dei valori* (1957) as a source for his own ideas about a more "advanced" criticism (Tafuri, introduction to *The Sphere and the Labyrinth*, trans. Pellegrino d'Acierno and Robert Connolly [Cambridge, MA: MIT Press, 1987], 7). As is noted later in this essay, the only previous use of the word "critical" that I have found in the title of an English-language architecture book is *Design, Nature, Revolution: Toward a Critical Ecology*, the 1972 English translation of Tomás Maldonado's *La Speranza Progettuale* (Turin: G. Enaudi, 1970); note that the word does not appear in the original Italian title.

15 Kenneth Frampton, *A Genealogy of Modern Architecture: Comparative Critical Analysis of Built Form*, ed. Ashley Simone (Zurich: Lars Müller Publishers, 2015).

16 My observations are in part based on my experience knowing Frampton over the past forty years, including several conversations about his interest in the Frankfurt School, and in part distilled from his writings and published interviews. Kenneth Frampton, telephone conversation with the author, May 16, 2016; Frampton, conversation with the author, May 21, 2018. For interviews, see Gevork Hartoonian, "An Interview with Kenneth Frampton," January 2001, *Architectural Theory Review*, 7/1 (2002), repr. *Global Perspectives on Critical Architecture: Praxis Reloaded*, ed. Gevork Hartoonian (Farnham, Surrey: Ashgate, 2015), 43–47; Allen and Foster, "A Conversation with Kenneth Frampton"; and Monika Mitásová, "Kenneth Frampton," January 19 and 25, 2010, in *Oxymoron & Pleonasm: Conversations on American Critical and Projective Theory of Architecture*, ed. Monika Mitásová (New York: Actar, 2014), 10–28. I have also drawn from the unpublished interviews by Talesnik (see note 4).

17 Kenneth Frampton, introduction to *Modern Architecture*, 8–9.

18 Allen and Foster, "A Conversation with Kenneth Frampton," 42. Frampton's essay "Industrialization and the Crises in Architecture" (*Oppositions*, 1 [1973]: 53–81) was written for a conference in honor of Hannah Arendt, which she attended.

19 Kenneth Frampton, "Maison de Verre," and Walter Benjamin, "Paris: Capital of the Nineteenth Century," *Perspecta: The Yale Architectural Journal*, ed. Peter C. Papademetrious and Stuart Wrede, 12 (1969): 77–125 and 161–72. Both articles were seminal in introducing new material to English-speaking architects and, more generally, U.S. readers. *Perspecta* republished the recent translation of "Paris, Capital of the Nineteenth Century" by Quintin Hoare, which had appeared in *New Left Review*, 48 (March–April 1968): 77–88, adding drawings by Grandville to illustrate the text. The magazine also included Ben Brewster's introduction to Benjamin's synopsis, "Walter Benjamin and the Arcades Project," which had also first been published in the same issue of *New Left Review*. It would not be until 1978 that the synopsis would be published in the anthology of Walter Benjamin's writings *Reflections*, ed. Peter Demetz, trans. Edmund Jephcott (New York: Harcourt Brace Jovanovich, 1978), 146–53.

20 Frampton, phone conversation, May 16, 2016.

21 Tomás Maldonado, who also taught at Princeton in the late 1960s, was probably responsible for alerting both Frampton and Colquhoun to Marcuse. In his interview with Allen and Foster, Frampton speculates that being in the United States also "politicized" Colquhoun and precipitated his turn toward Marxism (p. 41).

22 Kenneth Frampton, "The Volvo Case," *Lotus*, 12 (1976), repr. in Frampton, *Labour, Work and Architecture*, 75. Frampton had already used a passage from *Eros and Civilization* (New York: Vintage Books, 1962: 139) as an epigraph in his article "The City of Dialectic," published in *Architectural Design*, 39/10 (October 1969): 541, and he refers to the same passage from *Eros and Civilization* in his essay "America 1960–1970: Appunti su alcune immagini e teorie della città," "America 1960–1970: Notes on Urban Images and Theory," *Casabella*, 35/359–60 (December 1971): 34, 36.

23 Kenneth Frampton, "The Status of Man and the Status of His Objects: A Reading of *The Human Condition*," in *Modern Architecture and the Critical Present*, *Architectural Design* Profile (London: Academy Editions, 1982), 15, repr. in Frampton, *Labour, Work and Architecture*, 39.

24 In his essay "Place-Form and Cultural Identity," Frampton refers to Jürgen Habermas's essay "Technology and Science as Ideology" in *Towards a Rational Society* as a "a seminal work" and then states that "the later Frankfurt School remains" in his view "the only valid basis upon which to develop a form of (post) modern critical culture." Frampton, "Place-Form and Cultural Identity," 63.

25 Frampton, *Labour, Work and Architecture*, 25. The 1947 passage from Adorno's *Minima Moralia* is: "The only philosophy which can be responsibly practiced in the face of despair is the attempt to contemplate all things as they would present themselves from the standpoint of redemption; all else is reconstruction, mere technique. Perspectives must be fashioned that displace and estrange the world, reveal it to be, with its rifts and crevices, as indigent and distorted as it will appear one day in the messianic light."

26 Over the years Frampton has frequently expressed his sympathy for Clement Greenberg's argument in his 1939 essay "Avant-Garde and Kitsch." One of Frampton's most explicit rejections of mass-culture and popular taste occurs in his vehement exchange with Denise Scott Brown in the December 1971 issue of *Casabella*. Frampton, "America 1960–1970: Notes on Urban Image and Theory" and Denise Scott Brown, "Pop Off: Reply to Kenneth Frampton," *Casabella*, 359–60 (December 1971): 24–38, and 41–45. Besides the *New Left Review* (the source of *Perspecta*'s translation of Walter Benjamin's "Paris: Capital of the Nineteenth-Century"), a major source of translations of writings by the Frankfurt School and related theorists such as Siegfried Kracauer was the journal *New German Critique*, founded in 1973.

27 It was a young, precocious Argentine student at Princeton at the time, Emilio Ambasz, who was probably responsible for encouraging Dean Robert Geddes to bring Maldonado to Princeton to teach. Ambasz remains an important supporter of Frampton's research.

28 Monica Pidgeon, the editor of *AD*, accompanied Kenneth Frampton on this trip in 1963 to Ulm.

29 Claude Schnaidt, *Hannes Meyer: Bauten, Projekte und Schriften / Buildings, Projects and Writings* (Teufen: Verlag Authur Niggli, 1965).

30 Kenneth Frampton, "Apropos Ulm: Curriculum and Critical Theory," *Oppositions*, 3 (1974): 17. The essay, but not the introduction from which this quotation is taken, is reprinted in *Labour, Work and Architecture*, 45–63.

31 Tomás Maldonado, "Colloquium con Maldonado e Ohl," *Design-Italia III* (September 1972), 32, as quoted by Frampton, "Apropos Ulm: Curriculum and Critical Theory," 34. Maldonado was also influenced by the Marxist philosopher Ernst Bloch and the word "*speranza*" in his book title *La Speranza Progettuale* (The Principle of Hope) alludes to Bloch's *Das Prinzip Hoffnung*, which Maldonado cites extensively. See Maldonado, *Design, Nature, and Revolution: Toward a Critical Ecology*, trans. Mario Domandi, forward by Larry Busbea (Minneapolis: University of Minnesota Press, MN, 2019).

32 Claude Schnaidt, "Architektur und politisches Engagement," "Architecture and Political Commitment," *Ulm*, 19/20 (August 1967): 26, as quoted by Frampton, *Modern Architecture*, 285–86. The passage is the opening paragraph of a talk that Schnaidt gave at the Academy of Fine Arts, Hamburg, March 2, 1967.

33 Fredric Jameson, *The Seeds of Time* (New York: Columbia University Press, 1994), 188–205.

34 Ibid., 189–205, esp. 202–4.

35 Jürgen Habermas, *Knowledge and Human Interests*, trans. Jeremy J. Shapiro (Boston: Beacon Press, 1971). The original German book was published in 1968. Frampton said to me that he has not read this book.

36 Paul Ricœur, "Universal Civilization and National Cultures" (1961), in *History and Truth*, trans. Charles. A. Kelbley (Evanston, IL: Northwestern University Press, 1965), 276–77, as quoted by Kenneth Frampton in "Towards a Critical Regionalism," 16.

37 Frampton dedicates *A Genealogy of Modern Architecture* to Vesely.

38 Manfredo Tafuri, "Architecture and 'Poverty,'" in *Modern Architecture and the Critical Present*, 57–58. Tafuri writes: "It is hardly accidental that Frampton's critical sensibility enters into tension with the ethos that he has himself inherited from the 'tradition of the new.' Benjamin and Heidegger, in truth, are not irreconcilable. Yet still, a work of historical reconstruction is needed in order to open up a dialogue between them, the kind of work that hasty readers of Lyotard would barely be able to handle" (p. 58). Tafuri seems to imply that Frampton in "his excellent book" might have "cleansed" modern architecture even more, and have stated more forcefully the need for "destruction" and "poverty" as a precondition for new "paths." In his review, Tafuri cites Benjamin's essay "The Destructive Character" (1931), which had not yet been translated into English. Tafuri's title and argument also suggest Benjamin's essay "Experience and Poverty" (1932), which had also not been translated yet into English. Tafuri's willingness to consider a reconciliation between Marxism and phenomenology undoubtedly was spurred by Massimo Cacciari, who taught aesthetics at the University of Venice and who was deeply influenced by Nietzsche and Heidegger.

39 Frampton, "Towards a Critical Regionalism," 20.

40 Frampton's choice to structure "Towards a Critical Regionalism" as a series of points is also reminiscent of modernist manifestos, such as Le Corbusier and Pierre Jeanneret's "Five Points of a New

Architecture." Frampton's use of "Towards" also recalls—and was undoubtedly meant to evoke—the English title of Le Corbusier's *Vers une architecture*, *Towards a New Architecture*.

41 Allen and Foster, "A Conversation with Kenneth Frampton," 57.

42 Kenneth Frampton, "The Role of the Architectural Historian," unpublished interview with Daniel Talesnik, 48.

43 In the "Note to the Second Edition" of *Theories and History of Architecture* (n.p.), Tafuri dismisses all "sugary official 'Marxism,'" including the Marcusian school of proposing a "class architecture (an architecture 'for a liberated society')," arguing that it results in an ideology only serving the status quo.

44 Allen and Foster, "A Conversation with Kenneth Frampton," 57.

45 Manfredo Tafuri, *Architecture and Utopia: Design and Captalist Development*, trans. Barbara Luigia La Penta (Cambridge, MA: MIT Press, 1976), 170–82.

46 Frampton, "Interviewed by Gevork Hartoonian," 46. Frampton follows this passage by declaring, "I fail to see how my discourse preoccupied with regionalism and tectonics can be seen as perpetuating illusions as to the 'utopia of design,' to coin Tafuri's phrase."

47 Kenneth Frampton, "Minimal Moralia: Reflections on Recent Swiss German Production" (1997), in *Labour, Work and Architecture*, 331.

World Architecture and Critical Practice

Wang Shu

In 2012, after the announcement that I had received the Pritzker Architecture Prize, e-mails congratulating me on my award flew in like snowflakes. Of these, I was most impressed by two messages, both of which were particularly short. One of them was from my colleague Francis Kéré, who wrote: "Congratulations! This is the first time that a World Architect is awarded the Pritzker Architecture Prize." The other was from the respected Professor Kenneth Frampton from Columbia University, who wrote: "Congratulations to you! This is the victory of resistance architecture." The reason why I was most impressed by these two messages was because I realized that they were similar in their implications. I remember visiting Professor Frampton at Columbia University when I was in New York City. He invited me to participate in the seminar of his graduate students, the theme of which was "world architecture." I remembered we mainly discussed new architecture in South America. On that day, I was deeply inspired, and I suddenly realized that "modern architecture" does not mean "world architecture," and even that "modern architecture" could be said to be killing "world architecture." For quite a long time, Chinese architects have equated "modern architecture" with contemporary "world architecture," and have maintained "modern architecture's" claim of connection to the progress myth originating with the European Enlightenment. Perhaps that's why today I believe we need a kind of resistant or critical architectural practice. In 2009, the first solo exhibition of our practice, Amateur Architecture Studio, was held at the BOZAR/Centre for Fine Arts in Brussels. I named it *Architecture as a Resistance*, which was intended to pay tribute to Professor Frampton's ideas, since his essay "Towards a Critical Regionalism: Six Points for an Architecture of Resistance" was the theoretical reference for the exhibition title, and highlighted the fact that the essay had the greatest impact on my architectural thinking. In his message Kéré had called me a "world architect," a characterization with which I fully agree. It is important to emphasize that "world architecture" is not exclusively a part of "modern architecture," because "world architecture" should be current and reflect the diversity of contemporary practice. Even more important, based on my personal experience, is the fact that a critical sense of regionalism is awakening globally, one that can no longer be subsumed within the term "modern architecture." A critical practice is surely possible today, and is ever more urgently needed.

I recall my thoughts in 1993, when I first read Professor Frampton's "Six Points for an Architecture of Resistance." While the essay was about the profound crisis of urban and architectural development in the modern architecture movement in the Western world, and about the destruction of local civilizations that had already taken place, at the same time, I realized that the more recent changes in China, where the largest changes in the world's cities at the end of the twentieth century, and the beginning of the twenty-first century, were happening, had just begun. On the one hand, we are impressed by the profound foresight of theory and criticism, and, on the other hand, tragedy seems inevitable. The effects of high-rises and highways, the two iconic political tools of all globalized civilizations, have been magnified dozens of times in China. The local urban and architectural civilization in China, which originally highly valued nature, has completely collapsed in the city and is collapsing in the countryside. Whose victory is this?

Perhaps the impact of globalization on culture is more complex than we think. When Amateur Architecture Studio began the design of the Xiang Shan Campus of the China Academy of Art in Hangzhou in 2002, we used a thick-walled construction system combined with recycled materials to apply the concept of energy conservation and environmental protection in university campus building, and to promote a higher education lifestyle that does not rely on air conditioning (**19**). On this premise, we provided no more than one-third of the area in each building with air conditioning. We believed that although the area is hot in summer, the students were off campus at that time. If the weather is unusually hot during the semester, teaching activities can be concentrated in the air-conditioned area. Was this belief actualized when the buildings were put into use? Since 2005, when the campus was occupied, secretly setting up air conditioning has never stopped. I remember once we had a joint studio with an American university in June, early in our summer. It was already unseasonably warm, but the campus building was actually well-ventilated by breezes and was only slightly warmer than usual. I asked the American students and teachers whether it was too hot for comfort. They said it was a little warm, but it was a very comfortable heat (**20**). Yet the Chinese students thought that it was too hot to work! It is hard to imagine that air conditioning was rare in China before 1995. But from another perspective, in China, before there was air conditioning in summer, everyone was off work in those hot months.

I remember the hottest month of one summer, when it was too uncomfortable to sleep inside a room. Every family in the city put a simple bed at the door, on both sides of the street. The nighttime street became a huge city living room, which was also a children's paradise. Today, the weather has little effect on work habits. There are few people on the street in summer, and everyone hides in cool rooms. It can be argued that air conditioning has improved the efficiency of work to a certain extent, but it has also profoundly changed the way of living in each particular area. What's more, it has profoundly altered the methods of construction, because the energy-saving material layer of the wall breaks the continuity of the interior and exterior spaces. As a result, it is not only difficult to achieve authenticity of construction when employing contemporary building materials, but also the breathability of the natural

19 The Xiang Shan Campus, Hangzhou, China, designed by the Amateur Architecture Studio, 2007. Its energy-saving system utilizes thick walls and roofs.

20 The interior of the Xiang Shan Campus, with the corridor allowing air circulation in hot summers.

wall materials in regional traditions is now considered a negative element, leading to its inevitable removal in accordance with contemporary construction regulations.

In fact, compared to the time when Professor Frampton wrote "Six Points for an Architecture of Resistance," it is considered simple common sense in today's global architectural community to take into account sustainable development issues such as ecological materials and local climate. If we investigate the typical traditional courtyard houses in southern China with this view, we can find a type of dwelling that has existed for at least a thousand years—as a multistory collective residence, accommodating anywhere from several to dozens to even hundreds of family households. First, the use of the courtyard system solved the problems of neighborhood fire protection and the necessary boundaries between households in a community of mid-to-high density. Second, the orderly spatial arrangement of the courtyard had formed a good community way of life with a quality no worse than that typical of the modern style. In addition, the use of rammed earth, wood, stone,

21 A traditional village with rammed-earth houses in southern Zhejiang Province, China, 2013.

and clay brick—these easily available ecological materials—combined with easily replaceable technology assemblies made it possible for these courtyard dwellings to exist for hundreds of years and over many generations of a family (**21**). Owing to the intricate combination of varying exterior court sizes, outside air was able to flow through and cool the house even in unbearable heat, and as a result the whole building resembled a huge natural air conditioner. The difference was that this air-conditioning system was based on enabling a slight flow of air in and through the house, which is in fact contrary to the design regulation of "modern" space, which requires a completely enclosed, hermetically sealed space. The fact that these housing complexes had only portable toilets, and not flushing ones, is often seen, according to "modern" definitions, as a negative. Yet the older toilets also acted as an agricultural fertilizer recovery system, one that is in many ways very similar to the waste sorting and recycling that we see today.

It is also important to emphasize that there is no difference between the urban and rural examples of this type of housing in China. In fact, it is often the case that the standard of rural housing is higher than that of the city. Interestingly, if we don't predetermine the separation between tradition and modernity, it seems that these courtyard houses may be appropriately described as an ideal housing type and environment system for the future. In fact, in terms of the local culture of China, "modern architecture" is being realized in a completely different social background and context than that in which it originated, so that, due to the progress myth and technological improvement that come with "modern architecture," China today is completely dominated by the concrete-and-steel construction system. As a result, ninety percent of Chinese traditional buildings and cities that once existed as a comprehensive system have been destroyed during the past thirty years. China has demolished its future by striving to establish a modernity that in fact represents the past of Western modernity. Or rather, China has realized some crazy experiments that were impossible to achieve in the Western world, the result being what we can call an illusion of the future. In fact, we are more and more certain that the concrete-and-steel system of construction inherited from "modern architecture" is unsustainable, with negative consequences for the ecological environment. But the basic characteristic of the system is that, once widely adopted, it cannot be easily abandoned. The use of nostalgic renovation is just a cheap way to elicit sentimental feeling, and does not address the fundamental issues. It is painful that this crisis and its result were quite clearly stated more than thirty years ago in Professor Frampton's prescient essay, but that it still proved impossible to avoid this global tragedy, which has only been amplified dozens of times in China.

It is undeniable that the recent construction of large-scale infrastructure in China has provided unimaginable convenience for people's lives. In addition to the crossing highways and high-speed railway networks, in Zhejiang Province, where I live, each of the 30,000 villages is connected with concrete roads and internet access. That sounds good, but the problem is that the only asset capable of rapid return compatible with this large amount of financial investment in the short term is real estate. As determined by investment efficiency, the only viable mode of development is to build more and more high-rises, for which the city requires ever more land. Take the city of Hangzhou, where I live, as an example. It has expanded nearly twenty times during the past thirty years, but it is still short of land for development. Therefore, more and more local traditional buildings are being demolished to make way for new construction, creating a tragic cycle. Yet the people involved are happy because of their large compensation payments, a situation which seems to me quite comical. Ecological architecture is something similar. The so-called ecological and energy-saving regulations are instead promoting a new giant industry instead of ecological architecture. The mandatory requirement for the energy-saving wall fillers is a new weapon of extinction for the local architectural culture. If it is said that "modern architecture" has killed local architecture once, now the so-called energy-efficient architecture is killing it for a second time. Yet the emerging industry is booming.

This is an era that may be said to doubt whether there is still anything like a pioneer or avant-garde architecture. Yet even though the occurrence of modern avant-garde architecture in the West has had little to do with China, in 1989 Chinese architects were attracted by the modern avant-garde owing to its connection with progress, liberation, freedom, and drastic change. But this short-lived attraction soon experienced a double collapse: the American historicist postmodern architectural language was adopted as an effective prescription to prevent the end of Chinese architectural traditions, leading to the first collapse of any form of vanguard, Western avant-garde-inspired design; when this was combined with the increasing dominance of the real-estate-oriented urban planning and design style, the result was the collapse of any possible avant-garde consciousness, resulting in a complete devastation of progressive thinking. Faced with the first collapse, I wrote a long essay in 1987, "The Logic behind the Broken: The Crisis of Modern Architecture in China," which was never officially published, but was printed and distributed informally, and read by a few in the architectural community. My basic view was that we needed a true, humane avant-garde consciousness, and that any so-called historical style could not save the Chinese architectural tradition. The possible solution might be reconceiving the relationship between fundamental space types and ways of life in order to seek some kind of positive compromise between irresistible modern architectural production and localization. The key point was to think about what we could do amidst the destruction. And, a little later when Chinese market forces became dominant in the 1990s, I realized that for the architectural tradition of China, determined as it was by its relation to nature and craftsmanship, the destructive element in this new development was not some modern architectural concept, nor was it a matter of aesthetics. The key lay in the destructiveness of a professional architectural system that was in fact dominated by engineers.

Although Chinese architecture professors often talk about Chinese architecture, it was interesting to note that it existed only in architecture history classes. It was never mentioned in the design studios, because the professors themselves didn't understand it, and thus they were unable to teach the students about it. This situation remains the same even today. I made two decisions in 1990: first, I decided to rid myself of professional restrictions, and to work with the craftsmen so as to learn from them. The approach that I took was not just to make the shop drawings according to the needs of the craftsmen, but also to involve myself directly in construction management.

The projects I did in the 1990s were very symbolic. As a professional architect who graduated from the most highly ranked professional architecture department in China, I did what would not normally be considered real projects, but only several small-scale renovations and rebuilds. Then came the unprecedented waves of overheated demolition of existing buildings and their replacement by new construction that went on throughout China. All the work I did before Amateur Architecture Studio was founded in 1997 has in fact been demolished. At that time, in order to understand the full work of the craftsmen, I did not want to miss anything. At eight o'clock in the morning, when the craftsmen arrived at the site, I was already there. I would not leave until twelve o'clock in the evening after they finished work. My wife, Lu Wenyu, who was working in a large national design institute with 3,000 engineers at that time, came to the construction site after work in the evening and stayed with me until the end. Although it is a pity that these early projects were

22 The Tiles Mountain, located inside the Xiang Shan Campus, is a new rammed-earth building designed by the Amateur Architecture Studio, 2013.

23 The large tiled roof that protects the rammed-earth walls of the Tiles Mountain project.

demolished, the process of their construction was important to us because we were exposed to a completely different system of architectural activities. The premise of this system is not any abstract concept, but a familiarity with local materials and a deep understanding of a traditional construction system. The construction system has a special flexibility due to the extensive use of non-factory-produced natural materials. More interestingly, because the concrete-and-steel construction system has dominated the industry, craftsmen have been forced to make a compromise between traditional craft-defined qualities and contemporary building regulations. I realized that this compromise could be more positive, which would depend on both the understanding of the value of traditional materials and processes nowadays and on the architect's deep understanding of modern materials and construction systems. This dialogue between tradition and contemporary construction not only takes place at the structural level, but must also occur at the tectonic one, and extends to the whole construction system. And the man in between can no longer be considered just a professional architect. Instead, he is more like a builder in a special philosophical sense, because what he is doing is both modern and returning to the local origin (**22–23**).

When I recall that time, I remember that, in addition to practice, I was either wandering aimlessly in the city or reading. After so many years and so many experiences, the sources of my thought that I still remember clearly must be very significant to me: first, the French anthropologist Claude Lévi-Strauss's structural anthropology profoundly affected me. I got a clear idea of diversity from him, about the reassessment of local values, about the fundamental difference between craftsmen and engineers, about the concept of re-engaging the special value of craftsmen in urban activities, and about the important value of "Amateurs," as opposed to professionals.

The second important event in 1990 was the effect on me of the lectures on the gardens in southern China given by Professor Tong Jun from the university at which I studied. He proposed a question that struck me: where does nature end and where does architecture begin for almost any part of the garden that comes into

24 Natural stone structures placed within the perimeter of the buildings in traditional gardens, Suzhou, China.

25 New village houses designed by the Amateur Architecture Studio, Fu Yang District of Hangzhou, China, 2016.

26 Wencun Village, China, 2016; a stream flows along the village to form a complex irrigation system for rice cultivation.

contact with natural things (24)? His discussion of the originating inspirations for architectural activity also deeply influenced me. Architecture does not begin from any predetermined concept. Whether it is avant-garde or cliché, architecture should only begin as a hobby, as an activity of amateurs, as an avocation, which is more important than the technology of construction (25–26). Third, of course, would be the inspiration I received from Professor Frampton's "Towards a Critical Regionalism: Six Points for an Architecture of Resistance," in which one of his central statements remains effective and relevant today:

> Architecture can only be sustained today as a critical practice if it assumes an arrière-garde position, that is to say, one which distances itself equally from the Enlightenment myth of progress and from a reactionary, unrealistic impulse to return to the architectonic forms of the preindustrial past. A critical arrière-garde has to remove itself from both the optimization of advance technology and the ever-present tendency to regress into nostalgic historicism or the glibly decorative. It is my contention that only an arrière-garde has the capacity to cultivate a resistant, identity-giving culture while at the same time having discreet recourse to universal technique.[1]

Over the years, people have been interested in asking me, what did you learn from craftsmen in the 1990s? It seems they believe that I have some mysterious knowledge I am keeping as a secret. In fact, what I learned are some common technologies. The key is the perception of value and how to use the technologies. Over the years, I've distilled these issues into one question: how to build naturally and truly in this age, even if such an effort is in fact marginalized? To that point, in 1997, just before the removal of our series of small projects built in the 1990s, I wrote another long article entitled "Creating on the Edge." I remember writing at the beginning of the article: "True avant-garde architecture is anti-aesthetic, anti-symbolic and anti-iconic; it realizes itself belonging to the edge of the society." This article has never been officially published either. The draft still sits on my bookshelf, but it expresses a fundamental sense of resistance for architecture: China's pioneering architectural activities require a decisive beginning. The sense of pioneering depends first and foremost on experimentation. An experimental approach is meaningless if it is not thorough in its standpoint.

1 Kenneth Frampton, "Towards a Critical Regionalism: Six Points for an Architecture of Resistance," *The Anti-Aesthetic: Essays on Postmodern Culture*, ed. Hal Foster (Port Townsend, WA: Bay Press, 1983), 20.

Site-Specificity, Skilled Labor, and Culture: Architectural Principles in the Age of Climate Change

Wilfried Wang

> Today architecture can only be found in underdeveloped countries.
> Edvard Ravnikar[1]

Global climate change is impacting civilization's collective consciousness. The limits of conventional modes of living, of lifeworlds, have been reached; their continued validity is being questioned. Design principles that seek to show sustainable approaches to the transformation and development of buildings and settlements should be site-specific and employ skilled labor so as to make lasting contributions to their local cultures.

The process of autonomization as the primary form of globalization

Ways of confronting the world shape modes of living. The process of autonomization has made humankind independent from nature, climate, context, time, history, culture, and ultimately people from one another. Buildings have been means by which individuals and groups could not only protect themselves from predators or inclement weather, but also express this act in symbolic terms. Buildings and settlements constitute and represent respective modes of living or lifeworlds. While spatial organizations and formal expressions vary from one society to another, there are underlying structural similarities. As social organizations, private households and communal edifices reproduce the social organizations of their respective lifeworlds. Today, buildings and settlements are highly differentiated and articulated instances of the continuing process of autonomization. Adverse external conditions are overcome by building structures and technology. Contemporary lifeworlds extend to every corner of the globe. The process of autonomization has built the reality of the ubiquitous presence of humankind; as such, it is the primary form of globalization.

Similarities and variations in the outward appearance of these built realities express social solidarities and distinctions—they may be gathered in close proximity or spread over long distances. In the same way, the design of outward appearances of buildings may be developed at the place where these buildings are to be sited, their forms constructed of materials gathered in the vicinity and assembled by labor and techniques that have been developed and learned in the community. In other cases,

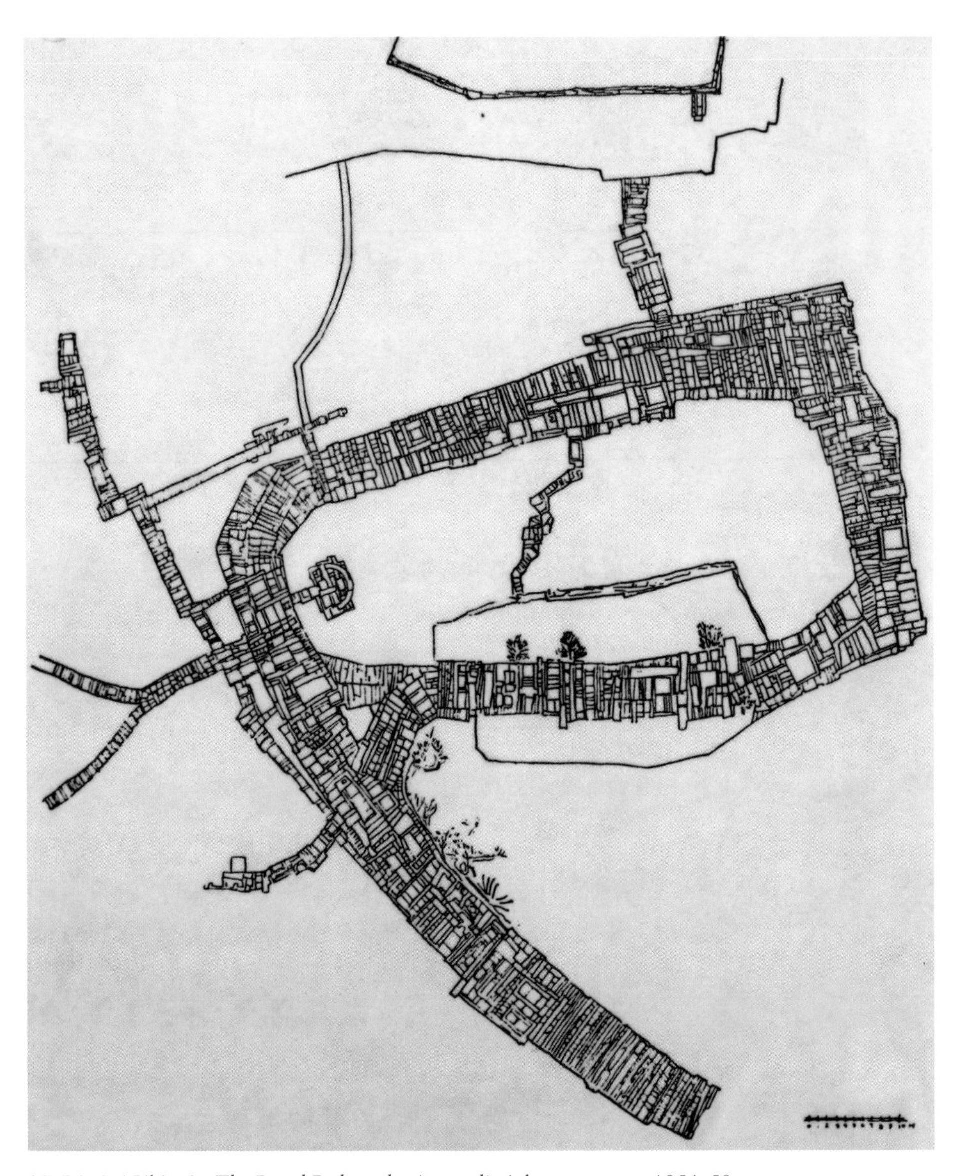

27 Dimitri Pikionis, *The Paved Path to the Acropolis*, ink on paper, *c.* 1954–58.

both outward appearances and the internal organizational structure or building typology, and even the materials and the techniques, have been transported. Empires have consolidated their rule through the construction of buildings and settlements; in colonies, the outward appearances and organizational structures of buildings and settlements speak of the origin of the rulership. Dominant lifeworlds impose outward appearances and organizational structures on less resistant lifeworlds, in some cases replacing previous built structures, in other cases imposing different use regimes, transforming parts of or adding layers to existing fabrics.

28 Dimitri Pikionis, detail of the Paved Path to the Philopappos Hill, Athens.[2]

29 Dimitri Pikionis, detail of St. Dimitris Loumbardiaris Church, Athens, 1951–57.

The process of autonomization of humankind co-opted other processes. For example, the development of civilization enabled people to live peacefully together in large and dense groups.[3] Scientific rationalism and the Enlightenment began to replace religious myths, thus separating individuals and groups of believers from cosmologies. The processes of industrialization,[4] standardization, mechanization,[5] and digitization secured technology's complete control over contemporary lifeworlds.

Architectural modernism, beginning in the early 1920s and later termed the "International Style,"[6] embraced the three early phases of technological change and

30 Álvaro Siza, Schlesisches Tor, sketch of Children's Day Care, IBA Berlin, 1984–87.

saw their application for buildings and settlements on a global scale. Urban structures followed the principle of functional segregation as set in the Charter of Athens of 1933; mass housing consolidated social segregation and the settlements' placeless character deracinated their inhabitants.[7] Key to the placelessness of mass housing was the systematic application of the technological processes of industrialization, standardization, and mechanization leading to the repetitive anonymity of individual dwelling units, the agglomeration of these into unarticulated configurations laid out in undetermined open space.[8] The end of conventional, composed "architecture" was marked by mass housing; this became the new paradigm of "building" as an organizational and management task without any claim to cultural significance.[9]

The bureaucratization of technology and the de-skilling of society

Over the last two centuries changes in construction technologies have been comprehensive. Besides the evident differences between a building of the pre-industrial era and that of the early twenty-first century, there are the invisible changes: first, the increased regulation of planning and building coupled with the increased codification of construction components and building processes; second, the increased division of labor that has resulted in architects no longer being in charge of every aspect of the building, although they may still determine the building's typology and its envelope; third, the shift in the design processing tools from paper to digital media

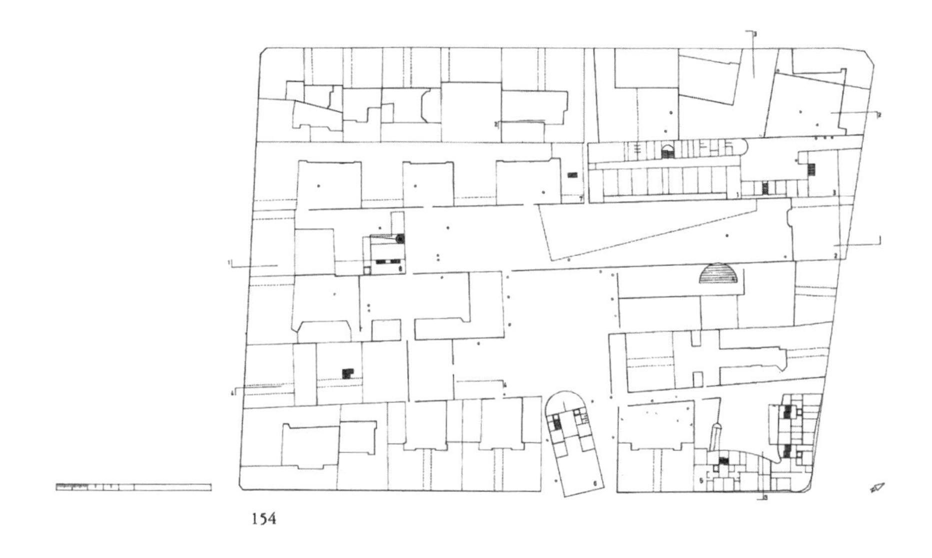

31 Álvaro Siza, Schlesisches Tor, site plan, IBA Berlin, 1984–87.[10]

(computer-aided design software including Building Information Modeling); fourth, the increased share of the dry assembly of pre-fabricated, standardized components and the decreased share of project-specific, in-situ construction (with the notable exception of cast-in-situ concrete); and fifth, the unceasing innovation, specialization, and monopolization of technologies for buildings with ever-shorter life expectancies resulting in the de-skilling of conventional contractors and the enslavement of users by monopolist technology corporations.

The inception and realization of buildings have therefore lost their early Enlightenment idealism to become degraded to just another, albeit complex, one-off business and legal transaction. The early twenty-first-century building industry in the so-called advanced nations has become a domain of optimized business administration from both the financing and the management points of view. The decision-makers in this optimized business administration would see themselves as agents in the real-estate industry rather than as clients commissioning architecture; that is to say, the notion of what the buildings and settlement fabrics might mean, what contribution these edifices might make toward the socio-cultural constitution of a place, is marginal at best.

While the building industry has fully adopted the technologically positivistic, technocratic corporatist regime, due to the nature of construction processes with their many unknown factors ranging from contaminated sites to late design changes, it is still only the unreliable and barely tolerated member of the pin-striped finance industry. The products of the building industry are, however, good enough as the

32 Álvaro Siza, Schlesisches Tor, "Bonjour Tristesse" apartment building, IBA Berlin, 1984–87.

raw material for such "processed" products as sub-prime mortgage-backed securities. Their widespread failure in 2008, coupled with the unrelenting land grab of the sprawling "American" suburban nightmare, has shown the world the economic and socio-cultural limits to the logic of this model. During the half century that followed the publication of the Club of Rome's *Limits to Growth* (1972), the rate of housing starts per month in the United States of America saw a spread from just under half a million (April 2009) to two-and-a-half million (January 1972), with no sign of change to this pattern of economic "growth" and consumption of land. Needless to say, there are few buildings of architectural merit among these millions of suburban homes, and needless to say this lifestyle persists in the United States of America and continues to be exported. This lifestyle encompasses the oversized, freestanding dream house with a triple-car garage, being the docking station for the daily commute to work, the shopping spree at the mall, the chaperoning of the kids to their friends' sleep-overs and so forth. Sustainability as a principle underlying alternative modes of living may have been the basis for the review of capitalist growth models in the early 1970s; however, the collective intelligence of enlightened democracies has not yet led to the fundamental alteration in their modes of living.

Over the last two centuries, changes in technology have enhanced the levels of comfort for those individuals who have been able to afford them and at the same time conditioned people to believe that, by definition, there are no limits to technological innovations. Technology is seen to be the miracle of civilization's own making; it has replaced religion; it is the *deus ex machina*. However, while technological systems have networked large areas of the world's surface, providing maximum access to a seemingly level economic playing field—a new flat earth[11]—they have pried open people's thoughts and behavior to the purview of these systems. The digital-technology-determined, current version of globalization is a very sharp double-edged sword, as it has not only liberated users in terms of communication (internet) and production (e.g., custom 3D printing), but has also brought them under the scrutiny of state and private corporations; it has enabled such corporations to evaluate and trade the users' meta-data.

Given the mining of private data, the public is experiencing the same estrangement from high technology as it had undergone with the Enlightenment.[12] So-called innovative technologies increase users' dependence on a black box, de-skilling both users and potential maintenance laborers. Some companies engaged in so-called innovative technology realize that they are working in a field whose limit to growth has long been reached and who therefore are following the business model employed by social network corporations in cultivating their customers as dependents.

With regard to the building industry, innovative technologies rarely deal with the existing built fabric. Thus, changes in technology have focused on the modernist conventional fixation on the spectacular new, the self-contained greenfield object. They offer little that is relevant to the improvement of the ninety-nine percent of existing structures. The built world does not need complicated, accident-prone, exclusive, copyrighted technology, but broadly accessible technology that anyone has the right to copy.

Site-specificity

The idea of Critical Regionalism in architecture can no longer rely on the certainties of previous discourses. Climate change will alter habits and habitats, will put into question any wise links of experience between local climate and responsive forms on which earlier, more rooted generations based their buildings in any given region. Architecture that seeks to be sustainable will need to be specific to the site, respect the impending climatic conditions, try to avoid sealing too large a proportion of the ground surface, and use the least processed, regenerative local materials in as direct an assembly as possible. Architectures that are easy to maintain by skilled labor using long-lasting, easily accessible technology, whose typologies and materials will permit change in use over a long period of time, would thereby make a sustained contribution to local cultures. Thus, designing architectures in the age of climate change could give rise to the creation of authentic identities that are based primarily on specific responses to the sites in their climatic, physical, and socio-cultural dimensions. Skilled labor with knowledge of and experience with regenerative or recyclable materials is needed to translate sustainable designs into credible and legible tectonics and construction details.

Kenneth Frampton's "Ten Points of an Architecture of Regionalism: A Provisional Polemic"[14] impacted global architectural discourse and practice in the late

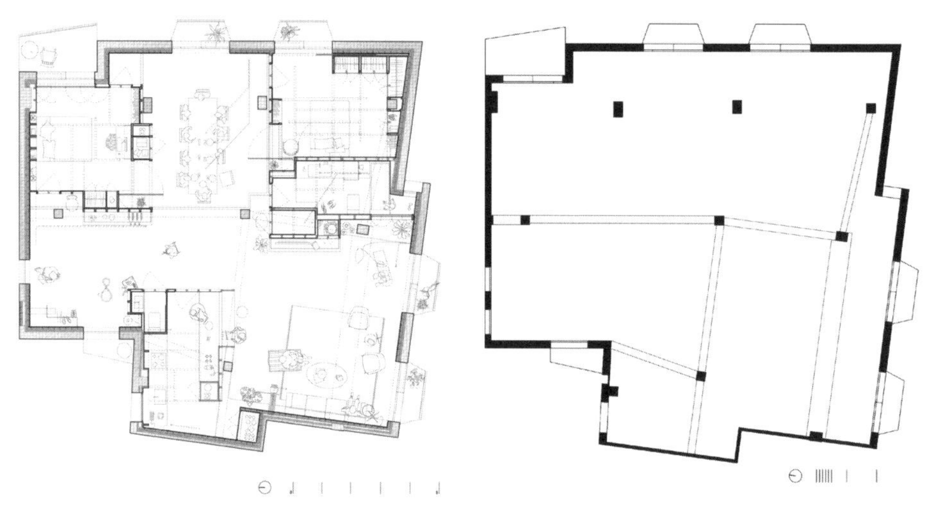

33, 34 TEd'A arquitectes, Can Gabriel, apartment before and after the renovation and transformation, Palma de Mallorca, 2012.[13]

1980s due to its analysis in defining what Critical Regionalism in architecture could be. Notwithstanding the controversies,[15] Frampton's "Ten Points" contain the principles for sustainable architectural practices. Given the realities of technologically homogenized "universal civilization,"[16] multicultural societies, global mobility, and climate change, emerging regional identities can be designed with references to the history of architecture as well as to the regional vernacular.[17]

Reviewing the "ground" that Frampton had laid in the "Ten Points of an Architecture of Regionalism," the changes in the last three decades have further diminished the relevance of nature, region, topography, and place for architects (Points 8,[18] 3, 6, and 5 respectively); precedents have become less relevant (vernacular form, modernism, and postmodernism, Points 1, 2, and 10); given the composite assembly of buildings there is no longer a logic of construction in contemporary practice (Point 7); and the visual mode of perception (Points 4 and 9) dominates the way buildings are received.

By regrouping Frampton's "Ten Points" in relation to the identified extensive changes that have taken place in the building industry over the last three decades, design principles can be defined to support twenty-first-century sustainable architectural practice. Rather than foregrounding the unchanging condition of civilization (Frampton's reference to Aldo van Eyck), it is time to recognize that architectural practice needs to bear its responsibility toward the larger physical context in which it seeks to operate. It is therefore not the condition of civilization, of any individual or collective, but the condition of the largest vessel, the world itself, to which architecture and environmental design need to respond—not with an attitude of technology-based autonomy, but with an empathetic symbiosis. For building and settlement design, the design principle that follows from this refocusing is that of site-specificity.

Skilled labor

Edvard Ravnikar's claim from the late 1960s that "today architecture can only be found in underdeveloped countries" is best understood in the context of technology's dominance over culture. In those years, forms of contract were in their infancy in underdeveloped countries. Planning regulations and building codes fit on a few pages. Lawyers were involved only in sales contracts. Construction companies and skilled laborers were still capable of reading architects' drawings and they were open to on-site negotiations to adapt and vary details without filing for change orders. Skilled laborers took greater pride in their trade and craftsmanship than in project management. Thanks to the skilled laborers' constructive attitude and knowledge, architects would treat them as key members of the team rather than automatons, whose hours on the project had to be minimized. In this way, architectural projects were well-crafted, enduring, open to repair by similarly experienced skilled laborers.

In some underdeveloped countries, these simple and direct conditions for the realization of anything, not just architecture, prevail. Ingenious improvisation, based on the understanding of complex structures, is brought to bear when barriers such as time, distance, resources, and money need to be overcome. Traditional trades in

35, 36 TEd'A arquitectes, Can Gabriel, view of partially complete interior, Palma de Mallorca, 2012 (left); detailed view (right).

underdeveloped countries show greater readiness in attending to "design" problems than in developed counterparts, where often the liabilities and the internal management of skilled labor preclude ad hoc interventions.

Improvisation and ad hoc interventions are nevertheless also needed in developed countries, often presupposing an even greater knowledge of the complex structures that require repair, maintenance, or renovation. The availability of skilled labor is a prerequisite for the continued life of the built fabric and is therefore a cornerstone of a sustainable building culture, since the wholesale replacement of the existing fabric, a conventional modernist dictum, is no longer defensible.

In terms of architecture, developed countries are confronted with the combined effects of corporate clients primarily concerned with a maximum return on investment and without cultural ambitions; restrictive building codes; digitized project management; and technocratic modernism with a limited palette of standardized components resulting in deracinated and sterile buildings. Given this uninspiring background of the real-estate building industry, schools of architecture in developed countries attempt to over-compensate for the lack of cultural ambitions by pretending to be the new avant-garde in the fields of digital image processing and esoteric theory. Both strands of the discourse—real-estate building industry and ivory-tower academia—pursue autonomous goals, unrelated to issues of sustainability.

Neither skilled labor nor architecture with site-specific identities can be brought into the real world without cultivated clients; developed countries are run by ignorant but ambitious politicians who enjoy being associated with star architects and under-educated middle managers who believe that track records are guarantors for design quality. This combination of clientship results in visual spectacles but cultural catastrophes, often celebrated by servile commentators as "iconic landmarks." Developed countries thus suffer from two extremes in building discourse: unambitious mediocrity on the one hand, and over-the-top and over-budget obscenity on the other. Hence, culturally appropriate, site-specific architecture constructed by proud skilled labor is more likely to be found in underdeveloped countries.

Culture

Culture in the age of climate change should mark the beginning of the reversal of the process of autonomy to a process of synergy between nature and humankind. In this necessary transformation, existing buildings and settlements play the main role; new buildings and new settlements should be the exceptions. Culture in the age of climate change needs to separate the real needs from the exceptional ones. The same sense of justice with which the issue of the per capita CO_2 emission is being discussed should be applied to the implementation of the universal right to a sustainable and identifiable, well-designed, if not also beautiful environment.

Advances in technology, in software programs, in artificial intelligence should be directed to serve this purpose; they should help in bringing such basic needs as clean water, sanitation, and universal free public health services and primary education to every community. The advances in technology should address the provision of shelter for the homeless.

Urban settlements need to be densified to become socially and functionally mixed. As a mixed development, each building should offer space for combined living, working, and leisure activities. Public space and infrastructure need to be adapted to provide space for sustainable modes of transport. Suburbia needs to be replaced by urbanized nodes on the one hand and productive landscapes in place of reclaimed territories on the other.

The conventional professional and mass media that serve the cult of star architecture should be eclipsed by truly open and critical analytical platforms to support the culture in the age of climate change.

The Modern Movement set out to fundamentally transform society through the built environment. After nearly a century, the architectural profession is realizing that, on balance, its legacy is negative. Mass housing, functional segregation, and less-than-mediocre design quality for much of what has been built according to its principles are the sobering result. There is less than a decade to implement the appropriate urban and architectural designs for the era of climate change. If and once it has been implemented, the resulting buildings and settlements will constitute and represent a transformed lifeworld.

1 Friedrich Achleitner, "On a Quotation from Edvard Ravnikar: 'Today architecture can only be found in underdeveloped countries'," in *Edvard Ravnikar*, ed. Aleš Vodopivec and Rok Žnidaršič (Vienna: Springer, 2010), 61.

2 "I will never forget my initial encounter with Pikionis when in 1959 I first visited the Acropolis and found myself walking almost by chance in the astonishing adjacent parkscape of the Philopappou Hill. There I sensed, with great surprise, the almost literal movement of the landfall as my frame was drawn by gravity and by the tactile grip of the paving, up and down the undulating labyrinth of the terrain; a site that was to be experienced as much by the body as by the eyes. More surprising still were the stone-paved way-stations and benches and, above all, the pine-wood-framed temenos and pavilion adjacent to the reconstructed Loumbardiaris church. These last seemed as though they had been drawn from Japan, over long eons of time, through Asia and the cultural sieve of Byzantium ... The last thirty years have changed our way of evaluating architecture. We now see back into our century over a much wider and deeper trajectory and while we are by no means anti-Modern, we are reassessing what our Modern culture has been and where we stand in relation to its multifarious strands. Thus figures that once were prominent now recede to a different level and those previously obscure and marginal emerge into the light. Pikionis is surely one of these latter-day luminaries, for his resonant work draws us back at once into a phenomenally concrete world, into a world of revealed radiance, where the 'thingness' of things, to coin Heidegger's phrase, comes into its own." Kenneth Frampton, "For Dimitri Pikionis," in *Dimitri Pikionis 1887–1968: A Sentimental Topography* (London: Architectural Association, 1989), 6.

3 Norbert Elias, *Über den Prozess der Zivilisation: Soziogenetische und psychogenetische Untersuchungen* (Basel: Verlag Haus zum Falken, 1939).

4 Gustav Adolf Platz, *Die Baukunst der Neuesten Zeit* (Berlin: Propyläen Verlag, 1927).

5 Lewis Mumford, *Technics and Civilization* (New York and Burlingame, CA: Harcourt, Brace & World, 1934).

6 Henry-Russell Hitchcock and Philip Johnson, *The International Style: Architecture since 1922* (New York: W.W. Norton, 1932).

7 Alexander Mitscherlich, *Die Unwirtlichkeit der Städte. Anstiftung zum Unfrieden* (Frankfurt am Main: Suhrkamp Verlag, 1965).

8 See the movie by Eldar Ryazanov: *The Irony of Fate, or Enjoy your Bath!* (Moscow: Mosfilm, 1976).

9 Hannes Meyer, "Bauen," in *Bauhaus 2* (Dessau: Bauhaus, 1928), 12–13.

10 If the rest of the Berlin International Building Exhibition (IBA Berlin) of 1984–87 was about superficial appearance in the manner of "recovering" the past, then Álvaro Siza's proposal for the renewal of the urban block in Kreuzberg remains to this day a paradigmatic case of an empathetic and appropriate comprehensive urban and architectural design, in which the inner world of the block interior—now publicly accessible—is shaped in a robust minimalism that pays its respect to the intense use and given the same amount of attention as the three realized buildings: the apartment building on the corner (the infamous "Bonjour Tristesse"), the old people's club, and the children's day care. Contrary to many external architects who had buildings realized in Berlin for the IBA, the complex for the Schlesisches Tor is the only design that offers site-specificity and transforms and enhances the existing cultural context.

11 Thomas L. Friedman, *The World is Flat: A Brief History of the Twenty-first Century* (New York: Farrer, Straus and Giroux, 2005).

12 Max Horkheimer and Theodor W. Adorno, *Dialektik der Aufklärung* (Amsterdam: Querido, 1947).

13 For the complete transformation of an apartment from the 1960s within an essentially orthogonal envelope, though haphazard arrangement of pillars, TEd'A arquitectes chose to insert three wooden boxes, thereby defining four other domains: an entrance foyer, a transition space, a dining area, and a living room. With a minimum of means, the architects have opted to articulate the wooden studs and panels to provide walls, recesses, wardrobes, and shelving. The contrast between the fine woodwork and the stripped surfaces of the old apartment not only reveals the original constructional system but also creates a relaxed domestic atmosphere. While this project is small, the architects have demonstrated a site-specific approach using skilled labor to create a lasting intervention in an existing architectural fabric, thereby ensuring a continued life of a number of decades.

14 Kenneth Frampton, "Ten Points of an Architecture of Regionalism: A Provisional Polemic," in *Center 3: New Regionalism*, ed. Lawrence Speck and Wayne Attoe (Austin: Center for American Architecture and Design, 1987), 20–27.

15 Keith L. Eggener, "Placing Resistance: A Critique of Critical Regionalism," *Journal of Architectural Education*, 55/4 (May 2002): 228–37.

16 Paul Ricœur, "Universal Civilization and National Cultures," in *History and Truth*, trans. Charles A. Kelbley (Evanston, IL: Northwestern University Press, 1965), 271–84.

17 "Modern ist das Haus, das alles in unserer Zeit Lebendige aufnehmen kann und dabei doch ein organisch gewachsenes Gebilde bleibt." ("Any house, that is able to absorb everything that is alive in our age and that still remains as an organically grown structure, is modern," trans. the author), Josef Frank, "Was ist modern?," in *Architektur als Symbol: Elemente deutschen neuen Bauens* (Vienna: Verlag Anton Schroll, 1931), 135.

18 Regarding "Point 8: Artificial/Natural," Frampton presciently decried the disconnection of modern buildings from natural surroundings on the strength of internally "optimized" technological systems that have a negative impact on their surroundings due to the "excessive energy consumption and the heavy pollution."

That Pesky Paradisiacal Instinct ...

Harry Francis Mallgrave

In 2018 an interdisciplinary group of planners and academics met in Davos, Switzerland, at the World Economic Forum. At the conclusion of the conference, they issued a short paper entitled "Towards a High-quality *Baukultur* for Europe," in which they pointed out "the lack of design values, including a lack of concern for sustainability, the growth of faceless urban sprawl and irresponsible land use, the deterioration of historic fabric, and the loss of regional traditions and identities." They countered with the need for "a holistic, culture-centered approach to the built environment and for a humanistic view of the way we collectively shape the places we live in and the legacy we leave behind."[1]

No one could disagree with such high sentiments, but then again, the voice seems almost disparate to our present era, in which the popular film and entertainment industries are obsessed with portraying our dystopian temper. It also appears during a rather odd period in architectural thinking—coming on the heels of the crashing of architectural theory at the end of the previous century, fostered by the decades of semiotic and poststructural pomposity and the hollowing out of humanist values. Architecturally, we are living the era in which the profession seems focused entirely

37 Empress Theodora and her entourage, Basilica of San Vitale, Ravenna, A.D. 547.

on the "culture industry" of the aestheticized object. The new, towering and crimped glass boxes of London—the Cheesegrater, the Shard, the Can of Ham—are our era's preeminent symbols for the failings of the design profession.

Nevertheless, the questions posed at the Davos conference raise other interesting questions. Just what is a "culture-centered" approach to planning and design? What in fact do we mean by the word "culture"? If we were to slip back another generation or two in anthropological thinking, we could define culture as a kind of ideological superstructure or self-imposed "extragenetic, outside-the-skin control mechanisms" for tamping down biological predispositions.[2] Yet within the context of what the humanistic and biological sciences have since revealed, such a definition no longer has credibility. I would prefer to take the word "culture" back to its original Latin root and define it as growing or cultivating something in soil or a prepared medium. In architectural terms, culture would be *the tending to the human organism within its built and social environments*, the inseparable medium in which our particular organism either thrives or languishes.

In line with this definition, I would like to append a comment that Alvar Aalto once tendered, when he noted that "architecture, too, has an ulterior motive always lurking behind the corner, the idea of creating paradise. That is the only purpose of our buildings."[3] I find Aalto's comment fascinating because its deeply felt sentiments, its quixotic aura, appear so contrary to the glass-and-concrete hyperreality of our age. Can anyone imagine an architect speaking in such terms today?

Nevertheless, I think it is time to resurrect the word "paradise." And in doing so, the first thing we need to do is to distinguish it from that even more troublesome word "utopia." For if we trace the latter's meaning—from Plato to Thomas More, from Francesco Patrizi to Francis Bacon, not to mention the later political writers—utopia has always been defined as the "cultural" imposition of a social or ideological structure on an existing civic body. Plato, through his ideal world, sought to define utopia entirely by himself. Yet from a contemporary phenomenological perspective, this utopian goal has little meaning because culture, within the humanities today, is no longer defined as an "outside-the-skin" event. Evan Thompson and Francisco Varela made this point quite forcefully when they noted that the nervous system, the body and the environment are highly structured dynamical systems, coupled to each other on multiple levels. Because they are so thoroughly enmeshed—biologically, ecologically, and socially—a better conception of brain, body, and environment would be as mutually embedded systems rather than as internally and externally located with respect to one another.[4]

Another well-accepted principle from the biological field of niche construction makes this same point. Just as we change our physical and cultural environments, these new environments alter the genetic, cognitive, and cultural patterns of who we are.[5] If one accepts this principle, then one must also accept that architects contribute to making the culture in which we dwell.

38 Assyrian relief, Garden of Ashurbanipal, Nineveh, 645–640 B.C.

The notion of paradise is different to that of utopia. The reason is that the human desire for paradise originates in a personal or inner yearning for greater happiness for ourselves and those around us. Paradise is a desire for peace arising from within, and it is not surprising that the idea has long been associated with the Arcadian atmosphere of the garden. The English word derives from the Greek word *paradeisos*, the related Median *paridaeza*, and the Old Iranian *paridaida*, which meant an enclosed or walled-off garden. The Akkadian word *pardesu* signified a "cool, shaded place." The concept, in its various enumerations, is, however, much more ancient.

It is tempting to take the idea back to the cave paintings of 30,000 years ago, or even to the early Anatolian settlements of Çatalhöyük and Nevali Çori—all of which record ritualistic beliefs of an afterlife. We are on firmer ground with the advent of Sumerian culture, divinely sanctified by the mythology of its creation. The oldest Sumerian city, Eridu, was reportedly built on the actual site of paradise, the garden "wherein grew a glorious tree," bearing fruit resembling "white lapis-lazuli."[6] Its founding architect, Enki, not only erected the first house but also planted the "tree of life" in a grove adjacent to his sanctuary. Another ancient city, Uruk, in mythology was attributed to Gilgamesh, another Sumerian king. In the *Epic of Gilgamesh*, it was he who planted the city's square-mile sacred grove, after returning from his Herculean pursuit of eternal life. It was on this quest that he visited the garden of the gods marked by carnelian and lapis-lazuli trees (**38**).

Because all Mesopotamian kings were anointed as demigods, their role was to observe the sacred rituals as well as to tend to the temples and sacred landscapes. Hence, they were given the title of "gardener."[7] It was from this tradition that gardens became such prominent features in Babylonian and Assyrian cultures. Assurnasirpal II, in rebuilding his capital city of Nimrud in the ninth century B.C., did so by "cutting through a mountain peak" and bringing water to the 900-acre city, which contained parks, farms, an arboretum, and zoological and pleasure gardens. The Assyrian king Sennacherib moved his capital to Nineveh and, adjacent to his massive palace, he constructed equally impressive terraced gardens. To raise water up into his terraces, he invented the Archimedean screw (350 years before Archimedes did), and thus his gardens became the famous "Hanging Gardens," which the Greek historian Diodorus Siculus and others mistakenly situated in Babylon.[8] The various Persian empires adopted the same love of the garden. The palaces of Cyrus the Great at Pasargadae, for instance, were surrounded with massive gardens. As one archaeologist reported from his excavations of the 1960s, "each inner palace with its stately colonnades and deep, shadowed porticoes was first glimpsed amidst a profusion of trees, shrubs, and grasses."[9]

It is this empyrean vision of paradise that finds its way into Judaic–Christian–Islamic cultures as the Garden of Eden. The Hebrew word *pardes* first appears in the post-exilic books of the Hebrew bible. In the Greek translation undertaken in Alexandria in the third century, the word *paradeisos* is used to refer both to *pardes* and to the older Hebrew word *gan* or "garden"—as in the Garden of Eden. This last garden, somewhere east of the city of Eden, was long believed to be an actual place on earth, at the confluence of the rivers Pishon, Gihon, Tigris, and Euphrates. Christopher Columbus, on his third voyage to the new world of 1498, believed he had found access to it at the delta of the Orinoco River along the Venezuelan coastline. When the turbulence of the waters prevented him from steering into the river, he reported that it was only by the "special grace of God" would one be allowed entry to the garden.[10]

The desert landscape of Palestine was hostile terrain for growing gardens, and it is interesting that the paradise in Hebraic culture transposes itself into the Temple of Jerusalem. The first Temple of Solomon was outfitted with paradisaical motifs throughout. Both the sanctum and main hall had pine doors carved with cherubim, palm trees, and open flowers overlaid with hammered gold. This temple was destroyed by Nebuchadnezzar II in 587 B.C., but the later Temple of Jerusalem, started by King Herod in the first century B.C., was similarly conceived as a garden. As the eyewitness Josephus relates, the gate into the temple had "golden vines above it, from which clusters of grapes hung as tall as a man's height."[11] By the time this temple was set afire by Roman troops in A.D. 70, the garden theme had been transposed by early Christian writers into the "New Jerusalem"—whose "brilliance was

39 Qian Xuan, detail from the painting *Wang Xizhi*, 13th century.

like that of a very precious jewel, like a jasper, clear as crystal," and whose river of life flowed "from the throne of God and of the Lamb down the middle of the great street of the city."[12]

The association of the garden with paradise is found throughout the East as well. Buddha found his enlightenment in a garden under a bodhi tree. Pataliputra, the city founded by the Mauryan emperor Asoka, was referred to as the "city of flowers," and the later Roman traveler Aelian insisted that its beauty was superior to that of both the Persian cities of Susa and Ecbatana. He went on to describe Pataliputra's parks and royal gardens, their tame peacocks, cultivated shrubs, and "shady groves and herbage," their boughs "interwoven by the workman's art."[13]

The cities of ancient China were invested with paradisiacal thinking. Beginning with the Zhou Dynasty from 1046 B.C., imperial cities such as Chengzhou were laid out according to the celestial principles of the *I Ching* and *feng shui*. This was the "golden age" to which Confucius later alluded and sought to reinstate. The Sui Dynasty's rebuilding of Chang'an in A.D. 582, for instance, was designed as a square with three gates on each side and its main axis running south to north. The axis led visitors to the imperial city and emperor's palace in the northern sector. The only two violations of the square were for a public garden in the south corner of the city, and the emperor's extensive gardens outside the northern gate of the city.

Seven hundred years later Kublai Khan, whom Marco Polo referred to as the "Great Khan," assembled the largest empire the world had ever seen. His capital city of Dadu, present-day Beijing, reflected his great love of nature. Here, the "Forbidden City" was located toward the southern side of the square, and to the west he built his vast paradise consisting of several lakes and islands, an artificial mountain, grottos, temples, pavilions, and exotic plantings from every region of his command.[14] It still survives today in part. The great Southern Song artist Qian Xuan was known for his blissful and idyllic landscapes (**39**). The same garden tradition can be found in Kyoto, Japan's capital city founded in A.D. 784. Two thousand temples and gardens survive today, built for both pleasure and meditation. The *Sakuteiki*, a garden primer written in the eleventh century for aristocrats and priests, sets out precise rules for paradise, everything from the height of garden waterfalls to the design of the tea house.

The West also has its garden traditions. Both Homer and Hesiod spoke of blessed isles—either from a golden age of the past or as a place where Greek war heroes would dwell. When the Greeks came into contact with the Persians, the garden took on a new character. The Academy at which Plato taught was outside Athens in a "well-watered grove," and the Lyceum at which Aristotle taught was similarly situated in a meadow north of the city. Alexander was the first Westerner to view the vast gardens of the Neo-Babylonian, Persian, and Indus Valley cultures, and it was left to one of his rival successors (his *diadochi*), Ptolemy I, to replicate such feats in Alexandria, with its urban ornaments of gardens, public buildings, and libraries. The city was so attractive that Julius Caesar considered moving the Roman capital there, and it similarly evoked the envy of Augustus. The latter's prime mover was Agrippa, who repaired and built aqueducts into Rome, through which he transformed the Campus Martius into a bucolic landscape in which he placed the Pantheon, the Basilica of Neptune, and the Baths of Agrippa. The baths, in fact, extended to the river Tiber, and contained exercise fields, a swimming canal, and a reflecting pool of a size to entertain small boats—much to the joy of the Emperor Nero. These areas were connected with a series of porticos, pleasure gardens, shade trees, fountains, promenades, and pavilions for lectures and poetry recitals. The Roman aristocrats, as Pliny the Younger makes clear, quickly caught the garden fever, but no one understood the possibilities better than Hadrian, who built his villa in Tivoli. It was a vast garden city erected for a population of one.

The rise of Islam in the sixth century focused on the garden, because its heaven quite literally was a return to the Garden of Eden. It was a lush and fragrant garden with shady vales, fountains, and rivers of pure water, milk, wine, and strained honey. The Islamic Mughal emperors of what is now Pakistan and northern India actually pursued the re-creation of paradise. Babur, in the early sixteenth century, built numerous garden estates, whose gardens he named after the great Muslim cities of Shiraz, Baghdad, Damascus, and Cairo. The mausoleum of Akbar the Great in Delhi was given the name "Abode of Paradise," and it was his son who built the Shalamar

40 Generalife gardens, Grenada, Spain, early 14th century, reconstructed 1931–51.

Bagh or "garden of bliss" along the shores of Lake Dal in Kashmir. No one, however, outdid Shah Jahan, who built the Taj Mahal, a mausoleum dedicated to his favorite wife. Few people today realize that the building was originally situated not on a mowed lawn but within an elaborate recreation of the Garden of Eden, one that extended across the Yamuna River to the "Moonlight Garden." Islamic conquerors also carried the garden motif across northern Africa and into Spain, where the famed gardens of Córdoba and Seville were built. The culmination of this development was the Alhambra in Granada, with the later addition of the Generalife gardens on the adjacent ridge (**40**).

Christianity, whose "New Jerusalem" Augustine shifted to the afterlife of our imperfect world, would seem to be anti-paradisiacal, but this is not true. Garden splendors were not unknown in Constantinople, and Constantine carried this Byzantine spirit to Ravenna. There, the mosaics of the Mausoleum of Galla Placidia, which later mesmerized Carl Jung, depict the Garden of Eden. And nearby in the church of St. Vitale, who would dispute that the setting for the Empress Theodora (**37**, **43**), standing among her entourage within a garden pavilion, is not paradisiacal? Certainly, this celestial inspiration can be compared with Oscar Wilde's infatuation with Sarah Bernhardt in 1884—that is, with her role in *Theodora* in Victorien Sardou's Paris production.

The early Christian monks referred to their monasteries as paradises, and Bernard of Clairvaux took the idea of paradise in a new direction in 1115 with his designs for the Cistercian abbeys at Clairvaux and Fontenay. He believed (like Augustine before and Leon Battista Alberti afterward) that simple musical harmonies could be translated into beautiful visual ratios, such as an octave (1:2), fifth (2:3), and fourth (3:4). He designed his bare churches of pointed barrel and cross vaults using these ratios. The result was an extremely high reverberation rate wonderfully fitted to the very precise phrasing of Gregorian chants. For the 100 or so monks attending a candlelit midnight office, the songs were no doubt experienced as emanating from no earthly place. Abbot Suger, in his design for the Abbey of St. Denis, was driven by a similar instinct, only his image of paradise was formed by the precious gems on the altar shimmering in the colored light of the stained glass. This intention was soon brought to perfection with the "reddish, violet light" that painted the interior of Chartres Cathedral. As Otto von Simson has noted, the guiding inspiration behind Gothic architecture was nothing less than to represent a "supernatural reality," to have its sanctuary serve as the paradisiacal "threshold to heaven."[15]

It remains to give the notion of paradise a more definitive architectural form, and I would like to do so in two ways. One is to provide an example of two towns that, for a while at least, approached terrestrial paradises. The second is to revisit a design principle that we seem to have lost track of in recent years, which is to view design from the perspective of dwelling.

The desire for paradise, as I have argued, is an instinct that rises from within, and it can also become manifest without any conscious planning or design. Every Eden, it seems, has to have original sin, and in the case of the English cities of Oxford and Cambridge the sins were many. Both towns were founded as monastic settlements, and in their early years there were local and often bloody conflicts between the "towns and gowns." The Reformation in the first half of the sixteenth century led to an abrupt theological reversal, and the two English Civil Wars of the 1640s led only to further mayhem. There is also the issue that for much of their existence, the two universities were closed to Jews, Catholics, and other non-Anglican faiths, to individuals not attending the requisite preparatory schools, and of course to women. In short, the two institutions with the legal monopoly of English university education throughout their early centuries came to epitomize the cult of male, Anglican snobbery. Yet the towns—not their founding ideologies—went on to become two of the more Edenic places on earth. What was the key to their success?

The foundation of the individual colleges took place in the thirteenth century and the building model was monastic—the orientation of a chapel, a dormitory, a dining hall, a library, and lecture halls around a central courtyard, or quadrangle. The small courtyard known as the "Mob Quad" at Oxford's Merton College, started in 1288, is the oldest example. With expanding student enrollment and need for space, these quadrangles eventually became larger, and when their limit was reached, the colleges began to build additional or adjoining courtyards. This novel planning principle assured at least half of the college land would always remain green.

By the sixteenth century, this principle was being implemented at full speed. For instance, Trinity College in Cambridge was founded by Henri VIII in 1546, and toward the end of the sixteenth century its Master, Thomas Nevile, demolished a few isolated buildings and created a "Great Court," entered through a gateway from the street. With the purchase of the land to the west, two later wings were extended, which were closed off in the last decade of the seventeenth century by Christopher Wren's majestic Palladian library. St. John's College, just north of Trinity, created a series of three courtyards from the east gate along old High Street, and when further expansion was needed, the college expanded across the river Cam to other courtyards—accessed by the "Bridge of Sighs" (**41–42**).

This process in itself was idyllic, but once the human paradisiacal instinct has a little room to run, it often gets greedy. Soon the Cambridge colleges along High Street realized that they could purchase land across the river and create permanent, private gardens for themselves—known as the Backs, each accessed by a private bridge. By the eighteenth century, most colleges in Cambridge and Oxford had at least three gardens: the Master's Garden, the Fellows' Garden, and the Scholars' Garden. Capability Brown, the theorist of the Picturesque, who designed the Master's Garden for St. John's College—the "Wilderness"—even proposed a plan to unite all of the Cambridge Backs into one large garden with meandering paths and a lake. For these colleges along the river, the percentage of green space to buildings had now climbed to around ninety percent.

Other colleges were not to be left behind. Christ Church College at Oxford, with the city's largest quadrangle, extended its courts and buildings eastward to obtain a panorama of Christ Church Meadow, a vast expanse of greenery that extends down to the river Thames. It miraculously remains intact today—after city officials, in the early 1970s, contemplated putting a four-lane highway through it. Magdalen College, with its bell tower perched at the historic entrance to the town, incorporated the land north of the main buildings to preserve a grove and deer park. Across the Cherwell River to the east, the area around the Water Meadow the college named "Addison's Walk," after the playwright and theorist of the Picturesque Joseph Addison, who daily enjoyed its natural beauty.

Yet there is more to Oxford and Cambridge. Except in a few cases, the thirty or so colleges in each town are not contiguous—that is, they are knitted together by a supporting urban network of inns, shops (with student rooms above), bookshops, restaurants, pubs, and other essential businesses. All these buildings, like the colleges, are generally three or four stories high, and collectively they provide a rich urban texture of different materials, styles, and colors. The architectural landmarks of the

41 Aerial view of Trinity College (center) and St. John's College north of it. Wren's Library is at the west end of Trinity's second courtyard parallel with the river Cam, Cambridge.

42 Christopher Wren, Library at Trinity College, 1676–95.

towns are also of a very high quality. Situated north of Oxford's High Street, among the colleges, are St. Mary the Virgin Church with its glorious spire, James Gibbs's Baroque Radcliffe Camera, the historic Bodleian Library, Nicholas Hawksmoor's Clarendon Building, and Wren's Sheldonian Theatre. All parts of the city are fitted to the pedestrian and connected with lanes, alleyways, passages, and minor streets. There are also nodes, promenades, and shopping streets with no sharp demarcation of residential from non-residential zones. Taking into account the towns' other cultural amenities—such as prestigious museums, botanical gardens, athletics fields, theaters, and the weekly musical performances at many colleges—one must conclude that the two towns, for a few centuries at least, had indeed become celestial for all who dwelt there. Yet paradise gained always seems to have the reprisal of paradise lost. Oxford and Cambridge have, in recent years, become overcrowded with tourists, and the ever-expanding endowments of the colleges have at the same time introduced the deadly virus known as the "building bug," as found in the many new technology parks that today overrun and bridle the two cities. They are now known principally for their snarling traffic, high rents, great disparities of wealth, and far too many people.

In his book *The Ecological Approach to Visual Perception*, James Gibson first put forth the notion of "affordance," which he defined as what the environment "*offers* the animal, what it *provides* or *furnishes*, either for good or ill."[16] Affordance implies a certain complementarity of the animal and the environment from which it has evolved, and the term has come into architectural currency in recent years. People generally prefer environments with a greater number of affordances. One likes to walk in the open air on a sunny day, and under a canopy on a rainy day. Environments should afford both. Yet Gibson made another distinction that I find more instructive, that between a *habitat* and a *niche*. A habitat, he notes, refers to "where" an animal lives, and a niche (which he defines as a "set of affordances") refers to "how" the organism lives.[17] This distinction leads me to a simple question: are we designing habitats or niches?

I think most will agree that for the past and present centuries our efforts have been focused on habitats. Shelter, food, and clean water are the most fundamental human needs, and both wars and the lack of economic development can bring these needs to a crisis stage. Yet even within the more economically successful countries, efforts have remained focused on our habitats. We regard our buildings as functional or aestheticized objects of formalist design, and our city as the accumulation of these artifacts. And in recent years, there has been an unparalleled construction boom of tall buildings in the major cities of the world, and television producers seem to take great pride in using their city's silhouette as a reporter's backdrop. Still, there is a cost to pay for this preening exercise. The Cheesegrater, the Shard, the Can of Ham—all creations of "leading" design offices—have added nothing positive to the character of London. They have created nodal points of high congestion that pollute the streets with high levels of ambient noise. They tower over Wren's St. Paul's Cathedral and more generally demean the historic scale and stately character of the city. The one positive factor is that they are for the most part restricted to the business sector, which means that the suited occupants traversing the rainy winds of the glass-and-concrete canyons can at least afford umbrellas with sufficient strength to withstand the gusty onslaughts. Is it possible to think of architecture in a different way?

The anthropologist Tim Ingold once made the distinction between the "dwelling perspective" and the "building perspective." The latter, he noted, is generally the outlook of architects: "first plan and build the houses, then import the people to occupy them."[18] In drawing upon Martin Heidegger, he went on to define the contrary "dwelling perspective," which reverses this way of thinking by situating the house (I prefer the term niche) within the life process itself—that is, the practical engagement one has with one's surroundings. "Through the dwelling perspective," Ingold notes in a later essay, "I hoped to shift anthropology away from the fixation with objects and images, towards a better appreciation of the material flows and currents of sensory awareness within which both ideas and things reciprocally take shape."[19] This is not entirely a novel idea within architectural theory, because a number of architects, from Aalto to Aldo van Eyck and Christopher Alexander, have articulated the same point in their writings. The focus of design should be around one's experience with the built environment, and not on the presumed aestheticized object.

Ingold's position is more radical than it might first appear. What he is attempting to do from his developmental perspective is to collapse the distinction between culture and nature—a long-standing distinction of the social sciences and one also implicit in the Davos "culture-centered" approach to design. Such a distinction, as I suggested earlier, presumes a cultural superstructure that rules above all else. Ingold is in fact echoing philosophical terrain also explored by Susan Oyama, who, in commenting on the most recent breakthroughs in genetic modeling, has argued that all organismic forms, rather than being directed by genetic programs or cultural forces—the nature/nurture divide—are better viewed as being in a continuous state of reconstitution with the input of multiple systems: genetic, epigenetic (the building or unbuilding of cellular and neurological circuitry), social, and cultural. From such a perspective, the human organism is never finished, as it were, and there can be no distinction between nature and nurture because, in Oyama's words, "Nature is the *product* of the *processes* that are the developmental interactions we call nurture."[20]

At first glance, this line of reasoning may seem to take us far afield from the practice of design, yet the opposite is the case because it allows us to advance Heidegger's notion of dwelling in a far more concrete way. What, we might ask, is dwelling? If it does not reside in the ideological, economic, or utopian objects that we conventionally view as our cultural habitats (where we live), where does it reside? I would like to suggest that dwelling resides precisely in the paradisiacal impulses springing directly from the well-considered and well-formed niche (how we live). Ingold once suggested thinking of building as a "modality of weaving," and this metaphor works well when considering the advances in our understanding of the genetic, epigenetic, social, and cultural aspects of our being over the past quarter-century. We are complex beings, and the point of these breakthroughs—a point I strongly emphasize—should be to assist designers in understanding the depth of our complexity, the presence of this paradisiacal instinct. More simply stated, everyone, from Hong Kong to Helsinki, does not fit into the same glass box.

How will these new models in the humanistic and biological sciences inform design? First, they underscore the fact that the experience of every environment is an embodied and multisensory (whole-body) event, one in which materials, forms, and spaces strike an empathetic and physiognomic accord (or discord) with the organism. The main lines of postmodern and poststructural theory in the last decade of the twentieth century viewed design almost entirely in conceptual or semiotic terms. Materials, or notions of form and space, were seen as abstractions without corporal weight or substance. We now know that tectonic culture, as Kenneth Frampton has referred to it, implicates our sensorimotor and mirror neuron systems in a process known as embodied simulation. This is not a theoretical supposition borrowed from some trendy school of philosophy, but a biological dimension of dwelling itself. Edward T. Hall's precocious notion of "tactile space" scratched the surface of this deep stream of native empathy with which we engage the world.[21]

Emanating from embodied simulation is the recognition that all architectural environments possess or modulate a mood. Environments that we construct are emotional, visceral, and hormonal; they come to life through the mist or atmospheres through which we engage them. Conventional psychology textbooks of only a few years ago viewed mood as some mysterious force swelling up from some equally mysterious place below. Today moods are recognized as endogenous kinaesthetic activities unto themselves, the very stuff through which we gain perceptual awareness. They are the predisposed movements and sensitivities that every organism maintains, and they cannot be distinguished from what we used to refer to as "rational" cognition. Emotion pervades cognition through and through, and, in the words of Giovanna Colombetti, emotion "is integral to both perception and action."[22] A stream of sunlight through a window, a waft of fragrance emanating from a garden, the height of the ceiling, the presence of a loved one—all affect the experience of a room, sometimes in a dramatic fashion. Such an understanding, of course, is not unknown to our better designers, but the fact that mood infuses every environmental niche should no longer be undervalued in our present-day design studios.

Perhaps the most consequential discovery in recent years is the recognition of our profoundly social natures, and there is no greater failing of architectural theory over the past half-century than its unwillingness to take up the matter. From an ideological or utopian perspective, there is little that we can do to stop the next Cheesegrater or Can of Ham from coming to fruition. Yet from a paradisiacal

43 The eyes of Theodora, Basilica of San Vitale, Ravenna, A.D. 547.

perspective, a small door is open. For instance, we are beginning to fathom the grounding of our sympathetic resonances and intersubjective contagions with others; we are exceptionally good apes at reading the minds of others because we are always rehearsing the subtle facial expressions that we perceive. More importantly, the growth in our understanding of evolutionary history has shown us that many of the behaviors that we formerly divined as cultural—music, dance, body ornaments, and the practice of architecture, in fact—are not cultural constructs of humanity but extend far back in time to earlier species than our own. They are artistic expressions deeply rooted in human dwelling, and they should be a focus of our environmental niches. One thinks in this regard of Hans-Georg Gadamer's exposition of the "festival," which, aside from its pleasing "sensuous abundance," knits people together into a community.[23] Gadamer also went on to argue that a building should fit into a community's way of life—that is, provide an "ornament, a background of mood, or a framework," as well as have an "enlivening effect."[24] How refreshing it would be for someone to put such a social intention into material form.

More instructive, and perhaps even tapping into the paradisiacal instinct, is Dalibor Vesely's desire for a "poetic mythos" for design—that is, acknowledging the role that significant gestures, rituals, settings, and conversations play in our social relationships.[25] We seem to be powerless to challenge the ideological structures of our age, and it is even more preposterous to believe that we can create a utopia through the symbolic or aestheticized trappings of our habitats. Yet we as designers can view those who inhabit our niches as dwellers with paradisiacal instincts. In its simplest form, this design program would amount to no more than a midday lunch or candlelit dinner for a party of two or more on a terrace. If this terrace were set within a garden, then we might legitimately claim, like Columbus before us, to have discovered the source of the terrestrial paradise.

1 Davos Declaration 2018: "Towards a High-quality *Baukultur* for Europe," January 20–22, 2018, https://davosdeclaration2018.ch/ (accessed December 9, 2019).
2 See Clifford Geertz, *The Interpretation of Cultures: Selected Essays* (New York: Basic Books, 1973), 44, 449.
3 Göran Schildt (ed.), *Alvar Aalto in His Own Words* (Helsinki: Otava Publishing Company, 1957), 215.
4 Evan Thompson and Francisco J. Varela, "Radical Embodiment: Neural Dynamics and Consciousness," *Trends in Cognitive Sciences*, 5/10 (October 2001): 424–25.
5 See John Odling-Smee, et al., *Niche Construction: The Neglected Process in Evolution* (Princeton, NJ: Princeton University Press, 2003).
6 Theophilus G. Pinches, *The Old Testament: In Light of the Historical Records and Legends of Assyria and Babylonia* (London: Society for Promoting Christian Knowledge, 1902), 71–74.
7 Geo Widengren, *The King and the Tree of Life in Ancient Near Eastern Religion* (Uppsala, A.-B. Lundeuistka Bokhandeln, 1951), 15.
8 Stephanie Dalley, "Ancient Mesopotamian Gardens and the Identification of the Hanging Gardens of Babylon Resolved," *Garden History*, 21/1 (Summer 1993): 1–13.
9 David Stronach, *Pasargadae: A Report on the Excavations Conducted by the British Institute of Persian Studies from 1961 to 1963* (Oxford: Clarendon Press, 1978), 109.
10 Cited from Charles Washington Moores, *The Story of Columbus* (Boston: Houghton Mifflin Company, 1912), 101–2.
11 *War of the Jews*, in *The Works of Flavius Josephus*, trans. William Whiston (Philadelphia: John C. Winston Co., n.d.), 5.5.4.
12 Revelation, 2:7, 21:11, and 22:2.
13 Aelian, *On the Characteristics of Animals*, trans. Alwyn Faber Scholfield (London: William Heinemann, 1959), 33.18.
14 For a description, see *Cathay and the Way Thither; Being a Collection of Medieval Notices of China*, trans. and ed. Colonel Henry Yule (London: Hakluyt Society, 1866), I: 128–29.
15 Otto von Simson, *The Gothic Cathedral: Origins of Gothic Architecture and the Medieval Concept of Order* (Princeton, NJ: Princeton University Press, 1974), xiv–xv.
16 James Gibson, *The Ecological Approach to Visual Perception* (Hillsdale, NJ: Lawrence Erlbaum Associates, 1986), 126.
17 Ibid., 128.
18. Tim Ingold, *The Perception of the Environment: Essays on Livelihood, Dwelling and Skill* (London: Routledge, 2000), 180.
19 Tim Ingold, "Anthropology Comes to Life," *General Anthropology*, 17/1 (Spring 2010): 3.
20 Susan Oyama, *Evolution's Eye: A Systems View of the Biology–Culture Divide* (Durham, NC: Duke University Press, 2000), 48.
21 Edward T. Hall, *The Hidden Dimension* (Garden City, NY: Doubleday & Company, 1966), 59.
22 Giovanna Colombetti, *The Feeling Body: Affective Science Meets the Enactive Mind* (Cambridge, MA: MIT Press, 2014), 63.
23 Hans-Georg Gadamer, *The Relevance of the Beautiful and Other Essays*, trans. Nicholas Walker (New York: Cambridge University Press, 1986), 39.
24 Hans-Georg Gadamer, *Truth and Method*, trans. Joel Weinsheimer and Donald G. Marshall (New York: Continuum, 1999), 158.
25 Dalibor Vesely, *Architecture in the Age of Divided Representation: The Question of Creativity in the Shadow of Production* (Cambridge, MA: MIT Press, 2004), 368, 373.

Paradoxes of Progress

Joan Ockman

> When the past speaks it always speaks as an oracle: only if you are an architect of the future and know the present will you understand it.
>
> Friedrich Nietzsche[1]

Fables of the future

"Now we're getting somewhere," cries an engineer. So Hermann Hesse begins his short story "The City." Written in 1910 and originally published in the German magazine *Licht und Schatten* ("Light and Shadows"), Hesse's tale distills the entire history of urban civilization into a couple of pages.[2] Two trains arrive at the end of the rail line, a desolate prairie on the edge of a mountain wilderness. They deposit a contingent of pioneers with supplies of food, tools, and coal. In short order a settlement is established. Shacks made of tin go up, then shelters of wood and, before long, of stone. The wild dogs and bison that used to roam the grasslands flee. Roads are cut and fields are tilled and planted. As the outpost prospers, workers from distant places stream in looking for employment. Churches, movie houses, department stores, and a temperance society open. Soon there are "broad smiling avenues lined with imposing banks and public buildings." In the shops "French wine, Norwegian herring, Italian sausage, English woolens, and Russian caviar" are on offer. In time the town develops its own culture, its own rules and rituals, a social hierarchy. Beyond the center, factories, fields, villages, and railroad tracks crisscross the former prairie. In summertime the wealthy repair to resorts in the nearby mountains or make excursions to the seacoast. "The days when the first hammer stroke had resounded, the first murder had been committed, the first religious services held, the first newspaper printed" recede into memory as the settlement grows rich and powerful and becomes the hub of a thriving region.

A century later, an earthquake levels the city. It is quickly rebuilt, this time with greater solidity and grandeur. "Architects and artists [embellish] the rejuvenated city with public buildings, parks, fountains, and monuments." The magnificent constructions, the splendid parks, and the museum of the city's history are admired throughout the world; "politicians and architects, engineers and mayors" come to visit and learn from its example. Students are taught "the great laws of development and progress: how the refined grows from the crude, man from beast, civilization from barbarism, and abundance from penury."

During the next hundred years the city reaches the apogee of its affluence and influence. But the urban idyll is rudely interrupted by "a bloody revolution" fomented by "the lower classes." The insurgents plunder the countryside, torching the region's rich oil fields and massacring the local population. By the time the troubles subside and the city recovers, it is no longer "the heart and brain of a world, the market and stock exchange of many countries." In the interim "a distant country beyond the seas" has begun to flourish, its cities attracting "the fallow energies, the strivings and ambitions" of the older one. Those who remain continue to live out their days in the increasingly moribund metropolis, subsisting amid "old moss-covered gardens," "weather-stained facades of vast buildings," "soundless squares." For a while the melancholy atmosphere has a romantic appeal for poets, painters, and lovers. Over the next couple of centuries, though, as all cultural impulses fade and the old families die off, life shifts "more and more to other continents." At this point the city falls into ruin, harboring only occasional "gypsies and fugitives."

Another earthquake devastates the region. It spares the city itself but alters the course of the nearby river. A portion of the already destroyed landscape turns into a pestilent swamp, the rest into desert. All trace of human inhabitation disappears now save for "a nondescript rabble, wild, unfriendly creatures." In due course these remnants vanish as well. Slowly the old forest rises again, creeping "down from the mountains, engulfing the crumbling remains of old country houses and stone bridges." Wild animals—fox and marten, wolf and bear—come back too. "A young pine tree had taken root in the rubble of a fallen palace," concludes the tale. "Only a year ago it had been the first harbinger of the approaching forest. But now, as it looked about, it saw new saplings far and wide. 'Now we're getting somewhere!' cried a woodpecker who was hammering at the trunk, and looked with satisfaction at the spreading forest and the magnificent green progress that was covering the earth."

Written four years before the outbreak of World War I, Hesse's tale reads as a premonition and parable of the demise of Old Europe and the ascendancy of an upstart civilization across the ocean. But the fable of "green progress" (*grünenden Fortschritt*) also belongs to a genre of utopian/dystopian imagination, of ecological speculation, that has existed since the advent of modernity, taking multiple forms of expression from literary to visual art, fiction to nonfiction, popular culture to philosophical reflection. A century after it was written, "The City" continues to speak, more powerfully than ever, to the concerns of the present: to a period that has retrospectively seized upon the name *Anthropocene* to describe the relationship between human history and natural history, chronological time and deep time, cities and the planet, finally awake to the impact of anthropogenic change on earth.

Among the recent literature that Hesse's tale prefigures is a best-selling book by an award-winning environmental journalist, Alan Weisman, published in 2007. *The World Without Us* undertakes a detailed imagining of what the earth would be like were human life suddenly to disappear.[3] While similar plot lines have long been a staple of science fiction, Weisman's thought experiment, acclaimed as a "nonfiction eco-thriller" and now optioned for a Hollywood movie, draws extensively on contemporary environmental research. It is worth quoting at length a passage from the chapter titled "The City Without Us," which explores a scenario that could one day play out in New York:

> In the first few years with no heat, pipes burst all over town, the freeze-thaw cycle moves indoors, and things start to seriously deteriorate. Buildings groan as their innards expand and contract; joints between walls and rooflines separate. Where they do, rain leaks in, bolts rust, and facing pops off, exposing insulation. If the city hasn't burned yet, it will now. Collectively, New York's architecture isn't as combustible as, say, San Francisco's incendiary rows of clapboard Victorians. But with no firemen to answer the call, a dry lightning strike that ignites a decade of dead branches and leaves piling up in Central Park will spread flames through the streets. Within two decades, lightning rods have begun to rust and snap, and roof fires leap among buildings, entering paneled offices filled with paper fuel. Gas lines ignite with a rush of flames that blows out windows. Rain and snow blow in, and soon even poured concrete floors are freezing, thawing, and starting to buckle. Burnt insulation and charred wood add nutrients to Manhattan's growing soil cap. Native Virginia creeper and poison ivy claw at walls covered with lichens, which thrive in the absence of air pollution. Red-tailed hawks and peregrine falcons nest in increasingly skeletal high-rise structures.[4]

Weisman notes that Manhattan's skyscrapers are solidly anchored into the city's hard schist bedrock, but their steel foundations were never meant to become waterlogged. He continues:

> Plugged sewers, deluged tunnels, and streets reverting to rivers ... will conspire to undermine subbasements and destabilize their huge loads. In a future that portends stronger and more frequent hurricanes striking North America's Atlantic coast, ferocious winds will pummel tall, unsteady structures. Some will topple, knocking down others. Like a gap in the forest when a giant tree falls, new growth will rush in. Gradually, the asphalt jungle will give way to a real one.[5]

The old philosophical conundrum of whether a tree that falls in a forest—or for that matter a tower that collapses in a city—makes any sound if nobody is there to hear it is here rendered moot. What Weisman's dramatization makes clear is that the impact of human activity will resound far into the future, even as the world goes on without us.

The central question that both Hesse's fable and Weisman's futurology raise has to do with nature's resilience. Yet while the German author can dream in 1910 of a return to a prelapsarian Eden, Weisman and today's scientific community—at least those who do not belong to the denialist fringe—know that perfect reversibility is a chimera. In a posthuman world some of the chemicals now contaminating our air and water will dissipate fairly quickly. But other human-made products, from glass to plastics, can take as long as 50,000 years to degrade, and nuclear waste can remain deadly for up to two million years. Weisman remains circumspect as to whether humanity is going to "make it through what many scientists call this planet's latest great extinction" and "bring the rest of Life with us rather than tear it down."[6] But it is clear that if we have any hope of doing so, we will have to abandon the anthropocentric view of progress that has underwritten Western thinking since the Industrial Revolution, perpetuating an instrumentalist approach to modernization and a positivist worldview.

The end of the world or the end of capitalism?

What exactly is in contention in the "Anthropocene debate"? A new name for the geological epoch we are currently living in, the period now being rebaptized the Anthropocene was known until recently as part of the Holocene. The latter began close to 12,000 years ago, in the aftermath of the last ice age. The new nomenclature was first seriously proposed by the atmospheric scientist Paul Crutzen just after the turn of the millennium to reflect the decisive impact that human activity has had on the earth's climate, geology, hydrology, and biosphere. While people disagree about when the Anthropocene began—arguments range from the early seventeenth century to the mid-twentieth—much more than a chronological dispute is at stake. Anthropocene is not just a name but also a narrative about history, a crisis theory, a prediction about the future, and an urgent plea for change. The term has also been rejected outright by some on both ends of the political spectrum, including intellectuals on the left. The latter argue that to lay blame for the current planetary predicament on the generalization "Man" is to indict the wrong culprit. Among the most outspoken representatives of this position, Andreas Malm has made the case that it is not some universal species-being—Anthropos—that has brought about the current crisis, but rather a specific historical system, namely industrial capitalism, and the fossil-fuel economy it has promoted ever since the invention of the steam engine for its own profit and benefit. While this political economy "has now become so entrenched that we recognize it as the only way humans can produce," it was a historical choice, not a foregone conclusion, Malm argues. Framing the history of social relations in terms of an innate property of the species has the ideological effect of "dehistoricizing, universalizing, eternalizing, and naturalizing a mode of production specific to a certain time and place," and ultimately of "block[ing] off any prospect for change."[7] As an alternative descriptor, he and others have therefore offered "Capitalocene," an unlovely word but a more accurate one.

Naming the system accurately may be the beginning of a response to the problem, but it is not a solution in itself, of course. Arguably, the ascription of blame for environmental depredation to capitalism rather than to Man is no less paralyzing and affords

44 Sinkholes in grazing land caused by overextraction of subsurface water for coal mining, Baorixile, Inner Mongolia, 2012. Photograph by Lu Guang.

people—among them architects—no more sense of agency. How can architects hope to contribute to repairing the planet if, as Fredric Jameson has quipped, it is easier to imagine the end of the world than the end of capitalism?[8] For those involved in the construction of the built environment, this may indeed be the most daunting problem. Centrally implicated in the global economy of oil and reliant on energy-intensive extractive processes and interlinked supply chains, buildings in advanced countries rank among the most voracious consumers of energy and most flagrant producers of global warming, using up to forty percent of the world's petrochemical resources and emitting nearly half its greenhouse gases. Yet short of wholesale change to the existing system of production, how to reimagine the practices of building so as to alleviate the crisis rather than deepen it? How to counteract the existing "hydrocarbon utopia"?[9]

This problem remains challenging for architects in multiple ways. As Kenneth Frampton, among the first and most consistent architecture critics to speak out against the building industry's abusive environmental practices, has long pointed out, only a very small proportion of the human-made environment is subject to the intervention of an architect: "It is the real estate and home-building industries—aided by banks, bureaucracies and our laissez-faire planning policies—that are jointly responsible for the dispersed and totally chaotic disaggregation of the environment."[10] Yet inasmuch as architects are complicit in this system—and, given their special expertise, should know better—they have an obligation to assume moral leadership and try to bring a measure of creativity to the most existential threat that we face.

At least two further obstacles to this project exist, though, and they are even more specific to the discipline of architecture. The first is an ingrained technocratic mindset, which Frampton has characterized as an affinity, inherited from the modernist avant-garde, for "high" or "optimized" as opposed to "appropriate" technology. The second is a no less reflexive, if more postmodernist, penchant for "scenographic" or spectacular aesthetics. Both of these proclivities have flourished under the contemporary regime of neoliberal globalization and digital culture.

Technocracy and the rhetoric of resilience and risk

Take the contemporary discourse of "urban resilience." The ability of life-forms to rebound and regenerate after trauma has long been associated with cities as well as nature.[11] Yet in recent decades, in a reverse anthropocentric projection, the metaphor of the city as a self-regulating ecosystem has been professionalized and popularized to the point that "resilience" has become a buzzword, taking its place in the policy lexicon alongside "green," "sustainability," and "smart growth."

The ideology of resilience confers an aura of naturalism on urban processes. Yet a city does not really behave like a beehive or a pond, even if it may be described as a complex and holistic system. More than ever today the city is a proving ground for profit-oriented managerial planning. According to an article titled "Urban resilience" in Wikipedia, a resilient city "is one that assesses, plans, and acts to prepare for and respond to hazards—natural and human-made, sudden and slow-onset, expected and unexpected." The article continues:

> Building resilience in cities relies on investment decisions that prioritize spending on activities that offer alternatives, which perform well in different scenarios. Such decisions need to take into account future risks and uncertainties. Because risk can never be fully eliminated, emergency and disaster planning is crucial. Disaster risk management frameworks, for example, offer practical opportunities for enhancing resilience.[12]

To translate the marketspeak, urban resilience is another name for risk management. From here it is but a short, bureaucratic step to the calculus of NIMBYism and outsourcing, as shown by Mark Schapiro in *Carbon Shock: A Tale of Risk and Calculus on the Front Lines of the Disrupted Global Economy*. Pittsburgh, once one of the most polluted cities in America, has now become a model of green urbanism, boasting a diversified economy of high-tech research, higher education, health care, banking, and tourism, as well as the highest concentration of LEED-certified buildings in the U.S. Meanwhile, 8,000 miles away, the city of Guangzhou has become a twenty-first-century Pittsburgh. A conurbation of over fifteen million people on China's southeast coast, it manufactures steel girders, bridges, auto

45 Bruce Mau and the Institute without Boundaries, *Massive Change*, Vancouver Art Gallery, 2004.

parts, and refrigerators for export to the American market. Guangzhou now has the largest carbon footprint in a country that is itself the world's largest emitter of carbon dioxide. "It wasn't just Pittsburgh's manufacturing jobs that migrated to China; the greenhouse gases associated with them went too," writes Schapiro. "The Chinese, in short, are producing greenhouse gases on our behalf."[13] When the German sociologist Ulrich Beck coined the term "risk society" in the mid-1980s to describe the unprecedented effects and increasing hazards of late-capitalist technological acceleration, he entertained the hope that a new "sense of planet"—a new cosmopolitan solidarity and compassionate collectivity—might emerge. What he failed to reckon with was the extent to which cynical reason and self-interest would remain defense mechanisms and weapons wielded by those in power and their agents.[14]

Anthropocene aesthetics

The second obstacle to an authentic and empathetic engagement with the current environmental crisis on the part of architecture and design culture is, ironically, architects' love of spectacular images and their talent for producing them. This syndrome has become manifest in recent exhibitions and books that mix an ostentatious display of "research" with dazzling, digitally facilitated presentation techniques. A landmark in this genre was *Massive Change*, an exhibition conceived and designed by Bruce Mau and his Toronto-based studio in association with the Institute without Boundaries that opened in Vancouver in 2004 (**45**), accompanied by a book of the same name.

Mau is a consummately talented graphic artist who previously collaborated with Rem Koolhaas on the tour de force volume *S,M,L,XL*. For the purposes of the exhibition Mau mobilized a full battery of sensory bombardment and visual seduction, wallpapering the gallery spaces with an overload of images and words. Proclaiming that "*Massive Change* is not about the world of design; it's about the design of the world," and aiming to offer "a wildly unexpected view of the future," the manifesto–project put forward a hubristically optimistic set of propositions:

> We will explore designer economies.
> We will tap into the global commons.
> We will distribute capacity.
> We will embrace paradox.
> We will reshape our future.[15]

These future-tense proclamations were elaborated in the companion book whose eleven chapters focused on different "economies"—Urban Economies, Movement Economies, Energy Economies, Information Economies, Image Economies, Market Economies, Material Economies, Military Economies, Manufacturing Economies, Living Economies, and Wealth and Politics. The chapters leapfrog through a vast array of subject matter and scales, from housing to health care, high-speed transportation to nanotechnology, grid computing to garbage. The through-line is a fervently proclaimed belief in progress through techno-scientific innovation, entrepreneurship, and design intelligence. Each chapter engages leading "thought leaders"—a new name for people who used to be called public intellectuals—in brief and provocative celebrity interviews. The sensational presentation, the confident "together-we-will-do-good" message, and the fabulous photographic imagery give the Anthropocene aesthetic a glamorous, cutting-edge, and progressive patina, one that cannot but prove irresistible to architecture students.

Yet while the exorbitance of the conception was no doubt an effort to subsume a big and complicated world in a *Gesamtwerk*, the effect of Mau's exhibitionistic virtuosity, the oscillation between zoomed-out aerial images and zoomed-in microscopic ones, is overwhelming and ultimately mind-numbing. To transform the looming crises of the twenty-first century into "visual splendor," as T.J. Demos has put it, is to turn aesthetics into anaesthetics.[16] More generally, in a recall of Walter Benjamin's famous admonition against the aestheticization of politics, it is to produce "abstract visual pleasure" at the expense of both in-depth understanding and any compelling argument for change.[17] Among the most egregious examples of this kind of spectacularization, skewered by Demos in his 2017 book, *Against the Anthropocene*, is the

46 Opening spread of chapter "Manufacturing Economies," from Bruce Mau, *Massive Change* (London: Phaidon, 2004). Photograph in background by Edward Burtynsky, "Oxford Tire Pile #1, Hamilton, Ontario, 1997."

photography of another Toronto artist, Edward Burtynsky. Several of Burtynsky's images appear in *Massive Change*, including a shot of thousands of discarded automobile tires in a vast dump in Ontario, reproduced on the opening spread of the chapter dedicated to "Manufacturing Economies." While Mau's overlaid text promises "a never-ending loop of improvement,"[18] the image affords the reader–viewer a "perverse enjoyment ... of our own annihilation" (**46**).[19]

Eyewitness evidence

In 1826 Germany's greatest nineteenth-century architect, Karl Friedrich Schinkel, embarked on a four-month journey to France and Great Britain in the company of his close friend Christian Peter Wilhelm Friedrich Beuth. The primary purpose was to survey and report back on the state of industrial advancement in the two countries, most especially England, where, in contrast to Prussia's still feudal agrarian economy, the Industrial Revolution was already in high gear. Beuth, an economic reformer with distinctly modern ideas of technocratic management and business entrepreneurship, was greatly interested in technological innovation and, in his capacity as chief official responsible for Prussian trade policy, was also a forerunner

47 Karl Friedrich Schinkel, view of industrial landscape around Dudley (near Birmingham), England, 1826.

48 "Manufacture of Glass for 'The Crystal Palace' at Messrs Chance's Works, Spon Lane Near Birmingham." From *Illustrated London News* (December 21, 1850).

in the no less modern business of industrial espionage, presumedly gathering secret information for his government. Thanks to Beuth's familiarity with the industrial geography of England and Scotland, Schinkel visited places to which he might not otherwise have had access, carefully recording his observations in notes and sketches and analyzing the new industrial processes with boundless intellectual curiosity.

49 Shexian Tianjin Iron and Steel Plant, She County, Hebei Province, China, 2008. Photograph by Lu Guang.

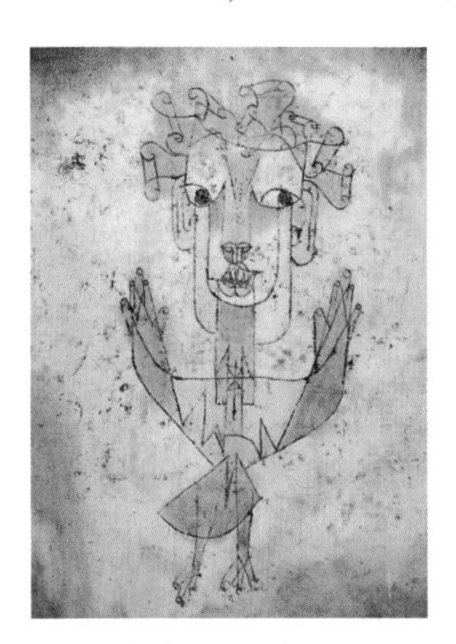

50 Paul Klee, *Angelus Novus*, monoprint, 1920.
51 Factory worker in Wuhai City, Inner Mongolia, April 2005. Photograph by Lu Guang.

He was most of all fascinated by England's factory buildings and engineering structures, their novel cast-iron skeletons and roofs and their machinery and installations. Yet as a small pencil drawing of the landscape around Dudley, a town near Birmingham, reveals, the sight of the devastated countryside evidently got the better of his emotions (**47**). "Overwhelming sight of thousands of smoking obelisks," he writes in his journal: ironworks "of horrific proportions."[20]

Schinkel, of course, was not the first to comment on the apocalyptic landscape of early industrial capitalism, and he would hardly be the last. A quarter-century later, in the era of the Crystal Palace, "factory tourism" enjoyed a heyday in England, drawing visitors curious both to learn about the new manufacturing processes and to gawk at the scene of smoldering chimneys and suffocating smoke. A vignette on the front page of the *Illustrated London News* of December 21, 1850, depicts a cavernous interior at Chance Brothers Glassworks in Spon Lane, Smethwick, near Birmingham, where the panes for Joseph Paxton's lucidly conceived and ethereally detailed architectural structure were being produced in record quantity, size, and speed (**48**). The dimly illuminated furnaces in which the glassblowers—many of them young boys—labored could hardly offer greater contrast with the iconic image of Victorian progress. This was truly the dark side of transparency.[21]

Fast-forward to the largest steel-producing region in China today, Hebei Province, where sulfur, nitrogen, and other noxious particulates in the air produce year-round smog (and where, in 1976, a devastating earthquake killed upward of 240,000 people in this seismically unstable zone). As of fall 2018, the steel plants have been required to install new equipment complying with "ultra-stringent" emissions standards. We can speak of belated modernization, or just of déjà vu. But it is sufficient to juxtapose Schinkel's drawing of Dudley with a photograph of industrial Hebei to behold the ironies of two centuries of progress (**49**).

Epilogue: history's angel

Photographer Lu Guang—three of whose images accompany this essay—disappeared in November 2018 while traveling in Xinjiang, an autonomous territory of northwest China where government authorities have recently cracked down on Uyghurs and ethnic Muslim minorities. His arrest was confirmed the following month after an international outcry. Freed on bail more than half a year later, he resides in his hometown in China at the time of writing.[22]

Born in 1961, Lu began working as a documentary photographer in the late 1990s. He has traveled throughout his native country, focusing his lens on the consequences of China's rapid development. Ranging in locale from resource-depleted mining regions in the north to polluted industrial zones in the east to drought-afflicted areas in the south, his images, some commissioned by Greenpeace Asia, have received numerous awards. His subjects include contaminated rice fields, toxic water sources, and "cancer villages"—impoverished communities stricken with HIV, birth defects, drug addiction, and other maladies brought on by environmental devastation.

Just as Lu's views of the infernal steel plants of Hebei recall the horror registered by Schinkel on seeing Dudley, his vistas of Inner Mongolia's bucolic pasture land—now pockmarked with sinkholes caused by the overextraction of water for coal mining—offer a twenty-first-century commentary on Hesse's fable (**44**). But no less eloquent are his more intimate shots of the people who inhabit these places, destroyed human beings who are themselves agents of the earth's destruction, who suffer the consequences of both social injustice and ecological catastrophe. The subjects captured by Lu's camera-eye are trapped in their tragic everyday lives just as they are also caught in the slipstream of the gathering planetary crisis (**51**). Like Walter Benjamin's angel of history, they are blown backward into the storm of progress (**50**).[23] Lu's photographs, daring to make visible realities China would prefer to suppress, constitute an ethical form of knowledge, essential for shocking us out of hubris and anaesthetic stupor, for reconciling seeing with being.

1 "On the Uses and Disadvantage of History for Life" (1874), in Friedrich Nietzsche, *Untimely Meditations*, trans. R.J. Hollingdale (Cambridge, U.K.: Cambridge University Press, 1997), 94.

2 Hermann Hesse, "Die Stadt," *Licht und Schatten: Wochenschrift für Schwarzweisskunst und Dichtung*, 1/12, unpag. [2–3]; English trans. by Ralph Manheim in Hermann Hesse, *Stories of Five Decades* (New York: Farrar, Straus & Giroux, 1973), 194–99, and by Jack Zipes in Hermann Hesse, *The Fairy Tales of Hermann Hesse* (New York: Bantam Books, 1995), 43–49. The quoted passages in the following extended paraphrase are taken from the Manheim translation, with slight modifications.

3 Alan Weisman, *The World Without Us* (New York: Picador, 2007).

4 Ibid., 32–33.

5 Ibid., 33–34.

6 Ibid., 346.

7 Andreas Malm, "The Anthropocene Myth," *Jacobin Magazine*, 30 (2015), https://www.jacobinmag.com/2105/03/anthropocene-capitalism-climate-change (accessed December 30, 2018). Also see Malm, *Fossil Capital: The Rise of Steam Power and the Roots of Global Warming* (London: Verso, 2016). For more on the Anthropocene debate, see Jason W. Moore, ed., *Anthropocene or Capitalocene? Nature, History, and the Crisis of Capitalism* (Oakland, CA: PM Press, 2016).

8 Jameson has posed this question on multiple occasions. See *The Seeds of Time* (New York: Columbia University Press, 1994), xii: "It seems to be easier for us today to imagine the thoroughgoing deterioration of the earth and of nature than the breakdown of late capitalism; perhaps that is due to some weakness in our imaginations." See also his review of Rem Koolhaas's book on shopping: "Future City," *New Left Review*, 21 (May–June 2003).

9 In the short term, the geopolitical threats posed by destabilizing the oil economy may be as great as the ecological ones. See Timothy Mitchell, "Hydrocarbon Utopia," in Michael D. Gordin, Helen Tilley, and Gyan Prakash, eds., *Utopia/Dystopia: Conditions of Historical Possibility* (Princeton, NJ: Princeton University Press, 2010), 117–47.

10 Kenneth Frampton, *Labour, Work and Architecture: Collected Essays on Architecture and Design* (London: Phaidon, 2002), 14.

11 For a historicized study of the concept of urban resilience, see Lawrence J. Vale and Thomas J. Campanella, eds., *The Resilient City: How Modern Cities Recover from Disaster* (New York: Oxford University Press, 2005), 3. Among earlier urban theorists to draw an analogy between cities and natural systems was Jane Jacobs, who described cities as systems of organized complexity in *The Death and Life of Great American Cities* (New York: Random House, 1961). For a recent and more nuanced interpretation, see Marina Alberti, *Cities That Think Like Planets: Complexity, Resilience, and Innovation in Hybrid Ecosystems* (Seattle: University of Washington Press, 2016).

12 "Urban resilience," https://en.wikipedia.org/wiki/Urban_resilience (accessed December 28, 2018).

13 Mark Schapiro, *Carbon Shock: A Tale of Risk and Calculus on the Front Lines of the Disrupted Global Economy* (New York: Chelsea Green, 2014), 113–14.

14 See "The 'Cosmopolitan Moment' of World Risk Society or: Enforced Enlightenment," in Ulrich Beck, *World at Risk* (Cambridge, U.K.: Polity, 2009), 47–66. Also see Ursula K. Heise, *Sense of Place and Sense of Planet: The Environmental Imagination of the Global* (Oxford: Oxford University Press, 2008).

15 Bruce Mau with Jennifer Leonard and the Institute without Boundaries, *Massive Change* (London: Phaidon, 2004), 16–19.

16 See T.J. Demos, *Against the Anthropocene: Visual Culture and Environment Today* (Berlin: Sternberg Press, 2017), 65.

17 Ibid., 69.

18 Mau, *Massive Change*, 181.

19 Demos, *Against the Anthropocene*, 70. For Burtynsky's latest undertaking, a multidisciplinary project in collaboration with Jennifer Baichwal and Nicholas de Pencier that encompasses photography, film, and virtual and augmented reality, see *The Anthropocene Project*, https://www.edwardburtynsky.com/projects/the-anthropocene-project/ (accessed December 9, 2019). The stated intent is to "immerse viewers in the new world of the Anthropocene epoch, delivering a sense of scale, gravity, and impact that both encompasses and moves beyond the scope of conventional screens and prints."

20 Karl Friedrich Schinkel, *The English Journey: Journal of a Visit to France and Britain in 1826*, ed. David Bindman and Gottfried Riemann (New Haven, CT: Yale University Press, 1993), 128–29.

21 On factory tourism in mid-nineteenth-century England, see Isobel Armstrong, *Victorian Glassworlds: Glass Culture and the Imagination, 1830–1880* (Oxford: Oxford University Press, 2008), 18–56. On child labor in the glassmaking factories, see Friedrich Engels, *The Condition of the Working Class in England* (Oxford: Oxford University Press, 1999), 215–16. With specific reference to the Crystal Palace, see "Manufacture of Glass for 'The Crystal Palace'," *Illustrated London News* (December 21, 1850), 470.

22 On Lu's disappearance, see, among others, Chris Buckley, "Acclaimed Photographer Arrested in Far West China, Wife Says," *New York Times* (December 15, 2018), A12. For a more recent update, see Xiao Yu, "China Releases Award-Winning Photographer Who Documented Nation's Dark Side," *Voice of America News* (September 12, 2019), https://www.voanews.com/press-freedom/china-releases-award-winning-photographer-who-documented-nations-dark-side (accessed December 17, 2019).

23 The figure of the angel of history appears in a passage in Benjamin's "Theses on the Philosophy of History" (1940). I quote it here from the opening of Kenneth Frampton's early essay "Industrialization and the Crises in Architecture," a Benjaminian reading of the relationship between architecture and technological development: "A Klee painting named 'Angelus Novus' shows an angel looking as though he is about to move away from something he is fixedly contemplating. His eyes are staring, his mouth is open, his wings are spread. This is how one pictures the angel of history. His face is turned towards the past. Where we perceive a chain of events, he sees one single catastrophe which keeps piling wreckage upon wreckage and hurls it in front of his feet. The angel would like to stay, awaken the dead, and make whole what has been smashed. But a storm is blowing from Paradise; it has got caught in his wings with such violence that the angel can no longer close them. This storm irresistibly propels him into the future to which his back is turned, while the pile of debris before him grows skyward. This storm is what we call progress" (*Oppositions*, 1 [September 1973], 58). The present essay is dedicated to Kenneth Frampton, with deepest gratitude for his inspiration over more than four decades.

Engaging the Lifeworld in Architectural Design: Phenomenology and Hermeneutics

Alberto Pérez-Gómez

Kenneth Frampton's writing about modern and contemporary architecture developed from a rigorous critical stance with its roots in hermeneutics. The outcome is a critical body of knowledge about practices that is nevertheless optimistic and generous. Architecture is valorized when it is responsible to societies and its innovative and poetic contributions are culturally recognizable. Architectural practice must not be an elitist and decontextualized "architecture for architects."

Meaning in artistic endeavors, whether figurative or abstract, explained philosopher Hans-Georg Gadamer in his famous essay "The Relevance of the Beautiful," takes place when there is a dimension of familiarity involved in present experience, allowing for true participation of the spectators or inhabitants in the work—rather than mere novelty or defamiliarization.[1] Both the familiar and the new must be present in great work, in work that is truly relevant and where beauty is coincidental with truth. Traditions are thus perpetuated and renovated, and memories created through the imaginative works of poets, painters, and architects. Gadamer calls this the true *symbolic* dimension of artistic artifacts: a *symbolon*, in ancient Greece, was a token or *tessera hospitalis*, which allowed a friend of the family to be recognized at some future time in terms of hospitality being offered. Good architecture must offer its inhabitants the possibility of *recognizing* themselves at home—while also challenging them to new modalities of being in the world, both ethical and poetic.

Frampton's preference has been for an architecture that acknowledges broad cultural values, but rather than being conservative or vernacular, it must also engage the technological tools of world civilization with its own positive social promises. Architecture must do both effectively. He has often opposed formalistic, self-referential, and self-consciously stylistic attitudes in architectural design. His understanding of Critical Regionalism, championing an architecture that truly acknowledges the lifeworld with all its complexities, has its origin in phenomenological hermeneutics, specifically in the famous citation of Paul Ricœur that he quoted extensively as an opening to his famous 1983 essay "Towards a Critical Regionalism: Six Points for an Architecture of Resistance."[2] In his own 1961 essay titled "Universal Civilization and National Cultures,"[3] part of the collection *History and Truth*, Ricœur explains how the modern world encompasses a dimension of universalization, which can be seen as an advancement, while at the same time constituting a "subtle destruction ... of the creative nucleus of great cultures, on the basis of which we interpret life." In other words, our instrumental architectural tools, both technological and formal, have the capacity to obliterate autochthonous values, spreading instead a mediocre civilization: "everywhere the same bad movie, the same slot machines, the same plastic or aluminum atrocities."

This observation demands that architects not impose arbitrary forms or concepts and efficient technological processes in their projects. Architecture is sited in specific *places* and is a promise for a better life for particular cultural groups. Inevitably, places have cultural and natural qualities that must be identified, valorized, and engaged; such given conditions are *primary* for design decision-making. Thus, architecture emerges as a practice that demands a broad and deep humanistic and historical knowledge, a grasp of what is valuable in traditions prior to global modernity by recognizing how past practices are not simply dispensable in the name of progress, but rather have provided answers to human questions that retain their relevance. This is what a hermeneutic approach to historical artifacts makes visible, valorizing with care that which matters cognitively and emotionally, rather than dismissing the past as something merely closed and distant, if not abhorrent in its values that may be contradictory to contemporary standards. Such understanding must be cultivated in practices and in education, over and beyond recent instrumental fads, technological obsessions, or the styles of famous practitioners. When engaging in architectural projects, hermeneutics demands that architects ask the right questions and engage in dialogue, acknowledging the semantic dimensions of local cultures first evident in their artifacts and languages, impossible to reduce to graphic tools, formal typologies, or mathematical functions and algorithms. The architect must learn to listen and remain attentive to the Other's answers—it demands that architects adopt an honest, humble position, quite at odds with the arrogance that is sometimes flaunted by some creative types.

One might imagine that an understanding of what is valuable in particular cultures is better grasped by local practitioners—Glenn Murcutt's Australian houses are a notable example, produced by an architect who has explicitly refused to engage in projects outside of his country while arguing a similar point. And yet, even in Murcutt's case, his ability to produce the masterpiece which is his mosque in Melbourne is the result of a practice driven by a hermeneutic imagination (**52–58**). The result is a building that is both novel, poetic, modern, and yet totally in tune with its traditional program, enabling a spiritual atmosphere both specific to the local Islamic community and ecumenical.

Let me emphasize: To understand the values, embodied in artifacts, poetic language, and habits, of those for whom one designs, it does not suffice to engage in brief site visits or draw cartographic projections and diagrams. History provides abundant evidence that for architecture to be appropriate and truly life-enhancing it must emerge from the bottom-up; this is clear in traditional cultures in which the physical environment constituted a sort of visual literacy for all dwellers. Nevertheless, the inescapable conditions of modern and contemporary practices require that the

52, 53 Glenn Murcutt and Elevi Plus, Australian Islamic Centre, Newport, Melbourne, 2019. View towards main entrance and ablution area (left); skylights, external detail (right).

architect accept their role as author, as creator, while understanding that cultures cannot be reduced to parameters, concepts, formal precedents, or clever ideas.

Thus, engaging the lifeworld in design processes is paramount, and far from a simple matter. Frampton has given us valuable clues in his writing about things to look for. In this regard, I would like to argue, it is most important to acknowledge the primacy of qualitative place over space, a complex issue sometimes misunderstood in view of the importance given in his writing to the tectonic aspects of architecture in relation to the problematic scenography of postmodern-style buildings, a contentious subject at the time when Frampton put forward his seminal ideas. The ontological primacy of place is a difficult philosophical problem which has been clarified by philosophers and critics working in the phenomenological tradition.[4] Architectural meanings do not simply emerge from geometrical or tectonic invention and their cultural pertinence is not merely imbued in the forms of the building as object, a frequent conceit of contemporary practices: places are qualitative, and a fundamental aspect of good architecture is its situatedness, rendered as *appropriate atmosphere*. The acknowledgment that meanings are already present in *places* is crucial, meanings that may originate in natural conditions and cultural uses. The manner in which such qualities must be made part of design decisions is also not a simple matter: a place cannot be reduced to a picture, to a diagram, or to a figure-ground site plan. Our difficulties in understanding such primary conditions are themselves culturally generated, and I have endeavored to explain such difficulties in some of my books.[5] They emerge from the rather universal concept that presupposes the existence of a homogeneous, isotropic geometric reality (a Cartesian space) as the domain of our

54, 55 Main prayer hall with stair to women's area (left); main prayer hall from women's area (right).

actions, regardless of our location in the world. Jeff Malpas has exhaustively explained the manner in which qualitative places are always primary for being human, and they abide in the contemporary world, one that is truly diverse as one changes locations, but they tend to hide in our everyday lives. The first challenge of a rooted architecture is to foreground those forsaken qualities as a primary dimension of architecture, enabling places for situations—spatio-temporal meanings—in appropriate atmospheres.

The lifeworld is first constituted at a prereflective level, in our motor engagement as embodied consciousness in the external world. We tend to mistakenly identify consciousness with attention, and the transmission of information with true communication. Human communication is primarily oral, gestural, erotic, and embodied, enabled by architectural and urban spaces; other modalities like writing and digital codes render information but can never fully convey such communication. We may think that all that matters is what we can represent, verbally or instrumentally. And yet, this is hardly the case: representational consciousness is like the tip of an iceberg. Enactive cognitive science estimates that about eighty percent of our consciousness is prereflective (not "subconscious" or "unconscious"), yet nonrepresentational, embodied in the body as habitual wisdom and thus enabling other forms of intellectual and affective cognition. Consciousness is yoked to life from its inception at the cellular level, and is always present whether we sleep soundly, dream, or act our awakened lives. And consciousness is "enactive," never passive. Even visual perception is not like the generation of a photographic image in the back of the retina: we see in high definition because our retinal vision is enabled by motor and conceptual bodily skills to contemplate such a world, which otherwise

56 Detail of calligraphy inscribed in concrete.

would appear sadly vague, full of holes, and literally pixilated. In other words, the architectural lifeworld is not primarily a question of intellectual attention, but of habit and gesture, and in continuity with the latter it possesses a physiognomy and includes natural languages. We actually dwell amidst an overwhelming constructed landscape and built environment, pervasive for the urban majority of our world's population. Alva Noë, prominent among philosophers and enactive cognitive scientists, has even suggested, loosely paraphrasing Goethe, that the city is made of frozen habits, as much as its good architecture might be like frozen music.[6]

Contemporary enactive cognitive science now recognizes what has long been a position of twentieth-century existential phenomenology: *that the environment is a constitutive part of animal and human consciousness*. Just like each animal has its own environing world that emerges with their organic morphology and biology—the same is true for humans. The world of the fly and the world of the monkey, for example, have little in common, if anything at all. They co-emerge for each organism as it acts out its own life seeking its particular modes of homeostasis: the equilibrium that allows the organism to prevail in life and which is its own modality of meaning. In other words: our personal consciousness is not our brain, it is both *embodied*—the entire sensorium of our nervous system with our particular bodily morphology and orientation, bipedal, with a distinct front and back, left and right, up and down, frontal vision and the ability to contemplate the regular motions of the stars—and, equally important, it is always in *place*. Despite the popular assumptions about the supposed interiority of consciousness, there is no human consciousness without place. Moods and emotions are effectively *in the world*: a seeming paradox explained by both Maurice Merleau-Ponty and more recently Nick Crossley, discussing the primacy of the social body.[7] The internal and external components of consciousness are always interacting through bodily motility; they constitute nonrepresentational knowledge in the form of cultural habits, for example, long before things come to our attention. Thus, internal and external components condition one another, *evolving* as they deploy themselves in time, along the path that is life and eventually becoming lasting cultures. The built environment qualifies our thoughts and feelings and contributes either to our well-being or, as I would argue in the case of many present dysfunctional architectural and urbanistic practices, to our collective psychopathologies. Grasping these complexities of the human lifeworld as presence is therefore fundamental for design practices to operate in view of the common good. The physical environment, cities, and their architecture matter in ways that would have been hard to acknowledge in earlier phases of modernity. It is not simply a matter of aesthetic preference or ornament. The human condition as such is at stake, and this involves much more than physical survival, comfort, hygiene, and ecological sustainability; it requires the preservation of linguistic differences and with it, true cultural diversity, gestures, and habits. It requires spaces for human communication with affective qualities, challenging and yet respectful of habitual action.

Adopting *atmosphere* as a central aesthetic concept in architecture facilitates an effective engagement with the lifeworld. The concept itself has phenomenological origins and has been extensively discussed by philosophers such as Gernot Böhme and Tonino Griffero, and architects Peter Zumthor and Juhani Pallasmaa, among others.[8] In my most recent book I addressed the concept's historical roots in our discipline.[9] I showed the association of *Stimmung*—the unique German term at the origins of present modern usage, implying both atmosphere and mood—with the traditional aims of architectural meaning since Vitruvius, encompassed by terms such as *harmony* and *temperance*, explaining how architecture had traditionally sought psychosomatic health, framing lived experience with order and stability congruent with local cultural values such as beauty and justice. This musical analogy referred to both tectonic qualities, the well-known desire for architectural beauty to emerge from the well-adjusted proportional relationship of parts to whole, and to its fundamental, experiential, life-enhancing qualities. The concept evokes the aesthetic quality of an architecture attuned to the human situations it frames. It involves form and also "program," the script for life which must respond to, further, and challenge particular cultural habits to offer a "home" for dwellers. Adolf Loos wrote that the great architect, a true artist, must first "identify a feeling for the effect he wants to create."[10] Appropriate effects such as "fear and terror in a dungeon, divine awe in a church, or gaiety in a tavern" must be clearly identified, and yet, Loos insists, "they originate in the material used and the form."[11] Atmospheres enhance moods that may be appropriate to focal actions like rituals and lived situations; they constitute cognitive and emotional communicative settings for human life. Thus, they stand beyond the common, yet failed definition of architecture as decorated shed stemming from the misunderstandings of eighteenth-century dualistic aesthetics and propose instead that architectural meanings are aesthetically *present*, in the mode of classical *aesthesis*—a form of emotional, multisensory bodily cognition which was primary for ancient Greek mentality. Indeed, the concept of atmosphere has the advantage of immediately leading us to question objectivist aesthetics, the common misunderstanding of aesthetic experience as aesthetic judgment (as famously defined for the discipline by Leibniz and Baumgarten).

The valorization of aesthetic atmospheres in modernity furthers a realization that architectural quality has very little to do with "formal style," whether connoting the identifying traits of an architect's work, a fashion, or a historical category. Issues such as formal coherence or semantic expression of any kind (regional difference, cultural identity, gender, ideology, marketing, etc.) may or may not contribute to such quality, but they can never fully subsume it. In other words, architectural meaning does not simply obey the rules of semiotics and its signifying pairs—its relationship with language will be shown to be of a different order. Not that these categories of communication are unimportant in themselves, but they must be understood as subsidiary. Architectural quality likewise is hardly the result of the formal novelty that secures the inclusion of projects and buildings in the latest journals or websites. Since architectural quality is separate from the particularities of style, it also precludes its reduction to formal categories such as simplicity versus complexity, frequently used today to justify computer-generated formal fashions.

Atmosphere, finally, is not a mere orchestration of effects, even if we must admit that human actions can deliberately change the given affective qualities of spaces and "create" atmospheres. Architectural atmospheres require a certain fixity and are therefore congruent with strong tectonic qualities; they involve materials, textures, colors, smells, and sounds. Their aesthetic effect may be initially grasped by prereflective perception, starting as a quasi-immediate sensation, and yet they must have the capacity of communicating enduring poetic images, in congruence with the continuity of embodied and placed consciousness, as described above.

Once it becomes clear what aspects of culture it is worth reinforcing, how is the architect to incorporate them in a design? How can we bring this concern with atmospheres—with spatio-temporal ephemeral conditions—to the sphere of architectural representation and design processes? As I have suggested, the authorial role of the architect is inevitable in modernity, and in fact crucial to acknowledge ethical responsibilities that should not be abdicated for some digitally produced pseudo-neutrality. Yet the impossibility of reducing the complexities of cultures to the

57, 58 Detail of structure and stair (left); nature captured behind the preaching area toward the sacred orientation (right).

mentality of a single individual is also evident. Local language is the primary mediation between particular cultural habits and intellectual understanding. Giorgio Agamben has suggested that *Stimmung*, or attuned atmospheres, lie precisely at the point of articulation between embodiment (in the form of habits) and language (which brings them to awareness and reveals their full affective and cognitive value), between *zoon* (biological life) and *logon* (linguistic, political life). The potential of stories to bring forward specific cultural values, habits, and metaphors during the design process is crucial. Here Frampton's insights meet again with hermeneutics and the understanding of the ethical imagination, as one that needs to be properly historical. Modern and contemporary practices have focused on functional diagrams, typologies, stylistics syntaxes, or staged revivals of historical forms. Despite their differences, all such options, present even at the inception of Functionalism in the books and teachings of Jean-Nicolas-Louis Durand, are ultimately pictorial. Durand famously asked his students to forget about the old problem of expression in architecture, based on linguistic analogies; a poetic architecture, like Étienne-Louis Boullée had intended, was out of the question. Architects fundamentally bypassed language as practices became increasingly more driven by instrumental tools of production, regardless of their particular stylistic leanings, from the early nineteenth century. If the desire is to truly acknowledge the lifeworld and preserve valuable cultural differences in design processes, it is imperative to listen with care to the poetic voice of others, to heed history and histories, and to incorporate narrative and poetic language into design processes.

1 Hans-Georg Gadamer, *The Relevance of the Beautiful and Other Essays* (Cambridge, U.K.: Cambridge University Press, 1986), 35f.
2 Collected in *The Anti-Aesthetic: Essays on Postmodern Culture*, ed. Hal Foster (Port Townsend, WA: Bay Press, 1983).
3 Paul Ricœur, *History and Truth* (Evanston, IL: Northwestern University Press, 1965), 271–84.
4 Significant among philosophers in the Heideggerian and phenomenological traditions are Edward Casey and Jeff Malpas. See Casey, *Getting Back into Place* (Bloomington, IN: Indiana University Press, 2009), and Malpas, *Place and Experience: A Philosophical Topography* (Cambridge, U.K.: Cambridge University Press, 2007). Within architecture, see Juhani Pallasmaa, Stephen Holl, and Alberto Pérez-Gómez, *Questions of Representation: Phenomenology of Architecture* (Tokyo: A+U Publishing, 1994), and Alberto Pérez-Gómez, "Place and Architectural Space," "Place is not a Postcard," and "Architecture and the Body," recently collected in *Timely Meditations*, 2 (Montreal: RightAngle International, 2016).
5 See, for example, Alberto Pérez-Gómez, *Attunement, Architectural Meaning after the Crisis of Modern Science* (Cambridge, MA: MIT Press, 2016), ch. 4, 107ff.
6 Alva Noë, *Varieties of Presence* (Cambridge, MA: Harvard University Press, 2012), 125.
7 Nick Crossley, *The Social Body: Habit, Identity and Desire* (London: Sage, 2001), 45.
8 The topic of atmosphere has a vast bibliography. See, for example, Gernot Böhme, *The Aesthetics of Atmospheres* (London: Routledge, 2017); Tonino Griffero, *Atmospheres: Aesthetics of Emotional Spaces* (Farnham: Ashgate, 2014); Peter Zumthor, *Atmospheres: Architectural Environments Surrounding Objects* (Basel: Birkhäuser, 2014).
9 Pérez-Gómez, *Attunement*, esp. chs. 2 and 3.
10 Adolf Loos, "Das Prinzip der Bekleidung," in *Ins Leere Gesprochen* (Vienna: Georg Prachner, 1981), 139–45.
11 Ibid.

PART II

Histories and Pedagogies of Architecture

The essays assembled in this section turn on two distinct areas of concern in Frampton's work: the history of modern architecture and architectural pedagogy. The essays draw from widely divergent voices that serve as a comparative backdrop to the more personal reflections by practicing architects in the final section. As with Part I, this section begins with a substantial piece which underscores the importance of Frampton's work within the vast field of the history of modern architecture: in this case, Jean-Louis Cohen's analysis of Frampton's writings on the history of the Russian avant-garde. The essay addresses Frampton's considerable contribution to the historiography of the movement, for example, his work on the Soviet avant-gardist El Lissitzky: a designer characterized by Reyner Banham as the great ideas man of the Modern Movement, given the very wide range of his activity—architect, painter, exhibit designer, polemicist, culture diplomat, and principal pioneer of modern graphic design.[1]

The second piece is Barry Bergdoll's review of the Bauhaus movement as it was addressed in 1938 by the Museum of Modern Art in New York City. The essay is offered to Frampton on the occasion of the centenary of the founding of the Bauhaus and in tribute to having learned from him about Hannes Meyer and his key role at the school. Frampton's serious investigation of the work of Meyer began with a very early piece titled "The Humanist versus the Utilitarian Ideal," based on the comparative critical analysis of two opposed designs for the canonical Société des Nations Competition of 1927, namely the entries by Le Corbusier and Pierre Jeanneret on the one hand, and by Hannes Meyer and Hans Wittwer on the other. The essay allowed Frampton to instruct readers as to the implicit values embodied in the different ways in which projects may be conceived, organized, and detailed—a method that formed the basis of his course "Comparative Critical Analysis" and the resulting book, *A Genealogy of Modern Architecture* (2015).

If Cohen draws upon the distinct culture of architecture in Russia, then in his essay, Ken Oshima brings to this discussion a distinct perspective drawn from the Japanese experience of new modern architecture. He focuses on the theme of Frampton's engagement with Japan in relation to his visits to the country and pursuant publications. The essay on the work and thought of the Japanese master Tadao Andō, written for the Museum of Modern Art's exhibition of Andō's work in 1991, is perhaps the best known to English speakers of Frampton's work on the Japanese masters. Frampton frequently wrote of Andō in comparison to the Portuguese architect Álvaro Siza, calling them "the twin magi" of the late Modern Movement in architecture.[2]

Further reflecting on Frampton's seminal contributions to the history of modern architecture, the next two essays, by Anthony Vidler and Richard Plunz, address the field of social housing and the heroic modernist urban vision. In his essay, Vidler provides a formative assessment of Frampton's comprehensive reappraisal of Le Corbusier's urban proposals and their influence. Pointing to Frampton's dialectical mode of thought, Vidler addresses the lasting importance of Frampton's radical reassessment of Le Corbusier's *Ville Radieuse*, seeing in it a nuanced critique of heroic urban utopias and a "critical and spatial knowledge" of housing. Vidler sees emerging from Frampton's reassessment of Le Corbusier the major themes that will engage Frampton throughout his career, namely "the spoliation of the environment, the breakdown of local cultures, and the loss of the art of tectonic design."

In a pivotal essay in Part II, Richard Plunz, a longtime colleague of Frampton, looks both to the topic of social housing as integral to Frampton's studies on modern architecture and to their collective pedagogical initiatives in this field. Plunz highlights Frampton's commitment to the subject of social housing as an integral part of architectural discourse and a source of innovation within the discipline, while also providing a valuable historical background on the housing curriculum initiatives in which he and Frampton were engaged during the 1970s at Columbia University's Graduate School of Architecture, Planning, and Preservation. Plunz also provides a rereading of two key European housing projects of the 1970s, which Frampton examined in an early comparative critical analysis, and which reflect his lifelong concern for this field, namely, Giancarlo De Carlo's Matteotti complex at Terni on the outskirts of Rome, and James Stirling's Southgate complex at Runcorn, Cheshire, England.

The second half of this section, encompassing five essays, is loosely grouped around the theme of architectural pedagogies. Here the focus extends far beyond the history of modern architecture in the twentieth century to address timeless themes of geometry, harmony, and proportion—themes which Juhani Pallasmaa writes are of lasting significance and of continued relevance to the discipline of architecture and the training of architects. Two other essays touch on enduring themes for the architect: in the first instance, manners or mannerism, as addressed by the late Robert Maxwell (Professor Maxwell died in January 2020 at age ninety-eight before the final completion of this volume); and in the second instance, Kurt Forster's discussion of the importance of conversation for maintaining a lasting "faith in the universality of ideas."

The final two essays provide assessments of pivotal moments in American architectural education by two leading figures, Rafael Moneo and Robert A.M. Stern. Moneo provides an in-depth reading of Robert Venturi's 1968 book, *Complexity and Contradiction in Architecture*—a work that Frampton resisted as "populism," yet nevertheless described as "Venturi's sensitive and sane assessment of the cultural realities confronting everyday practice."[3] Moneo's essay is a continuation of almost four decades of discussions he has shared with Frampton: their friendship as close colleagues is especially evident in their 2017 dialogue at Moneo's studio in Madrid, documenting their observations about the state of the profession today. In what might be a kind of personal summation shared between them, Frampton is recorded as saying: "Society is very unstable. And this is why I, however pathetic, think in terms of resistance. Not in the sense that one shouldn't change, but in the sense that architecture still has that potential to give to human beings, in their own short life, some kind of ground. Otherwise there is no ground."[4]

The final essay in this section is by another of Frampton's longtime interlocutors, Robert A.M. Stern. He is perhaps among the most unexpected contributors to this volume, given his long-standing ideological differences with Frampton. Their outspoken disagreements around the nature of the Modern Movement and the future of architecture came to public attention in 1980 in regard to the organization of the Venice Biennale, and subsequently shaped many of the parameters of architectural debates in the second half of the twentieth century. Nonetheless, Stern's essay on Paul Rudolph—and especially Rudolph's commitment to his students while he was chairman of the Department of Architecture at Yale—is a testament to the long professional relationship shared by Frampton and Stern, framed by their shared commitment to the value and consequence of architectural education.

1 Kenneth Frampton, *Labour, Work and Architecture: Collected Essays on Architecture and Design* (London: Phaidon, 2002), 106.
2 Ibid., 257.
3 Kenneth Frampton, *Modern Architecture: A Critical History*, 4th edition (London: Thames & Hudson, 2007), 291.
4 "Frampton and Moneo Interview," *Magaceen* (October 5, 2017), https://magaceen.com/en/interview/moneo-frampton/ (accessed December 8, 2019).

Kenneth Frampton's Elusive Constructivism

Jean-Louis Cohen

Rather than microwaving a frozen lecture or conference paper, this publication provides the opportunity to explore a significant aspect of Kenneth Frampton's early writings. During a period of more than fifteen years, he devoted his attention to the Russian avant-garde, in its artistic, architectural, and urbanistic dimensions. His thoughts were mainly contained in four essays published in the United Kingdom and the United States around 1970—the basis of this reflection—and in later forewords, as also in the chapter of his *Modern Architecture: A Critical History* devoted to the Soviet Union.[1]

Let's start at the beginning. The 1968 issue of the *Architect's Year Book*, an inspiring compendium of historical and critical texts published sporadically from 1945 to 1974 in London, contained no fewer than two articles by Frampton: "Notes of Soviet Urbanism 1917–1932" and "The Work and Influence of El Lissitzky," which I remember having read avidly a bit later, as I was looking for every piece of information on the 1920s in Russia.[2] During the same year, Frampton published in the *Art News Annual* his "Notes on a Lost Avant-Garde," which would be reprinted twice.[3] Finally, he rewrote in 1976 for *Oppositions*, the journal of the Institute for Architecture and Urban Studies where he was active, the lecture on "Russian Constructivism" that he had given late in 1972 in New York and early in 1973 in Detroit, under the odd and poetic title of "Constructivism: The Pursuit of an Elusive Sensibility."[4]

I will consider this group of writings as a *corpus*, an ensemble which had a pivotal part in Frampton's shift from his role as an architect and a critic toward the position of an historian, while reflecting an interest widely shared in his generation in episodes repressed in the Western consciousness of Soviet art and culture. In 1968, several years had passed between Nikita Khrushchev's vibrant critique of Stalinism in architecture, which had taken place late in 1954, and the appearance of the earliest Russian studies on the first fifteen years of the U.S.S.R.'s artistic and architectural production. The rediscovery of the Russian avant-garde, which was initiated in the late 1950s in the U.S.S.R., took place rather slowly in the realm of visual arts and literature. The rehabilitation of the forgotten architects was faster, thanks to the initiative of young people such as Selim Khan-Magomedov, who recalled as early as 1958 the project of the Constructivist group for a "reconstruction of the everyday."[5] The surviving members of the radical groups then joined forces with the young historians in order to compose anthologies of manifestos and programmatic texts, such as the books edited by Kirill Afanasev and Vigdaria Khazanova.[6] But the first monographs devoted to the main figures of the avant-garde were not released before the early 1970s. After that of Alexei Chinyakov on the Vesnin brothers, Khan-Magomedov was able to publish his own on Ivan Leonidov and Moisei Ginzburg.[7] Yet it was in East Germany, where the legacy of the Bauhaus was beginning to be acknowledged, that the first book on El Lissitzky's prolific oeuvre was produced.[8]

In the meantime, the legacy of the Soviet avant-garde had been reappropriated by several Western European architects—and not by historians, as if the works of the avant-garde had to be claimed first from within the profession. The Belgian modernist Victor Bourgeois was the first to greet the Constructivists in 1958 in the pages of the first issue of *Zodiac*, a journal then just created by Adriano Olivetti.[9] Italy became a fertile ground for the rememorating of Bolshevik Moscow's unbuilt designs and experimental buildings, thanks to the writings of the Milanese architect Guido Canella and his Roman colleague Vittorio De Feo.[10] But the main point of inflection before Frampton's 1968 essays was Anatole Kopp's *Town and Revolution*, written in 1967 by a maverick Russian-born architect, closely connected with the Paris leftist intellectual circles, where he had met Henri Lefebvre and many other

59 Anatole Kopp, *Ville et révolution; architecture et urbanisme soviétiques des années vingt* (Paris: Anthropos, 1967), cover.

thinkers interested in a revival of utopian thinking, including his publisher Serge Jonas (**59**).[11] The Roman Vieri Quilici's compendium *L'architettura del costruttivismo* was published two years later, after Frampton had written his own texts.[12] These books would be reviewed respectively by Robin Middleton, who considered Kopp's research "inadequate," and by Joseph Rykwert, more positive in qualifying Quilici's volume as a "major achievement."[13] Also, some Soviet authors were able to publish in the West. For instance, an article by Khan-Magomedov on Leonidov, which had been translated by Quilici in *Marcatré* in 1965, is mentioned by Frampton.[14]

In a conversation with Stan Allen and Hal Foster in 2003, Frampton recalled the circumstances of his first exposure to the Russian avant-garde, underlining the importance of Camilla Gray's *Great Experiment* of 1962: "Her book made me aware of the enormous energy of the Russian revolution from a cultural as well as a political point of view."[15] Frampton refers to this book as an antidote to the almost complete exclusion of the Russian scene from the most popular historical surveys, mentioning explicitly Sigfried Giedion's *Space, Time and Architecture* and Reyner Banham's *Theory and Design in the First Machine Age*.[16] But the role of Kopp's well-illustrated volume appears seminal in underlining the political dimension of the avant-garde's agenda in architecture.

The only original source that Frampton could tap was then Lissitzky's book *Russland: Die Rekonstruktion der Architektur in der Sowjetunion*, which had

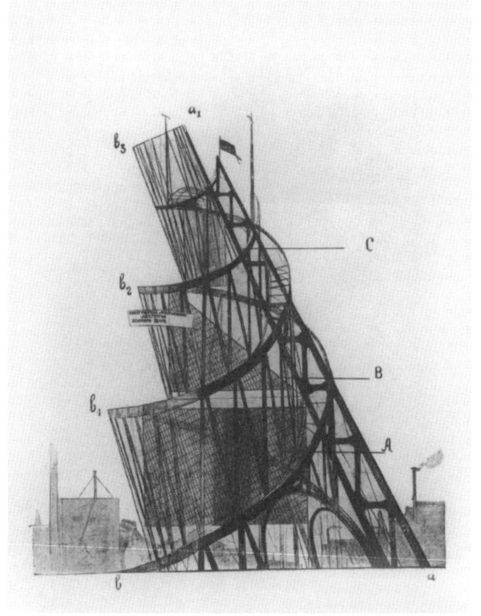

60 El Lissitzky, *Russland: Die Rekonstruktion der Architektur in der Sowjetunion* (Vienna: A. Schroll, 1929), jacket.
61 Vladimir Tatlin, project for a Monument to the Third International, 1919.

been reissued in 1965 by Ulrich Conrads in his Bauweltfundamente series (**60**).[17] He would repeatedly quote Lissitzky's commentaries on designs such as the Vesnin brothers' *Leningrad Pravda* competition entry of 1924 and recycle his illustrations. His analysis of the linear city uses, for instance, an interpretation of Arturo Soria y Mata's scheme found in the pages of the book. As he told Allen and Foster, Frampton also found a survivor from the period in the person of Berthold Lubetkin, whom he had met thanks to Gray and the German filmmaker Lutz Becker, after having read his article of 1932 in the *Architectural Review*—one of the few dedicated to Russia in the interwar British architectural press—and his disillusioned statement of 1956 in the *Architectural Association Journal*.[18]

Frampton's first quartet of essays can be considered as a single narrative devoted to the avant-garde, developed as a film composed of four shots: "Notes on a Lost Avant-Garde" is a wide shot locating the main agents and sites of the Russian avant-garde; "Notes of Soviet Urbanism 1917–1932" is a tracking shot from city to city, which depicts the unfolding of the Soviet planning doctrine; "The Work and Influence of El Lissitzky" is a close-up on a major protagonist and critic; and the fourth—"Constructivism: The Pursuit of an Elusive Sensibility"—is a movement backward, a final wide shot expanded, this time, to literature and the arts.

"Notes on a Lost Avant-Garde" considers panoramically a small group of projects, beginning with Vladimir Tatlin's 1919 Monument to the Third International, which is compared, among other designs, to Étienne-Louis Boullée's truncated cone mausoleum, published in 1952 by Emil Kaufmann (**61**). Frampton also pinpoints the relationship with the Eiffel Tower, on which he had just published an essay.[19] He writes on the Vesnins' 1924 *Pravda* project and on Leonidov's 1927 Lenin Institute, heavily quoting Lissitzky's *Russland*, while his consideration of Nikolai Ladovsky is based on Lubetkin's 1932 article (**62–63**). The programs of the avant-garde groups are quoted from an article by Camilla Gray.[20] The patchy map depicted is inscribed in the political context of the time, for instance when Frampton draws a parallel between the radical positions of the Productivists and the Maoist Red Guards.[21]

His "Notes of Soviet Urbanism 1917–1932" is the most seriously researched of the four articles. Besides the books of De Feo and Kopp, which are duly acknowledged, it is also based on Lissitzky's volume and Lubetkin's article, which generates some confusion. Following the latter, and De Feo, who had plagiarized Lubetkin's article, Frampton attributes to Ernst May the linear scheme proposed in 1930 by Leonidov for Magnitogorsk, without taking fully seriously Khan-Magomedov's and Kopp's clear attribution, which is acknowledged in a skeptical endnote referring to the *Marcatré* article by the Russian historian. This confusion reflects the rudimentary knowledge of the Western writers who had no access to the original Russian publications. More surprising is the credit given to Roman Heiligenthal for the drawing of the width-to-height ratio in housing that Walter Gropius had presented at the CIAM in Brussels in 1930. Frampton discusses in relative detail a set of urban plans such

62 Alexander, Leonid, and Viktor Vesnin, competition project for the *Leningradskaia Pravda*, Moscow, 1924, perspective view.
63 Ivan Leonidov, project for a Lenin Institute, 1927, in *Sovremennaia Arkhitektura*, 4–5 (1927).

as Trifon Varentsov's "Town of the Future," which he sees as "millenarist," going as far as publishing his own graphic interpretation of Ladovsky's Kostino *Siedlung* and of the ARU scheme for Avtostroy. This time, he sees in Leonidov's Lenin Institute a "suprematist" design. Suggesting a new parallel between France and Russia, Frampton recalls Claude-Nicolas Ledoux's Propylaea for Paris as a precedent for the *Wolkenbügel* of Lissitzky, emphasizing the latter's reflections on the notion of "open street."

Unsparing in his critique of Le Corbusier's positions on Soviet urbanization, Frampton in the end justifies the conservative turn of the 1930s:

> the extreme Russian utilitarians and visionaries were unsuited in a time of economic crisis and civil unrest. Russian planners and architects who were both competent and realistic (i.e. the designers of the SASS group) were also unacceptable to a party which was becoming subject to an insurgent nationalism. Hence the Party was compelled to seek the advice of the old prerevolutionary members of the academy who, although politically unreliable, were of proven if limited competence, and unlikely to be involved with internationalist ideals.[22]

As in the first article I have discussed, there is something rather touching in Frampton's attempts at making sense of unreliable fragments, as if one is witnessing the infancy of a research field.

The monographic component of the initial quartet is "The Work and Influence of El Lissitzky." The discussion of his "seminal role" is first related to Camilla Gray's earlier explorations of Lissitzky's typographic compositions.[23] This condensed biographical narrative takes into account Sophie Lissitzky-Küppers's thick anthology published in 1967, but derives principally from the Bauweltfundamente version of *Russland*, which included other texts reproduced in the article. Among these, Frampton devotes particular attention to the essay "K. und Pangeometrie" of 1925, in which Lissitzky suggests the notion of "imaginary space."[24] Frampton qualifies Lissitzky as an "international socialist-technocrat," underlining his opposition to the Constructivists' fetishism of the machine. The key design he considers from this perspective is the Lenin Tribune, which was then dated 1920, and has since been considered as probably designed in 1922. For him, "this work is characteristic of Lissitzky's non-utilitarian attempt to combine elementarist forms with 'engineered' mechanisms and structures."[25] Frampton's interest in utilitarianism transpired in his contemporary essay "The Humanist vs. the Utilitarian Ideal," in which he unearths the polemical exchange between Le Corbusier and "Kanel Tiege" (in fact, the Czech critic Karel Teige) apropos the architect's Mundaneum project, not knowing that Teige had completely plagiarized a scathing attack previously published by Lissitzky in Moscow.[26]

The fourth and last essay, "Constructivism: The Pursuit of an Elusive Sensibility," sees Frampton expand his horizons beyond architecture and graphic design toward a broader, more critical reflection, which derives from an attempt at breaking with a nominalist approach to the movement, best synthesized in the statement: "the importance of the term 'Constructivism' seems to have lain not in itself, but rather in the extremely volatile and elusive sensibility it came to evoke."[27] The essay explores the precedents of the movement in prerevolutionary literary production, reviewing the manifestations of Futurism in Russia and the emergence of *zaum*, or transrational language, in the poems of Alexey Kruchenykh and Velimir Khlebnikov. Frampton has shared with Stan Allen and Hal Foster the recollection that his awareness of Russian formalism had been acquired thanks to a series of friends he had in London—the artists Anthony Hill, Stephen Gilbert, Kenneth and Mary Martin, and Victor Pasmore, who defined themselves as "constructionists."[28] In addition to this literary excursus, he returns to his previous reading of Tatlin's Monument, underlining this time his "double preoccupation with utility on the one hand and with the culture, not to say the cult of materials, on the other."[29] He also tries to deal with the most elusive of all of this artist's works—his Letatlin flying machine of 1931, in which utility is no longer an excuse. In addition to Tatlin, Frampton scans at last the works of Alexander Rodchenko and Varvara Stepanova, whom he had ignored in his previous texts, and mentions Dziga Vertov's cinematographic montage. In the realm of architecture, the Vesnins' *Pravda* project is again brought to the fore, together with Konstantin Melnikov's Makhorka pavilion of 1923, unquestionably among his designs the closest ever to Constructivism, even if Melnikov can hardly be drafted into a movement he hated, as he would later affirm, for instance when I met him in 1973.

Again, Frampton tries to problematize the demise of the avant-garde, seeing in montage its main shared practice: "the revelation of the essential socio-cultural nature of productive synthesis through an explicit act of montage: this, perhaps, in the last analysis, was the essence of the 'Productivist–Constructivist' sensibility, a sensibility that depended upon a productive process of relative simplicity. Once this process became too complex then the sensibility could not be recovered."[30] In the end, he endorsed the analysis suggested by Lubetkin in 1956, according to which the primitiveness of the building techniques demoralized the radical architects and led to their withdrawal—an analysis since refuted by the historians of the period.[31]

In this essay, Frampton refrains from projecting his interpretation of 1920s architecture into the contemporary scene, as he had attempted in his "Notes on a Lost Avant-Garde," declaring then that "Leonidov shares with Lissitzky the honor of having anticipated much of our recent architectural avant-garde, as for instance the work of Wachsmann, Le Ricolais, Buckminster Fuller, Friedman, Otto, Price, Malcolmson, etc."[32] In a matter of a few years, he had assumed the role of the historian, becoming more cautious with respect to the relevance of the situations described.

In the four essays I have considered, one can see that Frampton's main points are derived from his fondness for a limited list of designs/buildings—from Tatlin's Monument to Lissitzky's tribune and *Wolkenbügel* (**64**), the Vesnins' *Pravda*, and Leonidov's Lenin Institute. The iconic force of the handful of images used to document them is undeniable, and Frampton's brave ability to draw conclusions from such a limited body of evidence is impressive. Unfortunately, he did not pursue his analyses in the following years, when a far more generous visual documentation of the avant-garde architecture became available, thanks to the indefatigable Catherine Cooke, who was the first British scholar to research and interpret original materials on Russia.[33]

He was perfectly aware of this new condition, as he was involved with Gray and Lubetkin in the exhibition *Art and Revolution*, organized in 1971, after an idea by Camilla Gray, at London's Hayward Gallery by its director of art, Robin Campbell, and the art historian Norbert Lynton, exhibition director for the British Arts Council. The exhibition was a watershed as, for the first time, original materials had been lent by the U.S.S.R.'s institutions, but it was also marked by a last-minute incident, when the Russian curator Oleg Shvidkovsky was summoned to the Soviet Embassy and forced to close the rooms in which Constructivist drawings were to be exhibited. He was nonetheless allowed to endorse the volume *Building in the*

64 El Lissitzky, project for a series of *Wolkenbügel* in Moscow, photomontage of the structure at Nikitskie Vorota, 1925.

U.S.S.R., 1917–1932, published in parallel to the show, a reprint of the articles featured in 1970 in an issue of *Architectural Design* edited by Robin Middleton and Monica Pidgeon, which probably triggered the exhibition.[34] His book featured biographies of the most significant architects of the period and marked definite progress with respect to the publications of the 1960s.[35]

By then firmly established in New York, Frampton continued to work sporadically on things Russian. At the Institute for Architecture and Urban Studies, he conceived with Joachim Mantel, Robert Slutzky, and Susan Wheeler the installation of a new version of the exhibition *Russische Architectuur en Stedebouw 1917–1933*, which had been put together in 1969 at the Technical University in Delft by Max Risselada and Gerrit Oorthuys.[36] Frampton had not only seen the show in Delft in that year, but also had written a short, albeit enthusiastic review in *Architectural Design*.[37] He assisted Risselada in publishing for the occasion a large, red, square catalogue, with an appendix featuring translations of a series of important texts of the 1930s (**65**).[38] The Delft presentation had also caught the eye of the young Rem Koolhaas, who embarked with Oorthuys on research on Leonidov's designs, the main result of this work being an article on his 1934 Narkomtyazhprom project, which was published in the Institute for Architecture and Urban Studies' journal, *Oppositions*, in 1974. In an unsigned prologue to the text by Koolhaas and Oorthuys, Frampton evokes again the "elusive" character of Leonidov's contribution and his "ethereal

65 Max Risselada, ed., with Kenneth Frampton, *Art and Architecture—U.S.S.R. 1917–32*, cover designed by Robert Slutzky (New York: George Wittenborn, 1971).

hedonism," detecting in echo to one of his own formed judgments on Leonidov's work the presence of a "distant but ever present master"—Kasimir Malevich.[39]

In addition to this significant essay, Frampton orchestrated the publication of several articles and documents on Russia's architecture in the Institute's journal, encouraging young North American academics active in the field. He asked Eric Dluhosh, who had translated Lissitzky's 1930 book, to review the substantial volume on the Soviet avant-garde published in Prague by the veteran Czech modernist Jiří Kroha.[40] He endorsed himself a long-awaited translation of Nikolai Miliutin's *Sotsgorod* by Arthur Sprague.[41] Among the significant manifestos of European modernism published regularly in the journal, Frampton pushed for the inclusion of major texts such as those of the ephemeral publication *Veshch*, or those commenting on Vladimir Tatlin's Monument.[42] Finally, in one of the last issues, he published side-by-side S. Frederick Starr's discussion of ignored visual and textual Soviet materials and a translation of my early essay on Le Corbusier's Soviet adventures.[43]

Four years after their *Oppositions* essay, Oorthuys and Koolhaas curated at the Institute for Architecture and Urban Studies an exhibition devoted to Leonidov, in which a model of the Narkomtyazhprom project was the most prominent feature. As a result, the Institute published in 1981 a catalogue in which texts by Khan-Magomedov and Quilici were translated.[44] On this occasion, Frampton published one of the earliest of the dozens of forewords he has not ceased writing to this day, and which could, as such, form an autonomous volume. In 1968, he had related Leonidov to the projects of the technology-minded designers of the 1960s, but by then the work of the "elusive modern master" took a different meaning. In Leonidov's early projects, repeating the points made by Lissitzky which he had endorsed, Frampton notes the "erotic and liberative dimensions" of images that "endure," equating Leonidov's designs to an "architecture degree-zero" which transcended the "culture of tectonic form," which he himself was then beginning to explore. Frampton notes that in the late vein of his work, Leonidov "turned toward the naive earthiness of the Russian icon, toward a kind of *zaumny* [transrational] Piranesian method of combining the old with the new—the towers of the Kremlin with the silos of the Narkomtyazhprom."[45]

If Leonidov had been the center of Frampton's attention since 1968, the leading theorist of architectural Constructivism, Moisei Ginzburg, had never drawn much notice on his part. Frampton seized the opportunity offered by the publication of Ginzburg's 1924 manifesto *Style and Epoch* in the *Oppositions* book series to catch up with new themes. Underlining the importance of the collective in the theory and the practice of Ginzburg, he insists on the divergences between him and Le Corbusier, both in Ginzburg's design for the Narkomfin communal house, which echoes the Parisian architect's ideas, and in his consideration of the machine.[46] Among the new themes Frampton touches upon is the use made by Ginzburg of Frederick W. Taylor's Scientific Management theory and his possible relationship with Alexey Gastev's Central Institute of Labor. For Frampton, *Style and Epoch* "remains a compelling and significant testimony to the promise of a modern architecture whose liberative potential remains as valid today as when it was first proclaimed."[47]

This position was rather remote from the 1968 considerations linking Leonidov to the designers of space structures. Some of the ideas contained in the Ginzburg foreword had already been expressed in the chapter "The New Collectivity: Art and Architecture in the Soviet Union 1918–1932" of *Modern Architecture: A Critical History*, the handbook he first published in 1980, mentioned in 1971 by S. Frederick Starr as "the first general survey in English to devote a full chapter to Russia," and announced as forthcoming that same year.[48] Almost exclusively illustrated by reproductions used repeatedly since 1968, this chapter appears at first sight to condense the articles previously published.[49] But this late retribution for the lacunae of Giedion's and Banham's histories also marks a shift in Frampton's view of Russia. Still celebrating the designs of Tatlin and Leonidov and the plans of Milyutin, he engages with the discourse of the "mature" Constructivism of the second half of the 1920s and its contribution to the "reconstruction of the everyday."

Paradoxically, in one of the most acid essays he has ever published, Frampton had failed in 1972 to detect the relationship between these projects and those of the new avant-garde which had emerged in the U.S.S.R. of Nikita Khrushchev and his

66 A. Baburov, A. Gutnov, G. Dyumenton, I. Lezhava, S. Sadovsky, and Z. Kharitonova, *Novyi Element Rasselenia, na puti k novomu gorodu* (Moscow: Stroiizdat, 1966).

followers. In a short review, he demolishes the American translation of the book *The Ideal Communist City*, published in 1968 in Milan in partnership with the Soviet section of the fourteenth Triennale by the NER, or Novy Element Rasselenia (New Element of Settlement) group, created by the architects Aleksey Gutnov, Ilya Lezhava, and Andrey Baburov around 1960 (**66**).[50] Basing his attack on a botched translation of the Italian version, in which the conceptual clarity of the Russian original had been lost, Frampton acknowledges that "what comes through are only the faint reverberations of bold initial intentions." He could not have missed, however, the earlier publications of their work by Kopp or in the pages of *L'Architecture d' aujourd'hui*, in which their ideas of decentralized urban structures allowing for better collective and individual interaction had been exposed. Rather, he saw in the book, whose title (*Idee per la città comunista*) chosen by Giancarlo De Carlo—who was an anarchist—for the Italian version had certainly an ironic dimension, "the conscious mystification of a potential model for some future socialist town."[51]

Frampton's salvo was unfortunately aimed at the wrong target. Far from being a "typical product of the 'cold thaw,' over which the spirit of Stalinism still lingers until today," or part of the "total cultural farce" which was taking place in the Soviet Union, over the dead body of the 1920s artists and intellectuals, the project of NER was, with its unquestionable naivete, proposing an alternative to the top-down urbanism and the production-centered space of the late Soviet Union. Out of nostalgia for the projects of the "lost avant-garde," Frampton had not been able to perceive a continuity that had not escaped the attention of Russian readers when the initial version of the book had been published.[52]

The corpus of Frampton's interpretation of five decades of Russian architecture condenses in its diversity and its displacements over time many aspects of his historical posture. Formalist considerations alternate with social ones, as architecture is never left suffocating in its professional ghetto. His essays on the Soviet scene deal with what the young British critic and ideologue Owen Hatherley has subsumed in the term "militant modernism."[53] But in doing so, they also illustrate a practice claimed by Kopp when he affirmed that "modernism was not a style but a cause."[54] Like his forerunner in things Russian, Kenneth Frampton found a cause not only in the episodes he narrated, but also in his own account of them.

1 My gratitude goes to Mary McLeod and Robin Middleton, who have read a first version of this essay and made extremely worthwhile comments.

2 Kenneth Frampton, "Notes of Soviet Urbanism 1917–1932," and "The Work and Influence of El Lissitzky," *Urban Structure: Architect's Year Book 12*, ed. D. Lewis (New York: Wiley Interscience, 1968): 238–52; 253–68.

3 Kenneth Frampton, "Notes on a Lost Avant-Garde," *Art News Annual*, 34 (1968): 96–103; also in *The Avant-Garde*, ed. Thomas B. Hess and John Ashbery (New York: Collier-Macmillan, 1968), 107–24; revised version in *Art in Revolution: Soviet Art and Design since 1917* (London: Arts Council of Great Britain, 1971), 20–29.

4 Kenneth Frampton, "Constructivism: The Pursuit of an Elusive Sensibility," *Oppositions*, 6 (Fall 1976): 25–43. Delivered under the title "Russian Constructivism" as a lecture at the Solomon R. Guggenheim Museum of Art in November 1972 and at the Detroit Institute of Arts in February 1973.

5 Selim Khan-Magomedov, "O roli arkhitektora v perestroike byta," *Arkhitektura SSSR*, 28/1 (January 1958): 45–47.

6 *Iz Istorii sovetskoi arkhitektury 1917–1925 Gg.: dokumenty i materialy*, ed. Kirill Afanasev and Vigdaria Khazanova (Moscow: Nauka, 1965). On this wave of publications, see S. Frederick Starr, "Writings from the 1960s on the Modern Movement in Russia," *Journal of the Society of Architectural Historians*, 30/2 (May 1971): 170–78.

7 Alexei Chinyakov, *Arkhitektory Bratia Vesniny* (Moscow: Izd-vo Literatury po Stroitelstvu, 1970); Selim Khan-Magomedov and Pavel Alexandrov, *Ivan Leonidov* (Moscow: Izd-vo Literatury po Stroitelstvu, 1971); Selim Khan-Magomedov, *M. Ya. Ginzburg* (Moscow: Izd-vo Literatury po Stroitelstvu, 1972).

8 Sophie Lissitzky-Küppers, *El Lissitzky, Life, Letters, Texts* (London: Thames & Hudson, 1968).

9 Victor Bourgeois, "Salut au constructivisme," *Zodiac*, 1/1 (1957): 193–95.

10 Guido Canella, "Attesa per l'architettura sovietica," *Casabella continuità*, 262 (April 1962): 4–16. Vittorio De Feo, *URSS architettura 1917–1936* (Rome: Editori riuniti, 1963).

11 Anatole Kopp, *Town and Revolution; Soviet Architecture and City Planning, 1917–1935*, trans. Thomas E. Burton (New York: George Braziller, 1970), initially published as *Ville et révolution; architecture et urbanisme soviétiques des années vingt* (Paris: Anthropos, 1967). On Kopp and Lefebvre, see my unpublished conference paper "La 'révolution urbaine' et le précédent soviétique," Paris, 2018.

12 Vieri Quilici, *L'architettura del costruttivismo* (Bari: Laterza, 1969).

13 Robin Middleton, "Ville et Révolution," and Joseph Rykwert, "L'architettura del costruttivismo," *Architectural Design*, 40/2 (February 1970): 108.

14 S. Khan-Magomedov, "Ivan Leonidov 1902–1960," *Marcatré*, 3/14–15 (May 1965): 140–54.

15 Kenneth Frampton, in Stan Allen and Hal Foster, "A Conversation with Kenneth Frampton," *October*, 106 (Autumn, 2003): 35–58; Camilla Gray, *The Great Experiment: Russian Art, 1863–1922* (London: Thames & Hudson, 1962), 39.

16 Allen and Foster, "A Conversation with Kenneth Frampton."
17 El Lissitzky, *Russland: Architektur für eine Weltrevolution* (Berlin: Ullstein, 1965), originally published as *Russland: Die Rekonstruktion der Architektur in der Sowjetunion* (Vienna: A. Schroll, 1929). An English translation based on the 1965 version would be published later by MIT Press.
18 Allen and Foster, "A Conversation with Kenneth Frampton," 39. Becker would author in 1972 a film derived from the *Art and Revolution* exhibition held the previous year. Berthold Lubetkin, "The Builders: The Planning of Towns," *Architectural Review*, 71/5 (May 1932): 196–208; Berthold Lubetkin, "Soviet Architecture: Notes on Developments from 1917–1932," *Architectural Association Journal* (1956): 260–61.
19 Kenneth Frampton, "The Work and Influence of Gustave Eiffel," *Midway Magazine* (Autumn 1967).
20 Frampton gives a rather vague indication, pointing to Camilla Gray's "Futurism, Constructivism, Suprematism," supposedly published in *Soviet Survey*, where it is not to be found. Frampton, "Notes on a Lost Avant-Garde," 102, note 2.
21 Ibid., 97, note 2.
22 Frampton, "Notes of Soviet Urbanism 1917–1932," 252.
23 Camilla Gray, "El Lissitzky, Typographer," *Typographica*, 16 (1959): 20–33.
24 Frampton, "The Work and Influence of El Lissitzky," 262–63.
25 Ibid., 255. This essay provided the base for the lecture "The Imaginary Space of El Lissitzky," delivered in 1969 at Harvard University's Carpenter Art Center.
26 Kenneth Frampton, "The Humanist vs. the Utilitarian Ideal," *Architectural Design*, 38/3 (March 1968): 134–36. This polemic was subsequently published by George Baird in *Oppositions*, also without any mention of Lissitzky: George Baird, introduction to "Karel Teige's *Mundaneum*, 1929, and Le Corbusier's *In Defence of Architecture*, 1933," *Oppositions*, 4 (October 1974): 79–82. Lissitzky's article was published as "Idoli i idolopoklonniki," *Stroitelnaia Promyshlennost*, 7/11–12 (November–December 1929): 854–58.
27 Frampton, "Constructivism: The Pursuit of an Elusive Sensibility," 27.
28 Allen and Foster, "A Conversation with Kenneth Frampton," 40.
29 Frampton, "Constructivism: The Pursuit of an Elusive Sensibility," 35.
30 Ibid., 42.
31 Lubetkin, "Soviet Architecture: Notes on Developments from 1917–1932," 260–61.
32 Frampton, "Notes on a Lost Avant-Garde," 102.
33 Cooke's doctoral thesis on the socialist city has unfortunately remained unpublished. Her main writings on the theme are: "Form is a Function X: The Development of the Constructivist Architects' Design Method," *Architectural Design*, 53/5–6 (1983): 34–49; *Fantasy and Construction, Iakov Chernikhov's Approach to Architectural Design* (London: Academy Editions, 1984); and *Russian Avant-Garde: Theories of Art, Architecture and the City* (London: Academy Editions, 1995).
34 *Building in the U.S.S.R., 1917–1932*, *Architectural Design*, 40/2 (February 1970): 69.
35 Oleg Shvidkovsky, ed., *Building in the U.S.S.R., 1917–1932* (London: Studio Vista, 1971). In the book, essays by Alexei Chinyakov on the Vesnins and by Yuri Gerchuk on Melnikov were added to those published in the February 1970 issue of *Architectural Design*.
36 Allen and Foster, "A Conversation with Kenneth Frampton," 45.
37 Kenneth Frampton, "The Russians at Delft," *Architectural Design*, 40/2 (February 1970): 71–107.
38 Max Risselada, ed., with Kenneth Frampton, *Art and Architecture—U.S.S.R. 1917–32* (New York: George Wittenborn, 1971). The initial version is Max Risselada and Gerrit Oorthuys, eds., *Russische architektuur en stedebouw 1917–1933* (Delft: Technische Hogeschool Delft, Afdeling Bouwkunde, 1969).
39 Unsigned prologue to Rem Koolhaas and Gerrit Oorthuys, "Ivan Leonidov's Dom Narkomtjazprom Moscow," *Oppositions*, 2 (January 1974): 95.
40 Eric Dluhosh, "The Failure of the Soviet Avant-Garde: A Review of *Sovětská architektonická avantgarda* by Jiří Kroha and Jiří Hrůza," *Oppositions*, 10 (Fall 1977): 31–55. Frampton's prologue "Commentary: Jiří Kroha and the Crisis of Post-Modernism" is on p. 29.
41 Kenneth Frampton, "On Nikolai Miliutin's Sotsgorod: The Problem of Building Socialist Cities," *Oppositions*, 9 (September 1977): 110–16.
42 Kestutis Paul Zygas, "*Veshch/Gegenstand/Objet*. Commentary, Bibliography and Translations," *Oppositions*, 5 (Summer 1976): 113–28; Kestutis Paul Zygas, "Punin's and Sidorov's Views of Tatlin's Tower," *Oppositions*, 10 (Fall 1977): 68–71; Nikolai Punin, "Monument to the Third International," *Oppositions*, 10 (Fall 1977): 72–74; A.A. Sidorov, "Review of Punin's Pamphlet about Tatlin's

Monument to the Third International," *Oppositions*, 10 (Fall 1977): 75–78.

43 S. Frederick Starr, "Le Corbusier and the U.S.S.R.: New Documentation," *Oppositions*, 23 (Winter 1981): 123–37; Jean-Louis Cohen, "Le Corbusier and the Mystique of the U.S.S.R.," *Oppositions*, 23 (Winter 1981): 84–121.

44 Selim O. Khan-Magomedov and Vieri Quilici, *Ivan Leonidov, IAUS 8* (New York: Rizzoli, 1981).

45 See Andrew Leach and Nicole Sully, "Frampton's Forewords, etc.," *OASE*, 103 (2019): 105–14.

46 Kenneth Frampton, foreword to Moisei Ginzburg, *Style and Epoch*, trans. Anatole Senkevitch, Jr. (Cambridge, MA: MIT Press, 1982), 7, 8.

47 Ibid., 9.

48 Starr, "Writings from the 1960s on the Modern Movement in Russia," 170.

49 Kenneth Frampton, "The New Collectivity: Art and Architecture in the Soviet Union 1918–1932," *Modern Architecture: A Critical History* (London: Thames & Hudson, 1980), 167–77.

50 On NER, see Sacha Goutnova and Masha Panteleyeva, eds., *NER—City of the Future* (Turin: Allemandi, 2018), with my essay "Fragments of History and Memory," pp. 24–49; and Daria Bocharnikova, "Inventing Socialist Modern: A History of the Architectural Profession in the U.S.S.R., 1932–1971," doctoral thesis, European University Institute, Florence, 2014, 157–98.

51 Kenneth Frampton, "The Ideal Communist City," *Architectural Forum*, 136/2 (March 1972): 13.

52 Andrey Baburov, Aleksey Gutnov, Georgy Dyumenton, Ilya Lezhava, Stanislav Sadovsky, and Zoya Kharitonova, *Novyi Element Rasselenia, na puti k novomu gorodu* (Moscow: Stroiizdat, 1966).

53 Owen Hatherley, *Militant Modernism* (Winchester: Zero Books, 2008).

54 Anatole Kopp, *Quand le moderne n'était pas un style mais une cause* (Paris: École Nationale Supérieure des Beaux-Arts, 1988); Jean-Louis Cohen, "Quand l'histoire était une cause; retour à Anatole Kopp," *L'Architecture d'aujourd'hui*, 271 (October 1990): 76–78.

Editing History: The Bauhaus at MoMA, 1938

Barry Bergdoll

On the occasion of the exhibition which I co-curated at New York's Museum of Modern Art with Leah Dickerman in 2009 for the ninetieth anniversary of the founding of the Bauhaus (and the eightieth anniversary of the founding of the museum), I delved into the museum's archives to shed light on the political context, as well as the complex logistics, of the museum's earlier Bauhaus exhibition staged in 1938. The museum's book that accompanied that important episode in the early reception of the Bauhaus in America remained the standard work on the school and its art philosophy in the English-speaking world until the publication of the English translation of Hans Maria Wingler's monumental *Bauhaus* in 1969. This essay, addressing the exhibition staged in New York and the misconceptions about the Bauhaus it set in motion for many years, is based on a lecture I gave at the exhibition symposium. It is offered to Ken Frampton—who first taught me about Hannes Meyer and his key role at the Bauhaus thirty years ago at Columbia—on the occasion of the centenary of the Bauhaus in 2019.

The Museum of Modern Art's founding director, Alfred H. Barr, Jr., wrote to Walter Gropius on September 15, 1938, in the lead-up to the museum's planned exhibition on the now defunct school that Gropius had founded at Weimar nineteen years earlier: "I regard the three days which I spent at the [Dessau] Bauhaus in 1927 as one of the important incidents in my own education."[1] Indeed, as has often been pointed out, the Bauhaus had had a profound influence on Barr's draft plans in 1929 for the structure of an unprecedented American museum of "the art of our time,"[2] with proposed departments of architecture, industrial art, photography, theater, and film. It also influenced Barr's mapping of the evolution of modern art movements, cogently diagrammed on the famous cover of the 1936 *Cubism and Abstract Art* catalogue. There, in the cover's celebrated diagram of the interrelationship of avant-garde movements, the Bauhaus was positioned as the synthesis of Expressionism, De Stijl, and Neoplasticism, and the flow of Cubism into Suprematism and Constructivism. Remarkably, however, its only outlet into the decade of the 1930s and the future—to judge from the diagram—seems to have been into "Modern Architecture," which Barr's chart would have consolidated at the very place where French Purism, Dutch De Stijl, and the German experimental school intersected to form into a coherent architectural movement at the center of his time line. But of course by the time this chart was drawn up, the Bauhaus itself was no more, having lived a tumultuous history: forced to move and then closed by the rising force of National Socialism, and largely erased from the German art scene, it was—as a school—dead.

Within a year of the publication of Barr's diagram, plans were afoot at the young New York museum for staging a major Bauhaus exhibition, catalyzed by two interlinked events of 1937. The first was the escalation of the German artistic and intellectual exodus, changing the face of American art and architectural education with the arrival, notably, of Walter Gropius at Harvard. He was one of many émigrés from Adolf Hitler's Germany who made the eight-year-old Museum of Modern Art an early port of call upon arrival in the New World. A single page alone of the Museum of Modern Art guest book for 1937 is revelatory, with its close juxtaposition of the signatures of László Moholy-Nagy, Marcel Breuer, Herbert Bayer, and Ludwig Mies van der Rohe, while raged controversy on the other side of the Atlantic generated by the Nazis' *Entartete Kunst* ("Degenerate Art") exhibition, staged in the newly completed Haus der Kunst, Munich, a design by Hitler's favored architect Paul Troost. It is hard to imagine a clearer statement of the National Socialist state's celebration of the dismantling of the Bauhaus project of modernist experiment. The Museum of Modern Art's purpose-built home, designed the following year and opened on the museum's tenth birthday in 1939 (it had been a nomad for that first decade), would indeed pay homage to the building that Gropius had designed to accommodate the Bauhaus in its second home city of Dessau, after it had been forced to leave Weimar in 1924. MoMA's new building was a veritable counter-model to the neoclassical architecture of Hitler's museum or, for that matter, John Russell Pope's contemporary National Gallery of Art in Washington (1938–41). By the time the Museum of Modern Art, designed by Philip Goodwin and Edward Durell Stone, opened at 11 West 53rd Street in 1939, the Bauhaus was but a memory, having been definitively shut by the National Socialists in 1933 in its last, makeshift home in a disused Berlin factory.

Even before the idea of MoMA emerged, Barr had been focused, as a young art history professor, on the German design school. He recalled in an interview in 1967 that he had been eagerly anticipating his visit to Dessau for some time before he was able to make the trip in 1927.[3] Already in 1926 he had invited the young architectural historian Henry-Russell Hitchcock to give a guest lecture about Gropius at Wellesley College, the progressive women's college where Barr's lectures on modern and contemporary art were pioneering, since most considered contemporary practice outside the purview of the discipline of art history. As he recalled:

> The Bauhaus idea did have an important influence on me well before I went to Dessau. Gropius's ideal of bringing together the various visual arts influenced my course in Modern Art at Wellesley ... It included architecture, industrial design, graphic arts, painting, sculpture, films, and photography. A few years later the Bauhaus also influenced my plan for the Museum of Modern Art ... I had looked forward with great anticipation to the Bauhaus ... among the ... things ...

I remember most vividly was the gentle charm of Klee, his interest in music, the sound of Frau Klee playing a Mozart sonata, his little collection of odds and ends of shells and minor curiosities, and his interest in children's drawings ... Moholy-Nagy's sullen expression when I asked him whether he or Lissitzky first used photomontage; the students at work on their various exercises, particularly *Formlehre*; Lux Feininger's enthusiasm for the Bauhaus jazz band; and Gropius's unsmiling earnestness ...[4]

Barr was not alone. Philip Johnson followed progress at the Bauhaus almost yearly on visits to Germany, writing in 1929, the year the New York museum was founded, that he had visited the Dessau school with a German friend, an interior architect, and had been shown around by Feininger. Johnson wrote to Barr: "I told Kandinsky about your writing about the abstract in art, and he thinks naturally he will be the hero of the book. Klee I found entrancing, the simplicity of a great man, without hide bound theories or illusions as to his greatness."[5] And he went on to speak at length in the same breath of figures who had left the Bauhaus and whom he met in Berlin:

Breuer, the young interior man whom you may have met ... is like Gropius, a utopian ... more interested in propaganda and education than in anything else, but ... if he had only invented that now famous chair of pipes, he would be something at his age of 26 ... Gropius was naturally most charming ... sees things in a big way, and [...] has the magnetism to draw people after him, never contented with a thing accomplished, always fighting for a new idea, now it is this business of ten story dwellings to save ground space and light. The Bauhaus suffers more and more without him ...[6]

Hannes Meyer, the director from 1928 to 1930, was not mentioned by name, nor is there any indication that Johnson met the architect/director. And Meyer was not to be included in what was the first documented Bauhaus exhibition held in America, mounted in 1930 by the Harvard Society for Contemporary Art: *Bauhaus Weimar Dessau*. Nor was Meyer included one year later in another small Bauhaus show at the Arts Club of Chicago. This omission set the stage for his exclusion again at MoMA in 1938 by Gropius, Herbert Bayer, and Breuer, all of whom had left the Bauhaus as Meyer took the reins in 1928. Meyer's leftist views in politics and his productivist vision of art education and art-making soon came to be seen as a critique of Gropius's curriculum and ethos, even though it was Gropius himself who had sought out Meyer in Basel to open the Bauhaus's long-delayed architecture department in 1927. Already during his directorship Gropius had begun his efforts to minimize Meyer's reputation as a formative figure in the Bauhaus.

For the exhibition at Harvard University, his alma mater, Johnson gave money, lent from his growing collection, and even wrote to Barr: "Dear Alfred, It comes to a pretty pass when the likes of us asks the likes of you for money. Yes—a subscription to our work—at the present we are having a Bauhaus show. At the present we are terribly hard up."[7] The investment banking firm Goldman Sachs (Paul Sachs, son of the firm's founder, was the teacher of Johnson, Hitchcock, Barr, and many others at Harvard) had chipped in, but not enough, Johnson reported. Lincoln Kirstein, who curated the show, which ran for six weeks in December 1930–January 1931, was "writing 200 personal letters in long hand asking for ten dollars apiece."[8] But with little success. The exhibition, as Nicholas Fox Weber later discovered, was afterward shown at the John Becker Gallery on Madison Avenue.[9] In summer 1930, Johnson again made the pilgrimage to Dessau, where Mies van der Rohe was now the new director after Meyer's recent ousting by the right-wing local government. On this return visit Johnson was accompanied by Hitchcock in preparation for *Modern Architecture: International Exhibition*, the new museum's first foray into exhibiting architecture. Barr wanted to float this as a trial balloon to convince the reluctant trustees that the new museum could have something all but unprecedented: a Department of Architecture.[10] The model of the Dessau building that Gropius and Bayer had prepared for their installation of the German section of the Werkbund exhibition in Paris in 1930 was sent on to New York to feature prominently in the 1932 show and was to travel throughout the country.

In autumn 1931, Johnson again journeyed to Dessau, this time on an architecture tour with the young American architect John McAndrew. McAndrew would become an influential teacher of art history at Vassar College and a curator in the Department of Architecture at MoMA, where he would assume the departmental directorship in 1937.[11] "Today naturally I am reminded of you," Johnson wrote in 1931 to Barr,

> ... We were really thrilled at the sight of the Bauhaus. It is a magnificent building; I regard it as the most beautiful building we have seen, of the larger than house variety. Perhaps the Hook [J.J.P. Oud's housing at Hoek van Holland which he had earlier called "the Parthenon of Modern Europe"] has what Hitchcock would call more lyric beauty, but the Bauhaus has beauty of <u>plan</u>, and great strength of design. It has a majesty and simplicity which are unequaled.[12]

They were led through probably by Howard Dearstyne, an American student: "He is in the second half of the program, that is working on chairs and things. The system impressed me as being a very good one indeed for such a school. This American did not seem to know it but he was getting, as John tells me, a much better architectural education than in any architectural school in our country."[13] Later in the day Johnson bought a few Klees at the painter's one-day show in a Dessau gallery.

During the 1930s, even after the Bauhaus was closed by Mies van der Rohe to preempt a definitive closing by the National Socialists, who had already raided the school, MoMA remained intimately linked to the defunct school through its former masters and students. Mies had emerged not only as Johnson's hero in his many visits to Berlin and to Dessau, but also as Barr's preferred choice as architect of the new building that the museum hoped to build in midtown Manhattan to declare its adherence to the principles of European modernist architecture. Many involved with MoMA were also personally involved in aiding the emigration of *Bauhäusler*, as the former masters and pupils continued to refer to themselves. Just weeks after the closing of the school in Berlin in May 1933, Eddie Warburg, another of the so-called "Harvard apostles" who had advocated modernism (and who through his family banking money was a major funder of their efforts), began a campaign to bring Josef Albers to the United States. He told Barr, then on sabbatical leave to treat the nervous exhaustion caused by the first four years at MoMA, "I cannot help but feel that getting Albers into this country would be a great feather in the cap of the Museum of Modern Art ... With Albers over here we have the nucleus for an American Bauhaus!"[14]

Johnson, like Barr, was again in Germany when *The Bauhaus Staircase* (1932) was purchased from Oskar Schlemmer's abruptly shut one-man show in Stuttgart. Barr recalled how "I missed the opening but got in afterwards by official permission as a foreigner. I was so enraged that I cabled Philip Johnson to buy the most important picture in the show just to spite the sons of bitches. Philip replied by buying the two biggest with Bauhaus subjects."[15] In January 1934, as the national tour of the *Modern Architecture* show came to a close, Johnson wrote to Gropius (on the letterhead, incidentally, of his next great venture, the *Machine Art* show which gave birth to the museum's Department of Industrial Design):

> I will be delighted to return your model of Bauhaus [*sic*] which has caused such great interest all over the country. I am enclosing a few excerpts of how it was received in the various cities. The whole Bauhaus idea has become much better known because of this exhibition and of course your name as well ... I am awfully sorry that you are having such a difficult time in Germany and I sincerely hope we will be able to have you come over here to give some lectures if you still think you would be able to give them in English.[16]

The model returned to Germany somewhat the worse for wear—"it was the worst built of any of the models we received from Europe," Johnson noted.[17] After Gropius had it restored, he packed it up for travel again in 1937 to Massachusetts as part of the first shipment of his household goods. "As soon as they have come, I shall be in touch ..." Gropius wrote to Barr, "I should be pleased to have that model permanently in the Museum of Modern Art."[18] So the model that featured in the window of the museum's temporary quarters in Rockefeller Center in 1938 was to join a growing collection of models out of which Barr hoped to create a permanent gallery of modern architecture in three dimensions (**67**).[19] This project was not to be; in fact, the model

67 *Bauhaus 1919–1928*: Installation in the Museum of Modern Art's temporary quarters in the Rockefeller Center Shopping Concourse, 1938. View through a shop window to the exhibition space.

spent much of its time in storage, or traveling to schools along with other MoMA models. By the mid-1950s Gropius requested its transfer to Harvard's Busch-Reisinger Museum, which he felt to be a better guardian of the Bauhaus flame than the Museum of Modern Art, whose focus had turned increasingly toward home matters—and to cultivating Latin America[20]—during the war and the immediate postwar period. Later he managed again to have it transferred to the newly formed Bauhaus archive in West Germany, first established in Darmstadt in 1960 and then moved to a purpose-built Gropius building in West Berlin in 1979, where it is still one of the prize exhibits. Ironically, it was too fragile to make a return trip to the United States for the 2009 exhibition *Bauhaus 1919–1933: Workshops for Modernity*.[21]

In summer 1937, as the "Degenerate Art" show began to make headlines in Europe, discussions began in New York—and in Gropius's rented vacation house at Buzzards Bay, Cape Cod, where Moholy-Nagy, Breuer, and Xanti Schawinsky gathered—of mounting a large-scale Bauhaus show at MoMA. McAndrew, who would officially join the museum in October that year as Curator of Architecture—and curator of the show—was already involved. Planned for winter 1937 (thus overlapping with the closure of "Degenerate Art" in Munich and the beginning of its tour around Germany and Austria), on Gropius's advice the American show was postponed to autumn 1938. It was delayed again, before opening in New York on December 6, 1938. But from the beginning the idea was clear: "Our purpose would be to illustrate, largely by means of objects produced at the school, the principles of education for which the Bauhaus stood."[22]

Strategizing for the exhibition went into high gear in September 1937 and was to be led on multiple fronts. In New York, McAndrew and his assistant Janet Heinrich began a massive letter-writing campaign to former *Bauhäusler*, seeking both potential loans and leads on the whereabouts of the Bauhaus diaspora. In Berlin, Herbert Bayer, recently returned from a trip to the U.S., was charged with assembling materials and tracking down *Bauhäusler* in Europe, the team having learnt that virtually nothing worthy of exhibition remained in Dessau itself. Responses began pouring in, but many were discouraging. For instance, Kandinsky regretted not being able to lend, since his own work was in storage. However, he recommended his former pupil Max Bill to join the effort from his neutral Swiss base in Zurich. Soon correspondence began to bifurcate, with letters sent within Germany referring to a show on "industrial art" and sometimes closing with approved sign-offs such as "with German greetings." The latter were, however, written entirely in lower-case Bauhaus style rather than in the neotraditional orthography of the Nazis.[23] Letters sent to possible lenders in the rest of Europe and in North America explicitly trumpet a Bauhaus exhibition, but the wording became ever more circumspect. Bill addressed a letter to MoMA, suggesting helpfully: "At the moment it is not well advised to carry on correspondence with Bayer about the exhibition since he is Austrian and since the Annexation of Austria has become a 'Reichsdeutscher' and thus carefulness is requested."[24]

By November the dragnet had been joined by former Bauhaus student Hajo Rose, in exile in Amsterdam, who helped arrange shipments, and by Hungarian architect Farkas Molnár, a former assistant in Gropius's Dessau architecture office, who gathered material including his own architectural drawings in Budapest. In writing to former Bauhaus students in America, such as the Chicago architect Bertrand Goldberg, the advertising designer Edwin Fischer (then working with Breuer on designs for a house outside New Hope, PA), and the American architect Howard Dearstyne, now at work in Wallace K. Harrison's office, where the design and construction supervision of Rockefeller Center was coming to a close, McAndrew laid out the basics:

> The show is going to be fairly large, filling all the space in this year's temporary quarters in the basement of Rockefeller Center. Gropius is supervising the whole show and authorizing it as a semi-official demonstration of what the Bauhaus was, and what it accomplished. Breuer, who has just gone to Harvard to teach under Gropius will also help. Bayer is in Germany right now hunting up material ... We are planning a fairly elaborate installation scheme, for the main idea of the show is to show what the Bauhaus was, rather than to be just an accumulation of objects produced there; to show this, all sorts of ingenuities of installation will be necessary. Bayer will see the catalogue through too.[25]

The highly political atmosphere was evident in Gropius sending Barr a newspaper clipping about a second degenerate art show in Dessau: "As the Museum at Dessau had very good pictures from the Bauhaus, it came to my mind that it might be worth your while to negotiate with these people about buying some of the pictures."[26] Nothing seems to have come of this provocative suggestion.

Throughout 1938 the hunt continued in Europe, while reconstruction of lost works got underway in America. Albers at Black Mountain College, North Carolina, and Moholy-Nagy in Chicago were working with students to produce reproductions of works from the Preliminary Course. Bayer, Bill, and Hajo Rose between them tracked down Ludwig Hirschfeld Mack and Otti Berger to London (later Berger would return to her native Croatia, only to die in a concentration camp).[27] Both agreed to lend fabrics, postcards, and Bauhaus books. Marianne Brandt in Chemnitz lent materials, which would be purchased or returned to her twenty years later in 1957, when she had become, de facto, a citizen of the German Democratic Republic. This formed part of the museum's ongoing efforts to return materials to lenders even two decades after the show. The most poignant case was that of Oskar Schlemmer. Bayer explained the project to him:

> an exhibition of industrial art, which is more or less a historical representation of precedents and also effects ... What I would like from you is everything that you consider important: theoretical, instruction, theater performances, life and events, parties, commercial graphics, etc. I am thinking also to reserve a part of the exhibition for "freien kunst" (as painting and sculpture and the nonutilitarian arts were called at the Bauhaus) especially for a selection of works that were carried out in Weimar and Dessau, including I hope yours ...[28]

Schlemmer noted:

> My situation in Germany is scarcely tenable, and anything that can extend my work over the borders is to be embraced. I am indeed already well known in the MOMA and represented there with my "Bauhaustreppe". I can't imagine that this picture won't be in the exhibition ... I am especially interested in theater; I want to turn entirely to that in the future, after painting has now been condemned to death.[29]

By August 1938 his tone was more desperate: "Please take as many of my things over there as you can, especially the Ballets."[30] He wanted to give three footlockers of costumes, and suggested displaying them in a harsh red light to make something dramatic, a "phantasmagoria." It would be fun, so he hinted, to be able to work with them in film, and maybe having the costumes in America could lead to further performances.

In the end much of the material would come from the émigrés: Alexander Dorner, now at the Rhode Island School of Design, lent textiles (and wrote an important text for the catalogue). From Black Mountain College, Schawinsky sent theater pieces, while Anni and Josef Albers provided not only textiles but also some of their household furniture, including a "steel arm chair" by Breuer. Gropius, of course, lent many pieces. Breuer, the last to make shipments, sent in late November 1938 an aluminum armchair and one of his bent-plywood tables. Both were produced not only after he had left the Bauhaus but after he had left Germany. The boundaries of the Bauhaus were clearly slipping, and the show was becoming perhaps less historical documentation than a new beginning, an embassy for the Bauhaus "idea" in America.

Soon it became evident that the full scope of the fourteen years of the school's existence could not be covered, or at least so it seemed since there is no indication that the gaps in available loans clustered chronologically. Gropius wrote to Barr:

> We are very anxious to put together all the material in an historic way, giving the actual facts, dates, etc; but in spite of all my endeavors, I couldn't manage to get my successors at the Bauhaus to cooperate ... In the case of Mies, it is chiefly the difficulties in Germany which seem to hold him back ... When I first saw him, months ago, ... he was still considering collaborating; but some weeks ago he definitively refused (in a letter) to take part in it.[31]

In fact, by 1938 Mies, too, had moved to America; but no attempt seems to have been made to see what he might have brought with him to Chicago, where he was taking over the directorship of the architecture school of the Armour Institute of Technology (today the Illinois Institute of Technology, or IIT). No mention was made of why it was impossible to include Meyer's years. The battle for the ownership of the Bauhaus was already well underway, as I have written in the 2009 catalogue, with competing presentations of it in 1930 by Gropius in Paris, Meyer in a traveling exhibition, and Mies in Dessau.[32] Gropius proposed the title *Nine Years Bauhaus 1919–1928*, to which Barr replied: "I am not unhappy about stopping the exhibition at 1928. The Bauhaus after you left did much excellent work but it seems to me that all the fundamental ideas were incorporated while you were still director and that we can do a more clean-cut and conclusive exhibition by concentrating upon the years of your tenure."[33]

Karen Koehler first underscored the exclusion of Meyer, who was already ignored in the presentation of the Bauhaus in Paris in 1930.[34] No attempt seems to have been made to get in touch with Meyer in Geneva, where he was living in 1937–38, having been expelled the previous year, like all other foreigners, from the Soviet Union. Mies, we have seen, decided in the end against participating, although he seems to have been at first considering it. Early drafts of a checklist include architectural drawings by his students, including Dearstyne, and Mies's own furniture designs. Others also opted out. Albers warned McAndrew from the outset that the museum would have difficulties: "many Bauhaus members will not dare to lend their material for political reasons."[35] Architect Fritz Schleifer in Altona responded that he had been a teacher since 1933 in the Landeskunstschule there and that his work was being published, so he could not see any point in participating: "for someone who has chosen to stay behind, you can imagine that it is not an easy matter."[36] Wilhelm Wagenfeld, on the other hand, explained that he did not want to exhibit his work in America for fear he might be copied.

More interesting, though, are both the maintenance of old rivalries and jealousies and the new ones produced by the division of Bauhaus émigrés between Chicago and Boston. Bayer had assured Schlemmer that the show would have nothing to do with Moholy-Nagy's New Bauhaus in Chicago, although in fact the third section of the exhibition ultimately included that successor institution prominently. The reaction of architect Bertrand Goldberg is perhaps most revealing. Already in September 1937 he wrote:

> I wish to stress my unwillingness to see the proposed exhibition, however, even under the expert guidance which the museum gives such things. There has been too much talk and action about Bauhaus here with too easy understanding of a principle dependent not upon a philosophy but upon actual work. I think in the last days of Johnson's Decline and Fall he realized this very thing, not that he did anything to stop it ... I think that exhibits such as you propose further the cause of philosophizing and emasculating Bauhaus, and promote the creation of a new temporary Bauhaus style in this country. This is a great danger and will cause Bauhaus to take its place with Modern, Functionalist, Internationalist, and the reminder of the ma-Holies.[37]

He was followed by photographer Walter Peterhans, who had just responded to the invitation to join Mies's faculty in Chicago:

> My own personal work and my teaching activities, in conjunction with that of my colleagues under the direction of Mies van der Rohe, were consistently kept away from the work of the original Bauhaus. I, therefore, believe particularly in consideration of my future activities in the United States, that it would create a false impression if my works were exhibited under a name whose goal can only be identified to a limited degree with my ideas.[38]

The show quickly began to take the form of a chronological leapfrogging. While the final five years of the Bauhaus, 1928–33, were excluded, recent and contemporary work from the United States was gaining new prominence. As early as November 1937 Albers, the earliest of the émigrés involved, sought to steer things towards the New World:

> I have come to the conclusion that this show should be more one of principle than an historical collection with results by now out of date. I think that the Bauhaus

68 *Bauhaus 1919–1928*, the architecture section with the model of Gropius and Breuer's Hagerty House, Cohasset, Massachusetts, 1938, at the left (on a shelf supported by a single column).

> is still living and after having been denied abroad we are apparently getting a new group of the Bauhaus movement in the United States. Therefore we could ask the American students of the Bauhaus how their work done here has been influenced by their studies at the Bauhaus, and maybe we should also besides their results, show some result of the Bauhaus teachers who have been working for years in this country ... I think therefore that Black Mountain College should have a place in the exhibition, showing its way of studying art problems.[39]

An amplified third section was to be devoted not only to Black Mountain College, but also to the mysterious and short-lived Laboratory School of Design in New York: asked at the last minute—twenty-four hours, so they claimed—and doubtless as a consequence were unhappy with their display. And then of course there was Harvard. The New York display included recent architectural commissions in Massachusetts of Gropius and Breuer, the Hagerty House in Cohasset and Gropius's own house in Lincoln, soon to become something of the Bauhaus embassy in exile (**68**). All of this is documented in the catalogue, beautifully designed by Bayer under Gropius's supervision. It deserves its own historiographical investigation.

Bayer returned to New York only on August 22, 1938, and rapidly began working on the installation of the show, now titled *Bauhaus 1919–1928*. Gropius appeared very rarely in the galleries in the underground concourse of Building 5 at

69 *Bauhaus 1919–1928* at the Museum of Modern Art's temporary quarters. View from student exercises display toward the section on architecture with the model of Gropius and Breuer's Hagerty House, Cohasset, Massachusetts, 1938, at the left (on a shelf supported by a single column).

Rockefeller Center, near 49th Street. On October 20, 1938, he told Bayer: "I have a terribly regretful feeling about leaving you there to work without any help, but it is absolutely impossible for me to be with you to help to build up the exhibition."[40] The installation photography is particularly rich and allows interesting comparisons of continuities and developments from Bayer's earlier counterpart at the Grand Palais, Paris, in 1930, also under Gropius's and Breuer's supervision. In New York the installation was more rough-and-ready, but an element of Surrealist humor entered in as well. Bayer not only incorporated elements from Surrealist painting in the graphic designs on the floor, but also pointing hands and other common techniques which he admired in American popular theater. The inspiration came about in his frequent strolls in New York's theater district of Times Square and along Broadway, and he unabashedly allowed a place for this in his handling of a Rockefeller Center storefront. For New York an exhibition was equally a sort of vaudeville sideshow, with arrows pointing in directions, and footpaths suggested by patterns of direction on the floor. Much of the material was photographic documentation, of architecture, of performances, of life at the Bauhaus, and, most importantly, of student work, since the aim was to expand the Bauhaus conquest of American art and architecture education.

The show was divided into six sections: "The Preliminary Course," "The Workshops," "Typography," "Architecture," "Painting," and "Work from Schools influenced by the Bauhaus" (**69**, **70**). Visitors entered the shopfront in the lower concourse—treated frankly as an advertisement in which Bauhaus and MoMA were emphatically linked. Wall labels were red, while the overall palette was creamy white, black, and gray, with accents of deep blue and red. Cords, thin support posts, and walls that didn't reach the ground added a sense of transparency and spaciousness. From Moholy-Nagy's "Light Prop" in the vestibule to the peep-show effects at the back of the exhibit, Bauhaus theatricality met Broadway techniques as Schawinsky and Schlemmer—in absentia—hoped to find new fields of operation.

The run was short—December 6, 1938, to January 30, 1939—but the attendance was large, the biggest ever in the temporary Rockefeller Center quarters, with an average of 402 visitors a day. And the press coverage was enormous. Politics were not admitted into the gallery, but they could not have been far from anyone's mind. Leading American architectural historian and sociologist Lewis Mumford noted:

> Dr Gropius, the father of the German objective architecture which attained international renown, is now chairman of the department of architecture at Harvard University. At a preview of the exhibition yesterday he was reluctant to discuss the political vicissitudes of his movement except to observe that the same architectural and aesthetic phenomenon is condemned in Russia as "western bourgeois" and in Germany as "Bolshevik," while it is acclaimed in Italy as "real Fascist style."[41]

But the reviews were for the most part skeptical to negative, and Gropius and Barr wondered if the best response was to change aspects of the show or to respond. Gropius wrote: "We are indeed somewhat disappointed at the rather low level of understanding among the present critics ... but we are also surprised at the critics' lack of familiarity with abstract painting, after having been so well prepared by you and your museum."[42] In turn, Barr noted: "We had a very hostile review ... by Henry McBride of the *New York Sun*. McBride is lazy and irresponsible. His taste is always strictly limited to Paris." Barr warned: "We must expect a certain amount of hostile criticism from four main sources: 1.) Pro-Nazi, anti-modern sources, 2.) Pro-French anti-German sources, 3.) American anti-foreign sources, and 4.) People who feel that the Bauhaus is too old fashioned to be worth the trouble." He noted further that the issue of anti-Semitism was not an exclusively German affair: "As we could have guessed, we have already heard reports that the exhibition is considered 'Jewish.' Many Americans are so ignorant of European names that they conclude that, because the Nazi Government has been against the Bauhaus, the names Gropius, Bayer, Moholy-Nagy etc. are probably Jewish Communists."[43]

Bayer's display seems to have created more confusion than clarity. James Johnson Sweeny, a great supporter of the Bauhaus as a historian and critic (and later an influential curator and museum director), noted in the *New Republic* that the Bauhaus produced "some of the finest industrial designs of the present century" but that "the Museum of Modern Art can scarcely be said to do justice to the ideas behind

70 *Bauhaus 1919–1928* at the Museum of Modern Art's temporary quarters. View of part of the display with, notably, Gropius's Chicago Tribune Tower competition design of 1922 and Farkas Molnár's Red Cube House of 1923, both shown in the 1923 Bauhaus exhibition in Weimar.

the Bauhaus and the influence it has exerted ... [A] greater critical frankness and more stringent selection would have been less confusing ... a more modest descriptive tone throughout the display might have made it clearer to the average viewer."[44] But Mumford, a major contributor to earlier shows at the museum, hailed the exhibition in the *New Yorker* as "The most exciting thing on the horizon," and added:

> We all have a lot still to learn from it; indeed it will probably take our schools of architecture another half-generation to catch up with it fully ... If Gropius, Moholy-Nagy and Breuer, who are now teaching in America, can reestablish the spirit of the Bauhaus here, they will be doing a good job. For this combination of imagination and logic is what our architects mainly lack; they tend to substitute memory for the first and precedent for the second.[45]

Plans were drawn up for two traveling versions, to the delight of Gropius, who esteemed the show a coup for his future plans, but to the chagrin of Breuer, who was eager to see the return of his living-room furniture for his new house in Lincoln. A large exhibition with most of the loans went to the art museums in Springfield

(Massachusetts), Milwaukee, Cleveland, and Cincinnati, where it finally closed on April 5, 1940, on the eve of the American debate over entering the European theater of the war. A small exhibition, *The Bauhaus: How it Worked*, traveled to school galleries—including the Addison Gallery of American Art and Phillips Academy in Andover, Massachusetts; and the University of Minnesota; Florida State University in Tallahassee; Louisiana State University; Harvard; the University of Washington; Mills College in Oakland, California; and finally Williams College, ending in June 1940.

By then even the protagonists were having doubts and disputes. When Gropius tried to get more money for Bayer for his work on the catalogue, Barr sent a sharp rebuke: "The catalogue also was by far the most expensive we have ever published on any exhibition—the cost far out of proportion to its interest, especially as it is both diffuse and confusing in character."[46]

To soften the blow Barr had ended his letter: "While we are speaking frankly about the Bauhaus exhibition I want to assure you that, although it was one of the most expensive, difficult, exasperating and in some ways unrewarding exhibitions we have ever had, we do not in the least regret having had it. At the same I think we should learn from it as much as we can." Barr felt that the critics might not have been entirely wrong: "the fact is that in the Bauhaus exhibition a good many works were mediocre or worse, so that the critics were naturally not impressed."[47] Gropius's suggestion that Americans were not ready to appreciate the Bauhaus rubbed the wrong way as the country's entry into the war seemed near.

But these are tensions buried in the archive. The book would remain in print for years (it was reprinted on several occasions), and Barr's preface would be read by thousands who had no notion of the display or the events of 1938–39. Indeed, it is that preface which set the tone for decades of Bauhaus reception in American art history and for the Bauhaus project in America. "Are this book then, and the exhibition which supplements it, merely a belated wreath laid upon the tomb of brave events, important in their day but now of primarily historical interest? Emphatically, no!" Barr answered his own rhetorical question thus, and asserted: "The Bauhaus is not dead; it lives and grows through the men who made it, both teachers and students, through their designs, their books, their methods, their principles, their philosophies of art and education."[48]

1 From Alfred H. Barr to Walter Gropius, September 15, 1938, "The Bauhaus 1919–1928," Registrar Exhibition Files, Exh. 82, The Museum of Modern Art, New York. Earlier considerations of this exhibition include Margret Kentgens-Craig, *The Bauhaus and America: First Contacts, 1919–1936* (Cambridge, MA: MIT Press, 2001), and Karen Koehler, "The Bauhaus, 1919–1928: Gropius in Exile and the Museum of Modern Art, NY, 1938," in Richard A. Etlin, ed., *Art, Culture, and Media Under the Third Reich* (Chicago: University of Chicago Press, 2002).

2 This was Barr's motto for the museum and the title of the tenth-anniversary exhibition which inaugurated the new building at 11 West 53rd Street in 1939. See also Harriet S. Bee and Michelle Elligot, eds., *Art in Our Time: A Chronicle of the Museum of Modern Art* (New York: MoMA, 2004).

3 Sybil Gordon Kantor, *Alfred Barr, Jr. and the Intellectual Origins of the Museum of Modern Art* (Cambridge, MA: MIT Press, 2003), 155, note 37.

4 Sybil Gordon Kantor, *Alfred Barr, Jr.*, 159, note 41, quoting Barr to Jane Fiske McCullough, February 6, 1967, "The Bauhaus 1919–1928," Registrar Exhibition Files, Exh. 82, The Museum of Modern Art, New York.
5 From Philip Johnson to Alfred H. Barr, undated letter, *c.* 1929, "The Bauhaus 1919–1928," Registrar Exhibition Files, Exh. 82, The Museum of Modern Art, New York.
6 Ibid.
7 Unsigned letter on Harvard Society for Contemporary Art letterhead, probably from Philip Johnson to Alfred H. Barr, December 16, 1930, "The Bauhaus 1919–1928," Registrar Exhibition Files, Exh. 82, The Museum of Modern Art, New York. See also Nicholas Fox Weber, *Patron Saints: Five Rebels Who Opened America to a New Art 1928–1943* (New York: Knopf, 1992), 118.
8 Ibid. Since this article was written the bibliography on Kirstein has expanded; see Samantha Friedman and Jodi Hauptman, eds., *Lincoln Kirstein's Modern* (New York: The Museum of Modern Art, 2019).
9 Weber, *Patron Saints*, 118.
10 On the show see Terence Riley, *The International Style: Exhibition 15 and the Museum of Modern Art* (New York: Rizzoli, 1992), and Barry Bergdoll and Delfim Sardo, *Modern Architects, Uma Intodução; An Introduction* (Lisbon: Babel, 2010). Since this essay was first published that introduction has been reprinted in David Hanks, ed., *Partners in Design: Alfred Barr, Jr. and Philip Johnson* (New York: Monacelli Press, 2015).
11 This was at a time when the small circle of the young museum was in shock after Johnson had thrown his financial support and energies to Father Charles Edward Conklin in Louisiana instead of to the nascent Department of Architecture, where he had footed much of the bill. Since this essay was first published a study of John McAndrew has appeared: Mardges Bacon, *John McAndrew's Modernist Vision: From the Vassar College Art Library to the Museum of Modern Art in New York* (New York: Princeton Architectural Press, 2018).
12 From Philip Johnson to Alfred H. Barr, October 16, 1931, "The Bauhaus 1919–1928," Registrar Exhibition Files, Exh. 82, The Museum of Modern Art, New York.
13 Ibid. On Johnson and the politics of the 1930s see Franz Schulze's *Philip Johnson: Life and Work* (Chicago: University of Chicago Press, 1996), and now Mark Lamster, *The Man in the Glass House: Philip Johnson, Architect of the Modern Century* (New York: Little, Brown & Co., 2018). On McAndrew see Keith Eggener, "Nationalism, Internationalism and the Naturalisation of Modern Architecture in the United States, 1925–1940," *National Identities*, 8/3 (September 2006): 243–58. See also Howard Dearstyne, *Inside the Bauhaus* (New York: Rizzoli, 1986).
14 From Eddie Warburg to Alfred H. Barr, letter, no date, "The Bauhaus 1919–1928," Registrar Exhibition Files, Exh. 82, The Museum of Modern Art, New York.
15 Alfred Barr quoted in Margaret Scolari Barr, "Our Campaigns," *The New Criterion*, 5/11 (August 1987): 44. See also Andreas Huyssen, "Oskar Schlemmer Bauhaus Stairway. 1932," in Barry Bergdoll and Leah Dickerman, *Bauhaus 1919–1933: Workshops for Modernity* (New York: MoMA, 2009), 318–21.
16 From Philip Johnson to Walter Gropius, January 29, 1934, "The Bauhaus 1919–1928," Registrar Exhibition Files, Exh. 82, The Museum of Modern Art, New York.
17 Ibid.
18 From Walter Gropius to Alfred H. Barr, April 20, 1937, "The Bauhaus 1919–1928," Registrar Exhibition Files, Exh. 82, The Museum of Modern Art, New York.
19 Barry Bergdoll, "The Paradoxical Origins of MoMA's Model Collection," in Mari Lending and Mari Hvattum, eds., *Modelling Time: The Permanent Collection 1925–2014* (Oslo: Torpedo Press, 2014), 159–61.
20 See Barry Bergdoll, "Good Neighbors: MoMA and Latin America, 1933–1955," in Thodoris Arrhenius, Mari Lending, Wallis Miller, and Jeremie Michael McGowan, eds., *Place and Displacement: Exhibiting Architecture* (Zurich: Lars Müller Publishers, 2014), 113–28.
21 See Michael Siebenbrodt, Jeff Wall, and Klaus Weber, *Bauhaus: A Conceptual Model* (Berlin: Hatje Kantz, 2009).
22 James M. Heinrich on behalf of John McAndrew to William Muschenheim, September 17, 1937, "The Bauhaus 1919–1928," Registrar Exhibition Files, Exh. 82, The Museum of Modern Art, New York.
23 See correspondence in "The Bauhaus 1919–1928," Registrar Exhibition Files, Exh. 82, The Museum of Modern Art, New York.
24 From Max Bill to MoMA, March 21, 1938, "The Bauhaus 1919–1928," Registrar Exhibition Files, Exh. 82, The Museum of Modern Art, New York.

25 From John McAndrew to Charles Ross, a former student, October 13, 1937, "The Bauhaus 1919–1928," Registrar Exhibition Files, Exh. 82, The Museum of Modern Art, New York.
26 From Walter Gropius to Alfred H. Barr, December 15, 1937, "The Bauhaus 1919–1928," Registrar Exhibition Files, Exh. 82, The Museum of Modern Art, New York.
27 See T'ai Smith, "Weaving Work at the Bauhaus: The Gender and Engendering of a Medium," Ph.D. thesis, University of Rochester, 2006, published as *Bauhaus Weaving Theory: From Feminine Craft to Mode of Design* (Minneapolis, MN: University of Minnesota Press, 2014).
28 From Herbert Bayer to Oskar Schlemmer, October 28, 1937, "The Bauhaus 1919–1928," Registrar Exhibition Files, Exh. 82, The Museum of Modern Art, New York.
29 From Oskar Schlemmer to Herbert Bayer, October 23, 1937, "The Bauhaus 1919–1928," Registrar Exhibition Files, Exh. 82, The Museum of Modern Art, New York.
30 From Oskar Schlemmer to Herbert Beyer, August 11, 1938, "The Bauhaus 1919–1928," Registrar Exhibition Files, Exh. 82, The Museum of Modern Art, New York.
31 From Walter Gropius to Alfred H. Barr, September 8, 1938, "The Bauhaus 1919–1928," Registrar Exhibition Files, Exh. 82, The Museum of Modern Art, New York.
32 Barry Bergdoll, "Bauhaus Multiplied: Paradoxes of Architecture and Design in and After the Bauhaus," in Bergdoll and Dickerman, *Bauhaus 1919–1933*, 59–60.
33 From Alfred H. Barr to Walter Gropius, September 15, 1938, "The Bauhaus 1919–1928," Registrar Exhibition Files, Exh. 82, The Museum of Modern Art, New York.
34 Karen Koehler, "The Bauhaus 1919–1928: Gropius in Exile and the Museum of Modern Art, NY, 1938," 287–315.
35 From Josef Albers to Janet Heinrich, November 19, 1937, "The Bauhaus 1919–1928," Registrar Exhibition Files, Exh. 82, The Museum of Modern Art, New York.
36 From Fritz Schleifer to Herbert Beyer, November 4, 1937, "The Bauhaus 1919–1928," Registrar Exhibition Files, Exh. 82, The Museum of Modern Art, New York.
37 From Bertrand Goldberg to Janet Heinrich, September 25, 1937, "The Bauhaus 1919–1928," Registrar Exhibition Files, Exh. 82, The Museum of Modern Art, New York. "ma-Holies" was a joke on the name of Moholy-Nagy.
38 From Walter Peterhans to Janet Heinrich, March 2, 1938, "The Bauhaus 1919–1928," Registrar Exhibition Files, Exh. 82, The Museum of Modern Art, New York.
39 From Josef Albers to Janet Heinrich, November 19, 1937, "The Bauhaus 1919–1928," Registrar Exhibition Files, Exh. 82, The Museum of Modern Art, New York.
40 From Walter Gropius to Herbert Bayer, October 20, 1938, "The Bauhaus 1919–1928," Registrar Exhibition Files, Exh. 82, The Museum of Modern Art, New York.
41 Article in the *New York Post*, quoted by Karen Koehler in "The Bauhaus, 1919–1928: Gropius in Exile and the Museum of Modern Art, NY, 1938," 300, note 45.
42 From Walter Gropius to Alfred H. Barr, December 15, 1938, "The Bauhaus 1919–1928," Registrar Exhibition Files, Exh. 82, The Museum of Modern Art, New York.
43 From Alfred H. Barr to Walter Gropius, December 10, 1938, "The Bauhaus 1919–1928," Registrar Exhibition Files, Exh. 82, The Museum of Modern Art, New York.
44 Cf. Alfred Barr, Jr., "Notes on the Reception of the Bauhaus Exhibition," Registrar Exhibition Files, Exh. 82, The Museum of Modern Art, New York; James Johnson Sweeny, "The Bauhaus—1919–1928," *New Republic* (January 11, 1959).
45 Lewis Mumford, "Bauhaus—Two Restaurants and a Theatre," *New Yorker* (December 31, 1938).
46 From Alfred H. Barr to Walter Gropius, March 3, 1939, "The Bauhaus 1919–1928," Registrar Exhibition Files, Exh. 82, The Museum of Modern Art, New York.
47 Cf. Karen Koehler, "The Bauhaus, 1919–1928: Gropius in Exile and the Museum of Modern Art, NY, 1938," 307–9, note 67: Alfred Barr to Walter Gropius, March 3, 1939, WGA, Harvard.
48 Alfred H. Barr, preface to *Bauhaus 1919–1928* by Herbert Bayer (New York: The Museum of Modern Art, 1938), 7.

Frampton and Japan

Ken Tadashi Oshima

While Japanese megalopoli seem to be as chaotic and alienating as any in the West, Japan has created an exceptionally rich architectural culture in the years that have elapsed since the completion of Kenzō Tange's Tokyo City Hall in 1957, a building that inaugurated a more civic phase in the reconstruction that followed the devastation of the Second World War. Directly or indirectly, the Japanese Government has played a prominent role in the rebuilding of the country, from the massive housing programmes of the Japanese Housing Authority started in 1945 to the latest State subsidies now being applied to the building of an international airport in the middle of Osaka Bay, together with a new terminal structure designed by Renzo Piano ... Throughout this period the patronage of the public sector has been complemented by private industrial and corporate commissions, which however paternalistic, have tended to be more socially conscious and civic-minded than is commonly the case with such agencies in the West.

Another predisposing factor affecting the quality of Japanese architectural production has been the unique capacity of the Japanese building industry to combine craft production with both rationalized industrial systems and high levels of self-sustaining research dedicated to the evolution of new materials and methods. This corporate *zaibatsu* approach to building, whereon many enterprises have their own architectural and engineering offices, is complemented on an ideological level by a number of influential magazines such as *Shinkenchiku*, *Kenchiku Bunka*, *A+U*, *Telescope*, *GA* and *SD*, and by the cultural activities of the major universities. While Post-Modern architectural fashions are as prevalent here as in any other advanced industrial nation, often with rather deleterious results, the country is still able to produce a considerable number of works that are conceived and executed at the highest level and often imbued with a critical as well as a poetic aspect.[1]

Kenneth Frampton, *Modern Architecture: A Critical History*, third edition, 1992

Together with that of Finland and Spain, the architectural culture of Japan constitutes the chapter "World Architecture and Reflective Practice" in the third edition of Kenneth Frampton's *Modern Architecture: A Critical History*. Published in 1992, this edition embodies Frampton's expanding knowledge/scholarship of the global extent of modern architecture situated within his personal constellation of England, the United States, and Japan through more than half a century. While the last part of the 1980 first edition included architects from Japan as "variations" of "The International

Style" and introduced Japanese Metabolists in its final section, "Place, Production and Architecture: Towards a Critical Theory of Building," such inclusion was limited.[2] The 1985 second edition included the work of Arata Isozaki (1931–), Kazuo Shinohara (1925–2006), and Toyo Itō (1941–), along with Tadao Andō (1941–) in the additional chapter on "Critical Regionalism." Then, in the fourth edition, Frampton proclaimed in the preface that "a disturbing Eurocentric bias has been evident in almost all the received histories of modern architecture, from Gustaf Adolf Platz's *Die Baukunst der neuesten Zeit* of 1927 to Reyner Banham's *Theory and Design in the First Machine Age* of 1960, to which this account has always been indebted."[3] Such a bias can be seen even further back in Banister Fletcher's "Tree of Architecture" in his *A History of Architecture on the Comparative Method* (first edition, 1896), in which Chinese and Japanese architecture is connected to a lower branch of the main trunk of Greek and Roman architecture leading to "modern styles" at the top.[4] Hence the sequential additions and revisions to *Modern Architecture* are part of Frampton's ongoing personal dynamic between practice and history as lifework.

Frampton noted in the 2002 introduction to *Labour, Work and Architecture*, "In addition to teaching, I am more strictly speaking a writer on architecture rather than an architect or even an architectural historian or, for that matter, a theorist or a critic ..."[5] Trained at the Architectural Association (AA) in London from 1950 to 1956, he practiced architecture in Israel, London, and New York. He began his teaching career at the AA in 1961 and his role in journalism from 1962 to 1965 as technical editor at the British journal *Architectural Design* (*AD*). Robin Middleton, his successor in that role, would commission him to write *Modern Architecture: A Critical History* in 1970.[6] Through the course of seven decades, Frampton's role as an architect, educator, journalist/editor, and historian would overlap and evolve as personal experiences became history.

Building on limited knowledge of and interest in the subject of Japanese architecture during his formative years in postwar England, Frampton would come to share sympathies with Japan and its built environment for the majority of his adult life. Even though both England and Japan are island nations adjacent to the respective continents of Europe and Asia, and both England and Japan suffered from extensive bombing during World War II, knowledge about Japan's built environment after World War II remained limited. As Reyner Banham described,

> Katsura-no-Rikyū—the Detached Palace—and Junzō Sakakura's pavilion at the Paris Expo of 1937 seemed to be the only two Japanese buildings that Western architects showed much interest in around 1950. If pressed conversationally, they might also recall a house by Antonin Raymond (but only because Le Corbusier had accused him of plagiarism) and some of them had discovered Bruno Taut's book, *Houses and People of Japan*, and, therefore, had some knowledge of the vernacular tradition of domestic building ...

The wish, therefore, was that Japanese modern would not develop in the same way as that of the West but would remain a kind of pure and uncompromised example of what modern architecture ought to be like in a perfect world, an exotic version of the work of Mies van der Rohe: spare, slender, light, and open. The wish was so powerful that it seemed to be treated almost as fact, a prediction of how the future of modern architecture in Japan must inevitably develop.[7]

Nonetheless, as Japan gradually recovered and rebuilt in subsequent years, interest in its architecture increased substantially. From 1954 to 1955, the Museum of Modern Art in New York presented the Japanese Exhibition House in its sculpture garden to illustrate how Japanese architecture dating to the seventeenth century was modern architecture. *AD* featured Japan in its April 1958 issue with text and photos by Irish architect/educator Noel Moffett (1912–1994).[8] For Moffett, this island country was a story of "two Japans": "the pre-Meiji Japan closed to the influence of the outside world and the Japan of to-day, open to progressive and up-to-date ideas." In February 1960, *AD* again published an issue dedicated to Japan, edited by Peter and Alison Smithson with Alison's essay on "The Rebirth of Japanese Architecture." This issue appeared in anticipation of the May 1960 World Design Conference held in Tokyo, which the Smithsons attended along with Louis Kahn, Paul Rudolph, and numerous other designers, and where the Metabolist architects would launch their movement. *AD* subsequently published a feature issue on Japan with Günter Nitschke's essay, "The Metabolists of Japan." In the same year Manfredo Tafuri published his early book, *L'Architettura Moderna in Giappone*.[9]

In this context, Frampton took particular interest in transnational figures within the architectural culture in Japan. In particular, the work of Antonin Raymond caught Frampton's attention, featured in Moffett's 1958 essay as a pivotal figure who traveled to Japan to work on Frank Lloyd Wright's Imperial Hotel and who practiced there before and after World War II to design works such as the Reader's Digest Building in Tokyo. Kunio Maekawa (who worked for both Le Corbusier and Raymond) was another architect of interest to Frampton.[10] Raymond's subsequent monographic issue in the *Architectural Association Journal* published in London in August 1962, together with Raymond's own monographs, confirmed Frampton's sympathy with the Czech-American architect's "preoccupation with combining the liberative ethos of the modern movement with the indigenous culture of Japan."[11] In 1963, Frampton, while working as technical editor at *AD*—and as the only person in the office on that particular day—first met a young Arata Isozaki, who visited in search of seeing James Stirling's work. This chance meeting would be the conduit to extensive contact and travel to Japan over the subsequent decades.

Frampton's journalistic and personal connections with Japan continued upon his move to the United States in 1965, particularly in his role as editor for the Institute for Architecture and Urban Studies (IAUS) catalogues and its journal, *Oppositions* (1976–82). Frampton's writings bridging practice and history would gain broad Japanese readership through their translation and publication in Japanese architectural journals from the 1970s to the present. His 1970 essay "Labour, Work and Architecture" was published in Japanese in 1972 in *Architecture and Urbanism* (*A+U*), and his 1971 essay "The Evolution of Housing Concepts 1870–1970" appeared in the same journal in 1977. Japanese journals featured his essays in English and Japanese on New York architects and their work (Peter Eisenman, *A+U*, November 1973; John Hedjuk, *A+U*, May 1975; and Raimund Abraham, *Space Design* (*SD*), March 1977), followed by his essays on Japanese architects (Toyo Itō, *A+U*, September 1986). Within this closely linked international architectural culture, Frampton's essay on Abraham was part of an *SD* issue on "Imaginary Architecture," edited by Arata Isozaki, who in his early days edited many special issues of architectural journals.[12]

Frampton and Isozaki's serendipitous meeting in 1963 would be followed by their collaboration some fifteen years later for the exhibition, catalogue, and lecture tour titled *A New Wave of Japanese Architecture* (1978) (**71**). This project was sponsored by the Japanese government to promote the country vis-à-vis the Japan Foundation established in 1973 and the Japan–U.S. Friendship Commission established in 1975. The "New Wave" consisted of eleven architects who ranged in age from Fumihiko Maki (1928–), then fifty, to Tadao Andō (1941–), in his late thirties. Arata Isozaki had assembled this group of architects and, as Frampton wrote at the beginning of his thirteen-page introduction to the book,

> At a mean point between them, there stands the extraordinarily spirited figure of Arata Isozaki—old enough to have been a member of Tange's Metabolist Studio that worked on the Tokyo Bay Proposal in 1960 and young enough to be the inspirer of a generation of conceptual architects, including such figures as Takefumi Aida, Tadao Andō, Hiromi Fujii, Hiroshi Hara, and Toyo Itō.[13]

While these architects would go on to have internationally prominent careers, the exhibition also included then relatively lesser-known figures: Monta (Kikō) Mozuna (1941–2001); Atelier Zo; and Osamu Ishiyama (1944–). The exhibition was held at the IAUS at 8 West 40th Street in New York, where Frampton was a fellow (1976–80) and Peter Eisenman was executive director. The exhibition was accompanied by "Five Japanese Architects on Tour to Ten American Cities," featuring lectures by Aida, Hara, Fujii, Minoru Takeyama, and Isozaki in San Francisco, Los Angeles, Houston, Miami, Washington, New York, Chicago, Minneapolis, Salt Lake City, and Seattle. Low-cost airfares and funding from the Japan Foundation enabled this whirlwind bicoastal series, but it had limited effect due to language challenges and small audiences.[14]

A New Wave presented an intersection of generations and cultures. Chris Fawcett, at the time an AA-based critic whose writings were referenced in the text and bibliography, observed that "the New Wave represents a backlash against

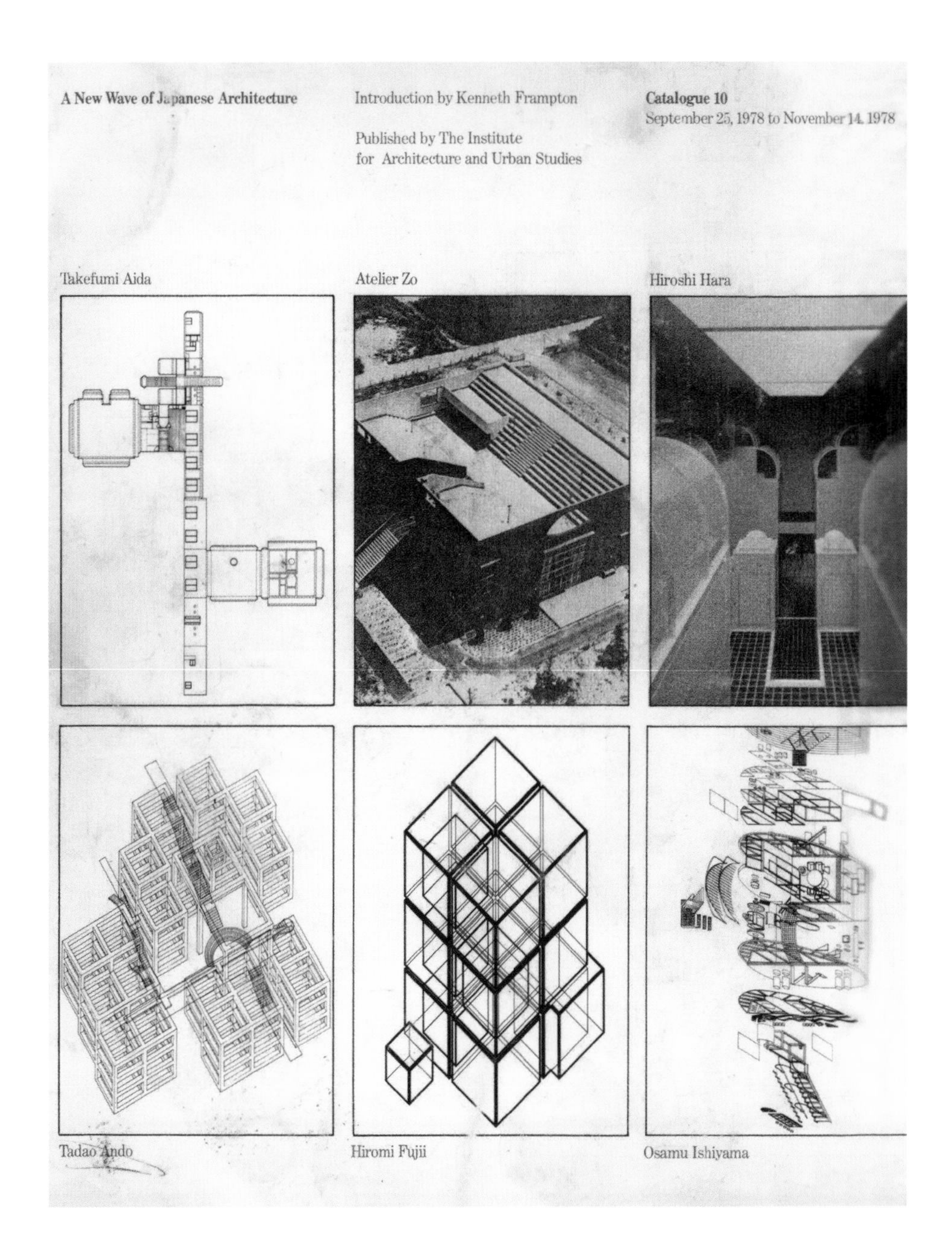

71 *A New Wave of Japanese Architecture*, ed. with an introduction by Kenneth Frampton (New York: Institute of Architecture and Urban Studies, 1978).

Metabolism."[15] Yet Frampton himself noted the complexity of such categorizations, as Maki, like Isozaki, was connected to the Metabolist movement yet remained "an architect whose response to the onslaught of industrial urbanization in the modern world was quite skeptical."[16] Frampton's essay was based on an extensive bibliography of the architects' writings and secondary criticism in English, but most importantly the exhibition provided the opportunity to juxtapose architects from both Japan and New York to make "intra- and international comparisons": Mozuna's Anti-Dwelling and Peter Eisenman's use of the mandala in his House X of 1975, or Isozaki's Yano House and Richard Meier's Douglas House, both completed in 1976.

The exhibition and catalogue received mixed reviews. *New York Times* critic Ada Louise Huxtable praised the New Wave's "most stunning and provocative expression" of this "active avant-garde."[17] As she noted:

> One of the most interesting aspects of this Japanese work—aside from its often exceptional quality—is the way which it simply abandons all the sociological and technological preoccupations that were a fundamental theoretical tenet of modernism through most of the 20th century. In their place is a blend of esthetics and philosophy in which the eye, and the idea, are all that count.

Yet Fawcett lamented that "Frampton's introductory essay condenses many of the architectural and formal operations of current Japan, but at the cost of a truly cultural perspective. The life of the buildings is interpreted as a mythos of significance, not as a frame for eating, living, and sleeping through the moebius strip of ritual cycles."[18]

While the *New Wave* exhibition was followed by Isozaki's exhibition, *MA: Space-time in Japan* at New York's Cooper-Hewitt Museum, at the age of fifty Frampton had the opportunity actually to visit work in Japan for the first time, in 1981. This journey was subsequently published as the three-part series "Modernism's Diffusion, Japan Diary: Summer '81" in *Skyline* from April to June 1982 (**72**). The detailed observation of his twenty-two-day journey, from June 20 to July 11, sponsored by the "Committee for the Year 2000" and organized by Isozaki, included stops in Tokyo, Kyoto, Osaka, Hiroshima, and Kitakyushu, with excursions and visits with architects including Arata Isozaki, Kazuo Shinohara, and Toyo Itō. Frampton's diary followed in a long line of published accounts of impressions of Japan and its architecture, including those of Ralph Adams Cram (*Impressions of Japanese Architecture*, 1905), Bruno Taut (*Houses and People of Japan*, 1937), Walter Gropius ("Architecture in Japan," *Perspecta*, 1955), and Noel Moffett's account in *AD*.[19] Frampton's trip followed the publication of the first edition of *Modern Architecture: A Critical History* and was in the same year as the publication of *Modern Architecture Vol. 1 1851–1919* (*GA Documents*). The diary clearly

26 Skyline April 1982

Modernism's Diffusion

Japan Diary: Summer '81

Kenneth Frampton with Yasuta Matsunaga (left) and Toyo Ito in front of The Imperial Hotel (F.L. Wright) reconstructed at the Meiji village (photo: Silvia Kolbowski)

Kenneth Frampton

Saturday, June 20: Arrival in Tokyo
Immediately struck at Tokyo airport by the Teutonic precision of the detailing and by the immaculate immigration officials and customs officers, by the white gloves and the white antimacassars lining the seats of taxis and private cars. We are met by Hiromi Fujii, ToyokazuWatanabe, and Makoto Uyeda. The seventy-minute ride to the center of Tokyo takes us along a rather narrow freeway through dense, small-scaled forest growth on either side of the road, which already looks like miniaturized nature. The entire highway from the airport to the center of town is lined with a sound-dampening barrier—an unexpected detail. Everywhere are sporadic paddy fields, bridges, rivers, industrial plants, baseball fields, and—as far as the eye can see—two- to three-story houses with small pitched roofs covered in tiles of ceramic or enameled metal: red, gray, green, and dark ultramarine. As one approaches the center of Tokyo, eight- to ten-story speculative office buildings and hotels stud the horizon. We arrive at the Hotel Okura, where we are met for dinner by Arata Isozaki, Aiko Miyawaki, and two friends of theirs from Los Angeles.

Sunday, June 21: Tokyo
We meet Arata and Aiko at the hotel and then go to Ueno Park for a quick visit to Le Corbusier's National Museum of Western Art, which, although it is hardly a work with a

difficulty in translating Japanese into English is the necessity to first eliminate all inflections indicating class and sexual differences, which are an integral part of the language. Clearly these inflections assume the age-old Japanese discipline and the acceptance of a normative social hierarchy.

I remark that I am surprised by the lack of evident aggressiveness in the streets of Tokyo, both in terms of traffic and pedestrian movement. The streets do not seem

twentieth-century equivalent of the nineteenth-century Japanese woodcut. What Ito has in mind is close to the "product" art of Andy Warhol (as in his House at Koganei; 1978). As far as he is concerned, a certain dimension of artistic hazard has to be present today in order to avoid preciousness. Through Ito and Matsunaga I become aware of the work of Kazuo Shinohara. For Ito,

72 Kenneth Frampton, "Modernism's Diffusion, Japan Diary: Summer '81," *Skyline* (April 1982), 26.

documented his perspective as a modernist discursively recording his visits, observations, and reflections. In describing his own interpretations and observations, Frampton noted in 2003 that:

> My preoccupations arise out of the direct experience of making buildings, at the societal as well as the professional level. Even though it's not explicitly elaborated, I tend to approach historical material through the eye of an architect: I ask myself what is the predicament faced by the architect in making a particular work in a physical setting at a given historical moment. That attention binds my two concerns together—place on the one hand and structural expressivity on the other.[20]

Naturally, the journey offered the opportunity to evaluate firsthand works that he had previously written about. In fact, he was questioned during the trip about "the validity of … making critical judgments on the basis of photographic reportage," which he admitted he had done regarding the work of Luis Barragán.[21] The visit provided the chance to consider the cultural implications of language, given that Frampton does not speak or read Japanese in order to be able to consider primary sources of architects' readings or Japanese critics' interpretations in the original language. As he noted from his conversation with Isozaki,

> [Isozaki and I] talk of recent research on the structure of the Japanese language which shows that, unlike Western languages, the vowels in Japanese have significance. I don't fully understand this argument, but the conclusion seems to be that due to the structure of the language in Japan, the left-hand side of the brain—the side usually dedicated to logical processes—becomes mixed with the right-hand or emotional side.[22]

The 1981 "Japan Diary"'s detailed account of visits both to traditional monuments such as the Ise Shrine and the Katsura Imperial Villa and to contemporary works is a particularly valuable document of the journey. In counterpoint to Kenzō Tange, who asserted that the Ise Shrine, as a "prototype of Japanese architecture," represents the peak in world architecture "along with the Parthenon,"[23] Frampton looked to the shrine's "presences":

> The monumentality of the Ise Naiku is completely unexpected, with its vast approach route and dramatic entry over the Isuzu River, the bed of which is lined near the bridge by a flat stone threshold that has the effect of calming the current on the upstream side of the bridge. The mirror-like surface of the water is regarded as a manifestation of the divinity. The way leads through a series of *torii* [wooden gates or arches] past a stepped stone esplanade leading down to the river's edge, where purification may be carried out—the *mitarashi*. The route then turns left and leads past the recently rebuilt center for sacred music, the *kaguraden*. There then follows a long drive, flanked by enormous cypresses, which finally leads to the entrance of the inaccessible main shrine, set on a small acropolis above the approach. The whole site is permeated by "presences": the elaborate tufted grass-and-stone edge of the route; groups of cockerels wandering within the grounds that mysteriously appear and disappear; attendant white-clad novices in black clogs and high black hats; the people arriving and clapping their hands before an imperceptible moving white veil, which signifies the presence of the spirit behind the multilayered fences.[24]

In contrast to Gropius, who looked to the Katsura Villa's potential for prefabrication, and to Le Corbusier, who noted the small size of the modular *tatami* mats,[25] Frampton looked to its shadows in reference to Jun'ichirō Tanizaki's *In Praise of Shadows*:[26]

> In retrospect I think of the Katsura Palace as essentially a gradation of shadows. I remember its inner volume as being hallucinatory; above all it conveyed a seductively destabilizing sense of varying size and relative distance: the subtly changing heights and levels; the ever-receding, endlessly unfolding sets of volumes; the shifting, sliding screens of translucent-versus-opaque and plain-versus-painted

> surfaces; the kaleidoscopic changing light ... Katsura reminded me of my childhood, when, with sudden unaccountable perceptual shifts in the apparent size [and] constancy of objects, one had the sense of being frighteningly small or large, a sense that was accompanied by illusory changes in the relative size of the environment, which became correspondingly colossal or inexplicably small.[27]

The 1981 visit to Japan also offered Frampton the opportunity to evaluate and experience the work of the "New Wave" firsthand. As he wrote,

> My last week in Japan starts with ... looking for the houses of the Japanese New Wave. The first stop on the tour is Hiromi Fujii's Pharmacy House, erected in the Chofu district in 1979. Fujii's monochromatic gray house is smaller than I imagined and has weathered rather badly. It is still a very exacting work, however, particularly the obsessively gridded fenestration and the interior. Fujii is without question the most intellectual figure of the New Wave; close to Eisenman, but with a feeling for formal resonance that is more syncopated.[28]

Fujii had been featured in the Fall 1980 issue of *Oppositions* 22, with the abstract axonometric drawings of his House/Pharmacy (1980) appearing on the cover, along with a black-and-white photograph of the facade as the first inside image (73). In its decontextualized abstraction, the design could certainly have been mistaken for Peter Eisenman's, as there was no caption on the photo and Eisenman's name appeared at the top of the opposite page. As Frampton's article on "Louis Kahn and the French Connection" was published just after Fujii's feature, the confluence of multiple interpretations could certainly be found both in *Oppositions* and in Frampton's personal experience.

Frampton's impressions of his visit with Hiroshi Hara at his own house match the mind and body of its creator with his physical expression:

> We visit Hiroshi Hara's own jet-black, timber-sided house of 1974 in Machida City. An anonymous pitched-roof box, with a symmetrical, stepped, white "microcosmic" interior, transforms the space of domesticity into a mythical urban realm. Hara is lean, diffident, and dressed like an Indian, wearing sandals and a rumpled white-linen, narrow trousered suit. His work reveals a preoccupation with anthropology and Islamic architecture. He has, it seems, a reputation as a mathematician and a Majong player; his much-thumbed paperback library contains the writings of the famous American mathematician George Birkoff; browsing briefly into this, I discover an essay entitled "The Mathematics of Aesthetics." Hara's concept of domesticity is romantic and all of his house interiors are rendered as "cities in miniature."[29]

Indeed, Frampton's observations go well beyond the interpretive gaze through photographs, ultimately rendering the subjectivity of Hara's design. Frampton's visit also confirmed his admiration for Kenzō Tange's work. As he described,

> We visit Kenzō Tange's still magnificent Kurashiki City Hall of 1958, which ... is surely a masterpiece of contemporary Japanese architecture. There is something almost Italian about the internal foyer in the center of the volume with its monumental stair and interior facades.[30]
>
> The next stop is Tange's National Gymnasia for the Tokyo Olympics (1961–64), which is undoubtedly the masterwork of his early career. The Olympic pool building is one of the most monumental modern spaces I have ever entered, and it is without doubt far superior to any of the many exotic structures designed by the late Eero Saarinen. After the cultural theory of Viollet-le-Duc, this structure posits "the great space" as the sign of a great civilization.[31]

Frampton's perspective on Tange was also shaped by Isozaki, his host for the trip and now longtime acquaintance:

> Arata follows with an eloquent account of his own position in the early 1960s and of his first meeting with me in 1963 at the London offices of *Architectural Design*. He talks of being influenced by both Kenzō Tange and Louis Kahn, but also of the way in which the concepts of structure in Tange and Kahn are entirely different, not only from each other, but also from his own recent development. What Arata objects to in Kahn is his priestly, didactic attitude. As far as Arata is concerned, there are many ways to create architecture, not just Kahn's ontologically exacting approach. Arata thinks that an assumption of an avant-gardist stance today can have nothing but negative connotations. It is not entirely clear what he means by this, but I take it that it has something to do with his concept that any architecture today has little choice but to make multiple, "pluralist" references and should be capable of directly expressing the fragmented nature of modern society.[32]

These comments preceded the completion of Isozaki's Tsukuba Center Building (1978–83), which was under construction at the time of Frampton's visit. The finished building, with its postmodern vigor and ironic references to Michelangelo's Campidoglio in Rome and Claude-Nicolas Ledoux, among many others, would prove to be too much for Frampton and subsequently marked a decided break between him and Isozaki.

Hence some architects and their buildings did not live up to expectations. Whereas Tōgo Murano has an almost cult-like admiration within Japan, the range of forms and subjectivity of his personal expression did not appeal to Frampton. As he described,

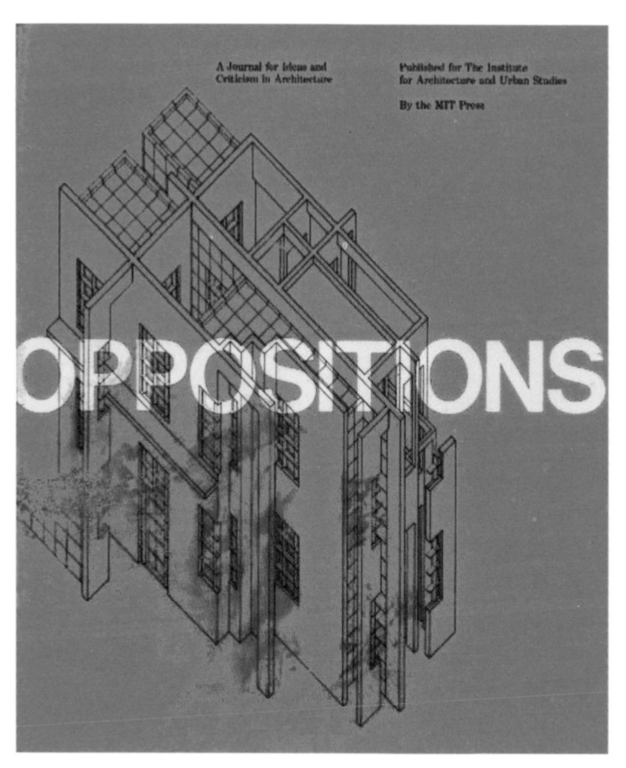

73 Illustration of Hiromi Fujii's House/Pharmacy, 1980, *Oppositions*, 22 (Fall 1980).

> Tōgo Murano's Shima Kanko Hotel in Kashikojima ... leaves one cold with its contrived play on the traditional single-story house piled up for eight floors and executed in reinforced concrete construction.[33]

> We visit Tōgo Murano's Chapel for World Peace (1953). Murano—the virtuoso eclectic—all too often is a disappointing architect.[34]

Other architects, such as Seiichi Shirai, would also prove to be not of Frampton's liking, as noted by Hajime Yatsuka, then a staff member in Isozaki's firm. Yatsuka guided Frampton to Isozaki's Gumma Museum, then subsequently presented his own interpretation of the Japanese architectural scene in *Oppositions*, not as a New Wave (as a reference to *The Great Wave* woodblock print, 1829–33, by Katsushika Hokusai), but rather as "an urban desert" in reference to author Kōbō Abe's "Ruined Map."[35] Yatsuka would further provide a counterpoint to Critical Regionalism in his own essay, "Internationalism versus Regionalism," in *At the End of the Century: One Hundred Years of Architecture*.[36]

The "Japan Diary" remains today as an invaluable record of Frampton's intellectual and aesthetic encounter with Japanese architecture, and of his observations of buildings and their architects. Since many of the buildings were subsequently torn down, this record is especially significant. Among those that are no longer extant are Kunio Maekawa's Harumi Apartment block (1958); Kenzō Tange and URTEC's Akasaka Prince Hotel (1972) and Hanae Mori shop (1976); Arata Isozaki's Oita Medical Center (1962) and House for Dr. Nakayama (1964); and Hiroshi Hara's Keisho Kindergarten (1968)—and the list continues to grow constantly. The relatively short life span of so many buildings in Japan would underscore the importance of their photographic record and publication in architectural journals, supporting the broad architectural culture in Japan that Frampton praised in the third edition of *Modern Architecture*.

In fact, in August 1981, soon after Frampton's tour to Japan, *GA Documents* published the fully illustrated *Modern Architecture Vol. 1 1851–1919* and *Modern Architecture Vol. 2 1919–1945*. The *GA* volumes were particularly accessible to the Japanese audience through the impact of Yoshio Futagawa's photographs and a text translated into Japanese. All of the works included were in Europe and America, except Wright's Imperial Hotel, and volume two included Junzō Sakakura's Japanese Pavilion at the 1937 Paris World Exhibition. They nevertheless were works particularly resonant with a Japanese audience, being built either in Japan or by a Japanese architect, along with sections on "The Chicago School of Architecture: The City and the Suburb 1830–1915," "The Structure and Symbolism of the Art Nouveau 1851–1914," and "Otto Wagner and the Wagnerschule 1894–1912," which reflected an era when there was strong interest in Japanese arts.

In the years following Frampton's journey to Japan, he incorporated the fundamental tectonics of the Japanese house in his conception of "Tectonic Culture" (given as lectures at Harvard University in 1985 and at Rice University in 1986, and published as *Studies in Tectonic Culture* in 1995). As stated at the outset of this essay, Andō would become a protagonist of "critical regionalism" with the inclusion of the Koshino House (1981), and Frampton's own experience of Andō's space through his own body (*shintai*), in combination with his conversations, formed the basis of his subsequent extensive writings on Andō.

In 1987, as the economic bubble rose to its peak, Frampton brought his interpretations of Japanese architectural culture to film in Michael Blackwood's project on "Japan's New Wave," which was released in 1989 as *Japan: Three Generations of Avant-garde Japanese Architects* (74).[37] Also in 1987, Andō taught his first studio at Yale University, exploring the proposition of reimagining Paul Rudolph's legendary Art & Architecture (A&A) Building as a Museum of Modern Architecture, for which Frampton would participate in the final review and write the introduction to the subsequent book (75).[38] As audacious as the studio may have appeared at the time (since Andō had no direct connection to Rudolph), Andō inherited the tradition of reinforced concrete in Japan and the A&A Building's bush-hammered concrete found inspiration in such a material expression as Tange's Kagawa Prefectural

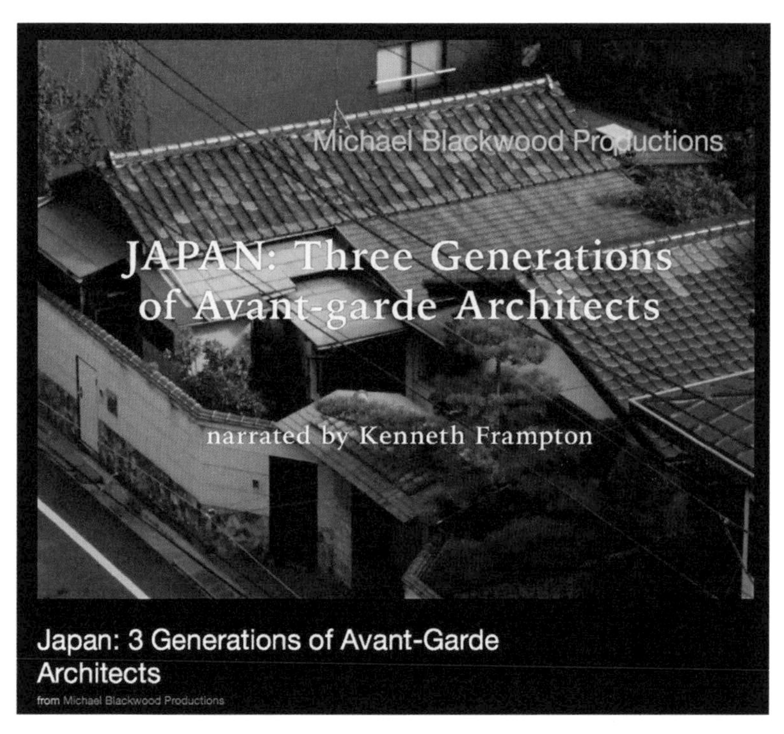

74 Opening image, Michael Blackwood and Kenneth Frampton, *Japan: Three Generations of Avant-Garde Architects* (DVD video) (New York: Michael Blackwood Productions, 1988).

75 Kenneth Frampton on the jury for Tadao Andō's 1987 Yale Studio, Tadao Andō, et al., *Tadao Andō: The Yale Studio and Current Works* (New York: Rizzoli, 1989), 134.

Office Building (1958), which Rudolph visited during the 1960 World Design Conference.[39]

Frampton's writings have had a lasting legacy and global impact through translation, especially in Japan. While journal articles were readily published in both English and Japanese, the complexities of translating Frampton's books meant that many of them were not translated until the twenty-first century: *Studies in Tectonic Culture* was published in 2002 (translators: Tsuyoshi Matsuhata, Sōtarō Yamamoto; Tōtō Publishing) and *Modern Architecture: A Critical History* appeared in Japanese as 現代建築入門. *The Evolution of 20th Century Architecture: A Synoptic Account* was published in 2016 by former *A+U* editor Toshio Nakamura. Architectural critic/historian Masato Kawamukai, a scholar of Gottfried Semper and fin-de-siècle Austrian architectural culture, published the 2015 book *Kingendai kenchikushiron* (*Modern/Contemporary Architectural History/Theory*), further elaborating on tectonic culture's expression in Japan through the work of architects including Kiyonori Kikutake and Kazuyo Sejima.[40] The resonance between the two authors can be seen to be mutual as Frampton himself has quoted Kawamukai when discussing the importance of material in the work of Andō.[41] In 2018, Frampton published a monograph on the work of Kengo Kuma, whose own tectonic construction of the V&A Dundee from hung precast concrete pieces reflects an almost boomerang return of ideas to the U.K. in what Frampton calls *répétition différente*.

Today, in a globalized world of architectural production, there remain mutual influences of modern masters including Frank Lloyd Wright, Le Corbusier, Alvar Aalto, Mies van der Rohe, and others on architects in Japan and the rest of Asia, as well as in the Euro-American context. The legacies of Frampton's "Labour, Work and Architecture" live on through the ongoing quest to realize tectonic construction sensitive to context, region, and craft shaped by life experiences. Frampton's journal publications from *AD* to *Oppositions* to *A+U* between the U.K., U.S., and Japan are now historical documents to be further unpacked. Indeed, Frampton noted in his "Seven Points for the Millennium: An Untimely Manifesto" that "Architecture as opposed to any other art form is irredeemably mixed up with the life-world. In this respect it is as much a context for culture and life as it is a cultural expression in and of itself..."[42] As he concluded upon leaving Japan in 1981,

> One thinks of Eliot's *Four Quartets* as the taxi rushes onward to the terminal: "Time present and time past are both perhaps contained in time future and time future contained in time past."[43]
>
> "Modernism's Diffusion, Japan Diary: Summer '81"

1 Kenneth Frampton, *Modern Architecture: A Critical History*, 3rd edition (London: Thames & Hudson, 1992), 339.

2 Frampton notes the first edition was limited by constraints of length by the publisher. Stan Allen and Hal Foster, "A Conversation with Kenneth Frampton," *October*, 106 (Autumn 2003): 46.

3 Kenneth Frampton, *Modern Architecture: A Critical History*, 4th edition (London: Thames & Hudson, 2007), 7.
4 Banister Fletcher, *A History of Architecture on the Comparative Method* (London: Batsford, 1896). For a further discussion of Fletcher, see Vimalin Rujivacharakul, "Ghosts of Asia Fergusson's Haunted Mansion and Architectural History of Asia in a Post-Said World," *Journal of Architectural Education*, 63/2 (2010): 161–65.
5 Kenneth Frampton, *Labour, Work and Architecture: Collected Essays on Architecture and Design* (London: Phaidon, 2002), 6.
6 Allen and Foster, "A Conversation with Kenneth Frampton," 35–58.
7 Reyner Banham, "The Japonization of World Architecture," in Hiroyuki Suzuki, Reyner Banham, and Katsuhiro Kobayashi, *Contemporary Architecture of Japan 1958–1984* (New York: Rizzoli, 1985), 16.
8 Noel Moffett, "Japan," *Architectural Design* (April 1958): 131–57.
9 Manfredo Tafuri, *L'Architettura Moderna in Giappone* (Bologne: Cappelli, 1964). For a further discussion of this book, see Ken Tadashi Oshima, "Manfredo Tafuri and Japan: An Incomplete Project," *Architectural Theory Review*, 8/1 (2003): 16–29.
10 Kenneth Frampton, "Belated Recognition," *Crafting a Modern World: The Architecture and Design of Antonin and Noémi Raymond*, ed. Kurt Helfrich and William Whitaker (Princeton, NJ: Princeton Architectural Press, 2006), 10.
11 Frampton purchased Raymond's own *Architectural Details* of 1938 in New York in the mid-1960s, followed by *Antonin Raymond: His Work in Japan 1920–35*. Frampton, "Belated Recognition," 10.
12 Isozaki edited many issues in the 1960s of *Kenchiku Bunka* (together with Teiji Itoh, et al., November 1961, December 1963) and *Toshi Jutaku* (January 1969), which he later published as *Kenchiku no Kaitai* (*The Disassembly of Architecture*) (Tokyo: Bijusu shuppansha, 1984). The latter featured chapters on Hans Hollein, Archigram, Charles Moore, Cedric Price, Christopher Alexander, Robert Venturi, and Superstudio/Archizoom.
13 *A New Wave of Japanese Architecture*, ed. with introduction by Kenneth Frampton (New York: Institute for Architecture and Urban Studies, 1978), 1.
14 Interview with program director, Andrew McNair, August 23, 2019.
15 Chris Fawcett, "Review: The Rites of Criticism Reviewed Work(s): *Beyond Metabolism* by Michael Franklin Ross; *Metabolism in Architecture* by Kisho Kurokawa; *A New Wave of Japanese Architecture* by Kenneth Frampton," *Journal of the Society of Architectural Historians*, 39/2 (May 1980): 156.
16 *A New Wave of Japanese Architecture*, 1.
17 Ada Louise Huxtable, "ARCHITECTURE VIEW; The Japanese New Wave," *New York Times* (January 14, 1979), section D, 27.
18 Fawcett, "Review," 155–56.
19 Ralph Adams Cram, *Impressions of Japanese Architecture* (New York: Baker & Taylor, 1905); Bruno Taut, *Houses and People of Japan* (Tokyo: Sanseido, 1937). The Gropius text is reprinted in Arata Isozaki, et al., *Katsura Imperial Villa* (Milan: Electa, 2005), 355.
20 Allen and Foster, "A Conversation with Kenneth Frampton," 48.
21 Kenneth Frampton, "Modernism's Diffusion, Japan Diary: Summer '81—Part 3," *Skyline* (June 1982), 24.
22 Kenneth Frampton, "Modernism's Diffusion, Japan Diary: Summer '81—Part 2," *Skyline* (May 1982), 27.
23 Kenzō Tange, *Ise: Prototype of Japanese Architecture* (Cambridge, MA: MIT Press, 1965).
24 Ise Shrine, Wednesday, June 24, 1981: Kenneth Frampton, "Modernism's Diffusion, Japan Diary: Summer '81—Part 1," *Skyline* (April 1982), 29.
25 Isozaki, et al., *Katsura Imperial Villa*, 355, 387–89.
26 Jun'ichirō Tanizaki, *In Praise of Shadows*, trans. Thomas Harper (New Haven, CT: Leete's Island Books, 1977).
27 Frampton, "Modernism's Diffusion, Japan Diary: Summer '81—Part 2," 26.
28 Frampton, "Modernism's Diffusion, Japan Diary: Summer '81—Part 3," 22.
29 Ibid., 22.
30 Ibid., 24.
31 Ibid.
32 Ibid., 25.
33 Ibid., 29.
34 Ibid.
35 Interview by the author, February 12, 2019.

36 Hajime Yatsuka, "Internationalism versus Regionalism," *At the End of the Century: One Hundred Years of Architecture* (Los Angeles: Museum of Contemporary Art, 1998), 166.
37 Michael Blackwood and Kenneth Frampton, *Japan: Three Generations of Avant-Garde Architects* (DVD video) (New York: Michael Blackwood Productions, 1988).
38 Tadao Andō, et al., *Tadao Andō: The Yale Studio and Current Works* (New York: Rizzoli, 1989).
39 Koji Kamiya witnessed Rudolph's visit to the Kagawa Prefectural Office Building in 1960. See Kagawa Museum, *Kenzō Tange—Tradition and Creation—From Setouchi to the World* (Tokyo: Bijutsu Shuppansha, 2013), 206.
40 Masato Kawamukai, *Kingendai kenchikushiron* (Tokyo: Chūokōron, 2015).
41 Kenneth Frampton, "The Work of Tadao Andō," *Labour, Work and Architecture*, 315.
42 Kenneth Frampton, "Seven Points for the Millennium: An Untimely Manifesto," *Journal of Architecture*, 5/1 (Spring 2000): 23.
43 Frampton, "Modernism's Diffusion, Japan Diary: Summer '81—Part 3," 25.

Dialectics of Utopia/Utopian Dialectics

Anthony Vidler

I first met Kenneth Frampton in the fall of 1965, arriving for a year-long research Instructorship at Princeton that was to stretch to twenty-seven years. I was fresh from the architectural diploma course at Cambridge; Kenneth was in the midst of delivering what was to be a landmark series of lectures on the architecture of the Russian Revolution, lectures that were to form the first English-language summary, "Notes on Soviet Urbanism 1917–1932," in the *Architects' Year Book 12* (1968).[1] In 1966, Kenneth developed his signature graduate seminar in Analysis, Criticism and Theory, devoted to the history of modern architecture—presentations that later became the foundation of his *Modern Architecture: A Critical History.* A year later, Kenneth structured an entire semester-long seminar reviewing the architectural and urban work of Le Corbusier, which resulted in articles on the Ville Radieuse and the Palace of the Soviets, and an edited double issue of *Oppositions* that brought together a wealth of new writing by Le Corbusier scholars. What follows is a brief reflection on Frampton's essay "The City of Dialectic," published in *Architectural Design* in October 1969, with heartfelt thanks for a lifetime of support and friendship.

> Il y a en tout utopiste un Le Corbusier qui sommeille, et qui ferait volontiers, comme l'éminent architecte, le projet de remplacer Paris ... par une trentaine de gratte-ciels. Inversement, dans tout urbaniste, il y a un utopiste qui ne demande qu'à s'éveiller.[2]
>
> Raymond Ruyer, *L'utopie et les utopies*[3]

There is no more dramatic display of the sharply divided debates that constituted British architectural discourse at the end of the 1960s than the October 1969 issue of *Architectural Design.*[4] In a year that saw the deaths of three "masters" of the Modern Movement (Ludwig Mies van der Rohe, Junzō Sakakura, and Walter Gropius), the editors, Monica Pidgeon and Robin Middleton, seemed intent on establishing an entirely new direction. The first section, "Cosmorama," opened with Nick Jeffrey's long article on "The Struggle for Environment," and a report on the International Congress of Cybernetics, ending with a new feature, "FiN (Future is Now:1)" with a list of "Futures organisations," classified according to country. The poison pill was in the margins: notes on the threatened demolition of two Modern Movement landmarks (Auguste Perret's Rue de Ponthieu Garage in Paris and Le Corbusier's Clarté apartments in Geneva) and the actual demolition of Le Corbusier's Villa Church, Ville-d'Avray (1927).

The heralding of a new era to be built on the ruins of the old was then celebrated with a series of articles on systems design: a program for the lattice design of "Multi-Strategy Buildings" by John Weeks; a study by J.G. Wanzel on "Systems and Society"; a review of new methods of "Forecasting Futures," by Joshua L. Taylor, followed by an examination of "Tensegrity Investigations" by A.J. Pugh; together with the more "hip" presentation of MEDIKIT's ("World Wide Medical System International Warehousing Agents") entry to the Paris Biennale.

This lineup is significant. The essay by Weeks, proposing what has since become understood as the power of the diagram, anticipated decades of parametric development, as he claimed of his lattice: "The diagram is translatable into building for a wide variety of physical situations, and while it may be distorted, its topological characteristics remain constant." Wanzel's take on the relation of systems to society is less positivistic, qualifying the distinctions and definitions of "user" and "method" and arguing against the celebration of "technique": "while 'technique' alone has its negative psychological, social and political implications each of these in turn gives rise to negative economies," quoting his reading of Jacques Ellul's *The Technological Society*. In a (satirical?) advertisement that is apparently smuggled in as a contribution, MEDIKIT takes this implied critique further, by employing an Archigram-like collage and graphic technique to suggest that its "propositions" for linking computer networks and social institutions ("links to group clinics") are deeply embedded in the New Society.

More importantly, and bookending these promotions for techno-systems, are three articles that hold the center of the issue: a contribution by Cedric Price titled "ECHOES. Environmentally Controlled Human Operational Enclosed Spaces," Peter Smithson's extraordinary photographic and meditative *randonnée* through Bath (still one of the best guides to the architecture of this Roman/Romantic neoclassicist town), and, as a historical/critical voice, Kenneth Frampton's radical reassessment of Le Corbusier's Ville Radieuse: "The City of Dialectic."[5]

These three essays form a telling statement on the question of architectural theory in the late 1960s. They can be roughly separated as Technology (Price), History (Smithson), and Critical Theory (Frampton). Here, nearly a decade later, the issues identified by Reyner Banham in his famous "Stocktaking" of early 1960 are brought up short: problems of technology, history, and sociology. Where Banham was eager to promote the improvement of scientific and technological knowledge as resistant to what he saw as the still pervading "academicism" (i.e. "formalism") of an architecture that had long run behind the Buckminster Fullers and John McHales of the world, here we have a renewal of Weimar critique based on an alliance between John Summerson and the Situationists (Smithson); the triumph of the iterative diagram based on the social premises of wartime reconstruction (Price); and the radical negativity of Theodor W. Adorno and Herbert Marcuse (Frampton). Whereas in the period 1957–63 the theoretical field was neatly divided between the "programmatic" (Summerson), the technocratic (Banham), and the formalistic (Eisenman), the culture of architecture has now shifted. Whether as a result of Frampton's recent move to the United States, or the quiet resistance to change for its own sake (Smithson), or the sense that architecture itself had disappeared without trace (Price), these articles in the context of an issue largely dedicated to technological innovation neatly pose the problem of an incessantly fractured discipline, always searching for a principle of unity.

In this context, Frampton's essay stands as a defense against the increasing systematization of the field: a critique of heroic urban utopias, but historically nuanced, and showing a respect for a utopia that had provided so much in terms of analytical and critical spatial knowledge to the field of housing, mediated by the understanding that it could not be dismissed outright. After all, Frampton implies, in the continuous struggle between utopia and anti-(or counter-)utopia that had defined the architectural discipline since the Renaissance, the consideration of an apparently outdated and outmoded urban model—the *ville radieuse*—might force the reconsideration of its epistemological bases; its relationships to still-strong ideals; and the struggle for light, air, and land common to all communities.

The title of Frampton's essay, "The City of Dialectic," opens up a larger question of interpretation, however. For it registers the fact that ideal cities, and the utopias they represented, were in some way or another always already dialectical. From Socrates, who pioneered the method in constructing his "city in words" for his listeners in the Piraeus, to Thomas More, whose two books comprising his *Utopia* established an opposition between an England corrupted by the enclosure movement, and a description of Utopus, the "No-Place" realm of Utopia, the genre had always insisted on its dialectical relation to reality. And with respect to the formulation of "ideal" cities, often authorized by utopian narratives, architects from Filarete, whose imagined city of Sforzinda was developed through "Platonic" conversations with his client, to the utopian socialist projects of the nineteenth century—Charles Fourier's Phalanstery, Robert Owen's New Harmony, Étienne Cabet's Icaria, and the Saint-Simonians' New Paris—all influenced the utopian aspirations of the Modern Movement toward building a new society. And Le Corbusier, the great eclectic, took them all under advisement as supports for his radical plans for city-building. The contemporary sources for Le Corbusier's grand plans—the syndicalist, proto-fascist, and fascist hierarchies of work and labor, as well as the idealistic revival of Neoplatonism in André Gide and Paul Valéry, Jean Cocteau and Jean Giraudoux—have been well researched since the publication of Mary McLeod's seminal article.[6] His *architecturally* formative influences, however, were deeply rooted in Saint-Simonianism and Fourierism, both of which underwent surprising revivals in the early years of the twentieth century.

These allegiances and derivations were obvious enough to Le Corbusier's contemporaries. Thus, the art critic Henri Focillon, thanking Le Corbusier for the receipt of Volume II of the *Oeuvre complète* (1929–34), remarked: "I don't believe I'm wrong in recognizing in you the inheritor of these Saint-Simonian architects, who intended to make of our towns, in their plan and their very configuration, a glorified image of humanity."[7] In a later letter, on receiving his copy of *La Ville Radieuse*, Focillon drafted an even more lofty encomium of Le Corbusier's Saint-Simonian city, which, he wrote, evoked those nineteenth-century "toolmakers of the last century," builders of "canals, towns, and railroads."

Le Corbusier's debt to Fourier was implied in his earlier housing schemes for the Ville Contemporaine (1923), with its apartment blocks around socially active courtyards and "*maisons à redents*" ("reticulated housing") that seemed to emulate Fourier's Phalansteries in a continuous ribbon, but it was stated openly with respect to his invention of the Unité d'Habitation, where he quotes from *Description du phalanstère et considérations sociales sur l'architectonique*, by Fourier's disciple, the engineer Victor Considerant.[8] For Le Corbusier, Fourier represents the "first visionary of the machinist era" who "judges his social constructions according to *joie de vivre*."[9]

The dialectics of *La Ville Radieuse* would then be played out in the inevitable contest between two fundamentally different versions of the ideal city: between the *machinist* utopia of the Saint-Simonians and the social and *communitarian* visions of Fourier and his followers.[10] That is to say, between the Saint-Simonian will to build the ideal city in the here and now—through infrastructural projects such as railroads, canals, and glass and iron temples—and Fourier's desire to withdraw from the city in carefully assembled, small-scale, self-supporting communities. In *La Ville Radieuse*, in a typical sleight of hand, Le Corbusier quite literally will build the one over the other, sliding the Fourierist countryside beneath the *pilotis* of the advanced technological Saint-Simonian city-machine, eliding the city–country opposition by the creation of a *ville-verte*. Fourier would be given a place in the prototypical "communitarian" projects for Nemours and Zlin (1934–35), but it was not until after the war that the "vertical phalanstery" of the Unité d'Habitation was built.

Frampton's balanced and comprehensive study of the Corbusian city is, for the late 1960s, somewhat of an intellectual achievement. Although ostensibly conducted as a review of the modernist legacy after Le Corbusier's death in 1965—and, in its concentration on urbanism, a follow-up to his Soviet researches—the article was written at a moment when the grand utopias of the Modern Movement were being subjected to serious critique, if not dismissal out of hand. From Theodor Adorno to Karl Popper, and already at a more popular level in Aldous Huxley's *Brave New World* (1932) and George Orwell's *1984* (1949), the very idea of utopia in the modern age seemed to have been thoroughly discredited.[11]

Karl Popper was the anti-utopian voice most listened to. *The Open Society and its Enemies* (1945), written in New Zealand during the war as a "contribution to the war effort," Popper said, turned the critique of utopianism toward a critique of the entire Platonic tradition and its historicization from Hegel through Marx—what

Popper saw as the entire "totalitarian" tradition. Indeed, Popper's first volume was entirely taken up with an attack on Plato, seen as the forebear of Adolf Hitler. Plato was "the first great political ideologist who thought in classes and races and proposed concentration camps," wrote Popper of Plato's suggestions for the isolation of malcontent citizens in the *Laws*. "The lesson which we should thus learn from Plato is the exact opposite of what he tries to teach us."[12] The Platonic approach, concluded Popper, represented a kind of utopian engineering. Opposed to this, the engineer–scientist Popper proposed a more gradualist and fragmented form of what he called "piecemeal engineering."[13] In France, the reaction against Le Corbusier's urban projects was even fiercer. The social historian of art and technology, Pierre Francastel, described in Popperian terms Le Corbusier's imagined world as a "*universe concentrationnaire*," where the individual is forced to experience happiness in a hive called a *machine à habiter*.[14]

By the mid-1960s, however, the climate had changed significantly. Indeed, in Frampton's London milieu, the discussion of utopian and ideal urban typologies had been advanced by the postwar debates over the housing question, and by British intellectual discussions over the form and role of Marxist approaches to reconstruction both within and outside of the London County Council. On the left, a serious resistance to Popper and the anti-utopians had developed, supported by the English translation of Karl Mannheim's *Ideology and Utopia*.[15] For the British left, Mannheim's sociological propositions were an acceptable counter to Marx's and Engels's critique of "utopian" socialism. As Robert Taylor and Tom Steele note, "Mannheim's pursuit of the goal of a broader notion of the social sciences, rather than simply a statistically based sociology, created an important new tome in academic circles."[16] Historians began to discover the utopian roots of the Labour movement: E.P. Thompson's *William Morris* (1956) was extremely influential on Michael Young and his circle of post-Fabians; and Raymond Williams explored notions of culture with respect to the working classes, giving a measured account of both Morris and Orwell in his influential *Culture and Society 1780–1950* (1958).

The interest in *architectural* utopia was equally evident, stimulated by the work of Emil Kaufmann, whose posthumous *Architecture in the Age of Reason* was a comprehensive review of neoclassical architecture in England, Italy, and France. Published in 1957, it was immediately adopted in England and the United States as the last word on the International Enlightenment in architecture. In Britain, Helen Rosenau at the Warburg Institute had already—following Kaufmann's early leads—published on Claude-Nicolas Ledoux (1946) and brought out a translation of Étienne-Louis Boullée's manuscript text on *Architecture: Essai sur l'art* (1953).

Perhaps the most influential discussant of utopianism in London in the early 1960s was the historian and critic Colin Rowe, briefly a lecturer at Cambridge University and whose article "Architecture and Utopia" had been published in the Cambridge review, *Granta*, in 1959.[17] In this special issue on utopia, he was accompanied by a brilliant roster of the newly graduated left social and political intellectuals: the editor James Cornford (son of John Cornford, the poet who had lost his life in the Spanish Civil War, and grandson of Francis Cornford, the celebrated Platonist), who wrote on William Morris; Robert Marris, a socialist economist; Richard Layard, who later gained a reputation in "happiness research"; and André Schiffrin, future publisher of Pantheon Books and an enthusiast of Mannheim.[18]

Rowe himself was perhaps the least enthusiastic. His article, in fact, was neither an endorsement of utopianism nor written from a left–Labour position. In *Granta* he traced a plausible-enough "descent" of the utopian idea in architecture, from its hybrid origins in "Jewish millennial thought" and Platonic forms, through its reification in the centralized star-patterns of Renaissance ideal cities, to the less "convincing" geometries of the Enlightenment, the "somewhat provincial" plans for redeeming "the lower strata" in the nineteenth century, and the divergent utopian impulses in modern architecture, split between the "mechanistic, vitalistic city of the Futurists," where life was premised on "an absolute orgy of flux," and Le Corbusier's Ville Radieuse, with its "boring," "schematic monotony." While Rowe admitted that there was inevitably an aspect of utopianism in every architectural project, it was the wholesale realization of the ideal in reality that disturbed him. Contesting Mannheim's definition of utopias as "orientations transcending reality ... which, when they pass over into conduct, tend to shatter, either partially or wholly, the order of things prevailing at the time," he countered, with reference to the ubiquitous effects of Le Corbusier's Ville Radieuse: "If we ask with what ideas an 'orientation' which 'transcends reality' is constructed we are obliged to wonder whether contemporary society can really tolerate such an 'orientation.'" Buttressing Rowe's skepticism was his enthusiasm for Popper, whose work, as he noted in an addendum to "The Architecture of Utopia" in 1973, while openly available, had been apparently ignored by the contributors to *Granta*.[19]

In London architectural circles, as illustrated by the articles in the October 1969 issue of *Architectural Design*, the disussion was spurred by debates over the role of technology against the nostalgia for lost history: between Cedric Price, for example, and the partisans of the *Architectural Review*'s "Townscape" polemics—or even between Price and Peter Smithson's "as found" attitude to historical contexts. In the end, however, it was the pervasive romanticism and neopicturesque formulations of Gordon Cullen and Hubert de Cronin Hastings that turned many of Frampton's generation against the rationalism and typological clarity of Corbusian solutions.

But the question of architectural utopia was equally on the agenda in the United States, and not only in terms of the "drop-out" movement. Indeed, Frampton brackets his article by two authoritative citations that draw on his then new U.S. experience. The first, from Herbert Marcuse's *Eros and Civilization*, speaks to the new culture of leisure opened up by the new organization of work. Frampton was a year later to develop this question through a reading of Hannah Arendt's distinctions between "Labor" and "Work" in *The Human Condition*, where in place of the third condition, "action," he substituted "architecture."[20] The second calls up Tomás Maldonado's critique of the wartime "ideology of waste" as a policy that delivers equitable housing and a "metabolically valid environment." Frampton's reference stems from his friendship with Maldonado, who had delivered a series of lectures at the Princeton University School of Architecture between 1967 and 1969, leading to the English-language edition of his book, *Design, Nature, and Revolution: Towards a Critical Ecology*, where he developed an advanced critique of environmental policy, design, and utopia, and an acute analysis of Marcuse's work on alienation.

Frampton's analysis of Le Corbusier's Ville Radieuse stands out as unique for its insistence on the integral connections between the diagrammatic form of the city plans and the sociopolitical structure envisaged for their operation. Rather than denouncing the architect for the "totalitarianism" implied by his geometric utopia—a common response in the postwar period—Frampton takes the time to read the heterogenous and fragmented text of the volume published in 1933, and tease out its complex, and often confusing, ideological superstructure set out in a series of apparently polarized themes that constitute a virtual "city of dialectic." First, Frampton notes that the book had been conceived after Le Corbusier's visits to Russia—its original title in fact had been "Réponse à Moscou"—and was firmly dedicated to rebut any idea that the Ville Radieuse was a utopia. Neither the "pre-machine age" utopia of the garden city, nor the "disurbanization" advocated by Soviet regional planning, Corbusier's city was urban: "to urbanize the town and to urbanize the country." At once denouncing the American garden suburb as "the organized slavery of capitalist society," he equally rejected the "colonizing" aspects of Soviet rural planning.

Drawing on the French tradition of Syndicalism and a mixture of utopian socialist ideas, Le Corbusier invented an organizing structure based on what he understood as technical fact, with evident political implications. Frampton explores these at length in a close reading of the text, as well as the stream of diagrams interspersed throughout the volume. One in particular draws Frampton's attention not only for its outline of hierarchical organization, but for its own formal interest, its oval center seemingly reflecting the plan of the assembly building projected by Tony Garnier in that earlier machinist utopia, the Cité Industrielle (1900–17) so admired by Corbusier.

Frampton's article stands even today, and after decades of scholarly publication, as a brilliant and evocative analysis of the text and illustrations of *La Ville Radieuse*, a text which he writes, "stands as a document of the greatest cultural importance, for not only does it illuminate the infinitely complex nature of its author's thought, but it also remains as a warning to our benighted present, rife as it is with both absurd affluence and abject poverty." Toward the end of his article, Frampton measures Le Corbusier's prophetic analyses of the relation between war and architecture, and the need for investment in infrastructure and urban renewal, against the conditions of 1969 in what he sees as the "tertiary state of rationalization": air pollution and oil industry profits; defense expenditure and lack of action in the cities; and what Le Corbusier called "the budding automobile" and the "instant Utopia of Los Angeles syndrome." In his ringing conclusion to this extraordinary essay, Frampton, ever the engaged historian, announces the major themes that will engage him throughout his career: the spoliation of the environment, the breakdown of local cultures, and the loss of the art of tectonic design. As he warns, in the words of Antoine de Saint-Exupéry: "We don't ask to be eternal beings, only not to see acts and things suddenly lose all their meaning."[21]

1 Kenneth Frampton, "Notes of Soviet Urbanism 1917–1932," *Urban Structure: Architects' Yearbook 12*, ed. D. Lewis (New York: Wiley Interscience, 1968).
2 "There is within every utopian a sleeping Le Corbusier, who would willingly, like the eminent architect, propose the project to replace Paris ... with thirty skyscrapers. Conversely, within every urbanist there is a utopian who asks only to be awakened."
3 Raymond Ruyer, *L'utopie et les utopies* (Paris: PUF, 1950), 43.
4 *Architectural Design*, 39 (October 1969).
5 Kenneth Frampton, "The City of Dialectic," *Architectural Design*, 39 (October 1969): 541–45.
6 See Mary McLeod, "'Architecture or Revolution': Taylorism, Technocracy, and Social Change," *Art Journal*, 43/2 (1983): 131–47.
7 "Je ne crois pas me trompe en reconnaissant en vous l'héritier de ces architectes Saint-Simoniens, qui entendaient faire nos villes, dans leur plan et leur configuration mêmes, l'image glorifiée de l'homme." Henri Focillon to Le Corbusier, ND. FLC B2-16-178. Cited in Pierre Saddy, ed., *Le Corbusier, le passé à réaction poétique*, exh. cat., Hôtel de Sully, 1987–88 (Paris: Caisse nationale des monuments historiques et des sites, 1988), 235. Focillon and Le Corbusier had in fact met a year before in Venice, in a symposium organized by Focillon for the League of Nations (where, on the topic of the machine, Le Corbusier had lectured on the functional form of the gondola). Focillon ended his letter evoking their shared "Palladian memories of the countryside of Vicenza."
8 See Le Corbusier, *Manière de penser l'urbanisme* (Paris: Éditions d'Architecture d'Aujourd'hui, 1946), 89; "Charles Fourier, premier visionnaire de l'ère machiniste," quoting from Victor Considerant, *Description du phalanstère et considérations sociales sur l'architectonique* [1834] (Paris: Librairie Sociétaire, 1848), 36. See also Peter Serenyi, "Le Corbusier, Fourier and the Monastery of Ema," *Art Bulletin*, 49 (1967): 277–86.
9 Le Corbusier, *Manière de penser l'urbanisme*, 35–36.
10 Jacques Rancière has described this difference as a fault line between the utopia of pure desire, the true no-place, and the utopian desire to build good-place *in* no-place: a contradiction in terms, between the prefix "u" and the "eu," then double negation—"it is not only the nonplace of place, but the nonplace of a non place." Thus, in Rancière's terms, there is a major difference between the dream of a world to come (Fourier) and the will to build it in the real world (Saint-Simonians). See Jacques Rancière, "The Senses and Uses of Utopia," in S.D. Chrostowska and James D. Ingraham, eds., *Political Uses of Utopia: New Marxist, Anarchist, and Radical Democratic Perspectives* (New York: Columbia University Press, 2016), 220; originally published as "Sens et usages de l'utopie," in *Raison Présente*, 121/1 (1997).
11 Huxley had cited from Berdiaeff's *Slavery and Freedom* in his epigraph: "Utopias seem much more attainable than one may previously have thought. And now we are faced with a much more frightening thought: how do we prevent their permanent fulfillment?" Aldous Huxley, *Brave New World*, from Nicolas Berdiaeff, *Slavery and Freedom*, trans. R.M. French (New York: Scribners and Sons, 1944).
12 Karl Popper, *The Open Society and its Enemies*, I (London: Routledge, 1945), 200.
13 Karl Popper, *The Poverty of Historicism* [1937] (London and New York: Routledge, 2002), 58–69.
14 Pierre Francastel, *Art et technique aux XIVe et XXe siècles* (Paris: Éditions de Minuit, 1956), 334–35.
15 See, for example, the special issue on utopia of the Cambridge review *Granta* (January 24, 1959), edited by James Cornford and including an article by Colin Rowe, "The Architecture of Utopia."

16 Robert Taylor and Tom Steele, *British Labour and Higher Education, 1945–2000: Ideologies, Policies and Practice* (London: Continuum International, 2011), 67.
17 Colin Rowe, "The Architecture of Utopia," *Granta*, 63 (January 24, 1959): 20–26.
18 "Utopia Supplement," *Granta*, 63 (January 24, 1959): 19–39.
19 Colin Rowe, "Addendum 1973" to "The Architecture of Utopia" [1959] in *The Mathematics of the Ideal Villa and Other Essays* (Cambridge, MA.: MIT Press, 1976), 215.
20 Kenneth Frampton, "Labour, Work, and Architecture," *Meaning in Architecture*, ed. George Baird and Charles Jencks (London: Barrie & Rockliff, the Cresset Press, 1969, 1970).
21 Kenneth Frampton, "The City of Dialectic," 541.

Kenneth Frampton: Apropos Housing and Cities

Richard Plunz

Although sometimes sublimated in diverse other questions, housing design has always been a key consideration within Frampton's critical assessments of modern architecture. In this, he is clearly aligned with those who value housing, and especially social housing, as a driving force in architectural innovation. Frampton's advocacy has been important in the American context, which on the whole has tended to exclude social housing from mainstream architectural discourse.

With the arrival of Kenneth Frampton in the architecture faculty at Columbia University in 1972, a robust initiative on "housing and cities" became important in the evolution of a new curriculum with a new generation of faculty. It seemed obvious that housing design could be a strategic thread in reweaving a new six-semester graduate design studio sequence. A number of options were tested, culminating in the third-semester housing studio being instituted in fall 1978 as an anchor midway in the curriculum,[1] a position that it still holds some forty years later.

Frampton played a crucial role in these deliberations, which included new housing design studios, sometimes in collaboration with myself and with other new faculty. And there were important related initiatives.[2] Already in fall 1973, at Frampton's suggestion, I offered a housing studio on "Extramural Manhattan. Low-Rise High Density." At the same time, in his writings he was referencing the "Alternative Suburbia" project at Penn State that I had completed previously.[3] Simultaneously, he was involved with the Urban Development Corporation (UDC) team that produced the low-rise, high-density Marcus Garvey Park Village housing in Brooklyn.[4] In the following year we jointly taught a housing studio focused on another UDC site in Harlem, under consideration for a similar development. "Low-rise" strategies continued to be a studio focus, including the semesters of spring 1978 in Harlem, spring 1979 in Coney Island, and spring 1981 for an "urban suburbia."[5] In fall 1975, with the initiation of a Rockefeller Foundation grant, the housing curriculum initiatives were expanded to an interdisciplinary seminar focused on the future of "Public Housing," with related studios, taught by myself in that semester and in spring 1976, both of which centered on New York City Housing Authority site redevelopment strategies.[6]

Which brings me to the 1977 lecture that Frampton and I jointly gave as part of a Rockefeller-funded project.[7] Under the rubric of "Emerging Directions in Housing Design," our focus was on low-rise, high-density case studies. I concentrated on the continuing relevance of the eighteenth-century prototypes deployed at the Bourbon utopian industrial town at San Leucio, near Naples, that I had studied previously.[8]

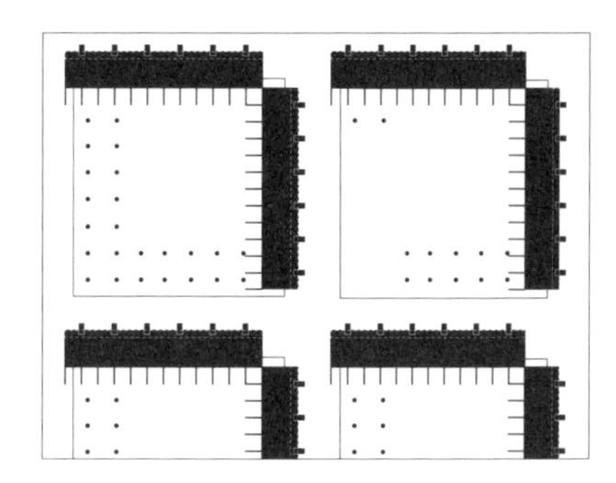

76, 77 Giancarlo De Carlo's Matteotti housing, 1970–75, at Terni, Italy (left), and James Stirling's Southgate housing, 1967–76, at Runcorn, Cheshire, England (right); fabrics at comparative scale.

Frampton focused on two recent European housing projects: Giancarlo De Carlo's 800-unit Matteotti complex at Terni, Italy, and James Stirling's 1,500-unit Southgate complex at Runcorn, Cheshire, England (**76–77**). Frampton's analysis captured well his concern with formal typologies and design methods, an approach that in many ways had been prefigured in his course, "Comparative Critical Analysis of Built Form," first taught at Columbia in 1973–74 and for many years thereafter.[9] Although Frampton's lecture centered on the design issues inherent to the Runcorn and Matteotti projects, his introduction revealed the extraordinary degree to which he could connect to larger questions related to global context, principally what he saw as the "crisis of the city." By 1977 there was an abundance of arguments to support crisis scenarios from the social sciences and urban planning, but it was Frampton's particular integration of the question within a tight formal typological analysis that stood out.

Frampton chose to introduce the lecture with a synopsis of a widely read paper by the economist Kenneth Boulding, which had been published in *Ekistics* in 1962 and was titled "The Death of the City: A Frightened Look at Post-Civilization."[10] It was an important "early warning" about the consequences of the emerging dominance of consumer culture and de-urbanization in the U.S. Boulding speculated that cities were suffering a transition from "civilization" to "post-civilization," with disruption and disturbance and "no end ... at present in sight." All of the conditions that gave rise to the "classical city" were said to have changed. Boulding's reasoning was prescient and related to what can now be seen as anthropogenic in nature; within a decade, for example, a prognosis affirmed by the determinations of the Club of Rome.[11] Boulding cited the impact of the automobile as a principal catalyst for the irreversible transformation of cities, a scenario given credibility by the transportation modeling of the English economist Ezra Mishan.[12] It was Boulding's scenario that Frampton chose to enunciate as it related to housing typology, with particular emphasis on urban fabric coherence as an antidote to the dispersive effect of the automobile. Within the realm of architecture, few other such critical connections come to mind, although as Frampton has noted, Serge Chermayeff and Christopher Alexander's *Community and Privacy* was important, although with little effect on the paucity of legislation to curtail "universal automobile ownership and rampant land speculation."[13]

Runcorn and Matteotti provided good catalysts for this discussion, in that both proposed low-rise, high-density enclaves while attempting to ameliorate the spatial disruption caused by the private automobile. They represented fundamentally different approaches, methodologically and typologically, with formal outcomes that indeed addressed Frampton's particular interest in how "architects' methods of working" affect the "loss of the city." The planning of both Runcorn and Matteotti was intended to be derivative of historic fabrics. Runcorn attempted a rather strict two-directional gridiron, in reference to eighteenth-century English Georgian residential squares that Stirling apparently admired.[14] But unlike the layout of the Georgian square, at Runcorn each square was contiguous to adjacent squares, such that the housing had to negotiate front and rear adjacencies, solved with repetitive "L" configurations. The ground plane of each square was defined by two sides of residential frontage and two sides of rear residential yards.[15] By contrast, Matteotti deployed linear strips of housing that could more flexibly interact with one another and the ground plane.[16]

Frampton began his formal discourse with the historical contexts of "traditional" and "modern" housing design. He contrasts the Georgian residential square (specifically citing "Bath") with the parallel rows of twentieth-century *zeilenbau* strip housing (specifically citing the "Weimar Republic"). He then argues that, as hybrids, both Runcorn and Matteotti represented neither and points to the difficulties of transformation, especially at Runcorn, where the spatial and social coherence of the traditional square was totally lost. As regards Matteotti, he is critical of the reinterpretation of the *zeilenbau* as a kind of "ragged operation," including the block ends. He contrasts the approach of De Carlo, which he argued lacked concern for the traditional city, with that of Stirling, which was too influenced by the traditional city. In both he sees "struggle."

Which brings us to Boulding's question of the automobile, and its disruption of traditional urban form. In both Runcorn and Matteotti, the necessity of automobile penetration was accepted, but with vertical sectional separation such that the traditional street was removed, with the automobile dominating the ground level and an upper level devoted exclusively to pedestrians, to the great detriment of "social gathering places." In this consideration, Matteotti deployed a more flexible section, with several options for how the automobile was to be integrated and housing accessed. Runcorn was without recourse, with "bridge streets" as a separation device. Frampton argued that the "street in the air" approach is a "nightmare legacy" and a problem that would plague housing design in the future.

Stirling was obliged to accept the conventions of British New Town planning, beginning with site selection as mandated by the Colin Buchanan 1963 report, *Traffic in Towns*,[17] which prioritized the automobile as a crucial transportation component: "the motor vehicle is here to stay." And Stirling was forced to respond to the strictures of the *Runcorn Master Plan*,[18] with its emphasis on the design of a "total environment," including the formulas for unit standards and configuration that were largely bureaucratic and universal, intended for an anonymous tenantry, such that the eventual occupants would have nothing to say about the character of the housing either before or after construction. This, when merged with Stirling's interest in prefabrication, could easily lead to a rather deterministic approach: what Frampton would characterize as a "contradictory juxtaposition of states."

By contrast, the circumstances at Matteotti allowed De Carlo to pursue an elaborate process for examining the programming objectives in conversation with the eventual occupants. For many years De Carlo had advocated "participation" in the design process, with housing as the most important priority for this process. By participation he meant straightforward joint collaboration such that architects plan *with* people, not *for* people. His manifesto to this effect, on "Legitimizing Architecture," was first published in *Parametro* in 1970 and was widely influential. His widely repeated admonition was that "architecture is too important to leave to architects," although he cautioned that "nevertheless, the world can never do without architecture."[19] The question was "whose architecture?"[20] Frampton had referenced the article in 1975 in a largely positive review of the Matteotti project.[21]

De Carlo's working method for Matteotti was his most elaborate manifestation of "participation." In collaboration with the sociologist Domenico De Masi, he managed to gain access to the future tenants through a negotiation with the private steel company, Italsider, which was building the project for its workers. The participation process developed the scheme for 800 homes, examining forty-five typological alternatives during "two months of daily meetings, one in the morning and one in the afternoon, which about seventy people at a time attended ... until over three thousand people were involved."[22] The apartments were conceived as being flexible, such that partition layouts could be altered in response to changing tenant needs.

With his "participation" strategies, De Carlo was defining protocols within this tendency in Europe. Slightly earlier in the U.S., a similar "participation" movement had evolved as "advocacy planning."[23] In 1972, the Dutch periodical *Forum*, which had earlier published De Carlo's "manifesto," devoted another issue entirely to "advocacy planning" with an emphasis on New York City.[24] In the U.S. "advocacy planning" had initially been encouraged by the Omnibus Housing Act of 1960 (S-3497), with the design professions most widely affected by the section under "Urban Renewal (Title V)," usually referred to as the Neighborhood Development Program, or NDP.[25] It was intended to engage urban communities in making decisions regarding design and construction. This provision was accomplished through the mandatory formation of "Project Area Committees" ("PAC Groups"). They were composed of community residents who were to serve as participants in expediting the work, and they were granted resources with which to hire professional advisers. Architects and planners were incentivized through federal government subsidies to work directly in empowering communities to control design decisions, an aspect that attracted many young graduates. Some 150 of these "community design workshops" were initiated. Academic participation was strong, leading to the optimism found at euphoric moments like the AIA-ASCA Teachers' Seminar devoted to "advocacy" in San Francisco in October 1969, with the enthusiastic participation of Frampton.[26] By 1970, however, the Nixon administration had already begun to drastically reduce the funding.[27] And by 1971 Frampton would observe that "there are dedicated twilight careers in advocacy planning where the agonies and ecstasies of community participation can be experienced in all their purity; often to no avail."[28]

With a significant degree of success in both the design process and in the occupation outcome, Matteotti had no equal in the U.S. In 1986 De Carlo related that "the families living in the Matteotti houses seem to have found their way to change the space into their place. They trusted the architectural configuration and began to inhabit it with intensity and perhaps some happiness." Today, many of the original families remain and are pleased with the maturation of both the social and natural environments, and have positive memories of both De Carlo and De Masi.[29] De Carlo had other concerns, primarily with the Italsider company managers, who did not allow completion of the project out of a fear that "the workers start with having a voice on the quality of their subsidized housing and then may end by asking to discuss the finality of their work." He also pointed to the public agencies who saw no reason for the "differentiated structure when long slabs or squat towers are proved to do very well." And he reserved comments for "some historians and critics of architecture ... [who] found it hard to range the Matteotti project on the chess-boards of types ... [and that it was not] synoptically classifiable in the books and magazines."[30]

Perhaps it was true that for most critics Runcorn was an easier read than Matteotti, and it received more immediate attention in the mainstream architectural media. As far as aesthetics was concerned, De Carlo's was not the rigid and hard-edged aesthetic of Stirling, but a kind of "ragged" assembly that his fellow Genovese, Renzo Piano, found to "have the virtue of managing to make cement soar, with its bridges and gardens, shattering the compositional rhythm, bursting it into a thousand fragments."[31] Indeed, there was some hint of a cultural distance at play between European Anglo and Latin cultures. De Carlo was the only Italian member of Team 10; in 1976 he organized the International Laboratory of Architecture and Urban Design (or ILAUD), undoubtedly in part out of frustration with the Team 10 milieu.[32]

Looking at Runcorn and Matteotti today, one realizes just how profound Frampton's critical dialogue was, and still is. His premonitions on the difficulties of Runcorn proved correct. By 1981 Stirling had received his Pritzker Prize, with little or no mention of Runcorn, already in precarious straits due to social dysfunction, exacerbated by typological and maintenance difficulties. Stirling blamed the constraints of the original Southgate Corporation brief that had suggested it was illogical to build housing in a new town using traditional means.[33] By 1990 demolition had begun. What scant notice its demolition received from mainstream architectural media was devoted to blaming the bureaucratic imperatives, more than the underlying design typology.[34] By contrast, however, Frampton remained insistent about the design conflicts first mentioned in his 1977 lecture. In a Stirling postmortem, he mentions, with some further clarity, the building's "front-to-back" issues and its corruption of the "morphological clarity" of the Georgian terrace, while shifting some culpability to the role of Léon Krier and German staff in Stirling's office.[35]

Although the 800 units at Matteotti would never be completed, Frampton included the project in his first edition (1980) of *Modern Architecture: A Critical History*, with "no doubt that this whole undertaking has resulted in housing of remarkable quality and variety, although the manner in which the users' desires were finally interpreted remains a controversial issue."[36] It is not clear which controversy is referenced, but incontrovertibly, the built fragment that remains today is as positive an exemplar for "emerging directions" as it was in 1977. One can imagine Ken's 1977 lecture being given only yesterday, but with added relevance today, given the present state of city and planet, and with the automobile still complicit in our accelerating anthropogenic condition. And to return to Boulding and the automobile, it is still safe to say that there is "no end ... at present in sight." As far as the third-semester Columbia housing studio is concerned, it is still with us. "Typology" was abandoned in its second trial year, quickly reestablished and then challenged by "phenomenology" toward the end of the 1980s, and is back again today, although in a much-mutated form. Experimentation on "low-rise" housing has remained, and the difficulties of integration of automobiles have had few takers among students and faculty.

Perhaps only from this point will the next decades witness a changing nature of the individual automobile. With enhanced social media and on-demand cars, perhaps things will more easily resolve themselves, without the necessity for the automobile to be slavishly integrated within living and public spaces. In Boulding's self-described "science fictional" scenarios for the future, the car does not retreat. But perhaps in the next seven decades, should anthropogenic considerations permit, there will be other options to consider; and Boulding did advocate that "in these days one must not despise science fiction as a way of keeping up with the news." As for Frampton, he has succeeded well in satisfying his often-repeated desire to "keep certain history alive."

1 The early Columbia housing studio curricula are found in Richard Plunz Papers, Department of Drawings & Archives, Avery Architectural and Fine Arts Library, Columbia University. A partial record of the early Graduate School of Architecture, Planning, and Preservation (GSAPP) housing studios also exists in the student publication, *Precis*, 1 (Spring 1979), 2 (1980), and 3 (1981).

2 I had joined the Columbia faculty in fall 1973, and became Acting Chair of the Division of Architecture by 1977, during this period of curriculum development.
3 Richard Plunz and Lawrence Regan, *Housing Manual for an Alternative Suburbia* (University Park, PA: Department of Architecture, The Pennsylvania State University, Spring 1971). On Frampton's suggestion, excerpts were published in the Italian review *Lotus* as "Alternative Suburbia. A Retrospective Rationalization," *Lotus International*, 10 (1975): 18–23. Frampton also made the argument for low-rise high density in the same number: "The Evolution of Housing Concepts 1870–1970," *Lotus International*, 10 (1975): 24–33.
4 See *Another Chance for Housing: Low-rise Alternatives; Brownsville, Brooklyn, Fox Hills, Staten Island*, exh. cat., Museum of Modern Art, New York, June 12–August 19, 1973 (New York: Institute for Architecture and Urban Studies for the New York State Urban Development Corporation, 1973). Also see Suzanne Frank, *IAUS, the Institute for Architecture and Urban Studies: An Insider's Memoir* (Bloomington, MN: Author House, 2010), 91–96.
5 Detailed early Columbia housing studio curricula are found in Richard Plunz Papers, Box 4, Donation 2004.02. See Folders A4006 Spring 1973; A4105 Fall 2074; A4006 Spring 1978; A4006 Spring 1979; A4006 Spring 1980; A4006 Spring 1981. For the first third-semester housing studios see Folders A4003 Fall 1982 and A4003 Fall 1983.
6 See Richard Plunz Papers: Folders AA4105 Comprehensive Studio V Fall 1975; A4106 Comprehensive Studio VI Spring 1976. Also see Richard Plunz, ed., *Housing Form and Public Policy in the United States* (New York: Praeger, 1980), ch. 16.
7 Kenneth Frampton and Richard Plunz, "Emerging Directions in Housing Design," lecture transcript for Architecture A4415y: The Future of American Housing Policy, March 31, 1977. Richard Plunz Papers, Box 3, Donation 2004.022. The Rockefeller grant was followed by a National Endowment for the Humanities grant in 1980 for development of a housing studies curriculum. See Plunz Papers, Box 1, Folder 39. Donation 2004.022. For a brief overview of the early GSAPP housing initiatives, see Marta Gutman, "The Housing Studio: Theory and Practice," *Precis*, 3 (1981): 44–45.
8 Richard Plunz, ed., *San Leucio: Vitalità d'una tradizione; Traditions in Transition* (New York: George Wittenborn and Company, 1973).
9 An extensive documentation of the seminar is found in Kenneth Frampton, *A Genealogy of Modern Architecture: Comparative Critical Analysis of Built Form*, ed. Ashley Simone (Zurich: Lars Müller Publishers, 2015). According to Frampton the genesis of the course was at Princeton. See Richard Oliver, ed., *The Making of an Architect, 1881–1981* (New York: Rizzoli, 1981), 255.
10 The paper was presented at the Conference on the City and History at Harvard in July 1961, and immediately published in *Ekistics*, the Doxiadis journal devoted to the "science of human settlements." Kenneth E. Boulding, "The Death of the City: A Frightened Look at Post-Civilization," *Ekistics*, 13/75 (January 1962): 19–22.
11 Donella H. Meadows, et al., eds., *The Limits to Growth: A Report for the Club of Rome's Project on the Predicament of Mankind* (New York: Universe Books, 1972).
12 The "Mishan Model" argued the irreversibility of the proliferation of the automobile once a critical mass is achieved. See Ezra Mishan, Appendix C, "A Note on the Interpretation of the Benefits of Private Transport," *The Costs of Economic Growth* (New York: Praeger, 1967).
13 Serge Chermayeff and Christopher Alexander, *Community and Privacy: Toward a New Architecture of Humanism* (Garden City, NY: Doubleday, 1963), 25. They had used an excerpt from Boulding and were undoubtedly on Frampton's mind, although by 1992 he noted that this "first extensively posited ... reformist strategy" had been to no avail. See Kenneth Frampton, *Modern Architecture: A Critical History*, 3rd edition (New York and London: Thames & Hudson, 1992), 342.
14 While it is difficult to trace the origins of Stirling's interest in the Georgian square, Werner Seligman described this antecedent for Runcorn planning in some detail in "Runcorn: Historical Precedent and the Rational Design Process," *Oppositions*, 7 (Winter 1976–77): 8–23.
15 An early detailed contemporary description of the Runcorn design was published as "Town Centre Housing. Runcorn New Town," *Lotus International*, 10 (March 1975): 105–23. Also see "Housing: Runcorn New Town," *Architectural Review*, 160/997 (November 1976): 282–88.
16 Frampton published (with Brian Brace Taylor) an early detailed description of the Matteotti design in the "Team 10 Plus 20" special issue, *L'Architecture d'Aujourd'hui*, 177 (January 1975): 38–43. Also see "Il nuovo villaggio Matteotti a Terni: una esperienza di partecipazione," *Casabella*, 41/997 (January 1977): 11–35.
17 Sir Geoffrey Crowther, et al., *Traffic in Towns: A Study of the Long Term Problems of Traffic in Urban*

Areas; Reports of the Steering Group and Working Group Appointed by the Minister of Transport (London: HMSO, 1963).

18 Arthur G. Ling, *Runcorn New Town: Master Plan; prepared for the Runcorn Development Corporation, with a Foreword by Vere A. Arnold* (Runcorn: Runcorn Development Corporation, 1967). For a summary of the bureaucratic constraints see Anthony Vidler, *James Frazer Stirling: Notes from the Archive* (New Haven, CT: Yale University Press for the Canadian Centre for Architecture and Yale Center for British Art, 2010), 164–65.

19 Giancarlo De Carlo, "Legitimizing Architecture: Revolt and the Frustration of the School of Architecture," *Parametro*, 1/3–4 (1970): 4–12, 98. It also appeared as "Legitimizing Architecture" in *Forum. Amsterdam*, 23/1 (1972): 3–20, within an entire issue devoted to De Carlo. A more recent, reedited translation is found in Peter Blundell Jones, Doina Petrescu, and Jeremy Till, eds., *Architecture and Participation* (London and New York: Spon Press, 2005).

20 Important in this question was Rudolfsky's 1964 MoMA exhibition. See *Architecture Without Architects: An Introduction to Non-pedigreed Architecture* (New York: Museum of Modern Art; distributed by Doubleday, Garden City, NY, 1964). In Italy, an important precedent was Pagano's exhibition in 1935, with the manifesto titled "Architettura Rurale." See *Casabella*, 14 (November 1935): 18–25. An English translation is found in Michelangelo Sabatino, "Pride in Modesty: Giuseppe Pagano's 'Architettura Rurale,'" *Journal of Architectural Education*, 63/2 (March 2010): 92–98. Also see Celia Tuscano, *Team 10: 1953–81, In Search of a Utopia of the Present*, ed. Max Risselada, Dirk Van den Heuvel, Team 10, and Nederlands Architectuurinstituut (Rotterdam: NAi Publishers, 2005), 370–71.

21 See Kenneth Frampton, "The Vicissitudes of Ideology," in "Team 10 Plus 20" special issue.

22 Domenico De Masi, "Participation and Project," *Giancarlo De Carlo: Le ragioni dell'architettura*, ed. Margherita Guccione and Alessandra Vittorini (Milano: Electa; Roma: Ministero per i beni e le attività culturali, Dipartimento per i beni culturali e paesaggistici, 2005). Also see Giancarlo De Carlo, "Afterthoughts on Terni: Reflections on its Participatory Process," *Leuven Seminar on Participatory Design*, ed. Jan Schreurs, Marcel Smets, and Lode Janssens (Leuven: Uitgeverji Acco, 1981), 26–28. And the interview with both De Carlo and De Masi, "Terni: Villaggio Matteotti per Società Terni 1970/1975," *Giancarlo De Carlo, Carlo Aymonino, Aldo Rossi, Vittorio Gregotti: Tre grandi progetti, Quattro grandi architetti, RAI SAT art, 2003*, https://vimeo.com/32628698 (accessed December 15, 2019).

23 A prominent argument for "participation" was the article by Paul Davidoff, "Advocacy and Pluralism in Planning," *AIP Journal* (November 1965), 331–37.

24 "Planning with People: Advocacy in East Harlem," *Forum. Amsterdam*, 23/4 (1972).

25 The plight of advocacy in the U.S., and the author's advocacy initiatives in Philadelphia, are recorded in Folder "Developments: 1968–70," Richard Plunz Papers, Box 5, Donation 2017.009. See also Richard Plunz, "Mini-School: Building with People," *Connection*, Graduate School of Design, Harvard University, 6/3 (Spring 1969), and Richard Plunz, "User Transformation of Pre-Existing Structures at Mantua, San Leucio, and Akcaalan, and How It Can Function to Plan for Future Evolution," *Leuven Seminar on Participatory Design*, ed. Jan Schreurs, et al., 46–49.

26 It was at this event that I first met Frampton, while presenting a paper, "Problems Involving the Academic Use of Community Design Workshops." See "AIA-ASCA Teachers Seminar, San Francisco, October 28, 1969," Richard Plunz Papers, Box 8, Donation 2017.009.

27 For an overview of the NDP program, see Plunz, "Developments: 1968–70." An extensive survey of CDC (Community Design Center) development is found in Henry Sanoff, *Community Participation Methods in Design and Planning* (New York: John Wiley, 2000).

28 Kenneth Frampton, "Polemical Notes on Architectural Education," *Architectural Education U.S.A.: Issues, Ideas, People. A Conference to Explore Current Alternatives* (New York: Museum of Modern Art, 1971).

29 Giancarlo De Carlo, "Terni, Mazzorbo," in *Year Book / International Laboratory of Architecture and Urban Design, ILAUD. 1986–87* (Florence: Sansoni Editore, 1987), 78–79. The author last visited Matteotti in August 2019 and found the project to be remarkedly intact, with a number of original families who were enthusiastic about their long tenures in residence. There were also positive anecdotes about De Carlo and De Masi. What was much in evidence was the deterioration in management and degradation of the public facilities that have suffered from disinvestment in recent years.

30 Ibid. Matteotti remains subject of considerable interest and study. For example, see Virginia De Jorge-Huertas, "Mat-hybrid Housing: Two Case Studies in Terni and London," *Frontiers of Architectural Research*, 7/3 (September 2018): 276–91, https://doi.org/10.1016/j.foar.2018.05.002 (accessed January 7, 2020).

31 Renzo Piano, "I Owe a Great Deal to Giancarlo De Carlo," *Giancarlo De Carlo: Le ragioni dell'architettura*, 22–24.

32 De Carlo's enmity within Team 10 is tracked in Annie Pedret, *Team 10: An Archival History* (New York: Routledge, 2013). Although the Smithsons refused to attend the 1966 Team 10 meeting in Urbino, they were among the few attendees at the 1976 meeting that De Carlo organized at Terni (Spoleto). Contentions apparently included the role of "history" in design practice. Also see Alison Smithson, ed., *Team 10 Meetings* (New York: Rizzoli, 1991), and Celia Tuscano, "International Comparisons: Team 10," in *Giancarlo De Carlo: Le ragioni dell'architettura*, 92–101.

33 "Stirling Says His Hands Were Tied," *Architects' Journal*, 189/9 (March 1, 1989): 9.

34 There was little public accountability as to the underlying causes leading to the razing of Runcorn. One useful source was Brian Hutton, "The Future in Ruins," *Blueprint*, 70 (September 1990): 46–50. Also see Anthony Vidler, *James Frazer Stirling: Notes from the Archive*, 163–64.

35 Kenneth Frampton, "On James Stirling: A Premature Critique," *AA Files*, 26 (Autumn 1993): 4.

36 Kenneth Frampton, *Modern Architecture: A Critical History* (London: Thames & Hudson, 1980), 288. Frampton also cites De Carlo's 1970 "Legitimizing Architecture" manifesto, 278–79.

Proportion and Harmony: Mathematics and Music in Architecture

Juhani Pallasmaa

Mathematical talent has been regarded as a prerequisite for studies in architecture. In *De architectura libri decem* (*Ten Books on Architecture*), the first architectural theorist in history, the Roman Marcus Vitruvius Pollio (84–14 B.C.), gives a long list of skills required of the architect. "Let him be educated, skillful with the pencil, instructed in geometry, know much history, have followed the philosophers with attention, understand music, have some knowledge of medicine, know the opinions of the jurists, and be acquainted with astronomy and the theory of the heavens."[1] He writes a paragraph on each one of these areas of learning and knowledge, and the realm of mathematics enters most concretely through the requirements of being "instructed in geometry," "understanding music," and "being acquainted with astronomy and the theory of the heavens." Vitruvius had especially gathered everything that was known about the art of building in Greece in accordance with the laws of music.[2] The mathematical ground of musical harmony was discovered by Pythagoras (about 569–495 B.C.), and classical Greek temples were proportioned in accordance with musical harmony (for example, the temple of Hera or Poseidon at Paestum). It is thought-provoking to realize that the interactions of architecture and music, based on a shared mathematical ground, are considerably older than Christianity, yet practically lost in the architectural theory, education, and practice in our time. The disappearance of the timeless relational, metaphysical, philosophical, and aesthetic mediation reveals how the art of architecture has gradually lost its connections with the world of cosmic ideas and the spiritual dimensions of human consciousness. In our modern age, it has turned into a secular and practical endeavor, and even beauty has lost its divine and eternal echo and turned increasingly into a manipulative aestheticization.

Mathematics in architecture

A fundamental and regrettable change has also taken place in the role of mathematics in the art of architecture. From the time of Pythagoras of Samos mathematics was part of the inner ideological and metaphysical substructure of architectural thinking and directly related to its higher purposes and meanings: the desire to connect human beings with an ideal world, both physically and mentally, through appropriately proportioned edifices. Architecture aspired to relate human constructions to the cosmic, mythical, and ideal worlds by means of mathematical proportionality that echoed the harmonic principles of the planetary system—the "Music of the Spheres"—the forms and growth patterns of nature, and our own measures and proportions. This mediating and relational role of mathematics in architecture has also been lost, and mathematics is today used only in the practical and technical calculations of structures and other technical systems.

Yet, mathematics and geometry are still part of architectural thinking and design practice in a multitude of ways, but now somewhat unnoticeably. Almost always the processes of construction imply the joining of distinct conceptual or material units or elements to one another in an additive manner. The reverse operation of subdividing larger entities into their constitutive elements—for instance, the total volume into structural units—is equally essential. These are mostly simple arithmetical and geometric routines, but the constant processes of relating units and entities, small parts and larger assemblies, as well as the processes and imageries of assembling and disassembling, are the inner structure of architectural thinking even today. Industrialization of construction has further concretized the idea of architecture as an assembly. The ideological mathematical ground of architecture is expressed in Colin Rowe's book *The Mathematics of the Ideal Villa* (1976), in which he compares the mathematical and geometric basis of the seminal Renaissance villas by Andrea Palladio and the modern houses of Le Corbusier.[3]

Connecting and fusing shapes and volumes requires a basic understanding of geometry, which may get rather complex, as in the case of Baroque and Islamic architectures, or certain projects of our time that are not results of simple additive or subtractive processes, such as Alvar Aalto's Church of the Three Crosses in Vuoksenniska, Finland (1955–58). Altogether, architectural design usually consists of mathematical and geometric operations carried out with material things and objects, structures and volumes. Architecture could be seen as a kind of applied situational, material, and embodied mathematics. The way that facts of physics are fused with beliefs and dreams, and logic with intuition and desire in architecture, makes one also think of alchemy, or "poetic chemistry," to use a notion of Gaston Bachelard.[4] A more demanding use of mathematics is required in the exact calculation of structures and their parts. But the reality of structures is usually dealt with "behind the scenes," as it were. The famous Mexican architect of concrete shell structures, Félix Candela (1910–1997), confessed in our conversation in 1963 that he could not calculate at all. He intuited the structural behavior of his designs, and the structures were engineered by his engineer brother. An example of the opposite relation to mathematics is the American mathematician and architect Richard Buckminster Fuller (1895–1983), whose projects arose from his unique "Dymaxion" and "Tensegrity" geometries. In this case, the mathematical structure is unchallenged and all other aspects, such as functional design and aesthetics, are subordinated. Fuller's structures continue to be the most efficient constructions by humanity in their relation of structural weight to the enclosed volume. These projects are structurally ingenious, but the mathematically perfect structure makes functional practicalities, such as fitting a door, or subdividing space into rooms, rather forced.

The tradition of proportionality

A significant aspect in architectural design is proportion, the aesthetic and metaphysical criteria of the appearance and meaning of architectural entities. Metric and proportional systems have been used in buildings at least since ancient Egyptian times. The Egyptians used two parallel systems of measurement, the royal cubit of 52.5 cm and the normal cubit measuring 45 cm. My professor and mentor Aulis Blomstedt (1906–1979), who was passionately engaged in modular and harmonic studies, calculated the dimensions of the great pyramids of Giza in royal cubits, and the dimensional and proportional logic of the pyramids of Kheops, Khephren and Mykerinus was revealed to be clear and simple; the inherent modularity and proportionality of the structures had been lost in their metric measurements (**79**). As Blomstedt designed a ceremonial golden knife and its juniper wood box for the Japanese Princess Takamatsu to open the exhibition of Finnish architecture in Tokyo in 1967, he dimensioned the object by the ancient Egyptian royal cubit. By the juxtaposition of the Egyptian system of measures, as applied in the great pyramids, on the

78 Pythagoras established the relations between number ratios and sound frequencies. This woodcut shows Pythagoras experimenting with bells, water-glasses, stretched cords, and variously sized pipes. His Hebrew counterpart, Jubal, uses weighted hammers on an anvil.

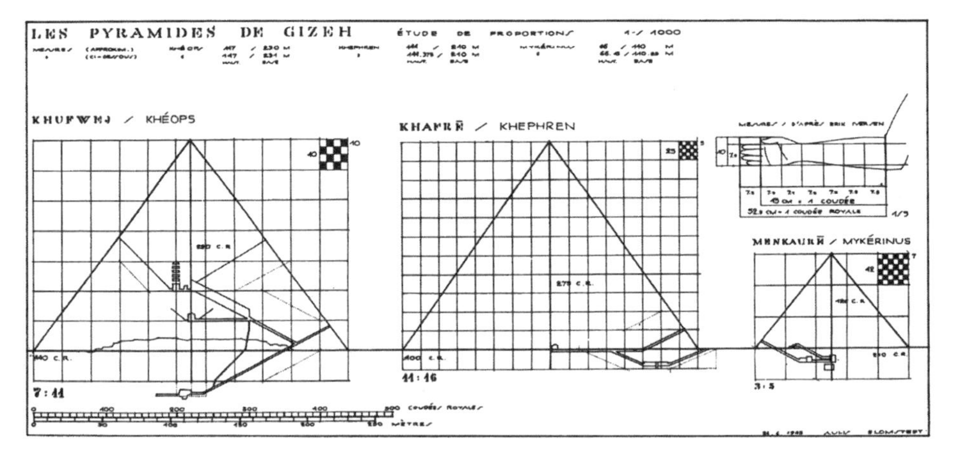

79 Aulis Blomstedt, dimentional and proportional study of the great pyramids of Giza, 1965. He observed that when the dimensions of the pyramids are given in ancient Egyptian royal cubits, the proportions appear very simple. The royal cubit was 52.5 cm, whereas the normal cubit measured only 45 cm.

one hand, and in Blomstedt's jewelry-like golden knife, on the other, I wish to underline the 5,000-year time span of proportional thinking, and the continued relevance of mathematical principles in the crafts of design and architecture, although lost in the ever more complex secular practicalities of today's design practice.

Rationalization of the standard measure

Proportionality, harmony, and metaphysical mediation, as well as the use of different devices or canons to assure dimensional coordination and harmony, were in fact central issues in architecture until the modern age. The ancient systems of measurement were related to the measures of the human body, and the inch and foot measures today still refer to it. However, the unfortunate agreement during the second half of the nineteenth century that the meter would be the universal standard unit of measurement implied a complete loss of the intrinsic connection of measures with the human body. We hardly know that 1 meter is one ten-millionth of the distance between the north pole and the equator through Paris, or 1/299,792,458th part of the distance that light travels in one second. Obviously, this measure has no internal connection with the human figure, sensory reality, or the innate situations in construction or the uses of buildings. This choice marked the secularization of measures and proportions in architecture, whereas relatedness and proportionality had been promoted by ageless practices in design and construction. We must conclude that the metric system is meaningless in the phenomenological sense. The decision on the standard measure took place after the poet John Keats had in 1817 accused scientists like Isaac Newton of having stripped the rainbow of its poetry through turning the magical perceptual phenomenon into a cold scientific fact.[5] This senseless rationalization of the standard measure also marks the detachment of artifacts from their dialogue with the world in any innate and experiential manner, as well as from mathematics as a relational system and mediation between the world and the human mind, the world of ideas and lived reality, the gods and the mortals. Historically, the use of proportional systems was intended to relate human construction with the dimensional logic of the universe through the ancient idea of the "Music of the Spheres." The Enlightenment era, however, turned buildings into solely rational and practical operations without inherent mediating tasks or metaphysical intentions. In the era of scientific classifications in the early nineteenth century, Jean-Nicolas-Louis Durand in France developed a fully rationalized system of architecture similar to Antoine Lavoisier's system of chemical phenomena and Carl Linnaeus's classification of flora. Architecture was here turned into a rational operation of joining together predefined units, either material or stylistic.

I am saddened to confess that today I do not know of a single school of architecture that would teach the ancient science of harmony, the oldest Western scientific tradition—although it is still taught in musical academies. Has architecture cut its ties with both the lived and idealized world? Yes, it has, and in doing that, it has turned from an art into a mere speculative service profession, which becomes increasingly aestheticized and self-centered. Architecture has become part of the "aesthetic capitalism" of consumer culture, to use a notion of philosopher Gernot Böhme.[6] This is the strategy of expanding consumption through aesthetic aging and repeated rejection of products and buildings.

The tradition of Pythagoreanism

Early Western architectural thinking was fundamentally based on the ideas of the great Greek mathematician and geometrician Pythagoras of the sixth century B.C. During the subsequent 2,600 years, the relations of architecture and mathematics have been decisively mediated through theories of music. Pythagoras discovered the numerical foundations of musical consonances using mainly the monocord as his research instrument. Pythagoreanism was developed, practiced, and guarded by secret societies, and their metaphysical reasoning remained largely a secret. However, in the second century after Christ, these ideas reemerged for a short period, but the Pythagorean science was again soon forgotten until Johannes Kepler (1571–1630), the mathematician and astronomer, dedicated most of his life to advancing the Pythagorean idea of the harmony of the spheres and to proving the mathematical and harmonical base of the universe. Yet Kepler is known primarily for his discoveries in astronomy, especially his three planetary laws.

The use of harmonizing systems had continued during the Middle Ages, as the construction of major buildings, especially of cathedrals, was dimensioned through harmonical devices, such as the Helicon Canon from ancient Greece, the medieval *quatratura*, and Villard's Diagram, devised by Villard de Honnecourt (the so-called "Sketchbook" of Villard dates to *c*. 1225–35). Villard's Diagram included musical equivalents for measures and proportions.[7] Although the diagram appears as a mystical alchemical device, it was related to musical harmony through Pythagorean harmonics. Studying architectural issues in the historical practice of alchemy, in the manner of James Elkin's *What is Painting: How to Think about Oil Painting Using the Language of Alchemy*,[8] could well reveal hidden ideas of architecture in medieval building practices and the internal sources of the extraordinary beauty of medieval architecture. Alchemy can be seen as a "soft science" or "spiritual science," comparable to Johann Wolfgang von Goethe's "Delicate Empiricism" (*Zarte Empirie*),[9] and it could valorize the hard-edged logic and scientific violence that we nowadays believe in and practice.

Harmonical principles of the Renaissance

Pythagorean ideas of harmonic proportionality and relatedness to human measures in architecture and music resurfaced in Renaissance times. Also, the famous "Vitruvian Man," which relates the human figure to the circle and the square, was redrawn by Leonardo da Vinci in 1487, and his version became symbolic of Renaissance humanist research and science. The origin of Leonardo's proportional scheme in Vitruvius, more than 1,500 years earlier, has not always been acknowledged regardless of the very title of Leonardo's drawing and his notes on the origin of his scheme. The great architects and architectural theorists of the Renaissance, Leon Battista Alberti (1404–1472) and Andrea Palladio (1508–1580), studied and demonstrated proportional harmony in architecture and its parallels in the field of music. In his treatise, *De re aedificatoria libri decem* (*Ten Books on Architecture*, 1443–52), Alberti assumes that harmony is not the result of individual aesthetic caprice, but of objective reasoning. A uniform system of proportion, based on the system of musical harmony developed by Pythagoras, should be maintained in all parts of a building. When discussing the correspondence of musical intervals and architectural proportions, Alberti stated, referring to Pythagoras, that "the numbers by means of which the agreement of sounds affects our ears with delight, are the very same which please our eyes and our minds," continuing: "We shall therefore borrow all our rules for harmonic relations from the musicians to whom such numbers are extremely well known."[10] This has also been the position of Hans Kayser (1891–1964), Aulis Blomstedt and other neo-Pythagoreans. "What is acceptable in music, must also satisfy architecture," Blomstedt remarked in his notebook.[11]

The mathematical arts

According to the authoritative scholar of the Renaissance, Rudolf Wittkower (1901–1971), "There was an unbroken tradition coming down from antiquity according to

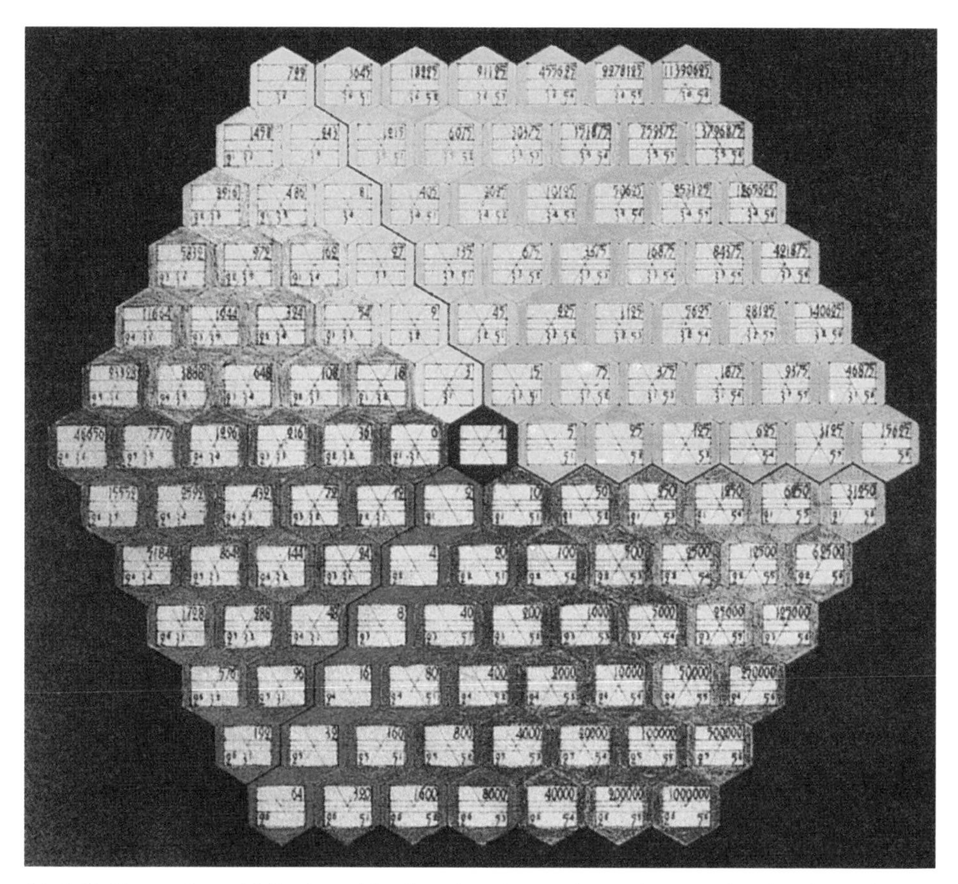

80 Aulis Blomstedt, multiplication table of numbers 2, 3, and 5 in a hexagonal grid. Colors indicate the numerical interaction of the three numbers. Undated.

which arithmetic (the study of numbers), geometry (the study of spatial relationships), astronomy (the study of the motions of celestial bodies), and music (the study of the motions apprehended by the ear), formed a *quadrivium* of the 'mathematical arts.'"[12] By contrast to these, the "liberal arts" of painting, sculpture, and architecture were regarded as manual occupations. In order to raise their identity from the level of the mechanical to that of the liberal arts, "They had to be given a firm theoretical, i.e. mathematical foundation, and that could be found in musical theory," Wittkower continues.[13] It is interesting to notice that in addition to the ideological and theoretical issues, the association of architecture with music, and its harmonic system, also had a political ground; architects wished their art to be recognized as a "mathematical art."

Since the late 1960s, the architectural profession throughout the world has increasingly abandoned its association with relational cultural signification and the fine arts by presenting its practice in professionalist, technical, and economic terms as a service of expertise. I wish to state as a reminder that already Vitruvius had listed music and mathematics among the fields of knowledge required of the architect.

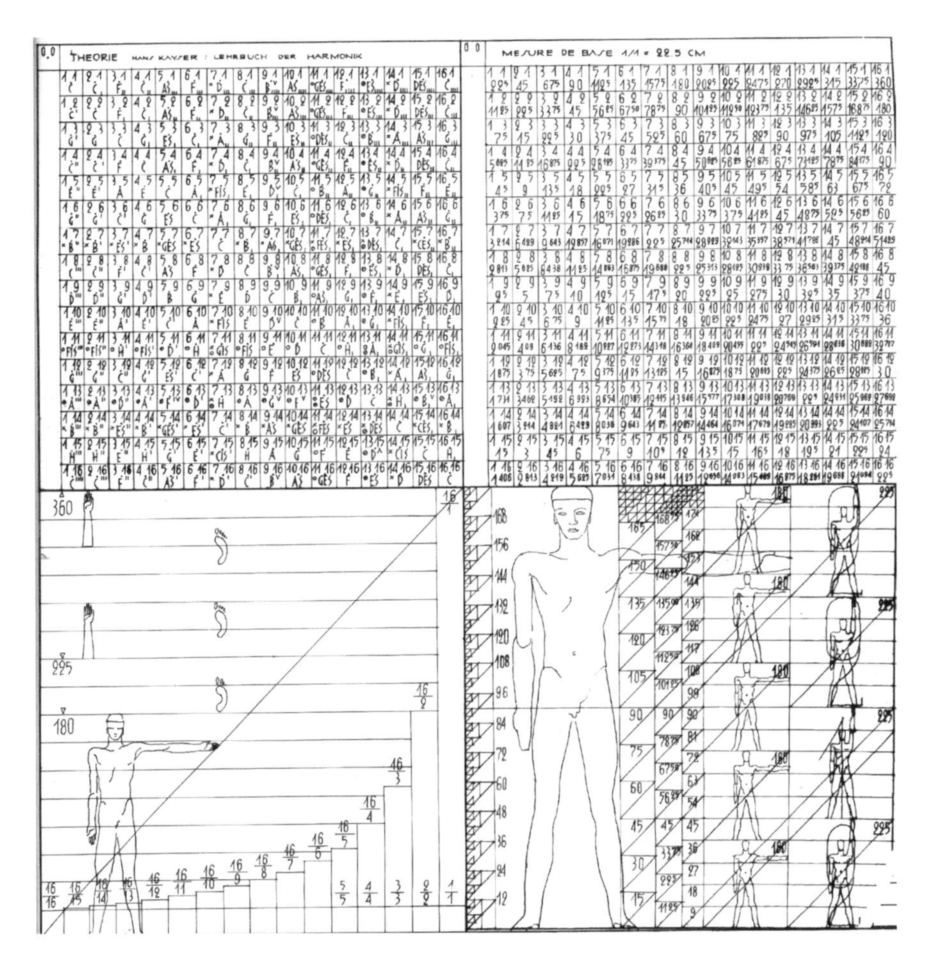

81 Aulis Blomstedt, Hans Kayser's Pythagorean harmonics applied to the human figure. Initial conceptions for an issue of the magazine *Le Carré Bleu*, presumably in 1958 when the theoretically oriented architecture magazine was founded in Finland.

The association of architecture and music was also made by the two German philosophers Friedrich von Schelling (1775–1854) and Johann Wolfgang von Goethe (1749–1832) in their definition of architecture as "frozen music" and music as "liquid architecture"; these expressions are usually credited to Goethe, but Schelling appears to have coined this idea earlier.[14] The research on harmony has been notably continued, expanded, and refined in the Academy of Music in Vienna through the life's works of Hans Kayser and his successor Rudolf Haase (1920–2013).

The golden section

At the time of the Renaissance a competing proportional system emerged, which has been called "The Golden Rule," "The Golden Section," or "The Divine Proportion."

It is evident that the golden section had already been known to the first Pythagorean circles. It is known that the school of Pythagoras was particularly fascinated by the geometric volume of the dodecahedron, which is related to the golden section. The dodecahedron is one of the five regular convex solids circumscribed by a sphere. In the antique way of thinking, its twelve regular facets corresponded to the twelve signs of the zodiac and thus it was the symbol of the universe. The point of intersection of the diagonals of the pentagon in the dodecahedron divides each diagonal into the golden section, and this would presumably have been noticed by the Pythagoreans. Alberti does not mention the golden section at all in his canonical *Ten Books on Architecture*. However, the golden section was reintroduced to the studies in harmony by Leonardo's friend Luca Paccioli (1445–1517), a gifted mathematician who wrote in his study *Divina proportione*: "First we shall talk of the proportions of man, because from the human body derive all measures and their denominations and in it is to be found all and every ratio, and proportion by God reveals the innermost secrets of nature."[15] Leonardo illustrated the book of his mathematician friend, published in 1509, and there have even been suggestions that Luca Paccioli's fine portrait (attributed to Jacopo de' Barbari (*c.* 1495) in the Capodimonte Museum in Naples) was painted by Leonardo. It is interesting to note that from its earlier cosmic perspective, related to the "Music of the Spheres," the harmonic system turned strongly to the human figure, as authoritatively illustrated by Leonardo's drawing. This seems to echo the novel human-centered thinking of the era. Leonardo also added a ratio of the golden section to the proportions of his scheme inherited from Vitruvius; the navel divides the overall measure of the man in the proportion of the golden section.

Wittkower writes: "With Renaissance revival of the Greek mathematical interpretation of God and the world, and invigorated by the Christian belief that man as the image of God embodied the harmonies of the Universe, the Vitruvian human figure inscribed in a square and a circle became a symbol of the mathematical sympathy between microcosm and macrocosm."[16] This image became also symbolic of the mathematical reality concealed in architecture. Renaissance artists adhered to the Pythagorean view that "all is number," and referring to the writings of Plato and the Neoplatonists, supported by a number of theologians beginning with Augustine, they were convinced of the mathematical and harmonic structure of the universe and all creation. To Paccioli, "even the divine functions are of little value if the church had not been built in accordance with correct proportions."[17] Placing architectural proportions above the Word and the liturgy indicates the high value placed on the mathematical ground of building.

Over the centuries, numerous scientists, scholars, and artists have investigated the presence of the golden section in the ratios, growth patterns, and rhythms of both organic and inorganic nature, as well as works of art. Regardless of the harmonic essence of musical consonances, the golden section also appears to be concealed in the harmonic overtones of music. The most notable supporter of the golden section in the twentieth century was undoubtedly Le Corbusier (1887–1965), whose influence can be seen everywhere in modern city planning, architecture, and theory. In 1954 Le Corbusier published a system of measures and proportions, which he called "Modulor," the golden module.[18] He actually used numbers of the Fibonacci series, which are approximations of numbers and ratios of the golden rule (golden section). He characterized his invention as "A range of harmonious measures to suit the human scale, universally applicable to architecture and mechanical things." In 1946 Le Corbusier had traveled to meet Albert Einstein at Princeton in order to gain the opinion of the mathematician–physicist genius on his invention. In the evening of their meeting Einstein sent Le Corbusier a note: "It's a set of proportions that makes the bad difficult and the good easy." Numerous architects after Le Corbusier have used—and are using—the golden section in dimensioning their buildings, most notably Steven Holl.

There are numerous studies that aspire to prove that the golden section is the proportional system in nature—nature's pattern of growth—as well as in different artistic phenomena, but Pythagoreans deny that claim and argue that the proofs are consequences of imprecise measurements. This was the view of Hans Kayser, and he spoke of "the specter of the golden section." Kayser, professor of harmonics at the Academy of Music in Vienna, was the most authoritative supporter of the Pythagorean ideas of harmonical proportions in the modern era with his remarkably thorough books, *Akróasis: The Theory of World Harmonics* (1950) and the monumental *Lehrbuch der Harmonik* (*Textbook of Harmonics*, 1950).[19] Kayser stated that it was unreasonable to assume that the visual aesthetic system of proportions would be based on the irrational golden section ratio (0.618 ...), and the auditory system of music on precise rational ratios, especially when the real differences between the two ratios are so small that the eye can hardly perceive them. The ear, on the other hand, differentiates the golden section ratios as discords.

Aulis Blomstedt's studies in harmony

I have already mentioned Aulis Blomstedt's remarkable studies in harmony. His interest in the use of modules in architecture was aroused during World War II by a lecture of Ernst Neufert in Helsinki on the octameter system, based on the 12.5 cm module. As I argued earlier, the decisions on the meter as the standard measure, and the later universal modular system based on the 10 cm module, regrettably lost entirely the significance of proportionality and the relational and mediating meaning of measures in architecture; measures turned into mere numbers. The Finnish Association of Architects was active in developing ideas and practices of standardization and the Standardization Institute of the Association was officially established in 1942.[20] The need to standardize construction practices was heightened by the immense reconstruction tasks after the war, which also instigated the industrialization

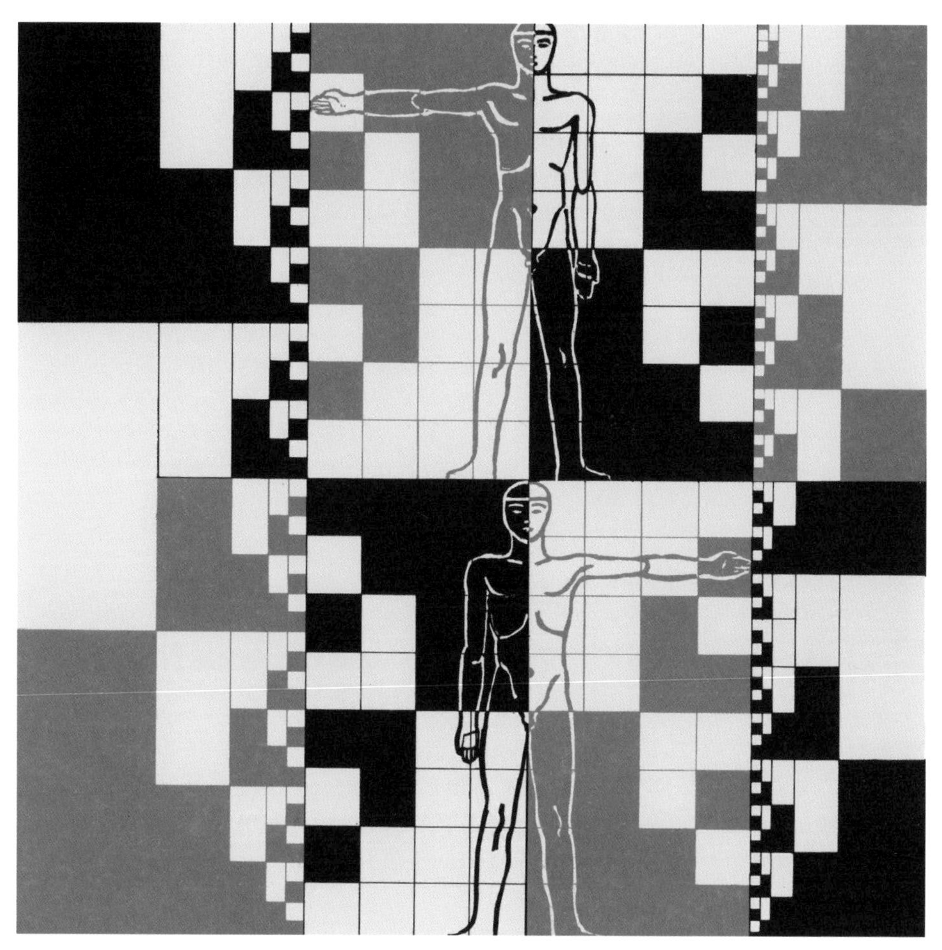

82 Aulis Blomstedt, study of Pythagorean intervals applied to the human scale. Undated.

of housing production. Alvar Aalto had a seminal initiating role in Finland in the research and practical programs concerning standardization.

Blomstedt continued his research on harmonical proportions along with his architectural practice during the 1950s. With admirable energy he devoted himself to the study of the multiplication and division of numerical series based on the multiples of small whole numbers and their relationships to human measures and musical harmony (**80–81**). He made endless graphic and color studies on the divisibility of numbers, their interrelations, and the relations of his proposed modular and number series to the human figure. The two starting points in his research were the practical work of the architect and the demand for harmonic proportions inherited from classical antiquity; his most important inspiration was Hans Kayser. The concept of the module itself was inherited from Hellenic culture, and originally it meant the division of half the diameter of a temple column into thirty parts. This module was used in the various dimensional details of the column itself and eventually

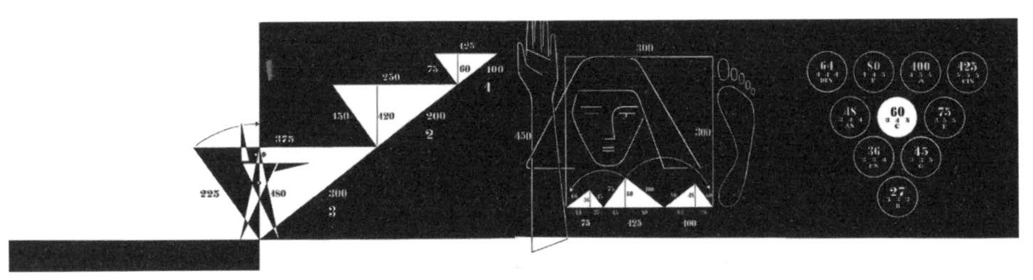

83 Aulis Blomstedt, "Canon 60", harmonical number system centering on number 60 with their musical equivalents, *c.* 1960. (1) The numbers of the triangle 75, 100, 125 in rapport with human scale. According to Blomstedt's own acknowledgment this illustration was added to the "Canon 60" scheme at the suggestion of Reima Pietilä to show its relation to the human scale. (2) In the center of the three triangles is a right-angled triangle 75, 100, 125 (3, 4, 5). On either side is a smaller triangle, composed of parts of the former. The sides of the three triangles are expressed by 10 different numbers. (3) The numbers of the triangles in the center image are arranged in a pattern according to their arithmetic properties. The harmonical musical equivalents are also shown.

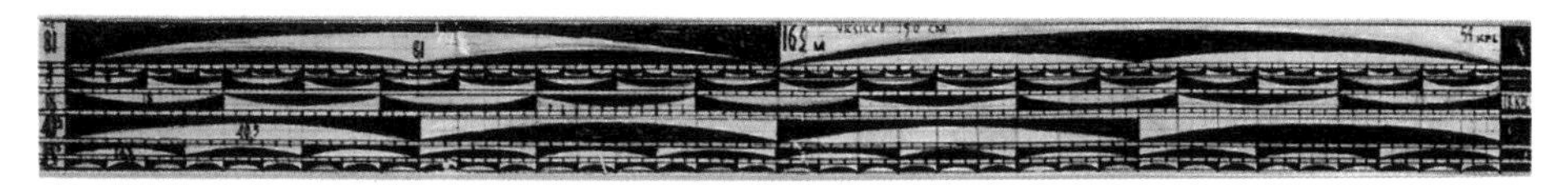

84 Aulis Blomstedt, a special scale stick developed for his project in an architectural competition. Basic unit 150 cm, scale 1:400. Undated.

the entire edifice. The module was thus originally relative and proportional to the specific size of each building, whereas the modern universal standard of 10 cm is the same in all tasks and only fulfills prosaic practical purposes of measurement. It is significant to realize that the antique notion of the module did not aim at a universal application.

Blomstedt explained his goal as follows: "In my studies of the module I have aimed at a remoter and broader goal than has hitherto been seen ... I have tried to find invariances, which would free architects to concentrate on essentials."[21] For him, the essential requirement was the choice of pretuned and harmonized numbers for every individual design task. His set of numbers was a kind of a preharmonized set of measures for design work, a tuned keyboard for the architect, as it were, to be used from the scales of planning and architecture all the way to objects like his golden knife. It is significant to understand that Blomstedt thought of numbers, not measures, because within his system based on musical harmony, the numbers of his harmonic series could be given any value as a measure, i.e. 36 could refer to millimeters, centimeters, meters, and so on, as all these multiplications of the unit are octave transitions in musical terms, and maintain their harmonic essence.

Through more than a decade of intense studies, Blomstedt devised numerous alternative number systems related to the human figure, especially a man 180 cm tall; he preferred this numerical value because of its multiple divisibility. Finally, in the early

1960s, he came up with a set of ten numbers, which have precise musical values, and create a logical and convincing system. Blomstedt called his harmonic system "Canon 60," with 60 (3 x 4 x 5) being the central figure (**83**). This number pattern satisfied his requirements so perfectly that he stopped making further harmonical studies. His later investigations showed that he had unknowingly been using the numbers of Canon 60 almost throughout his career.[22] In his design practice, a dimensional module, a basic number (the "grain" or "kernel," as he called it), was worked out specifically for each design project. The "kernel" was found through arduous studies of the site and contextual situation and its concealed dynamics, the design brief and its metric requirements, etc. Here he supported the relationality of the module as the Greek architects had done in dimensioning and proportioning their temples. He even made unique scale and measuring sticks with preharmonized measures for the specific dimensional conditions of his individual design tasks (**84**). In his design work, he always spent considerable time in the beginning defining the specific module or "grain" for the project, as well as studying the hidden inner dynamics of the task. These studies were casually made as compositional exercises in scale on the site plan, floor plan, or sectional drawings (**85**).

In the postwar years Kayser and Blomstedt were not alone in their research in architectural harmony. Other significant researchers in the modular and proportional systems in the modern era are Alfred Neumann, Ezra D. Ehrenkranz, Matila Ghyka, Yositika Utida, and R.M. Schindler (1887–1953). The Austrian-American Schindler's ideas, especially, were close to Blomstedt's in their integration of musical harmony, but the two were not aware of each other's work.

As construction is deeply engaged in geometric and mathematical operations, the geometric solids have been used in architecture throughout history. Geometry is the hidden frame or scaffolding of thinking in architecture. The association of geometric figures and solids with architecture is so evident that they suggest an abstracted architecture, and also they have a metaphorical reference to architecture even in visual arts, as Albrecht Dürer's etching *Melancholia I* (1514) suggests.[23] Geometric figures and volumes, and their combinations and intersections, are part of the vocabulary and syntax of architecture, as well as a means of generating architectural entities even in today's era of computerized design practice.

The architecture of geometry

The architect normally uses imaginary geometric figures and volumes in his or her design work as abstracted elements, or mental scaffoldings, in the composition. Geometry has also had its role in structuring architectural projection drawings as well as perspective constructions.[24] The optics of vision are essentially geometric. The story of how Filippo Brunelleschi (1377–1446) proved his theory of perspective in front of the Baptistery next to the Duomo in Florence is well known. On the other hand, perspective representation has supported a distinct static and pictorial

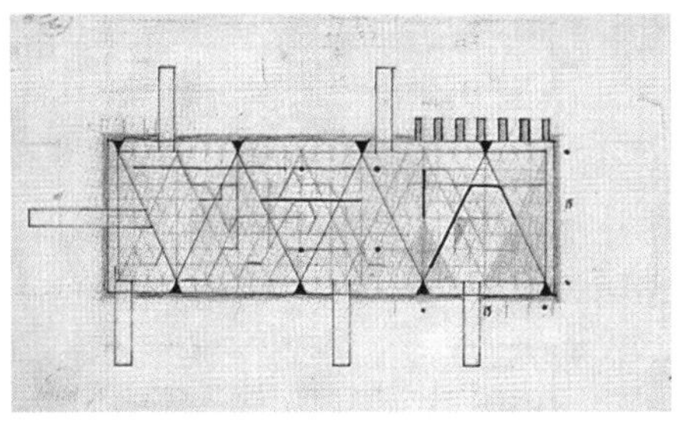
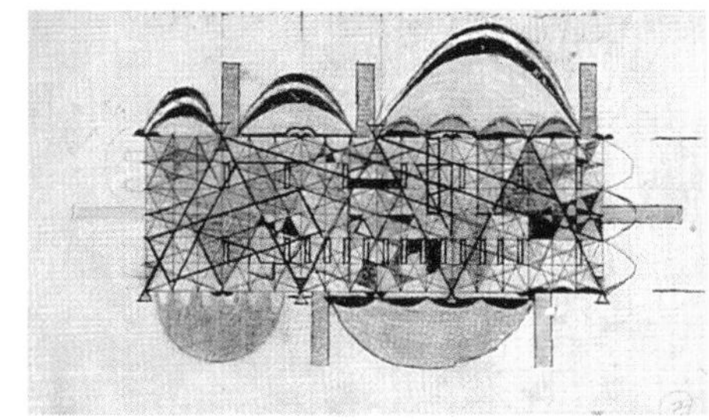
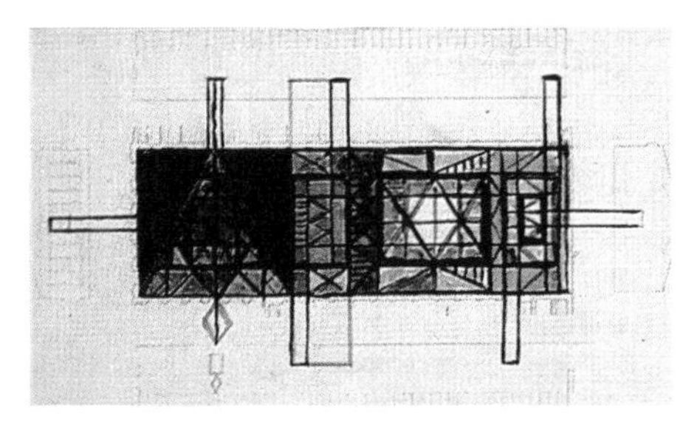
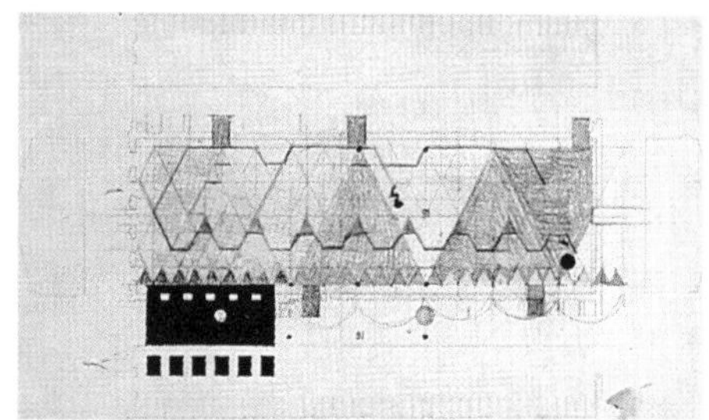
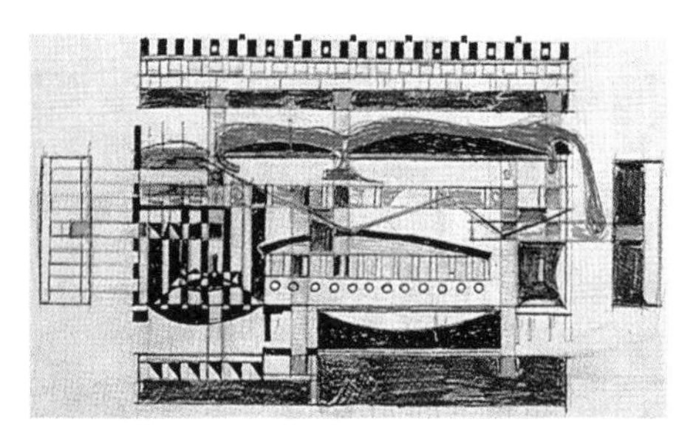
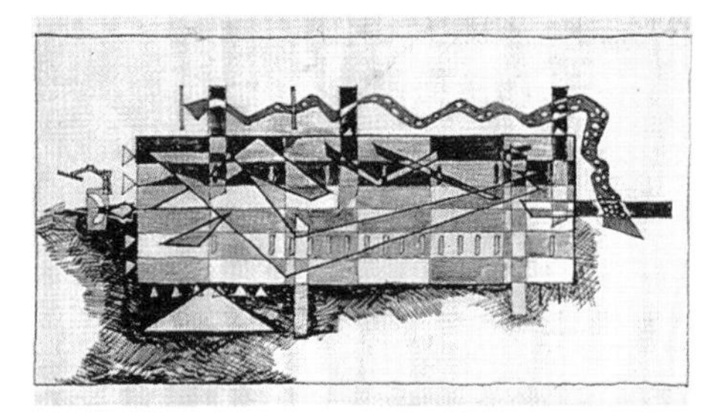

85 Aulis Blomstedt, studies for the exhibition of Finnish architecture at the Moderna Museet in Stockholm, 1960. The sketches are composition exercises juxtaposed on the plan and four sections of the exhibition hall to study the dimensional and dynamic characteristics of the space, entries, windows, skylights, etc., 1960.

understanding of vision as the central human sense, as well as an understanding of architecture as a formal discipline. These practices eventually seriously weakened the experiential multisensory reality in the art of architecture. Thus, while the vision-centeredness has been a focusing strength in the evolution of architecture, it has increasingly turned into a limitation. Also the true complexities of vision have only recently been revealed by research. A particularly significant point is that perspective construction, representation, and design thinking are based on the idea of a fixed eye, but that does not really exist outside the forced conditions of the research laboratory; the eye is constantly in motion. Today the emerging experiential and phenomenological orientation aims at grounding design in real and direct, multi-sensory experience and empathic thinking. This orientation also suggests a reevaluation of the roles of mathematics and geometry in architecture.

Altogether, mathematics has had a central role in the practices of design and construction, as well as the metaphysical and philosophical aims and aesthetics of architecture. The aspiration to unify the aesthetic proportionalities of architecture and music has been a strong undercurrent of this development. Here mathematics also had a significant role in elevating architecture into an art form from its historical understanding as a craft.

Architecture and digitalization

Today's architectural practices mostly take place in the mathematicized and digitalized universe of the computer and structures are even generated algorithmically, i.e. through mathematicized processes outside of human imagination. Many of the supporters of computerized design argue that this is the future of architectural design. I have my severe doubts about this, because architecture is primarily expected to create human experiences and meanings, atmospheres and attunements, and to provide us with our existential foothold in the world. Modernity has been obsessed with focused form, but there is an increasing interest in architecture as lived experience, atmosphere, and attunement. Architecture both arises from and addresses the body. The experiential emphasis fuses architecture and the human mind into a continuum in which the neuroscientific and neuro-phenomenological understanding of our evolutionary relationships with the world becomes seminal. The Pythagorean science of harmonics is the longest Western scientific tradition and I have no doubt in professing that after our surreal age of secular utility and the hegemony of economics, quasi-rationality, and manipulative aestheticization, the principles of harmony, mental grounding, and architectural mediation will again have their role in the studies and practices of the art of building.

1 Marcus Vitruvius Pollio, *Vitruvius: The Ten Books on Architecture*, trans. Morris Hicky Morgan (New York: Dover Publications, Inc., 1960), 5–6.
2 Rudolf Haase, "Harmonics in Architecture," *Abacus Yearbook 2* (Helsinki: The Museum of Finnish Architecture, 1980), 94.
3 Colin Rowe, *The Mathematics of the Ideal Villa and Other Essays* (Cambridge, MA, and London: MIT Press, 1976).
4 Gaston Bachelard, *Water and Dreams: An Essay on the Imagination of Matter* (Dallas, TX: The Pegasus Foundation, 1983), 46.
5 As quoted in Richard Dawkins, "Bar Codes in the Stars," *Olafur Eliasson, Your Lighthouse: Works with Light 1991–2004*, ed. Holger Broecker (Wolfsburg: Kunstmuseum Wolfsburg/Hatje Cantz Verlag, 2004), 13. In other sources the quote is credited to another poet, William Butler Yeats.
6 Gernot Böhme, *Critique of Aesthetic Capitalism* (Berlin: Mimesis International, 2017).
7 Haase, "Harmonics in Architecture," 103.
8 James Elkins, *What is Painting: How to Think about Oil Painting Using the Language of Alchemy* (New York and London: Routledge, 2000).
9 As quoted in David Seamon, "Goethe, Nature and Phenomenology: An Introduction," *Goethe's Way of Science*, ed. David Seamon and Arthur Zajonc (Albany: State University of New York Press, 1998), 2.
10 Rudolf Wittkower, *Architectural Principles in the Age of Humanism* (New York: Random House, 1965), 104.

11 As Aulis Blomstedt was married to the youngest daughter, Heidi, of Jean Sibelius, the famous Finnish composer (1865–1957), and his younger brother Jussi Jalas (1908–1985) was a renowned conductor, the world of music was close to him.
12 Wittkower, *Architectural Principles*, 117.
13 Ibid.
14 The coining of the phrase is somewhat unclear historically; it is usually attributed to Goethe, but Goethe credits Novalis around the year 1800. Johann Wolfgang von Goethe, *Maximes et réflexions* (Paris: Brokhauss et Avenarious, 1842). The phrase also appears in Friedrich Schiller (*Conversations with Goethe in the Last Years of His Life*) and Friedrich W.J. Schelling's lecture "Philosophie der Kunst," delivered in 1802–3, and published in 1856 (in English as *Philosophy of Art*, Minnesota: Minnesota University Press, 1989).
15 Wittkower, *Architectural Principles*, 15.
16 Ibid., 16.
17 Ibid.
18 Le Corbusier, *Le Modulor* (Boulogne: Editions de l'architecture d'aujourd'hui, 1948; in English *The Modulor*, 1964). Le Corbusier, *Modulor 2* (Boulogne: Editions de l'architecture dáujourd'hui, 1955; in English *Modulor 2: Let the User Speak Next*, 1958).
19 Hans Kayser, *Akróasis: The Theory of World Harmonics* (Boston: Plowshare Press, 1970), and *Textbook of Harmonics* (Santa Barbara, CA: Sacred Science Institute, 2001).
20 Elina Standertskjöld, "Alvar Aalto and Standardization," in *Acanthus 1992: The Art of Standards: The Yearbook of the Museum of Finnish Architecture* (Helsinki: The Museum of Finnish Architecture, 1992), 75–111.
21 Aulis Blomstedt, Notebooks, 1960s. The Museum of Finnish Architecture, Helsinki, Museum store, Blomstedt room.
22 See Juhani Pallasmaa, "Man, Measure and Proportion: Aulis Blomstedt and the Pythagorean Tradition," in *Acanthus 1992*, 23.
23 The engraving depicts an enigmatic winged female figure surrounded by carpenter's tools (hourglass, weighing scales, hand plane, claw hammer, saw) and other objects (geometric solids and magic square) related to alchemy, geometry and numerology.
24 See, for instance, Robin Evans, *The Projective Cast: Architecture and its Three Geometries* (Cambridge, MA: MIT Press, 1995); and Alberto Pérez-Gómez and Louise Pelletier, *Architectural Representation and the Perspective Hinge* (Cambridge, MA: MIT Press, 1997).

Mannerism Matters

Robert Maxwell

When we use expressions like "he's such a well-mannered man," or "it's a pity he has such irritating mannerisms," we are merely skirting a subject that I believe has now become an important aspect of human culture. The origins of mannerism are to be found in belief in a higher power, as expressed in art. Such belief appears to have been a fundamental need of early humankind, the first resort of primitive tribes that had just begun to think about ideas, as opposed to thinking about the other creatures with whom they were in competition for survival.

In historical times the word "mannerism" came into the language rather late. *Manneristi Toscani* (1944), by Luisa Becherucci, named a phenomenon that dated from the 1500s, in the work of such artists as Pontormo, Parmigianino, Bronzini—all Italian—and El Greco, who was Spanish. In their art, certain features, like long necks, were exaggerated or distorted, which had the effect of creating some ambiguity. But as a scientific age came nearer, the entire panoply of the Gods, named by the Greeks, taken over by the Romans, was treated more and more as a fact of life. As science grew stronger and more certain of its methods, Protestantism began to seem a step closer to the attempt to be objective, suggesting that, when it first set in with Martin Luther nailing his theses to the church door in Wittenberg in 1517, it presaged a certain overall weakening of faith. Did the artist really respect his religious subject? Or was he intrigued by a new possibility of not following appearances exactly, but of modifying them, a possibility that led in time to completely abstract art, such as we find in the work of Piet Mondrian. It was a new kind of freedom. It amounted to treating art as being more due to convention than to conviction. Not surprisingly, this led to a weakening of faith and a loss of belief.

As for mannerism in Britain, one of the earliest manifestations came with the writing of Laurence Sterne, who in 1700 wrote a picaresque novel, *The Life and Opinions of Tristram Shandy, Gentleman*, which fascinated Denis Diderot, a prime exponent of eighteenth-century mannerism in France, to the extent that he imitated the overall form and even plagiarized two passages in it.[1] In fine art it can be found, I believe, in the work of Henry Fuseli and Francis Bacon. But within architecture it is unmistakably present in the work of three English architects: Nicholas Hawksmoor, Edwin Lutyens, and James Stirling.

It was Colin Rowe who brought mannerism home to architects. In his essay of 1950, "Mannerism and Modern Architecture,"[2] he emphasized the idea of the blank panel: first in Palladio's Casa Cogollo, Vicenza, and again in Le Corbusier's Villa Schwob at La Chaux-de-Fonds. I think Rowe was intrigued by the change of style implied and loved the resulting ambiguity. However, the historian Howard Burns[3] has pointed out that at both these buildings the architects intended to display a new wall painting specifically intended for that site, making these panels no longer blank; moreover, the blank panel at the Casa Cogollo was backed by a fireplace, which blocked any idea of a spatial axis passing to the outside.

Michelangelo can be said to have invented the rules of mannerism. With him began an era of angst, leading over time to W.H. Auden's "age of anxiety." At the Sistine Chapel, his painted figures on the ceiling are at the same time full of emotion and utterly stylish, excessive in manner yet contained by form.

In the Cappella Sforza, attached to Santa Maria Maggiore, Michelangelo is working in the tradition of the centralized building; but, within its limits, every effort is then made to destroy that focus. At its center is a square space defined by four columns set on the diagonal, thus denying the Christian pull towards the altar and the ritual of the Mass. They (the columns) are supported by shallow apses of a form both definite and incomplete. Above is a dome-like space, broken into two parts, with windows that contradict the conception of a dome (it is actually a balloon vault). With this space furrowed by conflicting thrusts and engaged in active competition with the area of the sanctuary, there ensues not so much ideal harmony as planned distraction. The altar is placed opposite the entrance and is lit by small windows on either side.

The antechamber to the Laurentian Library in Florence is a typically mannerist space in that the staircase fills it so completely that the visitor is hardly acknowledged. The entrance delivers us to a side of the antechamber, while the axis of the staircase is focused squarely on the central bay of the right-hand wall. Unlike all the other bays, fully expressed as units in a sequence, with window-like entablatures emphasized by pediments and cornices, the central panel on the right-hand wall, which you face as you begin to descend the stairs, is blank, just as in Palladio's Casa Cogollo and Le Corbusier's Villa Schwob. The mannerism is present in the fact that you don't exit the library on axis under the blank panel, but have to turn sharply to the right, contradicting the formality, to exit by the side. On your way in, everything is unexpected, and ascending the staircase is made easier by the curves on the first few steps—one would hardly have been conscious of similar curves existing on the far side.

Mannerism in England

During the eighteenth century, England was seen by its continental neighbours as being far ahead of them in empirical know-how, possibly because of the common sense perceived in the work of Isaac Newton, and certainly because of the pragmatism conveyed by both the philosophers John Locke and Thomas Hobbes. Sterne, a clergyman by calling, is full of common sense, but he mixes it with fantasy. The *Tristram Shandy* story was described at the time of publication as a satire. In influencing Diderot, it was not just a question of the fantasy, but of the humor that is

86 West front of St. Mary Woolnoth, London, by Nicholas Hawksmoor, 1727.
87 St. George-in-the-East, Wapping, London, by Nicholas Hawksmoor, 1729.

mixed in with it: the enjoyment of treating a subject as both serious and amusing. As a clergyman, Sterne could not be seen as an agnostic.

In England, mannerism can be detected in the work of many Jacobean playwrights of around 1600: John Webster, Thomas Dekker, and Christopher Marlowe. Their contribution to mannerism may be summarized as the tendency to mix gore and bloodshed with convention and polite conversation. One example would be John Webster's *The Duchess of Malfi*, a grim tragedy written in 1612.

Some art historians see Henry Fuseli as a neoclassicist, as a precursor of symbolism, and even of Surrealism. After visiting Italy he changed his name from Füssli to Fuseli. He came to England, where he met Joshua Reynolds, who advised him to devote himself entirely to art. But it was Hawksmoor who really adopted the effects of mannerism, as we find it in London in his St. Mary Woolnoth or Christ Church Spitalfields, especially in their west fronts (**86**).

The mannerist effect is also evident in Hawksmoor's St. George's, Bloomsbury, where the pull towards the altar, familiar from medieval churches, was contradicted by the compression of this dimension; and best of all, in St. George-in-the-East, where little cupolas mark the four-square classical symmetry of the interior, in contradiction to the Christian idea of a dominant direction (**87**).

Hawksmoor was clearly still unaware of the idea of mannerism as such. He seems to have been instinctively drawn to the sort of contradictions that occur in

88 Garden facade of Homewood, Knebworth, by Edwin Lutyens, 1903.

mannerism. But, unlike James Stirling and Robert Venturi, he did not *know* that what he was doing would later be cited as mannerist. From Hawksmoor's work, it's but a small step in principle to reach Venturi's writing—his great essay *Complexity and Contradiction in Modern Architecture*, and his slogan, adopted around the year 2000: "new mannerism rather than old expressionism."[4]

There are many examples of mannerism by Edwin Lutyens. At the Viceroy's Palace in New Delhi, for example, the main staircase leads down on axis, but begins with two flights, symmetrically disposed right and left (**89**). When approaching this from the *piano nobile*, one finds that the upper flight is repeated on the other side, offering two ways down. And so there is an immediate problem: which side to take? One is forced to turn awkwardly to continue the descent—not unlike the awkwardness of leaving Michelangelo's Laurentian Library. In other words, the main axis is blocked. In this situation the smooth coved cornice around the space of this staircase takes on a certain blankness, a smoothness that is unexpected in view of the correct classical detailing found everywhere else. The effect is confusing rather than satisfying. In the context of Lutyens's amazing talent for giving the palace an "Indian" character this suggests a certain postmodernity *avant la lettre*.

In many of Lutyens's domestic buildings in England there are plenty of examples of the use of blocked axes: I give just one of them here. At Homewood, Knebworth, both entrance and garden side are symmetrical, but of different dimensions (**88**).

89 The staircase in the Viceroy's Palace, New Delhi, by Edwin Lutyens, 1912.
90 Detail of the Neue Staatsgalerie, Stuttgart, by James Stirling, 1984.

How Lutyens manages the transition is a masterly exposition of mannerism, with a staircase blocking the connection at the back of the dining room (itself symmetrical to the side facade) and with an exiguous loggia. Using classical symmetry, but contradicting it by some obstacle, is a frequent ploy that Lutyens uses, and this is clearly mannerist.

Mannerism in James Stirling

The death of James Stirling prematurely raised the question of his importance for world architecture: certainly, he was a world star, but has he been a major influence? The variety of the work has led to his being characterized in recent years as a post-modernist, not a label that he welcomed. In his own eyes he remained a modernist, as Venturi did. Nevertheless, his work seemed to respond to changes in the world. This is especially the case with the series of buildings he designed for German museums—beginning with the Museum of Art in Düsseldorf in 1975—which deal directly with the question of the role of architecture in the city, placing functionality at the service of a larger view of architecture as civic art. The context became as important as the function. Stirling's modernism can be seen as a response to the times rather than as a theoretical development for which he was himself responsible. At the same time, his work continued to assert an idiosyncratic view of architecture as a continuous personal evolution.

91 Gallery entrance, Clore Gallery, Tate Britain, London, by James Stirling, 1987.

Is architecture an art? It was once the "mistress art," but even in antiquity it was never accepted as an art free of practical constraints. Aristotle firmly places it among the useful arts, as opposed to the fine arts, whose task was to express myth as a living force and place it within history. With the rise of functionalism in the twentieth century, there was an attempt to make architecture an art through the very nature of its functional task. Revealing the function was considered the equivalent of revealing an inner necessity, in this way placing architecture under natural law. Architectural innovation was not seen as being under natural law, but as merely following rules, and the rules could be changed. For three-quarters of a century the myth of function served as the supreme justification for architectural form, and it was only with the advance of deconstructive architecture that the expressive weight of the architect's gesture was accorded the same primacy as in other forms of modern art.

The main thrust of Stirling's ideas seems to remain within a purely architectonic discourse. Stirling speaks to us in a limited way, not by verbal polemic, but through the works themselves. From the beginning he wished to practice a straightforward—even if sometimes daring—functionalism, pursuing technical innovation along with a devotion to the logic of the plan. We also see a frank interest in the resulting forms, not as the outcome of practical considerations, but as an opportunity to play with meaning. This playfulness, which resulted in Stirling becoming a figure of suspicion on the English scene, is nevertheless the main source of our continuing interest in his work.

92 Interior of the main entrance, Clore Gallery, Tate Britain, London, by James Stirling, 1987.

The coved cornice he used in the Neue Staatsgalerie in Stuttgart imitated Lutyens's use of it in the courtyard of the Viceroy's Palace in New Delhi; while Stirling preferred clear-cut and even classical diagrams, he always wished to apply a contradictory and subversive twist (**90**). As a result, the work is never predictable and never boring.

It is not that Stirling is naive about the use of classical precedent, expecting it to survive into his work unchanged by modern conditions. At the Schwartz Center for the Performing Arts at Cornell University, the banded stonework is proposed as veneer, not as structural masonry, and the fact is made clear—to the trained observer at least—by the insistence on open joints and the absence of mortar. At the Clore Gallery, Tate Britain, the main entrance is marked by a large pedimental opening ("as if a classical temple had been removed," said John Summerson) (**91**).[5]

Inside, beyond the reception desk, the stair up turns to the right, pointing away from the galleries, and the visitor has to pause at the top, reorientate, turn, and pass in the opposite direction along the side in order to enter the galleries through a brightly colored doorway (**92**).

Unlike that of many modernists, Stirling's devotion to function is not proposed as determining the outcome, thus freeing the architect from artistic responsibility. For if the outcome is to be entirely determined by function, architecture's status as a language of expression will be hideously deformed. To speak freely in the medium of cultural discourse, architecture must display elements that are arbitrary, and are determined only by the author within a total sensibility of architectonic forms and within a system of rhetoric that refers to an architectural tradition. In this sense, while Stirling rightly insists that his projects are founded on site and program, he does not deny that he practices architecture *as an art*.[6] He works consistently and rationally, developing formal sequences at No. 1 Poultry, which he puts to work at Carlton Gardens, where, in the residential section, the bowed gallery projects into a narrow space in a very mannerist way, but gives an effect of stunning beauty.

Like Alvar Aalto, Stirling has not been a force through his theories but rather through the inner conviction which radiates from the buildings he designed. If we compare him to Venturi, whose "gentle manifesto" provided a new theoretical approach to the problem of representation within modern architecture, we find no theoretical approach as such. His arguments were always made from a basis of functionality and, after Düsseldorf, from the basis of contextuality. Stirling seems lacking in ideology. Yet in contemplating the future of modern architecture without him, one has a sense of irreparable loss.

Mannerism in Francis Bacon and John le Carré

Art is both exploration and therapy: it aims to disturb at the same time as it consoles. No artist of our times has done this more succinctly than Francis Bacon.

All his work is suffused with a recognition of suffering, of the thin membrane that separates physical enjoyment from pain, the sentient body from the corpse. In the center of his pictures a human being is displayed in mortal captivity, sometimes screaming (the "screaming popes"), sometimes writhing in agony, sometimes amputated like butcher's meat, sometimes contorted in struggle, sometimes abandoned in unspeakable loneliness. These distortions are done to the subject by the artist not out of sadism, but in an attempt to seize more violently the sensation of the sitter's presence, of his having been there. This fleeting presence is only an image executed in pigment, and it arises in part through the accidents that can occur in working the pigment. Because the medium is thus incorporated in the message, the results have the status of works of art—not propaganda. The violence is calmed, and made accessible, by the way it is framed. The elements of this framing are a strict formality, strong and sweeping contours, colors of a lyrical sweetness, and certain abstract figures—a disembodied cube, an ellipse, an applied arrow—that have the effect of distancing the observer further from the agony depicted within. The result is an art that faces the postmodern condition, an art of first and last things that places together the heat of sensation and the cold of abstraction. It is serious, yet has the characteristics of a game: there is a distinct element of mannerism in this.

Bacon is a great artist; his work is widely recognized. How then can I consider him as a mannerist? While I accept his seriousness, I do feel that it contains an element of playfulness; there is more than one style within the canvas; the outer parts follow a semiabstract style, often deliberately beautiful; at the center is a human being, in principle treated more realistically, following Bacon's search for human contact—the fleeting presence of another being. There is a final juxtaposition, in which the central figure is "spoiled" by deliberate distortion (never done in the presence of the sitter), a stage where the overall meaning of the picture is transposed from the interesting to the enigmatic. And then he has an Irish side and from that comes an element of disrespect for authority. The whole thing may be just a joke. In Francis Bacon there is a mixture of high seriousness *and* tomfoolery. He knows how to suggest suspense beyond the boundaries of mere fashion. But at the same time, isn't he quietly enjoying himself and thinking what fools *we* all are?

John le Carré (the nom de plume of David Cornwell) is a popular writer of thrillers, which means that his writing is full of the kind of contradictions that turn up in the art of spying: the difference between normal life and the assumed "cover" of the spy. He obviously enjoys using this ambiguity, and when his character George Smiley is played by a superb actor like Alec Guinness, it comes close to a further case of ambiguity, like a textbook example of mannerism. In le Carré's *The Little Drummer Girl*, ambiguity arises because, to make things secure for everybody, those in the secret service have to commit crimes for the greater good: a prime contradiction. I doubt if le Carré ever considered mannerism as an aim; yet what his character Charlie says seems to be intentionally mannerist. The character Charlie, who is intelligent but easily influenced by feelings, falls in love with an Israeli adherent, and later with a Palestinian freedom fighter, who is later shot dead. In the end she is hopelessly lost between her two lovers, the Israeli and the Palestinian, each one convinced of the justice of his cause: ambiguity again.

Conclusion

These examples of mannerism, some in writing or in fine art, but most unequivocally in the art of architecture, all treat it as an interesting idea. But why is it so important for the world today? It seems to arise from the realization that our rules are not laws, that they may be unique to humankind and quite arbitrary, that we should not be too serious about them.

When primitive tribes started thinking about other beings, and began to be self-conscious, they had no idea about other worlds; there were just other tribes. With the discovery of writing, a new dimension was added: the idea of history took hold. This is evident in the Christian Bible: so-and-so begat X, who begat Y, who begat Z.

It was difficult to accept the finality of death, and that led to the idea that survival into an afterlife was possible: the concept of immortality began to beckon. Dead bodies were interred, or closed up in a tomb, or placed under a pile of heavy stones. One of the North American native tribes, the Navajo, believe in a principle of living in harmony with nature—they call it *hozho*. This fact links them to some more sensitive critics of today: Edmund Leach, who lectured at the Architectural Association in London in 1974 on the need to make *no growth* culturally acceptable; John Kenneth Galbraith, who put on a television series that was an undisguised criticism of capitalism;[7] and Naomi Klein, whose books *This Changes Everything* and *No is Not Enough* point to the finality of global warming, where an ever-increasing population is fighting to emigrate to the more temperate zones nearer the north pole. She is a hero of young people who are not set in their ways, and who want to see some practical innovation that faces up to the problem.

It was some time before the pile of stones could take on a more precise and sophisticated shape: in due course it became a Pyramid. It did not seem to matter that thousands of workers would be necessary to raise a massive structure to protect those surviving into an afterlife, a labour that would require years, whereas the food and drink provided for them would perish in a matter of days. Maybe that food and drink were symbolic. This idea came about in Egypt, but also in the western hemisphere with the Maya and other tribes. A simple pile of stones could be made more permanent by being cut with precision, and more important by being raised higher. That seemed proper for those at the peak of society—the king and his family.

In the end, the role of mannerism is clear: it provides us with an attitude, a way of facing up to the uncertainties of the human condition. It accepts the fact that there is no life after death. Its key factors—irony and ambiguity—allow us to come to terms with the approach of the end of our world. We may see the possibility of space travel, of electric airplanes; but these will need more time to develop than we can count upon. Scientists are no help, beyond suggesting that space and time came into existence together, so there can be no "before." In an age of uncertainty, mannerism gives some reassurance, allows us to think, momentarily as it may be, of more pleasant things. In our uncertain future, mannerism matters.

1 Denis Diderot, *Jacques the Fatalist and his Master*, rev. trans. with Introduction and Notes by J. Robert Loy (New York: Collier Books, 1962).
2 Colin Rowe, "Mannerism and Modern Architecture," *The Mathematics of the Ideal Villa and Other Essays* (Cambridge, MA: MIT Press, 1976), 29 (first published in the *Architectural Review* in 1950).
3 Howard Burns, in a symposium at the Royal Academy of Arts, London, on "Palladio and his Influence" (March 2009), answering a question from Robert Maxwell.
4 Robert Venturi and Denise Scott Brown, *Architecture as Signs and Systems: for a Mannerist Time* (Cambridge, MA: Harvard University Press, 2004), Section I: Robert Venturi, "Architecture as Sign rather than Space, New Mannerism rather than Old Expressionism."
5 John Summerson, "Vitruvius Ridens or Laughter at the Clore," *Architectural Review* (June 1987), 45, 46.
6 Marco Juliano, "Stirling Thinks," lecture given at Liverpool University on 15 October 2015: "As applied art, similar to furniture making or product designing (not styling) and therefore different from the 'fine arts' which have a greater freedom or arbitrariness and uselessness." As quoted in "Eight questions to James Stirling and James Gowan," *Polygon*, 5 (1960): 10–21.
7 John Kenneth Galbraith, *The Age of Uncertainty* (television series, BBC, CBC, KCET, DECA, 1977).

The Birth of Architecture from the Spirit of Conversation

Kurt W. Forster

Perhaps one of Kenneth Frampton's greatest virtues, and the hallmark of a great teacher, is his readiness to entertain a conversation at the drop of a hat. And since I've never seen him with a hat, it may take even less to draw him into the kind of exchange one remembers years after it occurred. While walking or lingering wherever it may be, my conversations with Frampton have helped me keep faith in the universality of ideas and in the fact that thoughts can never be owned or destroyed.

So as I attempted to put Karl Friedrich Schinkel and my reflections on his work between two covers, I grew to realize that his life can be thought of as one long conversation with others, with his surroundings, and with architecture.[1] What kind of conversation can engender such communion with things and ideas? And in what way is the *habitus* of interlocutors, their ability as *conversationalists*, necessary for the shaping of ideas, even the making of things that, in their turn, provoke vivid responses and intuitive musings?

Conversation is distinct from other forms of communication for its apparent purposelessness. Less an effort to get something across than to contemplate and examine a subject, slowly moving it before one's eyes and proffering one's view to others, conversation possesses a life of its own. No matter whether it is something tangible or just a passing thought, a piece of news, or the glimpse of an idea, a good conversation keeps moving and animating its subject without rushing to judgment. During a conversational exchange of views, not only differences of opinion but also different *notions of the subject* itself take shape.[2] Divergent opinions affect the subject being discussed; conflicting reactions alter its nature and propel it into further debate. The spirit of conversation makes allowances for this to happen, waiting for the right moment to take hold of another's intelligence and solicit feelings, not just challenging one's logical comprehension. Naturally, there need to be places that lend themselves to such conversing. A solitary wanderer may carry on a conversation with himself, as indeed many did, even committing their soliloquies to print in the expectation of finding an interlocutor, a *semblable*, a *frère*. Wandering freely promotes thought. There are many accounts of friends examining their ideas while hiking or resting on their way, even conversations that remained one-sided.[3] Two centuries ago, walking was still so common a means of getting around that one is not surprised to find travel diaries and letters brimming with accounts of such ambulant conversations.

Just as we converse with others, we're also able to do so with ourselves: where voices alternate with one another, a thought can propose its object from several vantage points. That is what the German writer Heinrich von Kleist must have had in mind when he reflected on "the gradual fashioning of thought while speaking ["über die allmähliche Verfertigung der Gedanken beim Reden"], if we wish to know something we cannot find meditating all by ourselves."[4] Thought seeks company and its object needs debate. Only in an exchange (of views) do we find the terms that make them tangible. "The transition from thought to expression" requires effort and causes a certain "excitement of our being."[5] Kleist recalled that the French have a saying to describe the phenomenon, not by chance but surely because conversation enjoyed special standing in French culture. The French adage *l'appétit vient en mangeant* lends itself to Kleist's parody as *l'idée vient en parlant.*[6] It's all about finding the turn of phrase and being able to do so while keeping the conversation going, perhaps with a little help from appropriate books, such as François de Callières's *Mots à la mode, et nouvelles façons de parler.*[7] Enlarged soon after publication and followed by other thesauruses that helped nouveaux riches *gentilshommes* find their way in elegant circles, these lexica nourished conversation. The theater of Molière and Marivaux furnished the dialogues, the rhythm and *tournure* of conversation in polite society, in journals and novels. Kleist reminds his readers that it was said that Molière's housemaid threw him expressions that vault over class barriers and add spice to the parlance of the educated. Conversation not only smoothed social exchanges of all kinds, but also set the tone for verbal media and guaranteed the French a long-lasting edge in everything requiring diplomatic exchanges. According to the experiences of Heinrich Heine, a conversationalist of passion and a poet of European rather than just German fame, the English were ill suited to the kind of conversation he admired among the French.[8] Since the early eighteenth century, in parallel to the affirmation of court etiquette, lexica with the term *conversation* in their titles appeared in astonishing numbers, soon spreading to other countries. In Germany, Johann Hübner's *Conversations-Lexicon* went through twenty-seven editions in the eighteenth century, producing numerous competitors along the way until the publisher Brockhaus took over Renatus Gotthelf Löbel's and Christian Wilhelm Franke's *Conversationslexicon* in 1808 and turned it into one of the most popular encyclopedias of modern Europe.

Today's crowded coffee shops with students conversing on their phones and ceaselessly messaging are only the latest descendants of the public houses that sprang up with particular frequency from the later eighteenth century onward. The autocorrect feature of computer programs and the numerous online resources supplying word choice descend from the thesauruses, as do the formulaic exchanges so essential to social media.[9] Two centuries ago, smoking and gaming rooms, establishments studded with the latest newspapers, were frequented by a clientele that chose them as their haunts and even turned them into coves of conspiratorial and revolutionary activity. Separate sections for playing chess or cards, and even billiard rooms, set the stage for a culture of conversation that excluded very few and extended very far. Conversation provided the running thread, beginning before one entered a public house and often migrating into letters and novels that were written or read there. Some of these novels consisted chiefly of dialogues or letters, plays traditionally drew on conversation as the lubricant of action, and a flurry of chatty *billets* constantly bridged the gap between one meeting and another, crisscrossing the geography of Europe no less hastily than did the armies of Napoleon and those of his opponents.

Karl Friedrich Schinkel (1781–1841) was born a few years before the French Revolution and died as many years before the short-lived bourgeois revolts of 1848–49. His education and the first years of his apprenticeship in architecture coincided with years of great political turmoil and cultural ferment. A trait of character he shared with many of his young contemporaries was a preternatural curiosity and an acute determination to take mental possession of what he wished to bring about in reality, even if that reality may at first have been one of images and daydreams rather than tangible objectives. Making a long story short and abbreviating quite an intricate process, one might say that his education tended to lodge knowledge in opinions, exposing him to a bewildering variety of points of view. Instead of fragments of information he typically had to contend with a bundle of impressions and arguments. Schinkel decided to leave high school before graduation and join a small group of young acolytes of the architect Friedrich Gilly. Gilly's father was a mainstay of architectural instruction in Berlin and his publication of a "Collection of Useful Essays" (*Sammlung nützlicher Aufsätze*, 1797–1806) revolving around new issues in architecture also gave a platform to his son Friedrich, who drew special attention to French architecture.[10]

The kind of social life that fostered conversation as an art for the many, almost a sort of collective performance, has been described by quite a number of its participants and, for Schinkel, most eloquently by the son of one of his important early patrons, the theatrical producer and promoter of panoramas Wilhelm Gropius: "Without formal invitation," reported Gropius, "a group of highly spirited people used to join Schinkel in his apartment on Friedrichstrasse. Clemens Brentano, Bettine von Arnim, Schinkel's brother-in-law Berger, the landscape painters Roesel, Karl Gropius, Rath Kerll and others gathered around Schinkel who, in [the] midst [of] the animated scene, would sit down and sketch."[11] For several evenings in a row, the writer and poet Clemens Brentano, a dazzling extempore narrator, would describe a romantic story in intricate detail and challenge Schinkel to capture it all on paper in a sort of "amicable contest" that drove these dueling minds into paroxysms of describing and picturing. While anecdotal and surely styled to celebrate the talents of these artists, the story captures important facts about conversation as both a social ritual and an artistic exercise. For obvious reasons, only words can give us a sense of these long-lost events, but images speak as eloquently of the settings in which such effervescent exchanges occurred and they convey, probably more immediately than do descriptions, the peculiar *Stimmung*, the powerful emotional undertow of this collective experience. I'll illustrate in a moment how this atmosphere coincided with one of Schinkel's ultimate aims, namely a calculated desire to turn buildings into emotional destinations.

Because this culture of conversation was by definition a shared experience, we need to look for records of encounters and descriptions that capture the particular effect that images and buildings were expected to achieve. In 1808, Schinkel's *Panorama of Palermo* stood out among the numerous exhibitions of these precinematic installations that were the rage all over Europe—soon to appear also in the New World.[12] To understand the clamorous success of panoramas one needs to accept that it depended on the experience they triggered in the viewer, rather than on the painter's talents. The landed gentleman and writer Achim von Arnim, Bettine's future husband and brother-in-law of Clemens Brentano, vividly conveyed his impression of the *Panorama of Palermo* in a letter to Johann Wolfgang von Goethe in 1809, praising this "marvel" as "one of the most exhilarating things to be seen in Berlin, along with some backlit scenes by Schinkel." Writing to his wife-to-be, Bettine, a week earlier, Arnim had given an enthusiastic account of his visit, moving from first impressions to a deeply felt response in his own imaginings: "I spent a serene hour in Palermo [in the *Panorama*] and was standing in the cloister garden, looking into the far distance across the blue sea toward Germany." Beholding something that was historically and geographically distant induced a keen longing in him, and this sensation put him in mind of his wife's country of origin, Italy, whence the Brentanos had emigrated only two generations earlier. This vague yearning for the past also filled him with ardor for his own country, which, in those years, was languishing under French occupation. These convoluted sensations, each predicated on distance, loss, or hope, also muddled geography, so that Arnim felt torn between yearning and nostalgia, letting his thoughts wander to the distant river Rhine, whose course he had followed with Bettine. From there he recalled his solitary exploration of Genoa and Milan, and the intimation of "alpine air that swept down from the gorges near Palermo."[13]

Bettine Brentano, who married Achim von Arnim in 1811, was one of the most sought-after *salonnières* at the time. She also entertained a wide-ranging correspondence with her lively circle in Berlin and farther afield. Susanne Schinkel and the architect himself became close friends of Bettine and of her brother Clemens, a relationship that on occasion stimulated the friendly competition between poet and painter I just mentioned. Bettine's intuitions far outran her logic. She frequently felt the blind force of events, the violence of change, and the tremors of fate. It is no surprise that she compared herself to a "billiard ball," adding that "I have always moved in the direction of the push I experienced" ["Ich bin wie eine Billiardkugel immer dahin gelaufen, wohin ich den Stoß erhielt"].[14] Often she wondered aloud about what might happen, as she did when she wrote to her husband about "whether the king would entrust the reconstruction of the Royal Theater to Schinkel," whose reputation was such as to suggest "he couldn't design a stable without turning it into a temple."[15] Bettine had taken drawing lessons from Schinkel and must have realized that this was an invidious rumor rather than the expression of serious reservations about the architect's abilities.

Conversational exchanges quickened many a subject and lent their pulse to arguments that would otherwise have been considered turgid. By the later eighteenth century, subjects of wider interest tended to be treated in the form of dialogues, especially when they sought to enlighten the public at large. Even thorny subjects and intellectually challenging theories profited from dramatization in dialogues: Francesco Algarotti popularized *Newton's Optics for Ladies* in a book that was quickly translated and imitated.[16] Entire novels took the shape of epistolary exchanges or *Briefromane*, especially when they mixed the sentimental and scandalous in contrived moral vexation, as was the case with *Hollins Liebesleben* ["Hollin's Love Life"] (1802), an anonymously published novel reputed in Schinkel's circles to be a work of Achim von Arnim.[17] To come closer to Schinkel himself, one needs to turn to one of his most enlightened clients, Wilhelm von Humboldt, who proved to be as much a mentor, friend, and advocate as a particularly stimulating interlocutor and tireless correspondent.

Humboldt had withdrawn from his ministerial office and was living on his ancestral estate at Tegel in the woods north of Berlin when he commissioned Schinkel to renovate an ungainly building that had served variously as a hunting lodge, a family retreat, and a caretaker's house for extensive holdings. Determined to dedicate his life to his studies and the collection of books and sculptures amassed during diplomatic assignments in Rome and Vienna, Humboldt may not have fully anticipated what Schinkel was to set before him: a complete overhaul that added three towers to the existing single one, preserved the oldest part of the lodge, doubled its footprint, and raised a spare but splendid three-story building with a roof terrace in the place of an awkward conglomerate of parts. The letters Humboldt wrote to his wife, Caroline, who meanwhile was taking the waters, as she often did, echo his conversations with the architect and with other artists in his circle.[18] "At Tegel Schinkel and [the sculptor] Rauch have given free reign to their passion for beauty," Humboldt told his wife, and went on to imagine a visit to a place "with four towers and a *gloriette* or rooftop pavilion in the Roman manner." Come fall of the following year, Humboldt was able to enjoy sunbathing on the warm, zinc-clad roof, a feature Schinkel applied to many of his buildings.

Long discussions had preceded the moment when Schinkel personally detailed his plans and explained their most ingenious features to his client, including the possibility of executing the work in such a fashion that the owners would be able to continue residing at Tegel while the transformation was underway. In a joyous *parlando* style Wilhelm wrote to Caroline as if he was taking his wife on an imaginary tour of their future residence, delighting in the architect's ingenious layout that provided not only for all the immediate needs but also created inspiring adjacencies and striking passages, opening up from a top-lit stairwell and linking study, library, sculpture gallery, and drawing rooms. Schinkel's watercolors for the central sculpture gallery enliven the walls with *faux marbre* revetment and provide for movable pedestals so that the antiques, both originals and in the form of casts, could be examined under ever-changing conditions. Humboldt proudly mentions that the sculptor Gottfried Schadow had bestowed praise upon Schinkel's proposal, and he even indulges in a bit of archaeological mystification when he imagines how much of a puzzle the presence of these ancient sculptures in the peat moss of Tegel will be to future excavators. Not only the near future of the estate but also the distant time of a later era ironically smile on Humboldt's fantasy. Wilhelm's letter to his wife is itself a piece of frozen conversation, preceded as it surely was by long exchanges between patron and architect, only to extend itself in later comments and reactions to the Humboldtschlösschen and its collection.[19]

In the years of Schinkel's work at Tegel, Johann Peter Eckermann, a kind of natural-born intellectual in search of a role in life, sought to fasten his ties with the admired writer Johann Wolfgang von Goethe. The account of their meetings and the extensive *Gespräche mit Goethe* ("Conversations with Goethe") did not exactly create a new genre but gave definition to the educational power of conversation.[20] Conspicuous are the locations in which their encounters took place and the seemingly casual circumstances that brought topics and issues to their joint attention. On the occasion of his first visit to Goethe in Weimar, Eckermann recalled,

> a chatty servant took me to the upper floor, opened the door after one stepped over the inscription SALVE as a portent of welcome. He led me through the room and opened the door to a second, more spacious one, asking me to wait here so I could be announced. Here was the coolest air in the house, a rug covered the floor and a canapé and two chairs upholstered in red made for a serene setting. On the side stood a grand piano and drawings and paintings of different size hung on the walls. Through yet another door, one caught a glimpse of the next room, also decorated with paintings. It didn't take long and Goethe, a most impressive figure, appeared.[21]

This was indeed the beginning of a great friendship, in the course of which Eckermann became the thoughtful chronicler of Goethe's late years and an interpreter of his more sibylline pronouncements.

The importance that Schinkel attached to conversation, not just for its social grace but also for the generation of ideas and, most of all, as the lubricant of critical examination, comes across in a project that remained on paper, but was beautifully illustrated on plate 66 of the *Sammlung architektonischer Entwürfe und Bauten*

("Collection of Architectural Designs and Buildings"). A terse text explains that a Lusthaus, a pleasure house in an isolated spot on a lake near Potsdam, "provides each of its four patrons with a separate cabinet [small room]."[22] Torchères in the niches that connect two cabinets to either side of the central stairs provide lighting in the evening both for reading and for the tea salon. The main purpose of the structure is to "bring the four participants together for tea in the evening." It goes without saying that an approach by land or by water adds attraction, as does the roof terrace and the exotic fowl in the sunken hen yard, but the principal aim is to engender convivial company. Why would one gather for tea, if not to regale one another with conversation? The peculiar purpose of the project calls to mind the four sons of King Friedrich Wilhelm III of Prussia who each went their own way for temperamental as well as dynastic reasons. Schinkel may have thought of changing all that by the simple English cure-all of afternoon tea. Be that as it may, the centrality of conversation to social life and, perhaps even more importantly, to the creative mind is slyly brought to attention in a project that may have to be ranked in a category of its own: teatime architecture.

To be sure, Schinkel could, and would, on numerous occasions, design something disarmingly modest while endowing it with architectural finesse. He did so for his lifelong colleague and friend Peter Beuth—head of Berlin's Technical School and an effective advocate of Schinkel's ideas with administrators and even the king. On Beuth's rural estate in present-day Niederschönhausen (now in Berlin), Schinkel added just a porch to the simplest of cottages. One may marvel at an imagination capable of rendering this addition of a roof over a small platform as an architectural set piece, but one cannot fault Schinkel for the thought he invested in the project. Completely forgotten until a few years ago, this veranda has been restored with the care worthy of a temple, but the result in no way overplays the hand Schinkel was dealt with the commission.[23] A shaded spot in which architecture seems to reveal its origins in the ritual adornment of its members, as Gottfried Semper was to argue in his *Style in the Technical and Tectonic Arts* a generation later, it also provides an ideal setting for conversation: surrounded by trees and gardens, the veranda transposes natural growth into the abstract language of ornament in vivid colors that are not naturalistic.[24] The posts are there to secure a roof over a company of kindred spirits and they are made to do so as stand-ins for the presence of architecture itself.

In 1810, Schinkel made one of his earliest experiments in the novel technique of lithography: at the bottom of the printing stone, on which an image of huge oak trees almost completely shrouding a Gothic church has been drawn, Schinkel added the caption, carefully penned in longhand, "An essay to express the sweet and yearning melancholy that fills the heart at the sound of a service wafting from the church ... drawn on stone by Schinkel" ["Versuch die liebliche sehnsuchstsvolle Wehmut auzudrücken welche das Herz beim Klange des Gottesdienstes aus der Kirche herschallend erfüllt ... auf Stein gezeichnet von Schinkel"]. What he set down for reproduction was a *Stimmungsbild*—a highly evocative image—of something that lends itself to describing rather than picturing. For who can build the sound, limn the affective response, and fathom the speculative analogy between trees and buildings? This recurrent theme touched on a range of associations Schinkel suggested in some of his pictures, for instance in large wall paintings for the court carpenter Glatz, and outdoors in landscape settings at Klein-Glienicke for Prince Carl of Prussia. These images engender a conversation between nature and society, between the unselfconscious majesty of battered trees and the ever-anxious human experience of time. A rupture in life, a break in the tranquil routine of things suddenly brings to the fore what is normally repressed. When, in the year Schinkel made his lithograph of the Gothic church behind trees, Queen Luise of Prussia died while the city was still under French occupation, he also, along with other artists, entered a project for a mausoleum. He never expected his idea to be realized and thus not only illustrated it in a beautiful large gouache but also delivered something of a "user's manual" along with it: "Approaching the Mausoleum," he wrote, "through a dense grove of ancient oak trees [actually the most ancient oaks!] advancing over a flight of stairs and entering, with a feeling of mild dread, into the penumbral porch, one will raise one's eyes toward the fan vaults formed by palms below which the departed rests in the glow of a sunrise."[25]

All of these instances point in the same direction: to the stage, to rapture, illusion, and an operatic consonance of means and effects. Equally as remarkable as Schinkel's groundbreaking work for plays and operas was the lavish publication of his stage sets by Count Redern, the director of the Royal Theater and also a private patron of Schinkel as an architect. If I were to illustrate my principal point in a single instance, I would point to Schinkel's practice of populating his plates with visitors. He started the *Sammlung architektonischer Entwürfe und Bauten* as soon as he had secured his first public commission, the Neue Wache ("New Guardhouse") in Berlin, in 1819 and ran it through more than two-dozen fascicles. As the title page indicates, he made a distinction between buildings that were executed and those that had been intended to be built but were not. It is not a facetious distinction, but one that justified including both variants of buildings that saw the light of day and those that remained on paper. Moreover, he gave himself room to advance arguments he may have lost at court or with the public, and he could put forward architectural ideas that, for one reason or another, would have disappeared without the printed page. In this regard Schinkel entered into a long and often painful argument about the merit of projects and the likelihood of their survival in the face of neglect or heedless alterations, and he also was able to render his buildings in the way he expected them to be seen and experienced.[26]

What most distinguishes Schinkel's plates are the thoughtful visitors to his buildings. Sometimes, they come in droves, as they do in the vestibule of the Altes Museum, and sometimes they are few. In the exedra of the raised garden parterre at Charlottenhof, there are just two: one gestures animatedly toward the villa, his hat still on, his cane to hand, while his companion sits back, takes in the view, and listens to what the other has to say. Sitting back, putting his fingers on his lips, he contemplates, weighs, and evaluates what excites the other. Two poles in the experience of architecture: heightened engagement, quiet reflection. It takes two for company, but it also takes the ability to step aside and reconsider, to immerse oneself before yielding to the temptation to act out and explain. In a word, you need to have a *conversation*, even if it should be only with yourself. Reading Novalis's novel *Heinrich von Ofterdingen*, the French writer Julien Gracq recognized the nature of its conversations that run their course not as "a striking exchange, but as a system of indefinably enriched and amplified echoes."[27]

If there is such a thing as a collective conversation, I would suggest it is the "hum" of the city. All the sounds that make it the place it is, swarming with people, crowded by vehicles, and, like a bank of mussels, constantly filtering its own life-giving substance and forever negotiating between the one and the many, between high and low tides, between spring and fall. The gorgeous plates of Schinkel's *oeuvre complète*—certainly a pioneering publication, able to record his professional vagaries while integrating and cumulating his ideas—may have been less than persuasive in their rendering of the urban transformations he advocated. When we take license and "colorize" the filigree of wiry lines in such an instance as the bridge to the island in the river Spree, enlivening the architect's drawing with the palette of his painter friend Eduard Gaertner, Schinkel's vision of the river bringing back the forest in its wake assumes a force to be reckoned with.[28] Letting the barges glide—for it is from the water level that the view is taken—the trees rustle, and the birds fly as the sun passes overhead, we'd have to add only the hooves of horses, the cranking of wheels, and Robert Schumann's piece titled "As If from Afar" ["Wie aus der Ferne"] to listen in on the town's own "conversation with itself."

1 Kurt W. Forster, *Schinkel: A Meander Through His Life and Work* (Basel: Birkhäuser, 2018). I recall with pleasure that an early draft of Frampton's *Studies in Tectonic Culture* opened with a quotation from an essay of mine on "Schinkel's Panoramic Planning of Berlin."

2 Useful sources for a theory of conversation have been assembled by Claudia Schmölders, *Die Kunst des Gesprächs. Texte zur Geschichte der europäischen Konversationstheorie* (Munich: dtv, 1979; 1986).

3 Paul Celan, "Gespräch im Gebirge," *Gesammelte Werke in fünf Bänden*, ed. Beda Allemann and Stefan Reichert (Frankfurt am Main: Suhrkamp, 1983–86), III, 169–73.

4 Heinrich von Kleist, *Werke und Briefe*, ed. Siegfried Streller (Frankfurt: Insel, 1986), III, 722–23.

5 Ibid.

6 Ibid.

7 François de Callières (1645–1717) was a most able diplomat and negotiator in the service of Louis XIV who cultivated the art of the deal and the mastery of vocabulary and expression in several treatises published during the 1680s and 1690s.

8 Henri Heine, *Reisebilder—Tableau de Voyage—précédée d'une étude sur H. Heine par Théophile Gautier* (Paris: Lévy, 1888), 239, where Heine observes that the "French cannot suffer those silent reunions they call *conversations anglaises*; instead they hurry from café to club, from club to salon in incessant conversation" [my translation from French]. The particular charm critics were quick to recognize in Heine's *Reisebilder* and in his poetry resides in their conversational *parlando*, the hallmark

of French *causerie*, see Rolf Hosfeld, *Heinrich Heine. Die Erfindung des europäischen Intellektuellen* (Berlin: Siedler, 2014), 169.

9 The very term has been captured by dotcom for word choice and usage that appears as the first item upon googling "thesaurus"!

10 See Kurt W. Forster, "Warum Karl Friedrich Schinkel kein architektonisches Lehrbuch geschrieben hat," in Jörg Trempler, *Schinkels Motive* (Berlin: Mattes & Seitz, 2007), 7–31.

11 Alfred Freiherr von Wolzogen, *Aus Schinkels Nachlass, Reisetagebücher, Briefe und Aphorismen, mitgetheilt und mit einem Verzeichniß sämtlicher Werke Schinkels versehen* (Berlin: Verlag der Königlichen Gheimen Oberhofbuchdruckerei R. Decker, 1862–64), II, 340; and *Karl Friedrich Schinkel und Clemens Brentano. Wettbewerb der Künstlerfreunde*, ed. Birgit Verwiebe (Berlin: Nationalgalerie, SMB, 2008), 9–27.

12 Kurt W. Forster, "Schinkel's Panoramic Planning of Berlin," *Modulus*, 16 (1983): 63–77.

13 *Achim und Bettine in ihren Briefen*, ed. Werner Vordtriede (Frankfurt am Main: Suhrkamp, 1961), I, 164.

14 Otto Betz and Veronika Straub, eds., *Bettine und Arnim, Briefe der Freundschaft und Liebe*, I, 1806–1808 (Frankfurt am Main: Knecht, 1986), 27.

15 *Achim und Bettine in ihren Briefen*, I, 84.

16 Francesco Algarotti, *Il newtonianismo per le dame, ovvero dialoghi sopra la luce e i colori* (Napoli [actually Venice], 1737).

17 *Hollins Liebesleben* (1802) enjoyed a *succès de scandale*, as had Friedrich Schlegel's *Lucinde*, conceived as the first of four novels, in 1799. The loose threads of Schlegel's *Lucinde* were taken up by other writers (Friedrich Schleiermacher, Johann Bernhard Vermehren, and Johann Wilhelm Christern), typically in the form of *Briefromane*.

18 For a detailed account see Forster, *Schinkel*, 197–210.

19 Among the most perceptive reactions to the Schlösschen (and its architecture) with its "shining figures" is a poem by the young painter and, later, writer Gottfried Keller who wrote a laconic poem on Tegel shortly after the middle of the nineteenth century, when still a student in Berlin, see Forster, *Schinkel*, 208.

20 Johann Peter Eckermann (1792–1854), whose *Gespräche mit Goethe* were published in 1836, is one of the most eminent exemplars of the educational power of *conversation*. Another preeminent conversationalist, the Bostonian Margret Fuller Ossoli, translated the *Gespräche* into English: *Conversations with Goethe in the Last Years of His Life*, trans. S.M. Fuller [Marchesa Ossoli] (Boston and Cambridge, U.K.: James Munroe and Company, 1839). Fuller also intended to write a biography of Goethe but health reasons and her political involvement in Italy prevented her from following through; see Nancy Craig Simmons, "Margaret Fuller's Boston Conversations: The 1839–1840 Series," *Studies in the American Renaissance* (1994), 195–226.

21 Johann Peter Eckermann, *Gespräche mit Goethe in den letzten Jahren seines Lebens* (Leipzig: Brockhaus, 1836), 16: "Das Innere des Hauses machte auf mich einen sehr angenehmen Eindruck; ohne glänzend zu sein, war alles höchst edel und einfach; auch deuteten verschiedene an der Treppe stehende Abgüsse antiker Statuen auf Goethes besondere Neigung zur bildenden Kunst und dem griechischen Altertum. Ich sah verschiedene Frauenzimmer, die unten im Hause geschäftig hin und wider gingen, auch einen der schönen Knaben Ottiliens, der zutraulich zu mir herankam und mich mit großen Augen anblickte. Nachdem ich mich ein wenig umgesehen, ging ich sodann mit dem sehr gesprächigen Bedienten die Treppe hinauf zur ersten Etage. Er öffnete ein Zimmer, vor dessen Schwelle man die Zeichen SALVE als gute Vorbedeutung eines freundlichen Willkommenseins überschritt. Er führte mich durch dieses Zimmer hindurch und öffnete ein zweites, etwas geräumigeres, wo er mich zu verweilen bat, indem er ging, mich seinem Herrn zu melden. Hier war die kühlste erquicklichste Luft; auf dem Boden lag ein Teppich gebreitet, auch war es durch ein rotes Kanapee und Stühle von gleicher Farbe überaus heiter möbliert; gleich zur Seite stand ein Flügel, und an den Wänden sah man Handzeichnungen und Gemälde verschiedener Art und Größe. Durch die offene Tür gegenüber blickte man sodann in ein ferneres Zimmer, gleichfalls mit Gemälden verziert, durch welches der Bediente gegangen war mich zu melden. Es währte nicht lange [...] so kam Goethe, in einem blauen Oberrock und in Schuhen; eine erhabene Gestalt!"

22 Schinkel, *Sammlung architektonischer Entwürfe und Bauten*, commentary on Lusthaus an der Havel, n.p.

23 Landesdenkmalamt Berlin, Schinkel Veranda in Niederschönhausen: to my knowledge, this beautifully restored veranda has not yet been adequately published.

24 The palette of high-keyed colors is derived from the recently discovered polychromy of ancient temples in Italy and Sicily; see https://www.archaeology.wiki/blog/2016/05/11/ancient-polychromy-sculpture-architecture (accessed December 22, 2019).

25 *Kataloge der Berliner Akademie-Ausstellungen 1786–1850. Quellen und Schriften zur bildenden Kunst*, ed. Helmut Börsch-Supan, 4 vols. (Berlin: Hessling, 1971), I, no. 189.

26 Kurt W. Forster, "Bau, Bild und Bühne: Wie Schinkel seine Architektur veranschaulicht," in *Karl Friedrich Schinkel: Geschichte und Poesie: Das Studienbuch*, ed. Hein-Th. Schulze Altcappenberg and Rolf H. Johannsen, published in conjunction with the 2012–13 exhibition presented at the Kupferstichkabinett, Staatliche Museen zu Berlin and the Kunsthalle der Hypo-Kulturstiftung Munich (Berlin: Kupferstichkabinett SMB and Deutscher Kunstverlag, 2012), 63–72.

27 Julien Gracq, "Novalis et 'Henri d'Ofterdingen'," in *Oeuvres complètes* (Paris: Gallimard, 1989), I, 993.

28 For an actual integration of color into Schinkel's prints, see Forster, *Schinkel*, 125–26, ill. 89, colorization by Boyuan Zhang.

On Robert Venturi's *Complexity and Contradiction in Architecture*

Rafael Moneo

The enthusiasm with which Vincent Scully read Robert Venturi's *Complexity and Contradiction in Architecture* is present from the very first lines of his introduction, when he states that it "is probably the most important writing on the making of architecture since Le Corbusier's *Vers une Architecture* of 1923,"[1] and it may be said that his opinion has strongly influenced the way we read Venturi's book. After the trivialization of the principles of the Modern Movement, the time was ripe for Scully to celebrate the discovery of a uniquely relevant book. And Venturi's book was truly unforeseen, freshly subversive and provocative, eagerly showing us that it was precisely the transgression, the anomaly, and the contingent where architecture achieved its great intensity and splendor.

That Venturi's text possessed a will to generate polemic is beyond question: "Orthodox Modern architects have tended to recognize complexity insufficiently or inconsistently. In their attempt to break with tradition and start all over again, they idealized the primitive and elementary at the expense of the diverse and the sophisticated."[2] Venturi shows his hand right from the beginning of the text and doesn't hesitate to cite Frank Lloyd Wright and Le Corbusier as examples of a manner of understanding architecture firstly for its simplicity and harmony and secondly for its primary forms, unmistakable and free of ambiguity, in contrast to the complexity and contradiction that he celebrates.[3]

Venturi's desire to present *Complexity and Contradiction in Architecture* as the antithesis of Le Corbusier, in Scully's opinion, should be his essential objective, confirmed by the twenty-two references made to Le Corbusier in Scully's preface. Scully believes that Venturi's proposals, "in their recognition of complexity and their respect for what exists, create the most necessary antidote to that cataclysmic purism of contemporary urban renewal which has presently brought so many cities to the brink of catastrophe, and in which Le Corbusier's ideas have now found terrifying vulgarization."[4]

Venturi's book, therefore, is a challenge to those architects of "urban renewal" who, in Scully's opinion, are "the more academic minded of the Bauhaus generation with its utter lack of irony, its spinsterish disdain for the popular culture but shaky grasp on any other, its incapacity and its preoccupation with a rather prissily purist aesthetics."[5] Here Scully presents Venturi's *Complexity and Contradiction in Architecture* as an alternative manifesto to Le Corbusier's *Vers une Architecture*.

For Scully, *Complexity and Contradiction* was also a quintessentially American book, to be celebrated as an alternative to those produced by the European avant-garde. As such, Scully is particularly satisfied to see Venturi attentive to such architects as Furness, Sullivan, Wright, Kahn, Giurgola, and Moore, who, while still holding to the tenets of academicism or the Modern Movement, reveal an independence and vigor that are genuinely American. Further accentuating its American character is Venturi's interest in Pop Art, illustrating how much he feels bound to the vision of American artists, and a culture where the "contemporary package" has such great importance. Venturi's book represents the ability of American culture, even with its debt to European precedents, to establish an independent and distinctive perspective. Ultimately, Scully's interpretation of *Complexity and Contradiction in Architecture* left certain aspects of the book behind which shouldn't be neglected.

Complexity and Contradiction was something more. *Complexity and Contradiction* could be read not so much as a manifesto but rather as a declaration of principles of how to see and understand architecture. *Complexity and Contradiction* could be understood not so much as a subversive provocation, ever attentive to the anomaly and celebrating the unique, but as a book with a clear notion of architecture and its role in history. *Complexity and Contradiction* could be understood as an ambitious attempt to explore and investigate the instruments that served the architects of the past and that still serve today. It is surprising today to see that critics did not pay more attention to Venturi's preface to the book, where he expresses explicitly his attitude and ideas, which extend beyond the reading offered by Vincent Scully.

And we would have to begin by saying that, in contrast to that of most of his contemporaries, Venturi's frame of reference—his way of seeing architecture—is based on an unabridged history of architecture. It is here, whether citing sophisticated architecture, or anonymous, popular constructions, that Venturi finds the examples that serve to illustrate his ideas and discoveries with respect to the means, processes, and instruments with which architects work.

The first lines of his preface in which he establishes the thesis of his argument are clear: "This book is both an attempt at architectural criticism and an apologia —an explanation, indirectly, of my work."[6] Venturi writes about architecture as an architect, "I am a practicing architect, my ideas on architecture are inevitably a by-product of the criticism which accompanies working."[7] Venturi concludes the book by presenting and commenting on his own work, returning to the custom typical of architects who, putting forward new theoretical proposals, provide examples from their own work.

And he recognizes from the very first moment that his critical perspective is based on the terms defined by T.S. Eliot in his 1919 essay, "Tradition and the Individual Talent," which claims that the critical work accompanies creative work, being "of capital importance ... in the work of creation itself."[8] A poet, like an architect, considers his work as something continuously subject to critical judgment. To emphasize this point, Venturi cites Eliot again, "Probably, indeed, the larger part of the labour of sifting, combining, constructing, expunging, correcting, testing: this frightful toil is as much critical as creative. I maintain even that the criticism employed by a trained and skilled writer on his own work is the most vital, the highest kind of criticism ..."[9] Eliot seems to distinguish here, in the process of a work's elaboration, an instrumental, critical aspect, and another that is strictly creative, and suggests that it is in this self-criticism that accompanies the creative process where we find the most valuable expression of what a critical attitude signifies. Venturi expresses himself in the same terms, saying "I write, then, as an architect who employs criticism rather than a critic who chooses architecture."[10] For Venturi, the critical reflection is necessary—even inevitable—as we can see in the following text: "Self-consciousness is necessarily a part of creation and criticism. Architects today are too educated to be either primitive or totally spontaneous, and architecture is too complex to be approached with carefully maintained ignorance."[11] Without this self-critical view of the work, it is not possible to understand it.

Venturi feels comfortable with Eliot, coincides with his aesthetic proposals, and returns immediately to cite his texts when he reminds us that analysis and comparison are the literary tools that he would also like to employ in order to understand his preferred works of architecture. The analysis and the comparative method should not be incompatible with architecture. Analysis implies fragmenting the apparent unity of an architectural work into elements, in pieces susceptible to be considered independently of the whole, allowing a critical appraisal of the buildings that presupposes the availability of an idea of what they are, a certain idea that precedes that which is architecture. The examination and the comparison of the terms of literary criticism do not appear out of place when talking of architecture: it would be enough to confirm such a remark in the characterization of architectonic elements as linguistic terms to define the styles. The task Venturi assumes for himself in his book is to identify those moments in which the knowledge and the critical spirit brought the architect to abandon the normative, and make use of their creative capacity. The transgression that comes as the combination of both—knowledge and creativity—should not be understood only as rebellion, as we will see shortly. Forsaking the normative, when challenged by certain contingencies, makes it possible for us to accept particular circumstances that foster the appearance of the unexpected, the singular, and the particular.

When the young Venturi tells us, "As an architect I try to be guided not by habit but by a conscious sense of the past—by precedent, thoughtfully considered,"[12] he presumes not only to enlist us in his valuable experience of architecture but also to make us see how he understands architecture, assuming that such knowledge appears both in the present and in the past. The defense that Eliot makes of how much the past weighs upon us—not allowing us to establish a clear distance between past, present, and future—is also employed by Venturi. To such a degree that Venturi finds it better to cite Eliot again rather than define these terms in his own words,

93 Rafael Moneo and Kenneth Frampton in dialogue, Madrid, May 10, 2017, interview published online by *Magaceen*, magaceen.com.

> we seldom speak of tradition ... Seldom, perhaps does the word appear except in a phrase of censure. If otherwise, it is vaguely approbative, with the implication, as to a work approved, of some pleasing archeological reconstruction ... Yet if the only form of tradition, of handing down, consisted in following the ways of the immediate generation before us in a blind or timid adherence to its successes, "tradition" should be positively discouraged ... Tradition is a matter of much wider significance. It cannot be inherited, and if you want it you must obtain it by great labour. It involves, in the first place, the historical sense, which we may call nearly indispensable to anyone who would continue to be a poet beyond his twenty-fifth year; and the historical sense involves perception, not only of the pastness of the past, but of its presence; the historical sense compels a man to write not merely with his own generation in his bones, but with a feeling that the whole of the literature of Europe ... has a simultaneous existence and composes a simultaneous order. This historical sense, which is a sense of the timeless as well as of the temporal and of the timeless and temporal together, is what makes a writer traditional, and it is at the same time what makes a writer most acutely conscious of his place in time, of his own contemporaneity ... No poet, no artist of any kind, has his complete meaning alone.

And Venturi adds immediately afterward, "I agree with Eliot and reject the obsession of Modern architects who, to quote Aldo van Eyck, 'have been harping continually on what is different in our time to such an extent that they have lost touch with what is not different, with what is essentially the same.'"[13] I believe that such an extended citation is necessary in order to understand Venturi's vision of architecture, and for that reason I find it pertinent here.

Venturi is aware that the objective of the book is to offer an answer to the puzzle of present-day architecture.

> Everything is said in the context of current architecture and consequently certain targets are attacked—in general the limitations of orthodox Modern architecture and city planning, in particular, the platitudinous architects who invoke integrity, technology, or electronic programming as ends in architecture, the popularizers who paint "fairy stories over our chaotic reality" and suppress those complexities and contradictions inherent in art and experience.[14]

But such an effort would not be possible without the influence of the past that inescapably affects us. And above all a recent past that contributed greatly to the configuration of the present reality in which we live. Venturi's ambition is to make us share his understanding of architecture as we read *Complexity and Contradiction*.[15]

Venturi wants to show us how he sees architecture, all architecture, making use of critical reflections developed by literary critics rather than critics of the plastic arts, including architecture. Venturi will not make use of the term "zeitgeist" in order to explain the building's appearance, like many critics had done after Sigfried Giedion, nor would he rely on the category of spatial evolution as did Bruno Zevi. His proposition was to see architecture without interpreting it as a progressive, temporal process. The examples that he uses do not obey a temporal order. They are opposed to a Hegelian historiography that seeks to discover the principles and laws that give meaning to an era: a history, ultimately, that is guided by the notion of continuous progress. As an alternative, Venturi defends a vision of architecture that does not distinguish between the present and the past. This is a vision of architecture that is understood in terms of timelessness once we see that it maintains certain interests over time even as its aspect changes. Again, it is pertinent to cite Eliot, when he writes that the writer, the artist—and even the architect we might add,

> must be aware of the obvious fact that art never improves, but that the material of art is never quite the same. He must be aware that the mind of Europe—the mind of his own country—a mind which he learns in time to be more important that his own private mind—is a mind which changes, and that this change is a development which abandons nothing *en route*, which does not superannuate either Shakespeare, or Homer, or the rock drawing of the Magdalenian draughtsman.[16]

Venturi resists a historiography that sees the evolution of architecture like an ascendant process, accompanying technological change. The authentic work of art, that which consciously or unconsciously was achieved by certain artists and architects in a given moment, has little to do with a vision that only seeks to understand the meaning of an artwork by situating it at its particular point in the course of historical development. The work of art, the work of architecture, should be seen within itself, absorbed in the infinite magma of the past that survives today and which, whether we wish it or not, incorporates the work of individuals at any given moment in history. It is a perspective that maintains the relevance of the notion of contemporaneity, a contemporaneity that constantly changes.

Complexity and Contradiction in Architecture shows us, through a series of architectural examples, the means, processes, and mechanisms used by architects—consciously or unconsciously—to respond to contingent situations, unforeseen responses that became works that earned the recognition as works of art. And although Eliot gave the term "monuments" a meaning that does not apply precisely to our notion of architecture, in the following quote it is still pertinent:

> The existing monuments form an ideal order among themselves, which is modified by the introduction of the new (the really new) work of art among them. The existing order is complete before the new work arrives: for order to persist after the supervention of novelty, the *whole* existing order must be, if ever so slightly, altered; and so relations, proportions, values of each work of art toward the whole are readjusted; and this is conformity between the old and the new. Whoever has approved this idea of order, of the form of European, of English literature will not find it preposterous that the past should be altered by the present as much as the present is directed by the past.[17]

I believe that Venturi would feel close to this declaration of principles with respect to the relationship between past and present. The past is here understood as a "whole," as if all that went before were included in the present. It is not so much to anticipate the future, assuming that one could foresee the trajectory of history, than to accept that works will form part of the "whole" to which Eliot alludes. Our past understood as testimony of who we were and the reality which we lived. Our work—legitimated, in the best cases, by provoking a change in the existing order—gives the work of art a dimension much different from that of a romantic omnipotence. A present in which we inevitably live and that will always be an enigma whose meaning escapes us. Something of this we understand when Eliot says, "I have tried to point out the importance of the relation of the poem to other poems by other authors, and suggested the conception of poetry as a living whole of all the poetry that has ever been written."[18] I read with pleasure these lines that help me to understand how Venturi would like us to see architecture.

To see the past, history, in this way, implies not seeking to establish a precise idea of what direction architecture will take in the future but rather recognizing the importance of the present and its significance for us. This is a much different proposition from that we find in most recent architectural history, in which the most important attribute of a work seems to be its condition as a precursor to another work or a linguistic invention.

Such a vision of the process of incorporation of the work to the patrimony entrusted to us by the past does not permit mechanical repetition, but, on the contrary, understands the new—continuous change—as something that can be such only if one is conscious of how architecture is produced. Eliot writes: "We must distinguish of course between taste and fashion. Fashion, the love of change for its own sake, the desire for something new, is very transient; taste is something that springs from a deeper source."[19] The new, including that which seems dictated by trends, is something inevitable, but that also requires us to introduce the notion of taste. Taste as instinctive, a personal and profound response to form, as the ultimate agent of change. Taste, therefore, as something closer to an aesthetic tendency, immanent, deep, which dictates the reaction—innate, or cultivated from experience—before a work of art or architecture.

With this vision of things we find ourselves in a book like *Complexity and Contradiction in Architecture*. The history of architecture, the panorama of the past, appears at once, without distinguishing styles or attempting to describe the causes of architecture's development. Venturi sees the history of architecture as a legacy that does not allow us to anticipate the future. Fortunately, what we build today does not determine what we will build in the future. Architectural history is a universe in which one encounters the works that help to explain the instruments and principles used by the most admired architects; works whose value becomes even more apparent when our eyes settle on specific aspects and episodes. Venturi is interested more in an understanding of the singular and contingent than in explaining the formal principles of a particular period or style.

> Nonstraightforward Architecture: A Gentle Manifesto. I like complexity and contradiction in architecture. I do not like the incoherence or arbitrariness of incompetent architecture nor the precious intricacies of picturesqueness or expressionism. Instead, I speak of a complex and contradictory architecture based on the richness and ambiguity of modern experience, including that experience which is inherent in art. Everywhere, except in architecture, complexity and contradiction have been acknowledged ...[20]

Venturi feels an attraction toward those works characterized by complexity, contradiction, not incompetent or arbitrary in their incompetence—ambiguous, rich, influenced by the work of other artists. Works that pertain to "nonstraightforward architecture," architecture that is not obvious and self-evident, and for which Venturi feels an irresistible attraction. There is, in fact, a straightforward architecture, direct, canonical, which imposes itself and that we accept without dissent: the Greek temple, the Gothic cathedral, or the Renaissance palace. But there are others that appeal to us that are not so straightforward, that do not impose themselves upon us imperiously, and that yet are pregnant with architecture. "I am for richness of meaning rather than clarity of meaning; for the implicit function as well as the explicit function. I prefer 'both-and' to 'either-or', black and white, and sometimes gray, to black or white."[21]

With this declaration of principles with respect to his taste and preference, and in spite of the fact that Venturi resists the use of other disciplines in his work when he states, "I make no special attempt to relate architecture to other things,"[22] it comes as no surprise that Venturi finds more kindred spirits among literary critics than among those architectural experts who established the canon of modernity in architecture, moved by the desire to establish norms and principles that, in their apparent rationality, seemed unquestionable. For this reason, it is not unexpected that Venturi cites a critic like William Empson, who in 1930 published his book—with a subsequent edition in 1946—*Seven Types of Ambiguity*. In it, Empson speaks of ambiguity as something present in his preferred poetry. Ambiguity, therefore, no longer as a pejorative term but rather a virtue, characteristic of the most intense moments of poetry; an experience that is defined by a certain ineffable quality.

The critical essay is the literary format that Venturi utilizes in *Complexity and Contradiction in Architecture* and explains what he understands by the terms "complexity and contradiction," compared to "simplification or the picturesqueness," and "ambiguity," to which he dedicates the first part of his book. For Venturi architecture, or at least the architecture that interests him, must be complex and clearly could be contradictory. The chapters that follow respond to the ways that elements can be manipulated, utilized, and exploited and how they change due to purely architectonic mechanisms, such as adaptation, juxtaposition, and contrast. In the last chapter of the book Venturi examines the definitive importance the concept of the "whole" has both for building and for architecture.

Repeatedly citing Empson at the beginning of his book, Venturi openly recognizes his debt. The architectural experience Venturi had travelling through Europe during his tenure at the American Academy in Rome seems to make him more comfortable with Empson's concepts. Like Empson, Venturi encountered elements of double significance in his architectural analysis, lending the term a meaning similar to Empson's in *Seven Types of Ambiguity*. Venturi also had perceived that a building's elements do not always serve a single end and that, just as in poems, not all similar words have the same meaning, in much the same way that in buildings elements can often be interpreted in different ways. And frequently the attraction we feel toward a poem or a work of art or architecture is rooted in the ambiguity of the elements,

94 Moneo and Frampton, Madrid, May 10, 2017.

capable of a wide variety of meanings. I imagine Venturi satisfied in seeing Empson speak of ambiguity when he says, "The fundamental situation, whether it deserves to be called ambiguous or not, is that a word or a grammatical structure is effective in several ways at once,"[23] suggesting the appeal of ambiguity in contrast to the banality of a strict application of norms and canons.

Venturi openly confesses his interest for particular works of architecture and celebrates the use of tools learned from the literary critics in their analysis of sonnets in expressing his thinking about a certain building. And a term like "ambiguity" figures prominently in his book in the same way that it had for Empson earlier. Venturi shows us that the term is also relevant in architecture, in those moments when works of architecture are characterized by complexity and the presence of contradiction. Thus, Venturi speaks of the ambiguity of the works he esteems, using—something that should not surprise us—as an argument of authority Eliot again, who "called the art of the Elizabethan poets an impure art … in which complexity and contradiction are exploited."[24] Empson takes particular notice of these poets who "dared to treat what had been regarded in poetry, imprecision of meaning, as poetry's chief virtue."[25] Venturi parallels Empson's ideas when he says that there are works of architecture, in his opinion, that should be comprehended this way in order to appreciate them. "Ambiguity and tensions are everywhere in an architecture of complexity and contradiction."[26] Venturi continues, "according to Stanley Edgar Hyman, Empson sees ambiguity as 'collecting precisely at the points of greatest poetic effectiveness, and finds it breeding a quality he calls "tension" which we might phrase as the poetic impact itself.'"[27] Ambiguity and tension, Venturi insists—absorbing, accepting, assuming the complexity and the ambiguity in architecture that interests him—is how he can incorporate the contradictions that serve as an obstacle to our understanding and appreciation of their intriguing and suggestive presence.

The ambiguity that Empson recognizes in a poem is much more obvious and pertinent in a work of architecture, in buildings that serve different purposes at the same time. Venturi cites Paul Rudolph's observation that, "Mies makes wonderful buildings only because he ignores many aspects of a building. If he solved more problems, his buildings would be far less potent,"[28] as an affirmation that it is not always possible to simplify in pursuit of a mistaken clarity. When Venturi pauses, at the beginning of the book, to comment on two works by Philip Johnson—the Wiley House and Johnson's own house in New Canaan—he cannot help but recognize that "They ignore the real complexity and contradiction inherent in the domestic program,"[29] and that in both houses there is "A diagram of an oversimplified program for living—an abstract theory of either-or."[30] In writing these lines, Venturi undoubtedly feels the support of Empson when the latter says, "I have myself usually said 'either ... or' when meaning 'both ... and.'"[31]

I do not believe that the value of Venturi's book is lessened by suggesting that its structure, when he speaks of manipulating the elements, relies so directly on Empson's *Seven Types of Ambiguity*. Venturi speaks to us of "contradictory levels; the phenomenon of both-and in architecture; the double functioning element; the conventional element; contradiction adapted; contradiction juxtaposed, and the inside and the outside."[32] Simply mentioning these words, one sees that there is an echo of the terms and arguments used by Empson to explain how and where poetic expression originates. One easily encounters in Empson's text such expressions as "a sentence can have different meanings";[33] that "two or more meanings are resolved in one";[34] that "actually I've said many times one or the other when in reality what I wanted to say was both";[35] and "certain types of ambiguity take place when the meaning of a word, the two values of ambiguity, are the two definitions opposed by the context."[36] Because Venturi's way of approaching architecture is similar to Empson's approach to poetry, we should not be surprised that both of them resort to the same terms and that we can equate Empson's "poetic expression" with what would be for Venturi the appearance in architecture, the authentic experience of architecture, where presence and knowledge meet.

Venturi's book concludes, as I mentioned, with a chapter dedicated to "The Obligation Toward the Difficult Whole,"[37] which I would say is of great interest as it is where the architect's objectives are most clearly shown. We hear Venturi's voice again,

> An architecture of complexity and accommodation does not forsake the whole ... The whole is difficult to achieve ... A complex system in Herbert A. Simon's

> definition includes "a large number of parts that interact in a non-simple way" ... The difficult whole in an architecture of complexity and contradiction includes multiplicity and diversity of elements.[38]

Once having accepted the elemental condition of architecture, reaching the whole implies giving meaning to the elements in different positions and at different scales. To indicate the way, the direction that allows the work to reach wholeness, Venturi introduces the notion of "inflection," almost identical to the Spanish word *inflexión*, at the same time alluding to the capacity to "bend," to adapt itself to specific circumstances, which appears to recognize also a certain debt to the Latin root (*inflectere*) when we recall the significance of words like declinate and modulate, adjusting the tenses of a verb to a precise position in a sentence. "Inflection in architecture is the way in which the whole is implied by exploiting the nature of the individual parts rather than their position or number."[39]

The whole is here understood as a result of the knowing juxtaposition of elements understood as fragments with their own particular life. The importance that Venturi sees in the whole leads him to cite Cleanth Brooks:

> It is not enough for a poet to analyze his experience as the scientist does, breaking it up into parts. His task is finally to unify experience. He must return to us the unity of the experience itself as man knows it in his own experience ... which, at his higher and more serious levels, triumphs over the apparently contradictory and conflicting elements of the experience by unifying them into a new pattern.[40]

Venturi helps us to interpret the meaning of "unity of experience," the whole, by offering us a variety of examples in different fields from the domestic to the urban. Venturi brilliantly illustrates how architects resolve with the "whole" the required "contradictions" and any one of the examples provided reveals his perspicacity and deep understanding of architecture. The whole comes to the rescue in the case of the difficult duality in the architecture of Sullivan and Vanbrugh, a complex duality that also appears in the work of painters such as Piero della Francesca, Morris Louis, or Ellsworth Kelly. The notion of inflection justifies, on the other hand, the inclusion of a work as polemic as Armando Brasini's Orfanotrofio (Orphanage of Il Buon Pastore), in which the diversity of its parts and its unsettling position are not an obstacle to our seeing the building as a whole: the "difficult whole" as the intuited final state when all the individual parts find their proper place. The Albertian resonances that seem to appear in an affirmation like this one disappear when we consider that the parts to which Venturi refers have nothing to do with the formal consistency which Alberti's organicism sought. The examples that he offers remove any doubt. From the whole one understands "the orgy of contrasting dualities of forms"[41] that we encounter in Gaudí's building, and even from the view of the whole one could ask, "is not Main Street almost all right?"[42] Accepting that it is, the whole that Venturi speaks of in *Complexity and Contradiction* allows us to anticipate the defense of Las Vegas that appears later in *Learning from Las Vegas*, written in collaboration with Denise Scott Brown in 1972.

We should pause now and examine the way in which Venturi proceeds and, even further, discuss his method. Again, we should cite Empson in order to explain what in my opinion is present in Venturi's method. Empson says, "The process of getting to understand a poet is precisely that of constructing his poems in one's own mind."[43] This is precisely what Venturi proposes: the ability to penetrate in depth the mind of the architect, who, consciously or unconsciously, used expressive processes, plastic inventions, and formal proposals, not so different from those used to confirm the theses of *Complexity and Contradiction*. And it will be offering us built examples to show us how architects proceeded, revealing which unexpected mechanisms were used to resolve particular and complex situations, as Venturi aims to make us see the authentic architecture. An architect is not so different from a poet with respect to their processes and rhetorical devices that contribute to the fact that for us their work has something novel, and it will be through the analysis of architectural work that most attracts him that Venturi makes us see how architecture reaches its greatest height of expression. In as much as a critic accepts the challenge of analyzing and evaluating works of architecture, Venturi appears much closer to the literary critics than any architectural critic. Demonstrating the coincidences in the sensibility between Venturi and the critics mentioned is my objective with this text, with the full understanding that Venturi's is not a mechanical translation of the processes introduced by the cited critics but rather a creative effort of interpretation that demands our respect and appreciation.

Venturi chooses, based on his instinct and considering their inherent value, moments and episodes in architecture characterized by complexity. He makes no claim to offer an exhaustive analysis of the examples he offers. He makes no allusion either to historic documents, construction details, or social conditions. Curiously, and in spite of the fact that he refers to literary critics, he does not seek to equate architectural expression with poetic expression. He does not speak of endowing buildings with "poetic content"; rather the contrary, he aims to reduce the experience we have of architecture to something very specific. He identifies a small aspect of the building, a particular point of view, the singularity of a detail that suddenly illuminates the work and makes present its architectural essence. He does not presume to offer us his experience or his knowledge in a systematic fashion. He wishes, by jumping from one example to another and emphasizing the discontinuity, to show us how architectural knowledge is present in the work, and how to a greater or lesser degree, it is present in all built work.

Obviously, he feels "partiality for certain eras: Mannerist, Baroque and Rococo especially."[44] He openly confesses his preferences. And he recognized his condition as architect/critic, coinciding again with Eliot: "one of the functions of the critic is to help the literary public of its time recognize an affinity with a poet, with a type of poetry, or with a poetic period instead of another." Discovering these affinities, the critic, the architect, is sharing with us certain works that invite his reflection. Venturi wants to openly oppose the architecture that he sees around him and he believes he has the arguments to do so:

> The desire for a complex architecture with its attendant contradictions is not only a reaction to the banality or prettiness of current architecture. It is an attitude common in the Mannerist periods: the sixteenth century in Italy or the Hellenistic period in Classical art, and is also a continuous strain seen in such diverse architects as Michelangelo, Palladio, Borromini, Vanbrugh, Hawksmoor, Ledoux, Butterfield, Soane, Furness, Sullivan, Lutyens, and recently, Le Corbusier, Aalto, Kahn, and others.[45]

The architects that interest him—varied and dispersed, in different countries and from different times—all tend to be rebellious and heterodox, sharing in a recognition of the value of complexity and contradiction in architecture.

With respect to the first half of the twentieth century, perhaps the most notable of these architects was Edwin Lutyens, to whom Venturi makes frequent reference, saving him from recent neglect. By so doing, I think that Venturi recognizes the value that a strict professionalism has had over the course of architectural history. We should thank Venturi for the fact that he allows us to enjoy an architect so well versed in his profession, seen in the solid basis of his plans on which Venturi focuses his arguments. With respect to more recent architects, the names of Le Corbusier, Aalto, or Kahn should not surprise us. In spite of the fact that Le Corbusier and some of his ideas are the targets of some of Venturi's critical observations, Venturi openly recognizes that the architecture of Le Corbusier is not necessarily simple, and he includes the Villa Savoye as an example of architecture that requires a double reading, and cites La Tourette and the Palace of Justice in Chandigarh as works in which the whole prevails.

Venturi finds in Alvar Aalto's architecture several pertinent instances that confirm his ideas. He sees Aalto's architecture as more sensitive to contingency, and this acceptance implies architectural inventions that celebrate and recognize, as when he says that, "Aalto seems almost to create the order out of the inconsistencies,"[46] or when, opposing Giedion's characterization of Aalto's work as "irrational," he states, "I prefer to think of Aalto's art as contradictory rather than irrational."[47] Venturi knows that he always has Aalto's work at his disposal to illustrate concepts like "inside/outside," whether in the Maison Carré, Bremen, Imatra, or in Aalto's own house in Munkkiniemi. The relation between Venturi and Kahn requires more careful consideration. It is more complex, since Venturi spent a short period working for

95 Moneo and Frampton in dialogue, Madrid, May 10, 2017.

Kahn after his time at the American Academy in Rome, where Kahn had also been. Venturi cites Kahn's aphorisms on more than ten occasions and they seem particularly well suited to defend Venturi's principles. An example is, "Architecture must have bad as well as good spaces; by order I do not mean orderliness; it is the role of design to adjust to the circumstances,"[48] but he also uses Kahn's work to illustrate his ideas, speaking of the Goldenberg House to underline the value of diagonals in design. Some of the examples he uses help him to maintain the polemical tone that he desired for the book. Otherwise, it is difficult to explain why he cites the work of Brasini on three different occasions—the previously mentioned Orfanotrofio, the Church of the Immaculate Heart in Rome, and the Forestry Pavilion at the EUR, Rome—or why he declares himself so close to the work of Luigi Moretti when he knew how out of favor Moretti was for his political ideas.

The careful and precise selection of examples and the skill with which Venturi chose the images that accompany the text contribute definitively to the interest and enthusiasm with which the book was received. The images may be said to be the origin of the text—images that at a certain moment were Venturi's sensorial and intellectual experience, later transformed into ideas that illuminate what he understands architecture to be—and a support for the discourse, as an inalienable complement to the text. And this would lead us to recognize the value of the immediate, the value of seeing something emerge, at a certain time and in a particular building, what architecture is capable of giving. Venturi flees from an academic discourse, purposefully avoiding the strictly pedagogical, to establish a discontinuous and direct dialogue, which moves from example to example and forces a reading that demands agility and attention in order to connect with the author's ideas. The text could be seen as a continuous use of techniques that, coming from case studies, end up revealing the value of filters, so consciously established by the author to scrutinize, from the deepest disciplinary registers, architecture. The text shows the extent of Venturi's rich experience of architecture and his acute critical sense, verifying the relevance of the examples chosen in relation to the epigraphs that head the different chapters of the book.

Venturi chooses well the illustrations that support his arguments, illustrations that have substantial value—something that the typography of the book emphasizes—and hence, in my opinion, it is the first edition published by MoMA that offers us the most attractive and eloquent version of *Complexity and Contradiction in Architecture*. The diversity of episodes translates into a broad range of architects and the fact that there is no intention to establish an order, be it chronological or stylistic, confirms that Venturi advocates a vision of timeless and non-style-based architecture, opposed to any understanding of architecture as the evolution established by an immanent previous idea. This is equivalent to considering architecture as the accumulated heritage of everything that has been constructed and which, nevertheless, allows us to talk about architecture as a discipline, without it being translated into a set of rules.

Although it may not seem like it, Venturi offers us a vision of an autonomous, disciplinary architecture, coinciding—despite the immense distance between them—with Aldo Rossi, whose celebrated book *L'Architettura della Città* (*The Architecture of the City*) was published the same year. *Complexity and Contradiction in Architecture*, a book that deliberately avoids the proposal of doctrines and offers an analysis of works in which architecture manifests itself in all its splendor, is the effort of an architect to explain how he understands the discipline. And to such an extent is Venturi's vision strictly disciplinary that we do not find any allusion to clients or to program, which explains why there is no reference to an interpretation of architecture from the ideological perspective. Nor does a vision of architecture developed from the evolution of constructive techniques seem to interest Venturi. As for Rossi, he intends to explain how the city is built by insisting on those aspects that allow us to see it develop from an idealist notion of immanence, to the point of being able to do without the individuals—the architects—who are responsible only for the monuments. On the contrary, for Venturi, it is the architects who, in the continuous exercise of their trade, recognize the contingent condition of reality and react to it by using a disciplinary knowledge that implies taking on both complexity and contradiction—contingency from which it is difficult to escape and that resists the orthodoxy imposed by the tyranny of languages and norms, being precisely in this transgression when architecture reaches its most intense instance of fullness.

But can it be said that the epigraphs that synthesize what is intended in each of the chapters have become canonical guidelines either for analysis, or for the project of architectural works, of buildings? Is Venturi's a book that provides criteria, principles, or even doctrine? These questions could be answered by admitting that Venturi's intention in including his works in *Complexity and Contradiction* was to prove the instrumental value of his critical discoveries. Venturi examines his works using the same criteria he used to analyze the buildings with which he illustrates his book: his works as examples of how much complexity and contradiction are almost essential components in any architectural work; his works as proof of the value of the principles he has discovered in the analysis of the works he esteems.

I quote literally from his texts. Expressions such as "contrapuntal rhythmic juxtaposition" and "contrasts between spatial filters" appear in the commentary on the Pearson House in Chestnut Hill, 1957; "Normal furniture and equipment are transformed by placing them unexpectedly," "harmony between the old and the new after the contrast of juxtapositions," in the James B. Duke House in New York, 1959; "A house without lateral facades: the main facade different from the later one to express the inflection towards the sea," "volume distorted both simple and complex at the same time," in the Beach House, 1959; "The complex position of the windows and the gaps in contrast to the simplicity of the volume," "circumstantial distortions," "juxtaposition of scales and forms," "the arc derives not from the nature of the materials," "but from its symbolism as entry," in the North Penn Visiting Nurses Headquarters, 1960; "Different things at once: an architectural walk in white marble," "a street that contrasts with the wide avenues," "a green grass embankment," in the F.D.R. Memorial; "Its new facade is a juxtaposition of one or two elements—again the game of duality appears," "the enormous letters create the scale and unity suitable for a public space," in the renovation of a restaurant in West Philadelphia. Venturi sees that his works, since the end of the 1950s, withstand an examination such as the one he performed on the buildings he has shown us, finding himself with the procedures that he identified with such critical insight.

In more ambitious and mature projects such as the Guild House, Venturi explains with even greater firmness the principles that inspire his work and the instruments he used when building them. I will now quote his words in greater length: see the Guild House as "a building in which the inflection dictates its shape, whose front facade is different from the back," "intricate mazes of walls that solve a very varied and complex program," "the corridor is an irregular space and varied," "economy dictated not by advanced elements of architecture but by conventional elements," "the tension appears with a change of scale of almost banal elements," "the television antenna shows [a] certain monumentality ... and can be interpreted in two ways: a sculpture by Lippold or as a symbol of the elderly who spend so much time watching television." Venturi sees his own work in a way not so different from the way to which he has accustomed us in his book. The proper handling of elements that are conventional—even vulgar, we could say—leads to them losing their meaning and acquiring that which the architect seeks for the unitary idea of the building, in this case, a building that pretends to adapt itself to the needs of older people.

But it will be in the house for his mother in Chestnut Hill where Venturi feels that he can best present us with an architectural work as an example of how he proceeds as an architect. The whole house serves those principles that he reveals in his book: utilizing them he designed the house:

> This building recognizes complexity and contradictions: it is both complex and simple, open and closed, big and little; some of its elements are good on one level and bad on another; its order accommodates the generic elements of the house in general, and the circumstantial elements of a house in particular. It achieves the difficult unity of a medium number of diverse parts rather than the easy unity of few or many motival parts, ... The front ... creates an almost symbolic image of a house ... The almost Palladian rigidity and symmetry is distorted ... And each of these elements, one essentially solid, the other essentially void, compromises in its shape and position—that is, inflects toward the other ... The stair, considered as an element alone in its awkward residual space, is bad ... The architectural complexities and distortions inside are reflected on the outside ... The house is big as well as little, by which I mean that it is a little house with big scale ... Complexity in combination with small scale in small buildings means busyness ... the big scale in the small building achieves tension rather than nervousness—a tension appropriate for this kind of architecture.[49]

Venturi employs the lexicon and the terminology he used in his book when examining his own work. It would seem that knowledge of the concepts, resources, and instruments that the discipline had used in the past and that he had shown us in his book continued to have value for him, as can be seen from his reading of his own work. His comments lead us to think that the complexity resulting from juxtapositions, distortions, contrasts, changes of scale, displacements in the use and meaning of the elements can be controlled from the project and that the contradictions that are incurred in accommodating these very different features can be anticipated in the design process. And that it is possible to incorporate all these concepts and mechanisms in a building from its inception, provoking situations and circumstances that foster architectural responses in which complexity and contradiction would be inevitable. Something that, in the end, implies that the architect can handle the contingent at will.

But was Venturi always faithful to the principles established in *Complexity and Contradiction*? I am afraid not. Venturi did not finally become the architect—in his professional practice—that embodied everything he promises, everything he suggests, in a book like this one. If, as we have seen, Venturi's first work served as an argument for the criteria and concepts he defended in his book, could the Venturi of later years illustrate a book like this with his later work? An in-depth examination of Venturi's work would lead us to see how acting on a contingency not dictated by immediate reality but inoculated by the architect in the design process leads to results much less convincing than those introduced in his book. We often have the sensation of finding ourselves before contrived epiphanies. But do we have to accept that contingency can be "manufactured"? Can this be "provoked" for the sake of achieving the purported complexity? Would it not be necessary to admit that the examples of architecture in which complexity and contradiction appear are architectural responses to real demands with which we find ourselves in situations not consciously posed? If we stick to the examples that Venturi offers us in his book we would have to admit that it is in the architectural response to the contingent where the poetic, architectural, desired tension is generated. That it is only in those specific situations in which the contingent forced the architect to forget the rules when the building was illuminated with the appearance of the authentic experience of architecture. And that is why it has been pertinent to ask the questions that we have asked ourselves.

There is a certain danger in designing directly with those formal mechanisms celebrated by Venturi in his book, as if they were concepts described in a manual, by confusing an established fictitious reality with a real contingent situation. In contrast to an invented contingency, voluntarily and consciously introduced by the architect, I consider that the true contingency, determined by specific conditions in time and space, offers a better foundation on which to build a work of architecture. And I say this without considering those works of Venturi in which he seems to understand architecture as a strictly communicative instrument, to the point of losing contact with traditional architecture. It should be concluded, therefore, that not all of Venturi's work was produced by serving the principles established in his book, and that the Venturi that the book anticipated became a very different one, which only at specific moments—for example, in the Sainsbury Wing of the National Gallery in London—retrieves the theses established in the book.

Venturi's book, seminal to the architectural thinking of the 1970s, was a breath of fresh air that allowed one to see the built world without the restriction implied by the tyranny of norms, in order to see the work of architects without being oriented by the relentless notion of progress that underlies the history of architecture as a stylistic evolution. Venturi's book inspired us to admit the singularity, to appreciate anomaly and the unexpected, and not to underestimate the contingent. All this allowed *Complexity and Contradiction* to be read as a book in which architects learned how to carry out their work without it being a manifesto. *Complexity and Contradiction* inspired architects to use resources with the greatest liberty as enabled by the discipline, but not to presume the use of doctrine. *Complexity and Contradiction* was a provocative book, polemical, that showed off before us the attractive panorama of architectural history, converting it into the key to understanding architecture itself. It was more than a simple judgment of modernism, as Scully would have us understand.

96 Moneo and Frampton in dialogue, Madrid, May 10, 2017.

Complexity and Contradiction was a violent reaction to the banality of what the Modern Movement had become, and Venturi became the defender of a process of renewal that, to his misfortune, led to the formation of the Postmodern movement. As I mentioned at the beginning of this text, Scully's reading of Venturi in the introduction had a disproportionate impact on the understanding of the book. Was this the most appropriate interpretation of *Complexity and Contradiction*? I would like to think that this essay offers a more appropriate idea of interpretations. That Venturi's book could be understood as a vision of the built world—inspired by T.S. Eliot's aesthetic ideas—of much broader horizons. That there was in the book the ambitious attempt to reveal what was behind the complexities of the built world, making sense of architecture. Venturi was not just an intelligent and provocative critic but also an architect who sought to explain to us, from built examples, in a definitive way, what architecture was for him.

1 Robert Venturi, *Complexity and Contradiction in Architecture* (New York: Museum of Modern Art, 1966), 11.
2 Ibid., 23.
3 Ibid., 13.
4 Ibid.
5 Ibid.
6 Ibid., 18.
7 Ibid.
8 Ibid.
9 Ibid.

10 Ibid.
11 Ibid.
12 Ibid.
13 Ibid., 19.
14 Ibid., 21.
15 Ibid., 18.
16 T.S. Eliot, "Tradition and the Individual Talent" [1919], *T.S. Eliot: Selected Essays* (London: Faber & Faber, 1999), 16.
17 Ibid., 15.
18 Ibid., 17.
19 T.S. Eliot, *To Criticize the Critic, and Other Writings* (Lincoln, NE: University of Nebraska Press, 1992), 21.
20 Venturi, *Complexity and Contradiction in Architecture*, 22.
21 Ibid., 23.
22 Ibid.
23 A.W. Empson, *Seven Types of Ambiguity* (Philadelphia: Stellar Books, 2014), 20.
24 Venturi, *Complexity and Contradiction in Architecture*, 28.
25 Ibid., 29.
26 Ibid.
27 Ibid.
28 Ibid., 24.
29 Ibid., 25.
30 Ibid.
31 Empson, *Seven Types of Ambiguity*, 81.
32 Venturi, *Complexity and Contradiction in Architecture*, 30, 38, 46, 53, 60, 71.
33 Empson, *Seven Types of Ambiguity*, 6.
34 Ibid., 48.
35 Ibid., 81.
36 Ibid., 102.
37 Venturi, *Complexity and Contradiction in Architecture*, 89.
38 Ibid.
39 Ibid., 91.
40 Ibid., 28, 29.
41 Ibid., 101.
42 Ibid., 102.
43 Empson, *Seven Types of Ambiguity*, 62.
44 Venturi, *Complexity and Contradiction in Architecture*, 19.
45 Ibid., 26.
46 Ibid., 47.
47 Ibid.
48 Ibid., 31, 46, 54.
49 Ibid., 117.

A Time of Heroics: Paul Rudolph and Yale, 1958–1965

Robert A.M. Stern with Leopoldo Villardi

I am pleased to dedicate this essay to Kenneth Frampton, my colleague at Columbia from the time of his appointment to the faculty in 1972 until my departure to Yale in 1998. It was Professor Frampton who helped me start documenting the Yale School of Architecture by encouraging me to write "Yale 1950–1965," which he later published in *Oppositions*.[1]

When I arrived in New Haven as an architecture student at Yale in September 1960, the old order of modern architecture was ending, marked by the death in 1959 of Frank Lloyd Wright, who had dazzled the world one last time with his idiosyncratic masterpiece the Guggenheim Museum (1943–59). But, as a result of Wright's individualistic romanticism, he was viewed by orthodox modernists as a sort of "anti-Christ," refusing to be part of the zeitgeist. Modernists who had established their reputations between the two world wars were losing force: I refer of course to Walter Gropius, Le Corbusier, and Mies van der Rohe. Le Corbusier had seemingly abandoned rationalism with his expressionistic chapel at Ronchamp (1950–55); Gropius had never recovered the rigor of his Bauhaus period; and Mies van der Rohe, with his Seagram Building (1954–58) behind him, was admired as the consummate skyscraper architect, but his work afterward seemed repetitious. As a result, these architects were both seen as masters as well as monsters by the young Turks of the postwar generation—Eero Saarinen, Philip Johnson, and Paul Rudolph—each eager to push them safely up on pedestals where they could do no more harm or, more to the point, get no more commissions. Notably this new generation of modernists was the first to be American trained.

Paul Marvin Rudolph was born in Elkton, Kentucky, in 1918, a key year in world history, as Sibyl Moholy-Nagy pointed out, when the old established rules of culture and artistic establishment had broken down following World War I.[2] As the son of a Methodist minister who, according to the rules of his denomination, was required to change parishes every two years, Rudolph grew up in a series of small southern towns throughout Kentucky, Tennessee, and Alabama. Though an accomplished classical pianist, Rudolph decided to pursue a career in architecture instead of music, and went on to study at the Alabama Polytechnic Institute (now Auburn University), where he received his bachelor of architecture degree in 1940 and whose faculty, he later observed, was best "when it left students alone."[3] Rudolph's first experience of a notable work of modern architecture came at the age of twenty-two in 1940, when he visited the recently completed Rosenbaum House in Florence,

97 Paul Rudolph (left) at Florida Southern College, *c.* 1941.

98 Frank Lloyd Wright, Rosenbaum House, Florence, Alabama, 1938–40.

Alabama, designed by Frank Lloyd Wright, which left an indelible impression on the would-be architect. As late as 1986, he described its living room as "one of the most sublime spaces in American Architecture,"[4] and spoke of various details of the house still in his memory: the cantilevered roof, the clerestory windows, and the piano hinges used on closet doors. Wright, too, had been the son of a minister, had grown up in a rural community, and had an affinity for the piano; and Rudolph went on to visit many of Wright's buildings as a young architect, including the campus at Florida Southern College (**97–98**).

In Rudolph's view, his architectural education didn't really begin with Auburn's Beaux-Arts curriculum (**99–100**), but rather with the Master's Program at Harvard's Graduate School of Design (GSD), where his classmates included Philip Johnson, Ulrich Franzen, John Johansen (three of the so-called New Canaan Five), Edward Larrabee Barnes, and Victor Lundy. However, after only six months, the outbreak of World War II interrupted Rudolph's education, prompting four years of service in the U.S. Naval Reserve.

While stationed at the New York Naval Shipyard (widely known as the Brooklyn Navy Yard), Rudolph was introduced to new materials and construction techniques related to shipbuilding and repair that stayed with him throughout his career. Writing some years later to the U.S. Department of the Navy, Walter Gropius—Rudolph's studio professor and chairman of the department of architecture at Harvard's GSD—described him as "one of the outstanding brilliant American architects of the younger generation ... well on his way to becoming internationally known."[5] After naval service, Rudolph returned to Harvard in 1946, was awarded his degree in 1947, and immediately began professional practice in Sarasota, Florida, partnering with the more experienced architect Ralph Twitchell, for whom Rudolph had previously worked after graduating from Auburn. After time spent in Florida designing in a version of the International Style favored by Harvard, Rudolph was awarded a Wheelwright Fellowship, enabling him to travel through Europe for a year—though he continued to work with Twitchell through correspondence.[6]

In 1952, Rudolph was recognized by Yale students as representing a new direction in architecture when they published some of his work and an essay in the inaugural issue of *Perspecta*, the student-edited Yale architecture journal. In that article, Rudolph described his time at Harvard, his time in the U.S. Navy, and his postwar travels through Europe as the "three major phases in [his] development as an architect."[7] Rudolph was not impressed with Gropius's American architectural work, but he admired Gropius as an educator who instilled a sense of direction and a foundation on which the young architect could build his own set of design principles.

Europe had a transformative effect on the young architect, reinforcing, in Rudolph's words, the "conviction of the necessity of regaining the 'form sense' which helped to shape Western man's building until the nineteenth century." Rudolph continued, "Other periods have always developed means of tying their architecture to

99 Paul Rudolph, Greek Temple, student project, Alabama Polytechnic Institute, 1937.

100 Paul Rudolph, Weekend House for an Architect, student project, Harvard Graduate School of Design, 1946–47.

previous works without compromising their own designs. This also is our task."[8] Perhaps most importantly, and setting himself apart from most of his contemporaries, Rudolph's year in Europe led him to conclude that "When you are really perplexed you can learn a great deal more from sound traditional [architecture] than from modern architecture."[9]

In Florida, Rudolph's work was almost exclusively limited to small houses, many of which took advantage of the new materials he had been introduced to in the Navy. Despite the small scale and provincial location of his work, Rudolph quickly became widely known within the profession in part due to his extraordinary draftsmanship, perfectly suited as it was to new printing methods then being adopted by architectural magazines.[10] He further enhanced his reputation through teaching stints at important northern schools of architecture, where his quick rise to national prominence as a residential architect had an unexpected side effect: according to 1949 Yale graduate and later faculty Charles Brewer, "students," seeking to emulate Rudolph, "decided they wanted to become famous the way he did—by designing houses ... that was the credential he came [to Yale] with. And that was what vaulted [Rudolph] to fame so quickly. That was a real shake-up."[11]

Even before his appointment in 1958, Rudolph had taught at Yale as a visiting critic in fall 1955, famously assigning a week-long design problem for a "Tastee-Freez" ice-cream stand (**101**). It was based on a project that he had proposed in Florida, although Rudolph somewhat aggrandized it in the design brief, calling it "the idea of the Pavilion in the Park." In so doing, he was calling for a conceptual richness, even among the most ordinary of building commissions. As he saw it, there were "so many ironies about it ... [It was] a pavilion on a sea of asphalt."[12]

Despite his youth, Rudolph had come to be so respected as an architect and teacher that in 1955 he was asked to succeed Mies van der Rohe as head of the architecture program at the Illinois Institute of Technology (IIT). In a letter to his parents, Rudolph wrote:

> This of course is for me a rather tremendous step, and I'm still very much on the fence about it. It is such a difficult problem in terms of human relations plus taking my own time. It is a real challenge for I know that it can be made the best in the middle west and nothing else would be good enough.[13]

Rumors of the impending appointment quickly circulated, and Rudolph initially agreed to take over as Mies's successor.[14] But after two weeks, Rudolph reneged on his decision. Despite his admiration for what Mies had accomplished at IIT, Rudolph would have felt obliged to take the school in a completely different direction as head of the program.[15]

Paul Rudolph assumed the position of chairman of the department of architecture at Yale in January 1958.[16] In short order, he not only rebuilt the program, but

101 Paul Rudolph, Tastee-Freez Ice Cream Stand, Florida, 1954.

also elevated it to greater prominence than it had enjoyed since the 1930s, drawing national and international acclaim as a rival to Harvard's GSD and attracting a remarkable number of students who would go on to their own celebrated careers as independent practitioners. He was thirty-nine years old at the time of his appointment—little more than a decade senior to some of the students, some of whom had their education interrupted by military service in Korea.

Though a well-known product of Gropius's Harvard, Rudolph surprised many by proving to be much more, as it were, in the Yale mode—that is to say, romantic and individualistic. In particular, Rudolph disdained partnerships, such as he had with Ralph Twitchell, and such as Gropius emphasized in his own professional firm, aptly named The Architects Collaborative. In an *Architectural Forum* interview at the time of his Yale appointment, Rudolph categorically stated: "architects were never meant to design together. Architecture is a personal effort, and the fewer people coming between you and your work the better ... If an architect cares enough and practices architecture as an art, then he must initiate design—he must create rather than make judgments."[17] Ten years later, Sibyl Moholy-Nagy, author of the first significant monograph on Rudolph's work, wryly commented that in his case, "The Harvard teamwork doctrine had been refuted by reality."[18]

Rudolph's popularity with students was immediate and they quickly came to revere their new chairman for his rebellious stance against corporate practice, deterministic functionalism, and other "isms" offered up as substitutes for genuine design insight. Both as an administrator and as a teacher, Rudolph's style, in fact his whole persona, was virtually opposite to that of his immediate predecessors. When he got to Yale, Rudolph immersed himself in the design studio where he was direct, brash, and refreshingly brusque. As British architect Tony Monk has written: "To Rudolph, the visual satisfaction of a design was far more important than a self-justifying intellectual debate. During a period when architectural theorists were developing their own complicated language, Rudolph described his design priorities in a refreshingly simple manner."[19]

Rudolph's obvious passion for building was deep and pure. "He brought an *emotional* love for architecture," remembers Charles Brewer. "He didn't come off as a practitioner. He came off as an artist. That shifted the emphasis. All the faculty suddenly looked very old fashioned and that became a problem."[20] Although unfailingly courteous with a soft Southern voice, he was in no way a "gentleman of the old school," nor even an "Ivy League type." He was not scholarly in any way; but it can be said that what he lacked in cultivation, he made up for in curiosity, and, perhaps above all else, hard work. Rudolph worked tirelessly, sometimes even obsessively, both at his architecture and his teaching, and expected everyone else around him to do the same. As Stanley Tigerman, who held both bachelor's and master's degrees from the school, put it, Rudolph's "architecture and life were inextricably intertwined. He lived, breathed, slept, taught and of course practiced architecture."[21] To this day, Allan Greenberg, a member of the 1965 post-professional class, believes that there "wasn't a person called Paul Rudolph. There was only the architect Paul Rudolph. His capacity to work was unlimited ... He measured his personal integrity by the integrity of his buildings. I don't believe he thought of anything other than architecture."[22]

Rudolph saw the studios as unique opportunities for students to work with the very best talents—the heroes of the day, many of them true masters, others still finding their way. Often students discovered that the heroes had feet of clay, that they weren't quite what students thought they were, and that what was published in the magazines wasn't always a true portrayal of what architecture is. To this end, Rudolph's great accomplishment was in taking advantage of the visiting critic system that had been the first of its kind when introduced at Yale in the early 1920s. Refusing to be ideologically hidebound, Rudolph invited talented architects from around the world, including Mies van der Rohe, who agreed to serve as visiting critic in 1958 at the behest of then Yale first-year student Phyllis Lambert.

As chairman, Rudolph's administrative role could be compared to that of ringmaster of an ever-changing circus of visitors. Rudolph cast a wide net in appointing visiting critics: the German engineer Frei Otto visited in fall 1960; Wilhelm Holzbauer from Vienna; Bernard Rudofsky, originally from Moravia (now part of the Czech Republic), in 1960 and 1964; Danish architect Henning Larsen in fall 1964; Italian-born Romaldo Giurgola, whom he had gotten to know while they were both visiting faculty at Cornell; and the little-known California architects Pierre Koenig and Craig Ellwood, not to mention many of his Harvard contemporaries.

By far the most significant visiting critic was James Stirling, who Rudolph first invited to Yale in 1959, and who would return at Rudolph's invitation several times before beginning an eighteen-year commitment as the inaugural Davenport Visiting Professor in 1966. Stirling would have a decisive influence on generations of Yale students. When he was hired, he was a rising star in the British architecture scene who had just begun to design the Leicester Engineering Building with his professional partner James Gowan—a project that would propel them to international fame.

Stirling and Rudolph were competing architectural stars in the eyes of the students. As Vincent Scully later pointed out, they were "very much alike ... They were both High Modern performers. Each one, each time, tried to do something that had never been seen on land or sea before, and to knock your eyes out. They were natural rivals."[23] But their personalities were completely different. George Buchanan, a 1962 graduate and later faculty, put it this way: "If Paul was head, then Jim was heart." The intensely shy Rudolph was awkward when he chose to socialize with students, while Stirling reveled in a shared camaraderie. Stirling "became 'Jim' to the students, but Rudolph, for the majority, remained 'Mr. Rudolph,'" although he was called "Big Daddy" behind his back.[24] Between Stirling and Rudolph, students felt they "were at the epicenter of architectural thought and practice," and, Buchanan continued, took their cues from the proclivities of both architects: "We thought a great deal of ourselves. We were a pretty arrogant lot. We were heavy-drinking, heavy-working."[25]

As a result of Rudolph's appointments, Yale quickly became recognized as the most cosmopolitan design program in the U.S., replacing Harvard as the "go-to" place to both study and teach. Years later, taking pride in his ability "to hold everything together ... I am very proud," Rudolph stated, "that ... I had brought the most diverse representatives of architectural ideas together at one time or another. I tried to be two different people—one un-opinionated, interested in others' ideas, helpful to their work ... but knowing all the time that this is the opposite of the life of a creative architect."[26]

At Yale, under Rudolph, the "debate" was focused in the advanced studios where his open-door policy for teaching appointments could be seen in the very different student projects. In *Perspecta* 5 he wrote, "the embryonic architect is seldom able to see that his own discoveries are usually restatements (often with complete validity). However, he has an uncanny ability to recognize that which is unique and significant in the work and thought of his peers."[27] To this end he endeavored to establish "an atmosphere and approach whereby the problems are defined and the students can commence the endless journey to find themselves."[28]

As a design critic, Rudolph was tough and he was brilliant, intent on conveying an approach that, though mindful of pragmatic issues, was principally concerned with formal expression. However, despite his own strong personal style, Rudolph was never dogmatic, believing that the teaching of architecture should be approached as a creative act, but that creativity cannot be taught.

Rudolph spent almost no time on department administration, leaving that mostly to engineer Henry Pfisterer. Instead, he typically took direct responsibility for the semester-long Master's Class studio each fall and then, typically along with King-lui Wu, taught the bachelor of architecture thesis studio in the spring. Under Rudolph, post-professional students were immersed into a studio culture that demanded intense concentration and high production. Rudolph's impact was immediately recognized and the Master's Class grew from ten students in 1957 to nineteen students in 1958.

Rudolph was determined to shake each Master's Class student out of a sense of security. He would assign programs and projects with which he was professionally involved—a decision that proved to be somewhat divisive. Norman Foster, who was a Master's Class student in 1961–62, "loved the way" Rudolph treated the Master's Class "as an extension of his office." But, as Foster recalled, "A lot of people thought that was really rather naughty."[29] On the first day of class in fall 1964, before students even settled into their desks, with Allan Greenberg and Thomas Beeby among the new post-professional class, Rudolph assigned a week-long design problem for a high school—with a program not unlike that of his recently completed Riverview or Sarasota high schools. The assignment had a seemingly impossible schedule, given the chairman's requirements for plans, sections, elevations, renderings, and details. Allan Greenberg recalled the assignment:

> If you spent the entire semester you could not fulfill the requirements of that program ... [after staying] until 3:00 or 4:00 in the morning ... All I had for our review was a series of freehand drawings on tracing paper ... I had done one section and a site plan. I was so terrified ... I said I've organized this building on a split level—you can see it in the section. Rudolph stood up. And he said, "Guys, this is what I was after. I didn't need all the plans, sections, elevations, because I knew you couldn't do them. It was a year's worth of work. I just wanted a week's worth of exploration. And a potential solution."[30]

Greenberg, like many others, was deeply impressed by Rudolph, finding him to be "the finest teacher [he] had ever encountered. Totally committed to architecture, he would often come into [the] studio at midnight to look at ... designs [by] the two or three students who were there. Although he was considered a ruthless critic," Greenberg welcomed his "honesty," which "stemmed from love of architecture and respect for his students." During one such midnight discussion, Rudolph examined Greenberg's designs for courtyard housing, such as those Greenberg had encountered while working for Jørn Utzon in Copenhagen.

Rudolph, who surmised that Greenberg had never walked through the courtyards of Yale's residential colleges, drew a map and said: "Walk through these courtyards on your way home tonight. Look at them again in the morning. They are superb."[31] It was a journey that Rudolph suggested other students might also benefit from, reflecting his complex relationship with traditional architecture, which he admired not for its stylistic tropes, but for its ability to shape public space, as well as its handling of scale and context.

Stanley Tigerman was probably the most representative Master's Class student of the Rudolph era. He was not a college graduate, having only studied at MIT for one year before dropping out and enlisting in the Navy. After military service, Tigerman worked for various architects, including Skidmore, Owings & Merrill in

Chicago, and then embarked on a less than lucrative independent practice followed by the decision to return to school.

Arriving at Yale as a thirty-year-old experienced, licensed professional, Tigerman found the pressure almost unbearable. His status as a registered architect in no way assured him of passing studio grades. If anything, he had to work harder to meet Rudolph's exacting demands. In one particularly cruel act of intimidation, Tigerman recollected being called into Rudolph's office when his work failed to meet expectations: referring to a "substandard grade," Rudolph said that Tigerman "seemed to have lost interest in architecture," and that "the architecture department would gladly undertake the responsibility of underwriting the cost of a battery of tests to ascertain what field [he] would be more suitably qualified for other than architecture."[32] Rudolph demanded that his students produce: "If there wasn't something to look at, a model, or a set of drawings, there was no conversation."[33] The pressure was intense. The penalties for failing were much more severe than they are today. Only fifty percent of Tigerman's bachelor's thesis class graduated on time; some students had to complete a remedial summer studio while others took an extra semester or year to complete their work. As well, there were always students who never received their degree.

Tigerman seemed always to be in the hot box, almost meeting his comeuppance at the end of his second year at Yale, when, for his thesis project in the Master's Class, he undertook a design for the University of Illinois's proposed Chicago campus, then slated to be built on Navy Pier. "I made a huge mistake," Tigerman recalls. "I finished ... sixteen thirty-by-forty ink boards a day and a half early, and [Rudolph] came around to my board before the jury and said, 'Why aren't you working?' And, like an asshole, I said, 'Well, I'm done.' He said, 'Really? Why don't I sit down and take a look at it. Do you mind?'"[34] Rudolph then "invited the rest of the Master's Class over to see the drawings since he felt there were some features he might like to discuss ... that could perhaps benefit the rest of the class generally and their own thesis presentations specifically." Tigerman had no choice but to agree to this, only to discover that Rudolph had invited the entire bachelor's thesis class to join the crit as well. Tigerman continued, "It was then that I knew that I was about to be given considerable grief for both the thesis and my cavalier attitude about finishing early." With all the students gathered around Tigerman's desk,

> Rudolph launched into an invective-laden tirade. He castigated [Tigerman] publicly, accusing [him] of treating both the architecture school and the project as if both came about as the result of a "blueprint reading course" as part of a vocational trade school curriculum. He threatened to withhold [his] degree if [Tigerman] didn't make striking changes to improve the project and then stalked off leaving [him] ... much diminished, as well as a stunned audience of both thesis classes in his wake.[35]

So Tigerman, like many of his classmates whom Rudolph would criticize at the eleventh hour, went back to work "and drew like hell."[36]

For Rudolph, rhetoric and reasoning were no substitute for completed drawings and models. If it couldn't be pinned up, it didn't matter. In an interview with Heinrich Klotz and John Cook, Rudolph explained: "I can assure you that what students, and I would also say many architects, describe about a given project often has little or nothing to do with its actuality ... The intentions in architecture and the results are two entirely different things."[37] Though he concentrated his teaching in the Master's Class and fourth-year design studios, Rudolph made it a point to participate in design juries at all levels. As a result, he had a strong impact on all the students in the program, turning what had been a relatively low-key gentlemanly pursuit into an intense, competitive blood sport.

Although the School of Art at Yale, from its inception in 1869, had admitted women into its programs in painting and sculpture, the department of architecture, founded in 1919, was an exclusively male domain. Dean Everett Meeks's decision in the 1940s to admit women students into architecture had little immediate effect until after World War II when female enrollment began to increase; students included Phyllis Lambert, who had enrolled in 1958 after finishing up her work on the Seagram Building, and the brilliant environmentalist Judith Bloom Chafee (**102**).

Six of the thirty-two students in my first-year class were women: M.J. Long (1939–2018; M.Arch. 1964) and Etel Kramer (1938–2001; M.Arch. 1964), both of whom had graduated from Smith; Joan Stouffer (Scharnberg); Harvard graduate Margaret Hansen (Smertenko); Judith Anderson (Lawler), from Mount Holyoke College, whose father was a prominent architect in Cambridge, Massachusetts, and was chairman and later dean of MIT's department of architecture; and Vivian Wei-Chu, who would soon transfer to graphic design; Lucinda Cisler had also been admitted to the school a year prior, in 1959.

To M.J. Long, who became one of the first woman critics in architectural design and taught on the Yale faculty for over forty years, Rudolph

> was tough as a critic, but he was very quick. Whereas most critics would sit around waffling, trying to find their way into something, he would very much more quickly than anybody say ... "I see what you're trying to do, which is this, but in your own terms you're inconsistent, here, here and here" ... "That stair doesn't correspond in plan and section." Nobody else would be doing things like that.[38]

Rudolph could be vehement in his opinions about a student's project but he was even more so about criticism offered by guest jurors at the department's well-attended open reviews. Very often, he would "sarcastically and explicitly" challenge guest jurors and resident faculty alike with what Tigerman remembers as "cutting commentary,"[39] before graciously hosting them at his High Street town house

102 Judith Bloom Chafee presenting her thesis before an all-male panel of design critics at Yale University, 1960. From left to right: Jean Paul Carlhian, Philip Johnson, Leonard Perfido (B.A. 1959, M.Arch. 1962), unidentified student, Paul Rudolph, Henry Pfisterer, and Judith Bloom Chafee (M.Arch. 1960).

apartment, which also served as his professional office (**103**). For students, the contact with so many wildly diverging points of view, always seen in relationship to Rudolph's own readily available opinions, was eye-opening, nurturing a depth of understanding and sophistication in the handling of architectural ideas that sometimes outstripped the student's ability to give them formal expression.

While it can be argued that Stanley Tigerman was in many ways Rudolph's most representative student, it was the Master's Class of 1961–62, the one following Tigerman's, that stands out as the most dazzling of the Rudolph years. That studio is now remembered as the "British Invasion," a term not coined until 1964 when the Beatles first toured the United States. In addition to Norman Foster, the 1961–62 Master's Class included British students Eldred Evans (another woman who would go on to lead a brilliant career), Richard Rogers, and Robert Alan Cordingley, who, as an undergraduate student at Liverpool University, had been an early collaborator with James Stirling.[40] Foster credits the rigor of his Yale education under Rudolph with instilling in him a "a sense of confidence, freedom and self-discovery."[41] And indeed, the organization of his eventual worldwide practice was very much modeled on the studio he took with Rudolph, as well as Rudolph's professional office in New Haven.

103 Paul Rudolph working in his professional office at 31 High Street in New Haven, 1962. From left to right: Frank Chapman (M.Arch. 1959), Jonathan Hall, Jim Weber (M.Arch. 1959), Paul Rudolph, John Damico (M.Arch. 1966), Bill Bedford, and Andrew Nastri.

"Consciously or subconsciously," Foster has said, "there is a very strong connection between [his] time [at Yale] and the way [he works in London] … the two are inseparable in a way."[42] In his 1999 Pritzker Prize acceptance speech, Foster recalled Yale as a frenetic, inspiring environment. "Paul Rudolph had created a studio atmosphere of fevered activity, highly competitive, and fueled by a succession of visiting luminaries. The crits were open and accessible and often combative. And it was a can-do approach in which concepts would be shredded one day to be reborn overnight."[43]

The open, loft-like studio at the top of the Art Gallery was the scene of memorable debates between the Brits and the Americans. As Foster's biographer Deyan Sudjic has described the situation, there was something of a divide between the two groups:

> The British were a little older, and preferred to debate and to argue rather than to draw … After one episode of more than usual provocative Anglo-Saxon prevarication, a placard appeared over their drafting tables. "Stop talking, start drawing," it demanded. The British struck back with a slogan of their own on the other side of the studio that urged the Americans to "Start Thinking."[44]

Although it may have seemed that British students dominated the master's program, under Rudolph talented students from all over the world were attracted to Yale.

Bangladeshi architect and planner Muzharul Islam went on to become one of the leading advocates of modernism in East Pakistan; and Shinichi Okada went on to become a prominent architect in his native Japan, best known as the designer of its Supreme Court in Chiyoda, Tokyo.[45]

At the end of the spring 1960 term, when Tigerman presented his bachelor's thesis to a stellar gathering of distinguished figures including Gordon Bunshaft, Jean Paul Carlhian, Harry Cobb, Ulrich Franzen, and Philip Johnson, there was only one juror who chose to speak out against the project: Serge Chermayeff. As Tigerman recalls, Chermayeff concluded his critical assessment with: "Now, young man, just between you and I [*sic*], if you had to do it over again, you *wouldn't* do it this way." Before Tigerman could say a word, Rudolph stood up and said, "of course he would, you ass. Next project."[46] Two years later, Rudolph surprised everyone by inviting Chermayeff to join the permanent faculty and lead one semester of the Master's Class.

Ideologically and pedagogically, Chermayeff was Rudolph's complete opposite. And that's exactly why Rudolph brought him to Yale. "It was my notion to get people who didn't agree with me," Rudolph boasted, "and he was certainly a good candidate. It was never dull when you were near Serge."[47] For Rudolph, Chermayeff was "someone who ... had the ability to think beyond the problems of the moment. And he was there as a complement to the faculty, as a thoughtful provocateur."[48]

While Rudolph probably did believe that Chermayeff would enrich the discourse, the reality, as Vincent Scully and others had predicted, was that he encouraged divisiveness in the department's approach to architecture, transforming what had been a debate between "functionalists" and "formalists" into an argument. In response to faculty protests, Rudolph insisted that he could control Chermayeff. "But he didn't," Scully recalled. "Chermayeff destroyed every place he came ...Chermayeff just divided and conquered. He tried to tear everything apart. He'd invite you to dinner just to conspire. It was horrible ... He was compelled to do this; compelled to run things; compelled to be in charge."[49]

Rudolph's influence at Yale could be felt not only within the confines of the architecture department, but also in the university's extensive program of adventurous new buildings being constructed with University President A. Whitney Griswold's encouragement. Dazzlingly inventive though the new buildings were, with only a few exceptions they made little collective sense. Modernist buildings were not place specific; they were program specific. Under Griswold, Rudolph sat on the Buildings Committee of the Yale Corporation, an appointment he deemed critical to his self-esteem, but also reflecting his belief that the leader of an architecture department should also be involved in setting the university's policies with regard to new buildings.

Rudolph's participation in the university's architect selection process was a definite departure from previous practice, where only donors and certain members of the Yale Corporation were typically consulted by the president. The story of the selection of Gordon Bunshaft as architect of the Beinecke Rare Book and Manuscript

Library illustrates how the new system did—and did not—work. According to Bunshaft, the selection process "started with Paul Rudolph calling me one afternoon and asking if I would be willing to be in a small group of four architects to do a competition to get the commission to do the Beinecke Rare Book Library." Bunshaft, however, believed that "it was Paul Rudolph's idea of having this competition," and "would have no part of it," concluding that it was "not the way to do a good building."[50] A week later, Provost Norman S. Buck confirmed the commission. Of course, it helped that the Beinecke brothers' father had owned the Fuller Company, and the family still had a financial interest in it.[51]

Though it was not part of his initial discussion with President Griswold, Rudolph was "delighted" when he was asked to design three buildings for the university shortly after his appointment as chairman: the Greeley Memorial Laboratory for the School of Forestry, Married Student Housing, and, most significantly, a new building for the School of Art and Architecture, which was to be his most enduring contribution to arts education at Yale, uniting the various departments of the school under one roof for the first time since the school had been founded in 1869.[52] It was an amazing opportunity to finally realize an American Bauhaus—not just a manifesto on the current state of architectural form-making but also a physical representation of a distinct philosophy of arts education. Rejecting the loft-like universal space of IIT's Crown Hall, Rudolph set out to arrange carefully defined spaces in an effort to unite students in all the disciplines of the arts in accord with a utopian, Bauhaus-like vision of interaction, if not collaboration.

Unfortunately this ambitious agenda proved unworkable. Students, especially those in painting and sculpture who moved into the new building in September 1963, struggled to adapt it to their own needs. Matters came to a head at the formal opening ceremonies that followed in November, when the hoopla of the enormous dedication party took a heavy toll on the energies of the school and on Rudolph. In the weeks preceding the dedication, the painting and sculpture students picketed in front of the building to protest the cramped quarters designed for them. These protests, which now seem so mild to us after the riotous activities of the late 1960s, caused no end of consternation at the school and were screened as far as possible from the press.

At the building's formal dedication, Nikolaus Pevsner, the eminent German-born-and-educated British architecture historian, delivered a rather negative assessment. He didn't like the building and what it stood for as a repudiation of the International Style modernism of the 1920s and 1930s, which, he averred, "could at least be imitated with impunity. Something reasonable, serviceable, non-aggressive would come out. But woe to him who imitates Paul Rudolph, who imitates Saarinen, Yamasaki, or Philip Johnson ... The result is disaster. The great individual, the artist-architect concerned with self-expression primarily, is inimitable."[53] Pevsner then went on to place the blame for the building's limitations on the fact that Rudolph was both its designer and client: "So, in walking round this building ... never forget that whatever you see and inspect is exactly as the brief demanded it. I find that a most stimulating and valuable lesson, and it is the lesson with which I want to end."[54]

Although Rudolph valued historic architecture and urbanism, his attitude to the discipline of architecture history itself was at best ambivalent, perhaps even hostile. Looking back, Rudolph expressed his feeling

> that one had to be clear about the relationship or attitudes of the would-be architect as opposed to the would-be historian and to have a balance between the two and to make clear that one is not to be intimidated by history and that everybody lives in their own time and has their own attitudes and that these are absolutely valid and must be respected.[55]

In particular, the charismatic Vincent Scully made Rudolph uncomfortable, largely because Scully was an important tastemaker with a national reputation, principally championing Wright, Le Corbusier, Kahn, and, later, Venturi, but not so much Rudolph. The chairman sought Scully's favor, frequently inviting him to join design juries, and often sitting in on his lectures—both those on Modern and Greek Architecture.[56] But the two men never grew close. As Tigerman remarked, Rudolph's "determination to shine as a bright star in the architectural firmament precluded deep friendships within the field."[57]

Rudolph remained at Yale for two more years until June 1965, during which time his influence over students was ostensibly as strong as ever. Thomas Beeby described that time as "the era of the great hero and everyone wanted to be a master architect." Yale was "the most energized place ... It was all about becoming a genius, ... where you're going to hone your skills and become one of the great architects of your period."[58]

The last jury attended by Rudolph in his capacity as department chair at the end of May 1965 not only marked the end of an administration, but also a changing of the guard in American architecture. The assembled faculty and critics included the old guard—Chermayeff—and the new establishment—Rudolph, Harry Cobb, and Scully—as well as a controversial figure who was beginning to challenge them all: Robert Venturi. These figures represented the debate between heroic form-making of the late International Style and the emerging semiological architecture. So did the student work. Peter Gluck proposed a redesign of New York's already constructed Pan Am Building, in which he revived the complex geometries of Kahn, especially as manifested in his tower projects of the early 1950s.[59]

My own thesis, also presented at this jury, proposed an alternative design for the new home of the Whitney Museum of American Art designed by Marcel Breuer in New York, then under construction. Following the same program given to the architects, I sought to combine the idea of the museum-as-monument with that of

104 Cover of *Progressive Architecture* (February 1964). Photograph by Robert Damora.

museum-as-warehouse, proposing three street-facing figural towers housing the permanent collection, and loft-like galleries for changing exhibitions accommodated in a back-building which was expandable in two directions.

On June 30, 1965, Rudolph officially stepped down, in order to, in his own words, "devote my complete time to the practice of architecture."[60] University President Kingman Brewster told the *Yale Daily News* that

> For several years Paul Rudolph has let the administration know that the time would come when the demands of professional practice would not permit him to continue as chairman of architecture at Yale. Yale has been fortunate to hold on to him this long and under his leadership architecture at Yale has gained an enviable reputation. This professional accomplishment has done much to make all of Yale a more creative and exciting place.[61]

Clearly, Rudolph was exhausted and disappointed by the reception of his building among Yale students and faculty, but outside New Haven, he had already profited in both professional and personal terms (**104**). "I suppose the Yale chairmanship made me a member of the establishment," Rudolph told Moholy-Nagy, but

> I now understand that I can never truly belong to these things and that I'll always be attacked as an outsider ... It took me eight years to really flex my own muscles. Now I must try to find myself. It means risking everything in order to find out who you are. That involves being wrong, but it's the most important thing I must do.[62]

In reaching beyond a documentation of his years at Yale, I venture to place Rudolph among his generation: Rudolph's most important accomplishment, even more than his teaching, was his demonstration that an American architect could overcome the "guilt complex" toward the validity of American architectural values that his generation of Harvard graduates had been indoctrinated with.[63]

While Harvard seemed to lose its way in the 1960s under Walter Gropius's urban-oriented successor Josep Lluís Sert, Rudolph was, as Sibyl Moholy-Nagy wrote to President Brewster in 1965, instrumental in upholding Yale's traditional emphasis on "architecture as the art of making buildings." According to Moholy-Nagy, Rudolph made it his mission to see that Yale "remained one of the few, if not the only school where a gifted student can sharpen [his or her] appetite and ... skill for creative design," while most others were becoming "technology-minded ... semi-competent training centers [that] abdicated design under the pretext of 'environmental study,' meaning city planning."[64] Leaning on Moholy-Nagy's observations, I feel comfortable concluding that, perhaps even more than his body of built work, his clear vision of what it means to train a young person for practice was Paul Rudolph's greatest gift to architecture.

1 "Yale 1950–1965," *Oppositions*, 4 (October 1974): 35–62. The current essay represents a portion of a talk presented at the Paul Rudolph Centenary Symposium at the Library of Congress, Washington, D.C. (October 25, 2018), developed with the assistance of Leopoldo Villardi. See also my work with Jimmy Stamp, especially "A Time of Heroics, 1958–1965," in Robert A.M. Stern and Jimmy Stamp, *Pedagogy and Place* (New Haven, CT: Yale University Press, 2016), 163–241.
2 Sibyl Moholy-Nagy, introduction to *The Architecture of Paul Rudolph* (New York: Praeger, 1970), 8.
3 See Russell Bourne, "Paul Rudolph," *Architectural Forum* (April 1958), 128–29, 192.
4 Michael McDonough recalling an April 5, 1986, interview with Paul Rudolph in Joseph King and Christopher Domin, *Paul Rudolph: The Florida Houses* (New York: Princeton Architectural Press, 2002). See also Paul Rudolph, "Excerpts from a Conversation," *Perspecta*, 22 (1986): 104–6.
5 Walter Gropius, letter to U.S. Department of the Navy (November 7, 1951), Paul Rudolph Heritage Foundation, New York.
6 Rudolph's early years were briefly described in Robert A.M. Stern's foreword to Paul Rudolph, *Writing Architecture* (New Haven, CT: Yale University School of Architecture, 2008), 6–7; see also Robert A.M. Stern, "Secrets of Paul Rudolph: His First Twenty-Five Years" (1965), republished in Robert A.M. Stern, *Architecture on the Edge of Postmodernism: Collected Essays 1964–1988*, ed. Cynthia Davidson (New Haven, CT, and London: Yale University Press, 2009), 5–20.
7 Paul Rudolph, "Three New Directions," *Perspecta: The Yale Architectural Journal*, 1 (1952): 19.
8 Ibid., 21.
9 Paul Rudolph, quoted in Sibyl Moholy-Nagy, "The Future of the Past," *Perspecta*, 7 (1961): 73.
10 See Mildred Schmertz, "Architectural Drawing for Printing Processes," *Architectural Record*, 133 (February 1963): 137–44.
11 Charles Brewer, interview with Jimmy Stamp, August 11, 2012.
12 Paul Rudolph, interview with C. Ray Smith, March 29, 1979, C. Ray Smith Manuscript and Research

Files on the Yale Art & Architecture Building by Paul Rudolph, MS-1948, box 1, Yale University Manuscripts and Archives, New Haven, CT.

13 Paul Rudolph, letter to his parents, April 12, 1955, Paul Rudolph Foundation, Library of Congress, Washington, D.C.

14 Colin Rowe, in a very long letter to Henry-Russell Hitchcock in 1955 in which he plots his escape from University of Texas, Austin, stated that "In the Mid-West I presume that the Paul Rudolph regime at I.I.T. (which is rumoured to be imminent) offers another alternative [to Harvard, MIT, Yale, Philadelphia, and North Carolina]." See Daniel Naegele, ed., *The Letters of Colin Rowe: Five Decades of Correspondence* (London: Artifice Books on Architecture, 2016), 103–4.

15 Paul Rudolph, interview with C. Ray Smith, December 28, 1977, C. Ray Smith Manuscript and Research Files on the Yale Art & Architecture Building by Paul Rudolph, MS-1948, box 1, Yale University Manuscripts and Archives, New Haven, CT.

16 Yale University News Bureau, Release #720, June 12, 1957; A. Whitney Griswold, letter to Paul Rudolph, June 3, 1957, RU-22, box 25, folder 232, Yale University Manuscripts and Archives, New Haven, CT.

17 Paul Rudolph, quoted in "Adolescent Architecture," *Architectural Forum*, 109 (September 1958): 177.

18 Moholy-Nagy, introduction to *The Architecture of Paul Rudolph*, 11.

19 Tony Monk, "Paul Rudolph: The Committed Late-Modernist," *The Art and Architecture of Paul Rudolph*, ed. Tony Monk (Chichester: Wiley-Academy, 1999), 8.

20 Charles Brewer, interview with Jimmy Stamp, August 11, 2012.

21 Stanley Tigerman, *Designing Bridges to Burn: Architectural Memoirs by Stanley Tigerman* (Singapore: Oro Editions, 2011), 53.

22 Allan Greenberg, interview with Jimmy Stamp, November 15, 2011.

23 Vincent Scully, quoted in Mark Girouard, *Big Jim: The Life and Work of James Stirling* (London: Chatto & Windus, 1998), 117.

24 George Buchanan, quoted in Girouard, *Big Jim*, 119.

25 Ibid., 123.

26 Paul Rudolph, quoted in *The Architecture of Paul Rudolph*, introduction by Sibyl Moholy-Nagy (New York: Praeger, 1970), 16.

27 Paul Rudolph, *Perspecta: The Yale Architectural Journal*, 5 (1959): 3.

28 Paul Rudolph, "The Architectural Education in U.S.A.," *Zodiac*, 8 (1961): 162–65; see also Russell Bourne, "Yale's Paul Rudolph," *Architectural Forum*, 108 (April 1958): 128–29, 192; and Paul Rudolph, "Six Determinants of Architectural Form," *Architectural Record*, 120 (October 1956): 183–90, in which Rudolph castigated the "early theory of modern architecture" for its limited ambitions. See also Paul Rudolph, "Changing Philosophy of Architecture," *American Institute of Architects Journal*, 22 (August 1954): 65–70; also Paul Rudolph, "Regionalism in Architecture," *Perspecta: The Yale Architectural Journal*, 4 (1957): 12–19. For varying assessments of Rudolph as an educator see Peter Collins, "Whither Paul Rudolph?," *Progressive Architecture*, 42 (August 1960): 130–33; and Henry-Russell Hitchcock, "The Rise to World Prominence of American Architecture," *Zodiac*, 8 (1961): 1–5. See also *Architectural Record*, 131 (January 1962), for an interview between Rudolph and architecture student Jonathan Barnett (b. 1937; B.A. 1958, M.Arch. 1963).

29 Norman Foster speaking with students in the William C. DeVane seminar series, Yale School of Architecture, October 8, 2001. Guide to the Yale School of Architecture Lectures and Presentations, Ru-880, Accession 2002-A-151, box 11, Yale University Manuscripts and Archives, New Haven, CT.

30 Allan Greenberg, interview with Jimmy Stamp, November 15, 2011.

31 Paul Rudolph, quoted in Allan Greenberg, "Introduction, Fragment of an Autobiography," *Architecture of Democracy* (New York: Rizzoli, 2006), 18.

32 Tigerman, *Designing Bridges to Burn*, 97.

33 Norman Foster, quoted in Deyan Sudjic, *Norman Foster: A Life in Architecture* (New York: Overlook Press, 2010), 71.

34 Stanley Tigerman, interview with Betty Blum, "Oral History of Stanley Tigerman," The Chicago Architects Oral History Project, Ernest R. Graham Study Center for Architectural Drawings, Department of Architecture, The Art Institute of Chicago (2003), 14.

35 Tigerman, *Designing Bridges to Burn*, 110.

36 Stanley Tigerman, interview with Betty Blum, "Oral History of Stanley Tigerman," 14.

37 John W. Cook and Heinrich Klotz, eds., interview with Paul Rudolph in *Conversations with Architects* (New York: Praeger, 1973), 107.

38 M.J. Long, quoted in Girouard, *Big Jim*, 116–17.
39 Stanley Tigerman, interview with Betty Blum, "Oral History of Stanley Tigerman," 15.
40 Anthony Vidler, *James Frazer Stirling: Notes from the Archive* (New Haven, CT: Yale University Press for the Canadian Centre for Architecture and Yale Center for British Art, 2010), 85, 87–90.
41 Norman Foster, remarks delivered on his acceptance of the Pritzker Architecture Prize (1999), https://www.pritzkerprize.com/laureates/1999 (accessed December 19, 2019).
42 Norman Foster speaking with students in the William C. DeVane seminar series, Yale School of Architecture, October 8, 2001. Guide to the Yale School of Architecture Lectures and Presentations, Ru-880, Accession 2002-A-151, box 11, Yale University Manuscripts and Archives, New Haven, CT.
43 Norman Foster, Pritzker Prize Address, quoted in Deyan Sudjic, introduction to *On Foster—Foster On*, ed. David Jenkins (Munich: Prestel, 2000).
44 Sudjic, *Norman Foster*, 74.
45 For Islam, see Zainab Faruqui Ali, *Muzharul Islam, Architect* (Dhaka: Bangla Academy, 2011).
46 Stanley Tigerman, interview with Betty Blum, "Oral History of Stanley Tigerman," 15; see also Tigerman, *Designing Bridges to Burn*, 100–1.
47 Paul Rudolph, quoted in Victoria Milne, "Nothing Trivial" (1994–1996), 49, cited in Alan Powers, *Serge Chermayeff: Designer, Architect, Teacher* (London: RIBA, 2001), 208.
48 Ibid.
49 Vincent Scully, interview with Jimmy Stamp, August 23, 2010.
50 "Oral History of Gordon Bunshaft," The Chicago Architects Oral History Project, Ernest R. Graham Study Center for Architectural Drawings, Department of Architecture, The Art Institute of Chicago (1990), 211; it is not likely that Saarinen was considered. He had just finished the Ingalls Rink, which was over budget, he was working on the university's master plan, and he had probably already been awarded the commission for two new residential colleges.
51 For more on this, see "A Time of Heroics, 1958–1965," in Robert A.M. Stern and Jimmy Stamp, *Pedagogy and Place* (New Haven, CT: Yale University Press, 2016), 213–15.
52 The decision to go forward with the construction of the Art & Architecture Building was officially announced on June 18, 1960, Yale University News Bureau, Release #515. The Beinecke Library was announced at the same time.
53 Nikolaus Pevsner, "Address Given by Nikolaus Pevsner at the Inauguration of the New Art & Architecture Building of Yale University, 9 November 1963," *Journal of the Society of Architectural Historians*, 26 (March 1967): 4–7.
54 Ibid.
55 Paul Rudolph, interview by C. Ray Smith, February 15, 1978, C. Ray Smith Manuscript and Research Files on the Yale Art & Architecture Building by Paul Rudolph, MS-1948, box 1, Yale University Manuscripts and Archives, New Haven, CT.
56 Vincent Scully, *The Earth, The Temple, and the Gods* (New Haven, CT: Yale University Press, 1962).
57 Tigerman, *Designing Bridges to Burn*, 102.
58 Thomas Beeby, interview with Betty Blum, "Oral History of Thomas Beeby," The Chicago Architects Oral History Project, Ernest R. Graham Study Center for Architectural Drawings, Department of Architecture, The Art Institute of Chicago (1998), 15.
59 For Gluck's project see Robert A.M. Stern, Thomas Mellins, and David Fishman, *New York 1960: Architecture and Urbanism Between the Second World War and the Bicentennial* (New York: The Monacelli Press, Inc., 1995); for more on Gluck see *Peter L. Gluck and Partners: The Modern Impulse*, ed. Oscar Riera Ojeda (San Rafael, CA: Oro Editions, 2008).
60 Paul Rudolph, quoted in James Adams, "Head Architect to Leave Yale for Own Firm," *Yale Daily News* (September 21, 1964).
61 Kingman Brewster, quoted in Adams, "Head Architect to Leave Yale for Own Firm."
62 Paul Rudolph, quoted in Moholy-Nagy, introduction to *The Architecture of Paul Rudolph*, 15.
63 Sibyl Moholy-Nagy, "The Future of the Past," 73.
64 Sibyl Moholy-Nagy to Kingman Brewster, November 16, 1964, Kingman Brewster Jr. Presidential Records, ser. 1, RU-11, box 25, folder 2, Yale University Manuscripts and Archives, New Haven, CT.

PART III

Operational Criticism, Landform, and Tectonic Presence

With the more conceptual and historical essays of the previous two sections as a context, this third section gathers reflections from contemporary architects on their own engagement with the challenges and guidance provided by Frampton as teacher, mentor, and critic. Some essays are quite self-reflective, expressing the authors' sense of personal gratitude toward Frampton and tracing their willingness to grapple with design challenges as an almost direct response to the inspiration which he provided to them.

Several themes stand out. The work discussed here represents a clear—and often literal—understanding of the ways in which Frampton's writings have provided a set of guidelines for the practitioner. Moreover, in some cases the professional success of these authors is in no small part due to Frampton's own criticism or reviews of their work and projects, and the scholarly attention he paid to their production—especially as it was understood by him as reflective of contemporary developments within the field. As a result, many of these architects are to some degree a product of what Frampton himself regarded (often with some regret) as his own *operational criticism*, referring to what Manfredo Tafuri regarded as criticism which largely served (for Tafuri, problematically) as an appraisal rather than a critique.

Three architects give broad appraisals of Frampton's impact on their own work: Steven Holl, Wiel Arets, and Brad Cloepfil. Then in their essay, "Architectural Osmosis," the Irish architects Yvonne Farrell and Shelley McNamara write about how Frampton's "Six Points Towards an Architecture of Resistance," from his important early essay, serve as a direct touchstone for their design process, and an inspiration for the constructive materiality of their projects. The architects and urban designers Marion Weiss and Michael A. Manfredi offer the transcript from a roundtable discussion they had with Frampton that expands upon the relation between megaform and landscape. Following from these examples of the importance of nature to the design process, Emilio Ambasz provides an account of his own concern with the situational environment in which his projects are located.

Ashley Simone, as a younger architect and designer, writes about her professional relationship with Frampton, having been his student at Columbia and there learning from him the art of reading images. She later worked with him on the conception, editing, and design of *A Genealogy of Modern Architecture*. Her essay reminds us of the fact that Frampton has a keen awareness of the influential role that photography has had on the development of modern architecture, both in highly interpretive images such as those by Hélène Binet, and in those that "draw a veil" over architecture, obscuring its authentic tactile and tectonic reality.[1] Finally, as a valuable coda for this volume, the architects Brigitte Shim and Howard Sutcliffe reflect collectively on the Frampton archives held at the Canadian Centre for Architecture, providing a sampling of key moments in Frampton's career and underscoring his convictions regarding what might be summarized as both the practical and theoretical competences of the architect.

1 Kenneth Frampton, *Modern Architecture: A Critical History*, rev. edition (London: Thames & Hudson, 1985), 312.

On Kenneth Frampton

Steven Holl

1974: A student from San Francisco

The first day I met Kenneth Frampton was in November of 1974 at Columbia University. Living in San Francisco, I had been accepted at three Ivy League graduate schools and had come to the east coast to investigate. At Columbia, I sat in the back of Ware Lounge and listened to the inspiring talk Frampton was giving on Le Corbusier. After the seminar, Frampton took the students to the Symposium, a Greek restaurant nearby. I followed, walking a block behind them. In the restaurant, when Frampton saw me sitting across the room trying to listen to the conversation, he said, "Come join us!" Forty-five years ago now, I first experienced his deep generosity as an inspired teacher.

1976: London

Thanks to director Alvin Boyarsky, I was accepted for graduate studies at the Architectural Association. I arrived in London on January 26, 1976. The motto on the AA shield reads, "Design with beauty, build with truth." Reflecting on these words today, I note that while so many others have forgotten them, Kenneth Frampton has kept these simple words like a flame.

I came to the AA at a time of turmoil and fascination. Charles Jencks had just published *The Language of Post-Modern Architecture*. Léon Krier had his manifesto in *Rational Architecture*, and Elia Zenghelis and Rem Koolhaas were finishing *Delirious New York*. Alvin had arranged free tuition for me if I would attend critical reviews in Unit 9 (which Elia Zenghelis encouraged). My second day at the AA I was a critic, along with Rem, applauding the "Architectonic" project of a former Léon Krier student from Baghdad, Zaha Hadid. We became lifelong friends.

1977: New York City

On New Year's Eve in 1976, I arrived in New York City on a twenty-one-day excursion ticket from San Francisco. I never took the return half. I was excited to attend the many events at the Institute for Architecture and Urban Studies, led by Kenneth Frampton and Peter Eisenman at 8 West 40th Street. I had been reading every issue of their journal *Oppositions* while in San Francisco and was especially moved by articles Kenneth wrote.

105 Steven Holl Architects, The REACH, The Kennedy Center for the Performing Arts, Washington, D.C., 2012–19. Revising concept sketch, three white concrete pavilions, 2015.

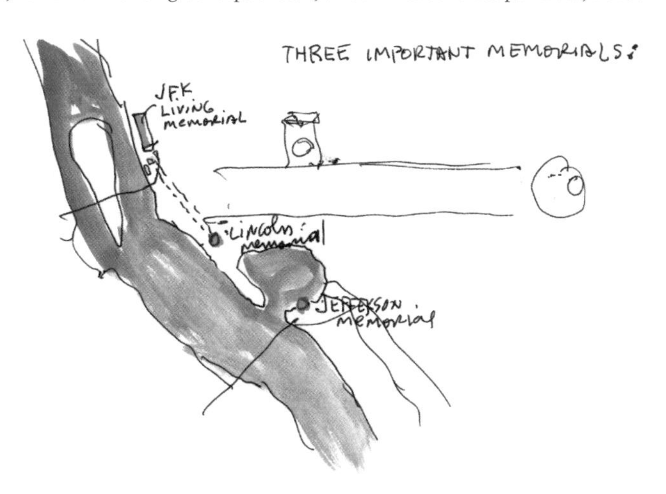

106 Competition sketch, Kennedy Center, 2012.

107 Entry Pavilion interior, Kennedy Center, 2019.

1981: Columbia University

A few months after being a critic in a heated review attended by Max Bond, Kenneth Frampton, and Robert Stern, I was offered a chance to teach first-year studio. Max Bond telephoned me three days before the fall semester start to ask if I could teach. He said, "We need articulate critics to counter Stern's historicism."

1986–91: Columbia: linear/planar/volumetric

In 1986, Kenneth Frampton and I spent the summer writing a new script for the first-year core studios at Columbia. We envisioned three interconnected problems to be built in basswood models: 1) Linear, 2) Planar, and 3) Volumetric. Kenneth, as chair, appointed me as director of first year, for which I wrote the following:

> First Year M Arch Design Studio
> Steven Holl, Director
>
> A central aim of the studio is to develop a poetic sensibility in the translation of thought into architectural composition. If questions raised in the studio are more difficult than those raised in vocational atmosphere—this is exactly fitting—but mere intellection is not the aim. The intuition of a composer, the artistic temperament must balance the intellect. Architecture must have both an intellectual and emotional dimension. "Architectonic thought is not merely invention

108 The REACH, Kennedy Center expansion, opened September 2019.

and combination, nor is it forming and molding in accordance with prescribed laws; rather it is a process which is a law unto itself ... We can recognize architectonic consciousness in the artistic sense only when an intellectual process of development becomes evident in the architectonic forms and active striving for an even purer intellectual expression appears in the development of these architectonic forms."—G. Semper

Limits: The focus of each of these exercises depends on limiting the elements in order to heighten awareness of basic compositional aspects. A beginning painter soon learns that when all colors are mixed together a murky gray appears—individual properties are annulled. Likewise, to begin again to study architecture, the individual properties of compositional elements should be contemplated.

Proportion: Proportional relations must be considered from the outset—even in a composition with two lines, the proportion of one to the other is established. A geometrical progression from the ratio 1:1.618 is an essential order of the geometry of natural forms—the nautilus shell, the pine cone, spacing of lateral veins on a leaf, etc. A bridge between natural phenomena and works of man—proportional analogues can be established in musical and spatial ratios.

Composition: Architectural composition engages the following aspects: symmetry-asymmetry/frontality-posteriority/path-obstruction/flank-border/central-peripheral/unilateral, bilateral, trilateral, quadrilateral/concavity-convexity/

109 River Pavilion and Reflecting Pool, Kennedy Center, 2019.

perpendicular-parallel/macro-micro/angularity-amorphism/straightness-distortion/sharpness-blutness/smoothness-roughness/expansion-contraction/verticality-horizontality/depth-shallowness.

Materials: Consideration of construction material and its expression is inaugurated in construction of scale models. Density, hardness, elasticity, and tenacity of construction materials can be paralleled in materials chosen for studio models. The degree of technical dexterity, together with understanding of properties of materials used, are essential ingredients to craft. The studio work serves as a beginning analogue for craft in architecture, striving toward craft, quality, and intensity of meaning before mere quantity.

Space and Light: Light is not studied as something abstract, it is definite and spatial in characterizing architecture. In the initial exercises, shadow, shade, twilight, and darkness should be considered as animating architectural form, space, and material.

Fundamental elements of architecture are studied in three cumulative problems. In these three studies, composition, proportion and clear concept stress *thinking* while the scale model work in different raw materials stresses *making*.

The sequence of problems is organized around the simplest elements of composition: point, line, plane, volume. The first problem characterizes horizontal

110 Glissando Pavilion interior, Kennedy Center, 2019.

movement on a flat plane. The second problem has a shift in horizontal movement, while the third characterizes vertical movement. The first problem is of shallow relief with unspecified section; the second is of medium relief with a specified section; while the third is of deep relief with specified section and plans. The first problem is of light construction, the second of heavy construction and the third joins light and heavy construction. The three models stand as crafted artifacts reflecting design concepts assembled as a trilogy in the final review.

1986: Atelier of Steven Holl Architects

During those years of dedicated teaching, I would return from Columbia to work in my cold-water loft at 655 6th Avenue. The Hugh O'Neill Building was then an empty department store (four or five artists occupied lofts), and my rent was $250.00 per month—perfect for an idealistic beginning architect. I slept on a plywood shelf over the office entry and showered after my 6.00pm workout at the local YMCA.

Frampton would come down and give me critiques on our projects. He came to criticize my first freestanding house. On Martha's Vineyard, it was a "linear construction" in balloon-frame wood: an exposed exoskeleton inspired by the Indians who long ago inhabited bark-covered whale skeletons according to a passage in Melville's *Moby Dick*.

I remember Frampton's critical words about the bedroom element sitting on the long linear composition. "Steven, you must reconsider this, it's like a dog house sitting on the roof!" I revised the design. The house won a "Progressive Architecture Award" before it was built, and an AIA National Award after it was built.

111 Corner stair skylight, Kennedy Center, 2019.

1988–89: "Anchoring"

Given the invitation by MoMA to show my projects at a two-architect exhibition in 1988, I struggled to write a little manifesto for the important occasion which developed into the book, *Anchoring*, published by Kevin Lippert of Princeton Architectural Press.

Kenneth Frampton wrote "On the Architecture of Steven Holl," the introduction to his monograph on my work, which began:

> The maturation of an architect's creative personality is an exhilarating moment although the indications that attend this process are often extremely subtle. One finds oneself asking at what point did Steven finally arrive at his present sensibility? ... As we have seen, two fundamental principles underline his architecture. The first of these is the "anchoring" of the building in its site, although, like the Portuguese architect Álvaro Siza, he believes that the architect has as much responsibility to challenge the site as to harmonize passively with its form. The second salient percept is Holl's need to integrate the conceptual level of his work with a phenomenological experience of its presence. The phenomenological for Holl amplifies and transcends in diverse ways the ideational.[1]

112 Simulcast projection on Glissando Pavilion, Kennedy Center, 2019.

The validity of these words thirty years later is amazing. The lucid clarity of Frampton's text and how it fortified my own challenge over thirty years of realizing architecture has been a gift for which I am humbly and deeply thankful.

1990–2019: Building and teaching

While teaching studio at Columbia for the last three decades, Frampton has repeatedly been the most lucid review critic. He has come down for "theory hour" in our Atelier at 31st Street and 10th Avenue, providing sharp critiques of our ongoing work. His influence has been realized in the Glasgow School of Art of 2014, the Campbell Sports Center at Columbia of 2013, and the University of Iowa's Visual Arts Building, opened in 2016, and the Kennedy Center Expansion, opened in 2019 (**105–112**).

I was thrilled when the Venice Biennale awarded the Golden Lion for Lifetime Achievement to Kenneth Frampton in 2018. I feel very fortunate to have developed my architecture over forty-five years parallel to teaching next to his deep wisdom and kind brilliance.

1 Kenneth Frampton, *Steven Holl: Architect* (London: Phaidon, 2003).

An Englishman in New York

Wiel Arets

When the Japanese novelist Jun'ichirō Tanizaki arrived in Kyoto in 1923, in order to leave behind a Tokyo devastated by earthquakes and to build a new home, it was also a turning point in his view of the West and the Japanese tradition. His former infatuation with the West had increasingly faded, in the face of the still-alive past of Kyoto, and the wistful memories of his former Tokyo, which had been irretrievably lost to the "Great Earthquake." The Kansai region—with Kobe, Osaka, and Kyoto—created ample new theses in him, such as shifts of cultural identities, modern and traditional sexuality, and other new class affiliations, which he controversially addressed in his 1925 book, *Naomi*. The translation into modern Japanese of the *Tale of Genji* is his expression of a deep interest in the ancient, seemingly lost culture of Japan, which he wanted to bring back into the light. The new edition of the eleventh-century classic, written by Murasaki Shikibu, into a then-modern Japanese translation, was a novelty of its time. In 1931 and 1932 he published two important works, "Love and Sensibility" and "Praise of the Mastery," in which he discusses important subjects in the fields of drama, dance, literature, eroticism, and painting in his home country. In Tanizaki's 1933 short novel, *In Praise of Shadows*, about Japanese aesthetics in the early twentieth century, he questions Japan's change of direction toward a Western society within a critical dialogue, which portrays moments of beauty in triviality, showing the slow, yet significant moments of change in Japan during the 1930s. One of his first books, *Shisei*, from 1910, shows how, early on, he dealt with issues of aesthetics, the dichotomy of East and West, and eroticism and nature, throughout his entire life.

In the 2019 movie *The Dead Don't Die*, the writer and director Jim Jarmusch, yet again, reveals his own reading of a world that shakes at its seams, and expresses his vision of the world we now live in, through the protagonists played by Bill Murray (city) and Tom Waits (nature). He enlists them to play the role of the conscience, as he criticizes the masses, who tend to pollute and clog the city as consumers who aimlessly wander, often discourteously, strolling, slavishly tied to the issues of their day, to the trends and fashion of the moment, from which they cannot escape, nor from which they are able to withdraw. His image of the manipulated human being as being physically fit, sporty, and athletic in his approach to success represents such a person who makes rather catastrophic life choices. He places the fear of crisis in perspective by indicating that we must look toward nature (Tom Waits), and that humanity must reconsider its position toward the brainwashed consumers roaming the streets of New York, who, while following their iPhones, are, in all actuality, victims: the drugged

113 Kenneth Frampton, 2014.

human being of the masses, which we have come to know in varying stages since the Industrial Revolution. The metropolis, with its fragile social order, seems to be the place where it becomes apparent that an environmental catastrophe is now imminent; it is central to the fate currently threatening the world, threatening our humanity. Humanity seems to be powerless, even as it writes its own scenarios about this state of mind. The metropolis as a cultural phenomenon, is, in consequence, in perpetual crisis mode in part due to those aimlessly wandering citizens of this divided world. Besides this "doomsday thinking," a realization must be nurtured that all of humanity must herald a new phase, wherein the understanding that humanity can never manipulate nature must be recognized. The fact that humans intervene through gene manipulation or, for instance, that they adapt bees, insects, plants, and perhaps even humans themselves will require us to ponder these issues. Humanity must come to terms with the fact that it is only a collection of dust particles in the larger violence of the universe.

It seemed there was, in the 1930s, according to José Ortega y Gasset, a consensus as to a self-declared modern humanity, in which the voice of the people was to be heard, and the masses strove for equality, which seemed to then be possible through technology's advancement. Yet after this, the masses quickly demanded speed, along with comfort. Technology progresses slowly, and thus it tends to become the weapon of the masses. Rather than the challenge of risk, the masses want immediate results; they are restless and ruthless. Respect for those who are specialists, inventors who deal with differences and attempt to develop new strategies, is thus gone. Therefore,

114, 115 Kenneth Frampton, 2014.

the avant-garde seems to no longer exist, for the masses now ask for—and reward—that which is *popular*. We must privilege slowness; we need time; the self-made person; and a new, non-ironic journalism.

In 1967 Jean-Luc Godard created the film *Week-end*, in which he displays his anarchical view on the "bourgeois morals" of the "sick" consuming classes. He had his actors recite lines from commercials: a woman mourns the loss of her Hermès bag, after her car had been involved in a brutal accident and had gone up in flames; and in another moment bloodstained, brand-name clothes are themselves mourned, while the seriously injured person in the accident receives but only a supporting role. The main character in *Week-end* is the car itself, produced as just one product for the consuming masses. It is at once both a symbol of freedom and progress, and it becomes a machine that can no longer be controlled. The dream of the car as the ultimate means of transportation for these masses—which also see the infrastructure created for the car, its highways, as a symbol of communication—is instead presented by Godard as a machine that stands still, thus causing destruction.

It was of course, no surprise after the collapse of the Berlin Wall, that the city of Berlin's backdrop was—and in just a short period of time—appropriated by the media: the imposing Coca-Cola billboard was placed on the rooftop of a D.D.R. building at the Spittelmarkt in former East Berlin, one of the most symbolic locations in the city. This was but one of the first actions then used to initiate the total brainwashing of the new consumer, in this new society, who wanted, so desperately, only to be *modern*.

The paradox of the D.D.R.'s urban planning was that the city streets were completely "over-dimensioned" in regard to scale, with hardly any cars driving in them, while the "Trabant" car, at least for the masses, belonged to some otherworldly, unrealizable—in their reality—distant dream. It can therefore be deduced that the word "interiority" is a term that we can use to express architecture's own ability to give a sense of space that rules out the reality of the exterior. We think verbally about our own perception of moving in public space or inside a building, but also of reading a book or watching a film. Interiority is a term we use to describe the intellectual and emotional multi-dimensionality of all named disciplines.

In 1910 Adolf Loos identified, after a few years of studying the work of Louis Sullivan during his long stay in Chicago which ended in 1896, a culture that found a balance between the world of humanity's interior and its exterior: that the only reasonable guarantee of authenticity is rational thinking and exchange. Loos attributed the farmer to culture, whereas the city dweller had become detached from such status, thinking that technology should instead be placed above nature, as it were human beings who could make their own artificial worlds. The architect, according to Loos, criticized, and, just as the city dweller, had detached himself from his own primal status, thereby causing the balance between the soul and the body to have been lost. Loos had his own opinion about the role of the architect, which he never hid. He makes a clear difference between public space—with the muted facades, or skin, of buildings—versus their interior, wherein he chose a range of raw/premium materials, such as wood, stone, mirrors, leather, and tapestries (which, he believed, belong to the whole).

It was Kenneth Frampton who, in 1991, described the paradox between global urbanization—which leads to a serious breakdown of the environment as a direct result of the expansion of technology—and the architect, who was relegated to a marginal position (**113–116**). In his texts, Frampton places as the protagonists the architects he writes about and with whom he feels a connection—allowing them to speak for themselves as much as possible. He truly wants to have a dialogue; he wants to pose questions; he is curious; he is fascinated; he maintains his wonder at what it is that he sees; he possesses a positive, critical standpoint, toward the quickly changing world that he inhabits. He has assumed this role since his very first writings: he looks, reads, and listens with a critical position toward realized works of architecture, as well as the statements of unrealized buildings of dreams that shape the reality of architecture. He is a true witness to humanity's own changing position, from the preindustrial era to today.

Scholars such as August Schmarsow and Wilhelm Worringer posited a belief in the division between an ephemeral body, on one hand, and an immortal soul, on the other; however, in the twentieth century, in part due to the notion of the "modern," the soul was replaced by the immortal machine. The twenty-first century's technological developments have allowed the virtual machine, with all its updates, to be loveless, aimless, and completely devoid of meaning. The human being, as it were, was robbed of its soul, and, through artificial intelligence, the body can now be repaired and can receive its own updates, and through this is able to pursue a true immortality. It was Andy Warhol who wanted to be the machine, and in doing so claim his own immortality. And by contrast it is Frampton who understands the nuances of accent, which could be expressed in the words of the musician Gordon Sumner (known as Sting): "Modesty, propriety can lead to notoriety, gentleness, sobriety are rare in this society, be yourself no matter what they say, I am an Englishman in New York."[1]

Frampton is an architect, who studied at the Architectural Association, at London's Bedford Square, the school he will always be attached to. The AA is a place of wading, a threshold where history is written, and a place that is dear to Frampton; not only because it is situated in London, but because it is a school that for him, as an Englishman, functions as a home of his own. It is an institute where one is filtered through its very self, every time one enters into it—which was certainly the case during the second half of the twentieth century. Frampton always wanted to be a practicing architect while there, an architect interested in "tectonic culture," wherein he sees the architect from the perspective of that of author, with realized work always fascinating him most. In many of his texts he writes from the perspective of the thinking of an architect questioning himself; he tries to crawl into and remain hidden within his own skin, and tries as much as possible not to come to his own theories regarding the disciplines of architecture and urbanism. This is also the reason why he tends to write essays about the work of architects, and not so much about an architect's own concept or concepts. In this sense, we could also consider Frampton to be an "illegal alien" within the architectural profession. He is a critical observer; a critical viewer who gives commentary on that which he sees, hears, and smells when he intensely preoccupies himself with a work of architecture. He analyzes a work just as a surgeon, tries to dissect it, and discloses what he sees through the use of his own texts. This is another reason why he writes essays about the works of architects as he, meanwhile, considers the division between architecture and urbanism as one of the biggest dilemmas architectural production faces, because in all actuality it can contribute very little to the identity of a metropolis. He is less concerned with writing the history of architecture itself, because he quite emphatically opines that it is concerned only with the moment in time when such a history is being written.

Frampton also uses every reprint of his texts as a means for modifications to his own self-reflection, as well as to provide his readers with new insights. He considers it a challenge to visit every work of an architect, as well as to discuss them, and enjoys challenging architects to a dialogue that serves as a "feast for the mind." A reversal of this position was when he himself was questioned—such as during a debate with Rem Koolhaas at the Berlage Institute in Amsterdam, which was rather uncomfortable. He was questioned by Koolhaas in the manner in which only a journalist would do, whereas Frampton wanted to think about architecture from his own critical standpoint. This in turn led to a moment quite reminiscent

116 Kenneth Frampton, 2014.

of the movie *Lost in Translation*, due to the duo's philosophical language conflict. That scenario is in direct opposition to the later interviews Frampton had with, for instance, Jacques Herzog and Pierre de Meuron, within the framework of their being Mies Crown Hall Americas Prize-winning architects. Another interview took place in the Mies-designed Farnsworth House with Álvaro Siza, also an MCHAP-winning architect, who was challenged by Frampton to make somewhat startling statements that created a situation allowing them to enter into proper dialogue. Both conversations consequently led to publications that, otherwise, would have never been possible to publish. One resulting book, *Treacherous Transparencies* (New York: Actar/IITAC Press, 2017) by Jacques Herzog, was preceded by a lecture by Jacques in Crown Hall in Chicago. And it was a two-day visit to Porto with Siza himself and his first two projects, and his own dialogue with Frampton, that led to the book *A Pool in the Sea* (New York: Actar/IITAC Press, 2018).

Frampton himself is more than conscious of the fact that the critical practice of architecture is the primary advantage of the progressive development of the architectural culture itself. It is thus, through the actual work of architects with whom he himself has a connection, that he is enabled to unravel his pen and form his vision, which in turn allows him to continually adjust that same vision. He is also critical and subjectively outspoken about all the works he chooses to write about. He wants to be positively critical, and place the works with which he is engaged within their architects' context of thinking, which in turn leaves them open to further consideration. Ultimately, however, he is self-critical, prepared to adjust his positions and even apologize to his readers and his listeners if he sees the reason not to discuss or even trust every work or subject on paper, or when he goes against his own opinion, or when his opinions are not consistent with his own arguments. Where he very clearly expresses himself is the challenge that he sees before the current generation of architects: that they should not exclusively concern themselves with the spectacular, ever-changing, and ever-fashionable aspects of architecture. This embodies his work with a certain *English humbleness*.

Frampton himself speaks to a humanist-oriented architecture practice, and since his time at Columbia University in New York has derived his opinion as to "modern" architecture from a continuous investigation of the Frankfurter Schule. His own position, that humanity is the architect of the "modern" and that technological development has alienated the self, keeps Frampton continuously preoccupied. His English roots, in which sensory empirical perception is key, place him in a position to resist devastating transgressions that technological modernization creates, which leads to the "other"—to use Frampton's own words.

What would be our world, or what would our world be, if we were not suspicious of technology? If we would listen more often to the human body and mind, instead of trying to change it until it is out of balance? Technology let us—increasingly less—train, exercise the body and brain; contrary to what ancient Greece would have us understand. Our society now seems to overestimate its own capabilities. The masses are being brainwashed and directed into dead ends. They are becoming lazy in many fields; our brains are shrinking, since it is indeed a muscle, like our heart—and like our lungs must be able to breathe fresh air. The misconception and promise that technology will make us more intelligent is a logical error. Why do we not use technology to assist us, to be used only in an emergency case? Why do we not understand and respect our cosmos in full, and intervene with the system of nature, every time we discover something new? We still do not understand that our civilization will never be able to gain control, since we ourselves are part of this cosmos as actors. The more our metropolis tends to depend on self-created, and even self-creating, systems, our civilization will be degraded. It will be a brainless, easy-to-influence conglomerate of brain constructs, which the consumer will most certainly believe in. Mother Earth will of course strike back, as she has done so many times, when all of life on the globe was wiped out; we will not be able to dominate, nor dictate, nature. The more we depend on technology—the more we believe in its updates—the less we believe in the trained muscle of the brain and the body, and the less we tend to understand that human beings have been forever competitive. We must—we now have to—understand that "the other" is a mindset that we should never underestimate.

1 Gordon Sumner (Sting), "Englishman in New York," from the album *Nothing Like the Sun* (A&M, 1987).

From the Field: Critical Regionalism and Tectonic Culture Applied

Brad Cloepfil

Entering Columbia as a postgrad architecture student from Oregon, I was accused of being an American romantic: in love with the landscape, bound to place and in pursuit of the sublime in building. My position was more a matter of passion, as I had been raised and educated in the powerful landscapes of the West. With the emerging digital focus in the academies favoring the procedural and formal over the visceral and experiential, I was assured that my position was retrograde. Then, in Kenneth Frampton's fall 1984 seminar, I was introduced to his essay "Towards a Critical Regionalism: Six Points for an Architecture of Resistance." His writings and teaching summarized everything I had intuited and subsequently came to believe in architecture. The historical connections he made, the concerns he framed, and the potential he revealed in them crystallized into a deeply personal architectural imperative. The "romanticism" I had been accused of was essentially part of a radical new position, Frampton's "arrière-garde." More than vindicated, I was utterly inspired. Here we have a critical position rooted in the nature of building and the influence of place, and an opposition to the corrosive forces of conformity and commodity:

> The tactile and the tectonic jointly have the capacity to transcend the mere appearance of the technical in much the same way as the place-form has the potential to withstand the relentless onslaught of global modernization.[1]

Cultural context

> Perhaps we are here in order to say: house, bridge, fountain, gate, pitcher, fruit tree, window—at most: column, tower ... to say them more intensely than the Things themselves ever dreamed of existing.
>
> Rainer Maria Rilke, from "The Ninth Elegy" in *Duino Elegies & The Sonnets to Orpheus* (1922)

To understand Frampton's impact on the field of practice, it is important to reflect on the state of the profession in the late 1970s and early 1980s. The death throes of international modernism were coming to a crescendo, or so it seemed. It was a time when the influences of the major corporate firms—SOM, Pei Cobb Freed, et al.—were waning (though significant commissions were still to come) and a new culture, of what I call "studio architecture," was just emerging on the streets of Los Angeles and New York.

In the academy, and in the battle for commissions, this discourse had become frozen between two poles: that of historic scenography as retro-commodity, as Frampton and Charles Jencks so aptly identified, and that of the emerging adoption of literary theory, under an array of labels from formalism to deconstructivism. The former saw architecture as a sort of semaphore, reduced to accepted symbols and variants; the latter applied theory and philosophy to architecture, creating a complicated composition in an attempt to prop up a romantic ideal of some lost avant-garde. In both, architecture was merely a vehicle to which historical pastiche or literary narrative could be applied in equally exaggerated amounts. Architecture was not regarded as a "thing in itself," as Rilke posed in his *Duino Elegies*; indeed, it had lost all autonomy. At the end of the last century, practitioners and theorists alike were locked in a desperate battle of association and borrowed authority.

Into this atmosphere, Frampton introduced the concept of a Critical Regionalism, in which:

> The primary principle of architectural autonomy resides in the *tectonic* rather than the *scenographic*, that is to say, this autonomy is embodied in the revealed ligaments of the construction and in the way in which the syntactical form of the structure explicitly resists the action of gravity.[2]

In this essay and throughout his reflections on built precedent, he asserted architecture—and specifically, a theory of Building—as a radical statement of practice. Building, in its material and structural potential, is the most potent act of architectural investigation. And in doing so, Frampton effectively asserted the very specific language of architecture as *the* critical cultural pursuit.

Frampton's place in the history of architectural discourse is primarily built upon his point of view, first and foremost as an architect. As such, he sees the work as a physical body, a construct of presence and inherent value. He believes deeply in building and its potential to manifest the critical character and values of our time. He is passionate about the domain that only building holds, the synthesis of structure, space, material, and the omnipresent ontology of the joint. For Frampton, the tectonic is not "a mechanical revelation of construction but rather a potentially poetic manifestation of structure in the original Greek sense of poesis as an act of making and revealing."[3] The building, the made artifact, can embody and transmit something true about its own construction, and by extension, the cultural forces at work upon it.

From classical Greece to nineteenth-century Germany to the present day, Frampton's historical insights seem effortless, even obvious—as hard as the avant-garde pushed for a rupture with the past, he persistently returned to the interconnectedness and shared inheritance of building. His critical propositions formed a bridge to the past and thereby cleared the only path forward for architecture as a discipline. More than the architects of the time, Frampton became a guide and mentor for me—with the questions of "why to build" and "how to build" coursing through all of my work. I regard his writing and instruction as something of a Fresnel lens—illuminating, multifaceted, painstakingly crafted, and providing critical guidance over time and distance.

Chronological regression and revelation

In the late 1970s the University of Oregon, where I studied architecture as an undergraduate, was a destination for a cadre of young architects—Thomas Hacker, Richard Garfield, Pat Piccioni, and Gary Moye—who had left Philadelphia and Lou Kahn's studio after his death in 1974. At the time I had no idea of my incredible good fortune. Immersed in Kahn's ideals and ethics—the nearly sacred nature of structure, the necessity of order—I left school with a deep respect for his poetic principles, and his ethics of building (**117**). Yet I longed to see how these ideas might evolve into new forms. In my nascent comparative searches, I was utterly uninspired by the modes of practice that I saw around me in the Northwest. Discouraged, I fled to Los Angeles.

In my first week in LA I passed a storefront office that had interesting models in the window. Inside I found Eric Owen Moss's one employee, and he spoke of

117 Louis Kahn, National Assembly of Bangladesh, Dhaka, 1982.

118 Mario Botta, secondary school, Morbio Inferiore, Switzerland, 1977.

the emerging scene there. On his recommendation I made the rounds: I applied at Morphosis, Craig Hodgetts's studio, and Frank Gehry's office—all had little to no work. With exhausted options I applied to SOM, where I was set to work designing office tower facades. Kahn's words echoed in my ears as I rendered elevations in various tartan grids of Prismacolor. I soon left, and when my girlfriend decided to intern for a judge in Anchorage, I followed. In the oil boom times there I quickly found work in a local firm.

It was in Alaska, at the apartment of two coworkers, both Harvard Graduate School of Design grads, that I was introduced to a series of small black and white books published by Electa in Milan. One was on Mario Botta, the other, Tadao Andō—names I had never encountered. I was transfixed. For the first time since Kahn, I saw work that revered structure and materiality, and specifically concrete. In Botta's secondary school at Morbio Inferiore and Andō's iconic Azuma House in Sumiyoshi, I saw new forms and poetics of structure (**118**). I borrowed the books, later to find that both had forewords written by Kenneth Frampton. This new work, and his words, revived my career and resolve. My life and work were forever transformed in that Alaskan evening. Six months later I wrote Botta a letter and, without waiting for a response, sold everything I owned and moved to Lugano.

After a year spent in Botta's office and Ticino—discovering the work of Livio Vachinni and Luigi Snozzi, as well as the vernacular architecture of the Swiss

119 Aurelio Galfetti, Bagno Pubblico, Bellinoza, Switzerland, 1970.

Cantons—I began to revel in the unlimited possibilities of an architecture of place. I saw the farmhouses that inspired Botta, and the brilliant works of civil engineering, both ancient and recent, that inspired Aurelio Galfetti's Bagno Pubblico in Bellinzona (1970) (**118**). It was all there, visceral and present. Botta's methodology of "building the site" merged tradition and innovation. The work came from the ground, from the stones and soil. As Frampton summarized about Botta and his contemporaries: "The specific culture of the region—that is to say, its history in both a geological and agricultural sense—becomes inscribed in the form and realization of the work."[4]

This experience was an object lesson in a movement that was emerging rather quietly, in locales across the globe. Inasmuch as cultural capitals can be centers of innovation, so too can the edges and ecotones. Frampton observed: "the Ticinese and Catalonians share in common the same experience of being a frontier ghetto, that is to say, of lying between two strong cultures and of not really belonging to either."[5]

I returned to the U.S., dreaming of a regional architecture in the powerful landscape and relative cultural isolation of the Pacific Northwest—itself a "frontier ghetto." After taking a position with a firm in Seattle, I again became discouraged by the state of American practice. Graduate school felt like a way out, possibly a last gasp. The only direction that seemed possible was New York, Columbia University, and Kenneth Frampton.

The education of an architect, Columbia University, 1984–85

As an undergraduate in the 1970s, I had been presented with the history of architecture as a continual evolution of visual style, clothing buildings from the Renaissance to the present. I was taught that history was created by individual genius, or perhaps divine intervention. The work itself and the cultures that created it were remote and unimportant. As a young student from suburban Portland, Oregon, I felt excluded from that history, believing I had lost the game before it began.

In the fall of 1984, walking into Frampton's "History of Modern Architecture" was a journey through the looking glass. He created a direct and continuous lineage of ideas, a built conversation through time. It was a deep dive into the work of Soufflot and Viollet-le-Duc, the Perret brothers, to Kahn, Scarpa, Utzon, Hertzberger, and their successors. It became, perhaps, a form of "gestalt therapy" where I was able to see my generation and myself as part of a lineage of architects with similar concerns and sensibilities. A foundation had formed, and therefore a place to stand on my own.

Even at the apex of Postmodernism and adjacent debates over style, Frampton, disheartened by the state of our cities and our built culture at large, pressed for substantial change:

> We are told that popular will demands the reassuring image of homely, handcrafted comfort and that "Classical" references, however abstract, are as incomprehensible as they are patronizing. Only rarely does this critical opinion extend the scope of its advice beyond the surface issue of style to demand that architectural practice should readdress itself to the issue of place creation, to a critical yet creative redefinition of the concrete qualities of the built domain.[6]

At Columbia, I was also introduced to the next generation of Swiss architects, notably Herzog & de Meuron and Peter Zumthor. Here were architects of unique vision and expression that clearly emerged from the history of ideas that Frampton presented. Many of my studio critics and professors were also beginning important practices, Steven Holl and Tod Williams among these. It was a time when practicing architects dominated the design studios—when the design of buildings, the drawing process, the necessities of construction, and the production of new ideas were intrinsically linked and critically important.

At the beginning of the second term, I volunteered as a research assistant. It was January 1985 and Frampton was just beginning work on a new essay for a Cullinan Lecture at Rice University. He asked me, with no German language skills and scant experience, to research two German architects I had never heard of: Gottfried Semper and Karl Bötticher. Through them, I was introduced to a new and more generative reading of the "primitive hut"—an elemental architecture that resonated with the poetics of fire, earth, sky, and the tie that binds them. As Semper wrote,

> Architecture, like its great teacher, nature, should choose and apply its material according to the laws conditioned by nature, yet should it not also make the form and character of its creations dependent on the ideas embodied in them, and not on the material?[7]

Here was an alternative, constructive archetype, a counterproposal to a more formal or nostalgic Vitruvian style, which appealed to the "frontier" sensibilities of my Northwest origins and the ethics of craft and structure with which I was reared as an undergraduate.

Theory into practice

> I have lived many places. Now I am here.
>
> Per Petterson, from *Out Stealing Horses* (2003)

The "Sitings" project

Soon after my time at Columbia, I began my practice. That meant a return to Oregon, to the refuge of a place and landscape that I cherished. To support my practice I started the University of Oregon Summer Studio with my close friend John Cava, the future editor of Frampton's *Studies in Tectonic Culture* (1995). In that studio, we asked students to propose specific built responses to sites across Oregon and Washington. The ideas explored in this studio, and represented in a show of student work at the Maryhill Museum of Art in Goldendale, Washington, would later evolve into an essay titled "Sitings: Five Reflections on Architectural Domain" and my first significant built work. As I wrote in the 1994 introduction:

> This project proposes that the realm of architecture be made more exclusive in its consideration and expression so that it may re-establish a sense of domain in our environment; a "here" and a "there". ... The five projects will be considered as reflections on a location, architectural analysis of distinct places with unique opportunities for a built response.

Here and there, a wall in the desert

"Sitings" was proposed as a direct response to the ideas raised in "Towards a Critical Regionalism." From the original series of five propositional sites, three were designed and one built: The Maryhill Overlook, completed in 1998 (**120**). The Overlook is an 8-foot x 150-foot site-cast ribbon of concrete, situated on a bluff overlooking the Columbia River. It provides measure and reference in this vast landscape, taking the form of a Heideggerian bridge consisting of eight

120 Allied Works, Maryhill Overlook, Goldendale, Washington, 1998.

volumes, a single piece of structure operating as shelter, observatory, and ruin. It stands as a marker and boundary, yet one that is hollow and occupiable.

A seismic figure in the void

During the construction of Maryhill, I was asked by the advertising agency Wieden+Kennedy to renovate a warehouse on a full city block for their world headquarters in Portland, Oregon (**121**). My response was to introduce a clearing into the heart of the masonry and timber structure, an 80-foot x 100-foot void filled with two structural interventions. The first, a site-cast concrete seismic frame rising from basement to penthouse, diminishing in steps from 16 inches to 8 inches in thickness as the structure rises upwards, is an expression of the structural performance. The alternating and stacked openings in each "facade" of the box allow for views across the clearing and introduce daylight into the workspace. The second intervention fills the interior of the box with a pinwheeling figure of columns and beams linking the floor plates of the building back together. Collectively, it is a dialogue between wall and column as distinct and spatially expressive entities, one holding and one expanding against this embrace.

Structure as domain for art

In the Contemporary Art Museum St. Louis (2003) and the Clyfford Still Museum in Denver (2011), beam and wall converge into a system of large spans and cantilevers —a structural "house of cards" that is both abstract and figural—creating open fields of transparent space that simultaneously bind and hold (**122, 124**). In the case of St. Louis, the walls define the urban site boundaries and turn inward, their monumental order holding a place in a vanished city fabric. At the same time, the building invites the urban landscape to flow through it. For the Still Museum,

121 Allied Works, Wieden+Kennedy World Headquarters, Portland, Oregon, 2000.

122 Allied Works, Contemporary Art Museum, St. Louis, Missouri, 2003.

plates of structural concrete create an open matrix of rooms scaled and tuned to Still's work. The entire building reads as one body, defining sequence, establishing proportion, creating spatial relationships, and modulating light across its striated board-form surface and through a perforated structural ceiling grid. It is a bound building that dissolves in light.

Structure as consecration

The National Veterans Memorial Museum (2017) in Columbus, Ohio, was located in an open field bordering an as yet to be developed neighborhood (**123**). The building had to literally create its own site. The primary language of construction is a series of large cantilevered concrete bands or "arches" that touch and overlap. Within each band, the reinforcing steel is closely woven and held by the enclosing concrete, and a continuous structural ring at the top unites the entire system. In lifting an open-air amphitheater/sanctuary above the ground plane, the building binds earth and sky. It is a service memorial that holds its ground, on one level a metaphor, on another, simply a demonstration of principles. It is an act of structure consecrating the site for memory.

On concrete

> It's important, you see, that you honor the material that you use.
>
> Louis Kahn, Master Class at Penn, 1971

Concrete has been the focus, the métier of my poetic investigations into structure: its inherent alchemy, its curing and finish as a result of weather, the color given by local sands, the art of placement and the power of hydrostatic forces, the craft and construct of formwork that imparts a visceral scale for hand and eye. It is a material in its very essence of the earth and weighted with shadow, and yet it can rise organically, as one body, blurring the bounds of earth and sky. The possibilities of expression and experience—visceral, physical, and ephemeral—are limitless. There is something in Frampton's reading of Kahn, the sense of "a 'timeless archaism,' both technologically advanced and spiritually antique," which has always pressed me to continue this exploration.[8]

Conclusion

> By the end of the last century the average human being in a country such as ours, saw as many images in a day as a Victorian inhaled in a lifetime.
>
> Pico Iyer from "Chapels," *Portland Magazine* (2010).

123 Allied Works, Construction of the National Veterans Memorial Museum, Columbus, Ohio, 2017.

124 Allied Works, Clyfford Still Museum, Denver, Colorado, 2011.

Thirty-five years and counting after the publication of "Towards a Critical Regionalism," the precepts and propositions therein still ring true. Whereas Frampton's original critique was aimed at internationalism and visual affect, in our current context one could say that the stylistic notes have changed but the song remains the same. The branding and marketing of architectural style is rampant; cities and institutions across the globe compete to acquire the latest fashions, and the places where people live and work possess identical forms of placeless consumerism. This loss of distinction and definition contributes to the global crisis of identity and the rise of reactionary neonationalism. As I posited in my introduction to "Sitings": "This project proposes to investigate architecture as a particular endeavor that produces buildings whose meaning is not assignable to, or defined by, other cultural media."

The more the realm of architecture expands to compete with consumer culture—the expedient, the expendable, and the quickly forgotten—the weaker its position and potency. It is through the lens of time and enduring meaning that the true measure of architectural value is calculated. What we are seeing in the profession today is merely improvisation in service of the "new"—a mode that speaks in pop cultural signifiers and nods to the in-group, essentially, the evolution and apotheosis of what Frampton was fighting against in 1983 and has been ever since:

> When architecture is reduced to large sculpture, it is not only formalistically reductive but also an acritical mode of expression that may pass muster as art but is hardly architecture ... Unlike music, painting, sculpture, literature, or even photography and film, architecture cannot convincingly attain or aspire to the critical autonomy of modern art.[9]

What Frampton proposed was a reversal: looking *into* architecture and its inherent domain, rather than *out* to mass culture. His position is based on the history of execution, and the ideas embedded in building expression. Perhaps his work is a call for limits—a revision of how we view the domain of architecture in the twenty-first century.

Rather than focus on what the architect has to say, we might ask what architecture can offer. What can the space reveal, the construction elevate, the experience amplify? What question can a building pose, or its position clarify? The dueling poles of image versus tectonic and global versus local may now beg larger questions of what a building can serve: the notion of an "architecture in service of" neutralizing both auteur and object, and elevating a calling to "the other"—insight and enduring meaning.

At this stage in our culture and world economy one might also ask, why build at all? Is building truly the answer sought by cities and institutions? If one understands the potency of the built act, it quickly becomes clear that the potency of architecture is derived by its limits—the means of expression and visceral and physical contact.

The challenge today is to create an architecture of nearness, rather than one of distance. "Thus one may assert that building is *ontological* rather than *representational* in character and that built form is a presence rather than something standing for an absence."[10] In effect, it is a search for the reason to bring a building into the world, to disrupt the land, employ labor and material energy, consume capital and time. Buildings, in their literal expense, are precious. Therefore it is incumbent that a building justifies its existence in the greatest sense.

What Frampton has created through his years of deep introspection and reflection illustrates a reverence for architecture at its most potent and elemental. More than historical analysis, he has crafted a conversation of shared ideas continually renewed over time by the completed work of architects. Looking back, his writings can be seen as a paean as much as a call to arms, an invitation to practitioners and theorists alike to consider possibilities of architecture to construct a world, and a worldview, with inherent integrity, meaning, and wonder.

1 Kenneth Frampton, "Towards a Critical Regionalism: Six Points for an Architecture of Resistance," *The Anti-Aesthetic: Essays on Postmodern Culture*, ed. Hal Foster (Port Townsend, WA: Bay Press, 1983), 29.
2 Ibid., 27.
3 Kenneth Frampton, "Rappel à L'Ordre: The Case for the Tectonic," *Architecturally Speaking: Practices of Art, Architecture, and the Everyday*, ed. Alan Reed (London and New York: Routledge, 2000), 178.
4 Frampton, "Towards a Critical Regionalism," 26.
5 Emilio Battisti, Kenneth Frampton, and Italo Rota, eds., *Mario Botta: Architetture e progetti negli anni '70 / Architecture and Projects in the '70s / Monografie* (Milan: Electa Editrice, 1979), 8.
6 Kenneth Frampton, *Modern Architecture: A Critical History* (London and New York: Thames & Hudson, 1980), 10.
7 Gottfried Semper, *The Four Elements of Architecture and Other Writings*, trans. Harry Francis Mallgrave and Wolfgang Herrmann (Cambridge, U.K.: Cambridge University Press, 1851), 102.
8 Frampton, "Rappel à L'Ordre," 187.
9 Kenneth Frampton, "Seven Points for the New Millennium," *Architectural Review*, 206 (1999): 77.
10 Frampton, "Rappel à L'Ordre," 179.

Architectural Osmosis

Yvonne Farrell and Shelley McNamara

When we, as curators of the sixteenth International Architecture Exhibition at the Venice Biennale of 2018, were asked by the President of the Board, Paolo Barrata, to put forward a name for the Golden Lion for Lifetime Achievement Award, our first and immediate choice was Kenneth Frampton: architect, critic, historian, and educator.

Through all our architectural lives, we had witnessed his work, being aware that he occupies an important position within the world of architecture—valuing him as a person with extraordinary insight and intelligence, combined with a unique sense of integrity. Kenneth Frampton stands out as the voice of truth in the promotion of key values of architecture and its role in society. His humanistic philosophy in relation to architecture is embedded in his writing. He has consistently argued for this humanistic component throughout all the various, often misguided "movements" and trends in architecture in the twentieth and twenty-first centuries. His experience as a practicing architect has given him a deep understanding of the process of designing and crafting buildings. This makes him both more sympathetic and more critical of the various forms of the practice of architecture. As an esteemed and hugely influential writer and commentator, as a teacher and researcher, he has affected and inspired generations of students and architects.

His seminal works include the essay "Towards a Critical Regionalism: Six Points for an Architecture of Resistance," which was a leader in influencing architects to

125 President of the Venice Biennale Paolo Barrata and Kenneth Frampton, 2018.

reevaluate context, place and culture. His book *Studies in Tectonic Culture* was a key work in highlighting the connection between the language of construction and the language of architecture. In *Labour, Work and Architecture*, he puts philosophy, politics, and sociology right at the heart of the thinking and critique on architecture. The book is symbolically dedicated to the memory of Hannah Arendt. In *A Genealogy of Modern Architecture: Comparative Critical Analysis of Built Form*, he captures with incisive clarity the inner workings of projects, decoding them to make them legible for us all, revealing their architectural strengths from ideas to structure and construction. His consistent values in relation to the impact of architecture on society, together with his intellectual generosity, position him as a uniquely important presence in the world of architecture.

Recently, when we opened—yet again—our battered 1980s copy of *Modern Architecture: A Critical History*, we noticed for the first time that the dedication of the book simply reads: "To my parents." These three words are powerful. They possibly reveal the strength of the springboard from which this unique human being evolved. We do not know the circumstances of Frampton's youth, but we witness this adult living his life *tending* architecture, valuing the built envelope of human lives as being of the highest cultural importance. Whatever happened in the early days of his life, the deep respect built into those three words, "To my parents," is loud and clear, with repercussions that continue to affect our architectural lives.

Wondering about the origins of this respect and resilience, we can imagine that it is because of those early foundations that Kenneth Frampton can stand rod-straight in the changing storms of global architecture. His work brings him back again and again to the "stripped-bones" nature of architecture. The early experiences of life in the Britain of the 1930s onward certainly engraved a deep and palpable sense of social justice.

London is only a short distance from the town of Woking in Surrey, where Frampton was born. That amazing capital city must have been extraordinary in the early 1950s as it recovered from the effects of World War II, when Frampton became a student there and trained as an architect at the Architectural Association, less than thirty miles away from his hometown.

Just two years before Frampton was born, Thomas Hardy died. Hardy had trained as an architect, before becoming a novelist. Hardy's writings have a palpable physicality. His skill as a storyteller brings places alive: words craft the shape of stones, the span of bridges, the enclosing walls of imagined villages. Language impacts the landscape where Hardy's characters stand. Frampton could also be described as a storyteller, in the sense that he has the ability from the inside of the profession of architecture to bring work alive in order to allow us to be simultaneously aware of the intellectual basis and physical realities of architecture. Frampton crafts words. He peels back the layers of a building to reveal its meaning, to understand its relevance, to evaluate its impact. Frampton inhabits the world between thinking and doing, observing what is being done, analyzing why, aware of possible outcomes, keeping a watchful eye on the state of things. For Frampton, "the history of modern architecture is as much about consciousness and polemical intent as it is about buildings themselves."

As a result of being asked to write this essay and because of the impact the manifesto "Towards a Critical Regionalism" has had on Irish architecture, we downloaded the "Critical Regionalism" pdf, photocopying it and carrying it around with us, reading it at various opportunities. Two particular things are striking in that essay: one is the density of thought with his depth of influence. The other—we now realize—is that, as young architects at the beginning of our architectural journeys, we skimmed over the top of his manifesto, absorbing his thoughts by a type of osmosis, finding inspiration and courage from his words.

We chose aspects in a kind of *à la carte* manner, taking certain ones particularly to heart: "Critical Regionalism ... may find its governing inspiration in such things as the range and quality of the local light, or in a tectonic derived from a peculiar structural mode, or in the topography of a given site." Local light, a tectonic derived from a peculiar structural mode, the topography of a given site—these are aspects of architecture that we continue to "mine" for inspiration. Our work has been inspired by this text where our aim is to trap local light, find an appropriate structural tectonic, and respond to the topography of a given site.

When considering the influence of Frampton's writing, one must recognize that it is intertwined with so much that has infiltrated deeply into our unconscious over the years of practice. After so many years, it is startling to read again in Section 5 of "Towards a Critical Regionalism" the following: "The bulldozing of an irregular topography into a flat site is clearly a technocratic gesture which aspires to a condition of absolute placelessness, whereas the terracing of the same site to receive the stepped form of a building is an engagement in the act of 'cultivating' the site."

In 2002, when we were designing a new high school for 900 children on a sloping site on the edge of the town of Ballinasloe, Co. Galway, in the west of Ireland, our initial discussions involved whether we should flatten the site to accommodate the 4,000-square meter (43,000-square foot) footprint of the proposed new school or keep the slope, incorporating the hilliness into the experience of future students, placing the memory of the undulating ground into the muscles of students as they negotiated the varying levels (**126**). The wish to keep the slope and to "live the section" was explored and this was what we built.

Frampton refers to Martin Heidegger's 1954 essay, "Building, Dwelling, Thinking," as providing a "critical vantage point from which to behold this phenomenon of universal placelessness." Heidegger argues that the phenomenological essence of space/place depends upon the concrete, clearly defined nature of the boundary, for, as he puts it, "A boundary is not that at which something stops, but, as the Greeks recognized, the boundary is that from which begins its presencing."

126 Grafton Architects, Ardscoil Mhuire, Secondary School, Ballinasloe, Co. Galway, Ireland, 2003.

When we were asked to develop a theme to be the focus of the 2018 Venice Biennale, we wrote *Freespace* as our manifesto. When we again read Frampton's references to Heidegger, our weave of thoughts, which had begun many years ago and was influenced by his critical thinking, became interestingly apparent. Among the many aspects emphasized in *Freespace* was that architecture encompasses the freedom to imagine, the free space of time and memory, binding past, present, and future together, building on inherited cultural layers, weaving the archaic with the contemporary. It reinforces the importance of going beyond the visual, emphasizing its role in the choreography of daily life. *Freespace* provides the opportunity to emphasize nature's free gifts, with the earth as client, bringing with it long-lasting responsibilities. Architecture is the play of light, sun, shade, moon, air, wind, gravity in ways that reveal the mysteries of the world. All of these resources are free. In the manifesto, we referenced Jørn Utzon's concrete and tiled seat at the entrance of Can Lis, Majorca, which is perfectly molded to the shape of the human body for comfort and pleasure. Spatially, that entrance is a "word" of greeting, of welcome (**128**). Also mentioned is Angelo Mangiarotti's and Bruno Morassutti's beautiful building at 24 via Quadronno, Milan, Italy, to which there is a gently sloping path, with a seat at the entrance threshold which "holds" each person who arrives and welcomes them home from the city. To participate in the Biennale, we chose concrete examples of generosity and thoughtfulness in architecture throughout the world, believing that these qualities sustain the fundamental capacity of architecture to nurture and support meaningful contact between people and place. Focusing attention on these qualities celebrated the intrinsic attributes of optimism and continuity. Architecture that embodies these characteristics and does so with generosity and a desire for exchange is what is at the core of *Freespace* (**125**).

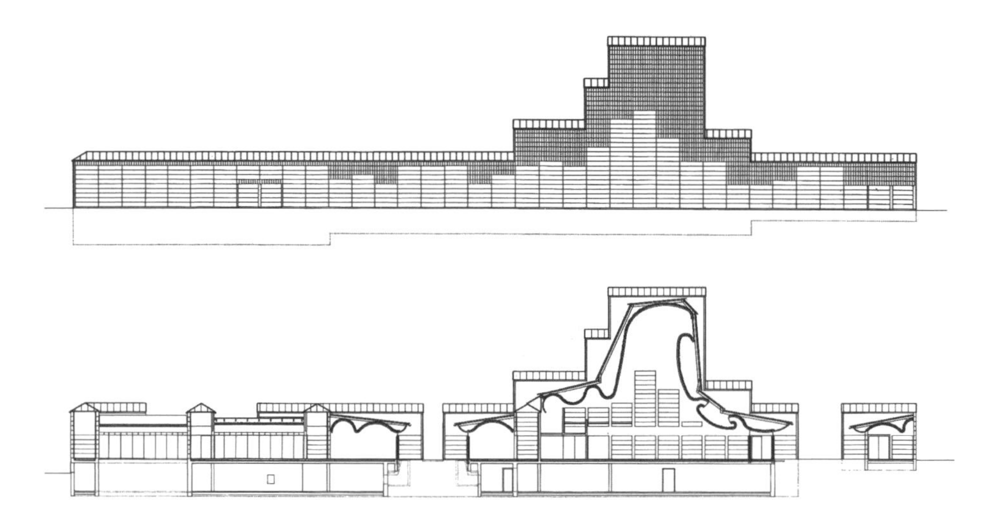

127 Jørn Utzon, Bagsværd Church, Denmark, 1976.

128 Jørn Utzon, Can Lis entrance seat, Majorca, Spain, 1971.

129 Grafton Architects, Université Toulouse 1 Capitole, France, 2019, brick wall.

In Section 3 of "Towards a Critical Regionalism," Frampton gives concrete examples and displays an incisive intellectual ability to take a building, dissect it, and give it to us architecturally *cooked*, so to speak. Like a master chef, he sets out the ingredients of the building like a wonderful meal, thereby challenging each of us to "cook" any new building, as good, if not better! In this section, he takes the physicality of Utzon's 1970s Bagsværd Church in Denmark, itemizing the ordinary ingredients of that complex work: the regular grid, concrete blocks, in-situ concrete frame, precast concrete wall units, patent glazing, whisking it with a little "cream" of "the rationality of normative technique and the arationality of idiosyncratic form," ... topping it all off with the cherry ... "Regional reaffirmation providing ... some form of collective spirituality ..." (**127**)!

In Section 5, Frampton takes the art gallery as a building type to explain clearly the impact of ways of thinking on our experience of architectural space:

> Until recently, the received precepts of modern curatorial practice favored the exclusive use of artificial light in all art galleries. It has perhaps been insufficiently recognized how this encapsulation tends to reduce the artwork to a commodity, since such an environment must conspire to render the work placeless. This is because the local light spectrum is never permitted to play across its surface ... The converse of this "placeless" practice would be to provide that art galleries be top-lit through carefully contrived monitors so that, while the injurious effects of direct sunlight are avoided, the ambient light of the exhibition volume changes

130 Grafton Architects, Université Toulouse 1 Capitole, France, 2019, main entrance view.

131 Grafton Architects, Medical School, University of Limerick, Ireland, 2013.

under the impact of time, season, humidity, etc. Such conditions guarantee the appearance of a place-conscious poetic—a form of filtration compounded out of an interaction between culture and nature, between art and light. Clearly this principle applies to all fenestration, irrespective of size and location. A constant "regional inflection" of the form arises directly from the fact that in certain climates the glazed aperture is advanced, while in others it is recessed behind the masonry facade (or, alternatively, shielded by adjustable sun breakers).

As we build our own work, this "regional inflection" has become embedded deeply into our thinking and strategies. Our Université Toulouse 1 Capitole Building in Toulouse, France, for instance, pleats its Roman brick facade to protect the research offices from the hot sun; or we modified the elevational surfaces of our Urban Institute in University College Dublin with a folded wall of red clay tiles; and we protected the Medical School in the University of Limerick from the wind and rain of the west of Ireland with stone folds of granite (**129–131**).

Frampton refers to the term *a structural poetic*, which captures and condenses material, craftwork, and gravity. He infers that the "wrapping" of the structure of many contemporary buildings means that the potential for expressing the inherent strength, of finding a fusion of the structural system and the volumes with the expression, becomes difficult. Regarding structure as space maker and the impact of material and gravity in our own research, both the Bocconi University Building in Milan, Italy, and the UTEC University in Lima, Peru, allow the rhythm of structure to hold space and form platforms for life. In both cases, these buildings, set into their respective and very different cities, carve into and anchor themselves into their unique locations on the earth—one in a Rationalist city in Europe, the other into a desert city, 12 degrees south of the equator (**132–133**).

The title of Section 6 of Frampton's essay is "The Visual versus the Tactile." Here, Frampton makes us aware again that we are human beings with skin and emotions. He discusses the effect of light, darkness, heat and cold, humidity, the aroma of material, the type of surface beneath our feet. He refers to the Italian film-maker Luchino Visconti and his insistence that real wooden parquet be used in the floor of the main set for the film *The Damned*, so that the actors would respond by giving authentic and convincing performances.

In a similar way, Frampton's incisive revelations in Section 3 regarding Utzon's Bagsværd Church continue in Section 6, making us aware of Alvar Aalto's brilliant orchestration of movement within the Town Hall of Säynätsalo in Finland (**16**, p. 36.) Frampton's sensual description of Aalto's route from brick steps to springy deflection of the timber is a powerful reminder to us all as practicing architects that what we specify has impact; what we describe becomes real; what we imagine has physical and emotional implications. Just in case we might forget in this busy, digital world, Frampton's words remind us that people *experience* architecture.

132 Grafton Architects, Università Luigi Bocconi, Milan, Italy, 2008.

The main thrust of these "Six Points for an Architecture of Resistance" is to make sure that we do not forget the value of our senses, encouraging us to remember our impulse to touch, encouraging us as architects to value the totally immersive *poetics of construction*.

With regard to Frampton's ability to transmit the understanding of the legacy of architecture and to share his vast knowledge with both architects and students of architecture, a most memorable conversation took place at the School of Architecture, University College Dublin, at a final review of fifth-year students' work some years ago. The visiting critics were Kenneth Frampton and Eric Parry. There was a preponderance of ramps in the student projects. At a certain moment during the review, Kenneth Frampton "took flight" and delivered a treatise on the importance of the staircase in the history of architecture. His delivery was poetic, scholarly, and passionate, ranging through all ages and cultures. The criticism of the seemingly "fashionable preference" for the ramp was made by elaborating on the time-honored element of the staircase. His thought-provoking words spoken at that review in Dublin are like himself—unforgettable and wise.

133 Grafton Architects, UTEC University, Lima, Peru, 2015.

Public Natures: A Roundtable Discussion

Kenneth Frampton, Marion Weiss, and Michael A. Manfredi with Justin Fowler

First published in 1999, Kenneth Frampton's *Megaform as Urban Landscape* articulated a need for delimited large-scale interventions within the incoherent placelessness of the neoliberal megalopolis. Equal parts historical survey and projective manifesto, Frampton's tome suggested an architecture that would take on a unifying formal character verging on the topographic: megaforms that are integrated into the urban fabric. The concept of megaform builds on Reyner Banham's notion of megastructure, but it emphasizes intrinsic spatial order and program, rather than structural expressivity. As Frampton further clarified the idea of the megaform in a lecture given in 2009, "What is more pertinent in the case of the megaform is the topographic, horizontal thrust of its overall profile together with the programmatic place-creating character of its intrinsic program."[1]

Frampton's work is cogent in the current conversations about large-scale urban projects, particularly the relationships between nature and urban form, and social and environmental values. To continue the discussion in contemporary terms, Frampton sat down with Marion Weiss, Michael Manfredi, and Justin Fowler to discuss the future of the remedial megaproject and its place within the urban centers of today's cities. The conversation followed a series of continuous studio investigations titled "Evolutionary Infrastructures," conducted by Marion Weiss and Michael Manfredi at the University of Pennsylvania, Yale University, and the Harvard Graduate School of Design that built on issues related to their built and speculative projects. The studio investigations sought to reenvision dense urban thresholds, layered with complex interplays of constructed and natural systems, testing the potential of an evolutionary, inhabitable, and hybrid form of infrastructure—a new megaform. One such site focused on the highway corridor spanning from the George Washington Bridge to the Alexander Hamilton Bridge in Upper Manhattan—an armature described by Reyner Banham in his 1976 book, *Megastructure*, as "the largest and most visually convincing of all accidental megastructures."[2]

Nearly four decades after Banham's anthology for the megastructure, this infrastructural found object, with its Pier Luigi Nervi-designed bus terminal and highway-straddling housing towers from the mid-1960s, remains a functioning, yet underperforming urban complex. This recently reedited conversation takes the site investigation as a starting point to address the evolution of the architectural megaproject.

Marion Weiss: The term "evolutionary infrastructures" was intended to invoke a more open-ended understanding of what a megaform might be, particularly as it relates to systemic operations that are either embedded in (a part of) or invented for (on behalf of) a territory like this. We have a suspicion that the megaform is not yet doing enough work. The section is not quite holding up its end of the bargain and infrastructures remain too monofunctional. As it relates to our academic investigations, the real question was, what would we add or take away if we were to somehow reengage, fifty years later, the potential promise of the visions that were never realized? It's right by a park, it's near the water, and it's embedded within the city. The latter is quite unusual, since most of these strange concoctions are always on the edges. So what would we do? And that's one of the questions of our transformative intervention position. But the other one asks, is there anything prototypically compelling about the situation—and the situational change over time—that we might invoke in some other parts of the world?

Michael Manfredi: Frampton's *Megaform as Urban Landscape* essay also offered an informative lens to focus the trajectory of our work. What interested us in the shift from megastructure into megaform was the emphasis on the horizontal and topographic character of the projects. We also wanted to introduce into this conversation a means by which to systematically pursue an ecological agenda. Given the imperatives of connectivity and the implication of operating at a megascale, we could privilege ecological systems and energy patterns in a more holistic way. We are also drawn to the hybrid, programmatic capacity of the megaform and its potential for an embedded public presence. By sheer virtue of size, multiple public and private programs could coexist and function simultaneously.

Justin Fowler: What was it that drew you to this site and how did you see it relating to today's urban condition?

MW: We were certainly seduced by this strange assemblage of pieces that amounted to a de facto megastructure. Taken piece by piece, there are moments of real architectural quality. Nervi's George Washington Bridge bus terminal is exemplary, but even the four housing towers have a kind of power in their seriality. At the regional scale, it's a piece of transit infrastructure, yet for the neighborhood of Washington Heights, it's a home for thousands of people. Banham understood this project as a megastructure, yet it was a piecemeal utopia particular in many ways to the American context.

MM: The Port Authority of New York owned the land, so the project was actually one of the first major public–private initiatives in this country, utilizing air-rights development transfers to support housing for displaced residents above the expressway. The project was not only radical as an economic model, it also embodied merging infrastructural and architectural ambitions. The Nervi bus terminal, for example, with its serially serrated roof, is an extraordinary combination of structural bravura, multilevel traffic engineering, and passive venting of bus exhausts. The four residential slabs just east of the terminal span the highway and, in so doing, restitch the neighborhood with the terminal, creating this hybrid megastructure.

MW: We wanted to investigate the familiar images of classic megastructures in order to suggest that its history is not as tidy as we might now believe. All of this became an interesting trigger for us to take stock of this site some fifty years later to consider how its formal, material, and economic legacies might serve as a point of departure for considering the future of large-scale remedial transformations in the city.

Kenneth Frampton: If my *Megaform* essay were to turn into a real book, it would need a lot of work in terms of adding other examples. It would also need to define how the idea of a megaform could be interpreted as a realistic strategy. In 1999, a task force headed by Richard Rogers produced a paper titled, "Towards an Urban Renaissance." The group's primary task was to anticipate the building needs for the United Kingdom over the next twenty years [from 2000 to 2020]. Some smart aleck in the team wrote that ninety percent of what will exist in the year 2020 has already been built. I find that statement to be a really terrific rhetorical game, and I've no doubt that it's right. The proliferation of freestanding objects in the megalopolis *ad infinitum* makes it nearly impossible to negotiate the whole urban environment without the aid of graphic signs. There are so few genuine landmarks. With the arrival of portable GPS devices and smartphones, perhaps this is less of an issue. Nevertheless, the contrary role of the landmark can hardly be considered obsolete. That aspect of the megaform as landmark would be one of its virtues as a critical intervention in the urban environment.

MW: And landmark has to be distinct from icon?

KF: You could say landform as well, perhaps. What's important is the horizontal continuity of the form and that it's recognizable and understandable as such—meaning outside you can see it and inside you can experience it. It is a sort of compensatory project, which compensates for the privatization of the megalopolis, as compared to the balance of public and private found in traditional urbanism. I think it was Jean Nouvel who said, rhetorically of course, that urbanism is no longer possible, period. It's gone, it's over. I suppose what he has in mind is so-called "traditional urbanism." Where historical cities are still in place, one can still operate within an identifiable urban fabric that has a public aspect. Once one is out of this, into the megalopolis, then it's all privatized—it's like the provisional title of [Frank Lloyd] Wright's 1932 book on the city, *The Industrial Revolution Runs Away*.

What I've just been saying is not very well articulated inside the *Megaform* document. I find it difficult to unpack the current situation.

I would hesitate to put the emphasis entirely on "infrastructure." It is key of course, and you could say that some of the projects illustrated in *Megaform* take infrastructure as the primary driver of the form. Look at Le Corbusier's incredible intuition with his project for Algiers. And then you have the pathos of the Smithsons' London Road Study, much later on, where they also realize that the permanent civil engineering operation is to receive the automobile. With Le Corbusier, because he's so intuitive and intelligent, he realizes very early on that infrastructure is a very strong aspect of the emerging reality and tries to capitalize on that. It's incredible when you see the perspective of the project: the roadway is in the middle of the block. And then he stacks into the framework all these Spanish colonial houses and any old stylistic kitsch you want. I find it incredible he would do that, because he recognizes, after all, that it doesn't really matter if you load the frame with stuff because the frame will have such a big presence at this scale that the trivial kitsch wouldn't matter. That's obviously what he understands. But at the same time, it's very utopian. Well, we didn't build it, did we?

MW: No, although the Pedregulho social housing project in Brazil pulled off something within earshot of Le Corbusier's vision. Affonso Reidy built a slice of that larger figure around the topographic edge of the site (**134**).

134 Affonso Eduardo Reidy, Pedregulho Housing, Rio de Janeiro, 1952.

KF: But he didn't make it into a road; it just imitates the form of an infrastructural spine. The inherent problem with the autoroute, however, is that it is a processual extrusion. Le Corbusier was the first who recognized that, to a greater extent than the railway, it constitutes a new geography: a kind of artificial ground upon which one could build. This is the obsessive vision leading from the first sketches for Rio of 1929 to the Plan Obus for Algiers of 1930. Despite the fact that the car seems to be quite literally at one's doorstep, it is not so easy to access the multistory block above the roadway. I think there is a lot to be said for dense hybrid structures that are served by the autoroute system. However, such structures don't have to be built directly over the route. For example, the L'Illa block in Barcelona is built to one side of the Avenida Diagonal and not over it. This is an argument I attempt to advance with the idea of megaform, a concept inspired by the L'Illa block.

JF: At the moment, there appears to be an uneasy alliance between your project of megaform and perhaps the more infrastructural project of landscape urbanism, which seem tenuously united beneath an umbrella aesthetic of the "topographic." In many respects, the formal manifestation of landscape urbanist projects is a didactic transposition of the systemic processes at work (suggesting a one-to-one correspondence between an economy of performance and expression). Yet the megaform is buttressed by your advocacy for the "tectonic," which has a rational material logic, but also a surplus poetic effect or some sort of irreducible element. How would you characterize the relationship between the ecological ambitions of landscape urbanism and the formal drive of the megaform?

KF: If you accept that it's a question of remedial strategy, then—and I feel this very strongly—architects have more to learn from intelligent landscape architects than the other way around. I particularly admire Michel Desvigne and the landscape school in Versailles founded by his mentor, Michel Corajoud, but what do we actually know about it? We have schools of architecture, we encourage people to do research, and yet all over the place there is material that no one ever touches. Two things come to mind: one is that landscape school and the other is Curitiba. Jaime Lerner was mayor there for fifteen years, and I was struck by a line from his lecture where he said, "as a figure of power, I have to work fast to defeat my own bureaucracy." This attitude has a certain relevance in the context of the megaform discussion. We desperately need to expand our frame of reference and absorb some of the lessons from these situations, particularly as it relates to strategies of implementation.

If we come back to landscape urbanism and this question of megaform as urban landscape, I think I know the work that Charles Waldheim has done, and also James Corner. Waldheim has pushed landscape urbanism as a didactic framework, but one really has to work at it to tease out the substance. It is clear, however, that they're productively engaging with the idea of remedial operations in a megalopolis that is already built-out.

MW: However, there seems to be an antipathy towards architectural form that's intrinsic to the remedial project.

KF: It doesn't have to be that way. What you did with the Seattle Olympic Sculpture Park provides a necessary kind of architectural gesture through the material of large-scale earth manipulation (**135**). It's a sort of extraordinary thing you've produced, breathtaking from so many points of view. It's also an achievement vis-à-vis infra-structure. It repairs a rift and brings people from the city to the water. This is landscape urbanism, but as is true in this profession in general, given that techno-science rules the world, these kinds of humanist fields have always looked to legitimize themselves by evoking techno-science. What is interesting about architecture is that it's a very quixotic and durable practice. It remains at this crucial interface where it cannot simply be reasoned away. Architecture touches reality like no other profession.

JF: To continue along this thread on the human aspect of the architectural endeavor, one of the striking things about your position is that the megaform requires a decisive authorial stroke across the urban fabric. In many respects, this kind of language is

135 Weiss/Manfredi, Olympic Sculpture Park, Seattle, Washington, 2007.

not at all dissimilar from Robert Somol's defense of the "shape" or "logo" project. I'm thinking specifically here of his line that, "neither natural nor necessary, the plasticity of the graphic can only be artificially asserted and subsequently played out."[3] This statement leads me to believe that the distinction between megaform and shape, or even "bigness," is less a formal one and more about the kinds of political values that underwrite their respective "assertions." Clearly, there's as much topographic manipulation in a large-scale project by BIG or MVRDV as there is in the most exemplary urban work of Moneo or Holl, so the difference might require some articulation in terms of values beyond form. Given that there seems to be an urgent appeal to political necessity in your [Frampton's] work, how would you characterize this dimension of the megaform project as it relates to the issue of shape?

KF: There are two words that I think the architecture profession has been somewhat uneasy about for a long period of time. One was "beauty" and the other was "form." For me too, if you look at what I've written, form doesn't feature that prominently. Given my personal history, I realized the importance of form rather late in the game. But this question of form and image; you can't dismiss this question.

But I think what you're saying is very important, which is this issue of necessity. I am very prejudiced about this. I think, for example, that inside many contemporary buildings there is nothing, literally nothing, because their architects are not interested at all in what's in the buildings. Whatever the program is, they just stuff it in there. All they're interested in is the shape and the surface. I'm being very prejudicial, but I think I'm right. The question of what the space is, and the program of the space—what is inside the building—is crucial. It doesn't mean that the form/image issue is not important. If one is going to invoke "landmark," obviously form and image are of consequence. That's why I think this step formation of L'Illa Diagonal by Moneo and de Solà-Morales gives the block a character or profile which is identifiable, and that's important (**136**).

MW: Lately, we've been preoccupied with this notion of sequence and section and the belief that these are things that start to temper or catalyze the legitimacy of a megaform or megastructure, particularly as it relates to a larger urban scale. This potential is part of what we were teasing out in the "Evolutionary Infrastructures" studio investigations—the sense that something larger is at stake. Something larger is at stake politically and materially because a host of systems seem to be completely in conflict with each other. At the Trans-Manhattan Expressway site, for instance, the improbable juxtaposition of an expressway cutting through the city with twenty-three-story towers spanning ten lanes of traffic raises the question of what additions and transformations need to be introduced to create common ground to these seemingly incompatible systems.

136 Rafael Moneo and Manuel de Solà-Morales, L'Illa Diagonal, Barcelona, 1993.

MM: In this project, the image of the figure and its scale remain central. Because you can see the towers from as far away as Central Park, you can begin to understand their relationship to the city: their east/west deployment marks the route of the highway, yet each tower is rotated north/south to mark the predominant grain of the grid. The lesson for us is the way the form of this project aligns with its geographic orientation to register at multiple scales.

KF: There's this beautiful Le Corbusier project for the Paris Exposition of 1937, which consists of four Y-shaped Cartesian skyscrapers of the same height. In the sketch you see he established a new datum by bringing them all to the same height, which is of course the same idea as the Ville Contemporaine. You could say that the main virtue of these four slabs was that they share the same datum. It's strange how rare this is. A comparable example might be the London County Council's Roehampton Estate project from the 1950s.

MM: Wallace Harrison did something similar with his towers in Albany, albeit for a more civic purpose. Seriality and repetition are played out to amplify this civic effect (**137**).

137 Wallace Harrison, Empire State Plaza, Albany, New York, 1976.

KF: The question is: does it or does it not establish a new datum? Is that new datum something that could be read visually as a landmark with a certain horizontality as opposed to being a product of this open-ended capitalist development where everything is coming to a different height according to what one can get away with?

JF: One thing we haven't touched on is who, namely the body politic, animates this idea of the megaform as a means of resistance. The proliferation of triumphalist narratives of the city, such as those by Richard Florida and Edward Glaeser, seems to suggest that cities are primed to receive a new wave of people, both young and old, who see certain benefits to living in an urban environment. At the same time, though, the accommodation of this influx appears to entail reproducing an image of suburban life within city centers through a kind of amenity urbanism, where what's being offered in terms of public space does not really challenge the status quo.

In this context, your concern with Hannah Arendt's distinction between labor and work is particularly interesting because it speaks to the issue of social character and the need for political resilience in the face of perceived technological or economic inevitability. Here, the megaform serves as a proxy in this broader debate over social values, and, in many respects, its remedial aims are primarily social since the formal repair of our cities has to be underwritten by a renewed ecological consciousness.

KF: There are some new projects in Hong Kong that offer an interesting take on that challenge. I recently came across the work of architect Rocco Yim. The interesting thing about the high-rise buildings he has constructed in that incredibly dense city is how they're organized to relieve monotony. For instance, he has designed a twenty-five-story building for the Hong Kong Polytechnic University, consisting of a sixteen-story hotel on top of an eight-story teaching facility, which is also supposed to be a hotel school. What he does in some of these high-rise buildings is to build into the block, some way up the height of the structure, a breakout space or green space, which consists of a gymnasium or swimming pool or other kinds of amenities.

MW: It acts as a kind of public datum that's not at the level of the street but is shared for recreation.

KF: Yes, I find that fascinating. You can say that one of the beautiful aspects of the high-rise type is the tower quality, but on the other hand, what is somewhat discouraging is the endless repetition of one floor after another. It's an interesting formal and programmatic issue to think through how to create variety within a tall building and how to mediate or transform a group of them through new kinds of spatial connections.

MW: You're raising an issue about cities that is very important. In cities we have compressed footprints; we need to move vertically and once we move vertically, the idea of a datum, which is public but is not at the street level, becomes fraught. It's privatized immediately when it's raised. To what degree do we find public life and private ties in these secondary datums?

KF: In the 1960s there was a big debate about whether the space within a mall was public space. It took place, if I remember correctly, at a legal level because of the restrictions imposed by mall owners on public activities in their spaces. It was decided, of course, that it isn't public space. But I don't think it means that one should take an unrealistic attitude toward the potential socializing benefits of semipublic space in an otherwise commercial space, since it is in some sense a semipublic space as well. Also, from the point of view of entertainment and pleasure and other activities, you could say that the provision of such space remains a strategy that is open to society to compensate for increasing privatization. The fact is, it's not public in the sense that the agora is public, but there are still positive opportunities to be leveraged.

MM: I want to return to this whole idea of the relationship between work and play, because we're seeing it played out in both urban corporate campuses such as Novartis, in Basel, Switzerland, and also in the urban university settings such as Barnard College in New York City. You might bring your food into the library or go to a coffee shop to study. Work and play are comingled in surprising and interesting ways. If the city is relevant as a place to enjoy this programmatic interplay and level of "authenticity" that you don't get elsewhere, I wonder if the opportunity to bring "authenticity" into semipublic space is also partially a function of scale and density. Paradoxically, programmatic variety might be more possible in big hybrid projects.

While there is an assumed consensus in current architectural and urban thinking that incremental, fine-grain urban development will yield social benefits, it is productive, especially given the magnitude of our environmental challenges, to consider that the megascale is an equally robust catalyst for social engagement. We believe the scalar affinities between the city structure and the megastructure might sponsor the emergence of broad solutions difficult to achieve within more conventional urban or suburban planning models. Intrinsic to this potential is also the recognition that to achieve systemic solutions we must leverage all the disciplinary tools available to architects, landscape architects, ecologists, and infrastructure engineers.

For instance, with our design for the Olympic Sculpture Park in Seattle, the design is a constructed hybrid—ecological, cultural, infrastructural—reinvented through the lenses of geometry and topography. Our intent was to create an open urban armature that nurtures unexpected uses, activities, and environmental benefits.

MW: You can't have intensity without some density, and that's the real issue.

MM: A discovery we made in the context of researching urban campuses occurred when we went over to the new Google headquarters here in New York, which is located in a former Port Authority industrial building and is the city's largest horizontal building. What Google realized is that there are a greater number of employees that want to move from their suburban campuses in California to that urban location. Obviously, this stems from a need for social interaction at the urban scale. Their workforce is comprised of sophisticated and technologically savvy employees, yet there is a hunger for some of the "dirt" of the city with its frictions and unpredictable interactions. For us, the New York City Google headquarters can be described as a dense default megaform, an alternative to their homogeneity of the sprawling suburban corporate campus. In this context, the urban campus can be seen as a program or type uniquely conducive to the characteristics of the megaform.

KF: That situation also has to do with the argument that the spontaneous face-to-face interaction of bright people produces unpredictable results in terms of scientific experiments and knowledge exchange. That's a fairly old story, in terms of justifying the design of campuses.

MW: The shape of many contemporary cities has been unduly impacted by the monofunctional demands of transportation infrastructure, or conversely, that of postwar mass housing. Ultimately, what we're trying to arrive at is the question of why such megaprojects are relevant today in the context of existing cities and how they can be retooled to accommodate a higher quality of life. If you consider ambitious proposals, such as Le Corbusier's 1931 Algiers scheme, Kenzō Tange's 1960 Tokyo Bay project, and Paul Rudolph's 1967 study for the Lower Manhattan expressway, their promise of a systemic coexistence of infrastructure and inhabitation has still gone largely unfulfilled. Those ambitions were powerful and, in some ways, more carefully calibrated and crafted compared to what's actually being realized today. So, the question that we're really interested in is how do we bring in these older examples in order to think critically about this issue today? Is there something we are taking forward that really can be recast? Terms like landform, megaform, megastructure, landscape—these are all rubrics that have loose-fit overlaps with one another. What is relevant for us to consider now as we go forward?

KF: Clearly Tange's Tokyo Bay of 1960 is a remarkable work, but in the end it derives from Le Corbusier's postwar Unité planning strategy as manifest in his 1945–46 proposal for La Rochelle-Pallice, an anti-suburban model allowing one to accommodate a large number of people in the countryside without destroying it in the process. The Unité d'Habitation in Marseille is a communal dwelling still viable even now. As to today's imperatives, the primary directive is to live closer together to minimize movement and conserve energy.

Maybe it's too discursive or speculative, particularly in relation to the ubiquity of high-speed informational exchanges, but I think this question of the social—what is left of the capacity of the human species for acting collectively—is of great relevance to the future of the species, which is very precarious in many ways. If one were to persist with the culture of architecture and the built environment, and with the potential to provide for social and symbolic space, then the argument about relevance has to begin there. It has to be assumed axiomatically that architecture still has bearing and import, otherwise you can't even begin.

1 Kenneth Frampton, *Megaform as Urban Landscape* (Champaign, IL: University of Illinois, 2010), 11.

2 Reyner Banham, *Megastructure: Urban Futures of the Recent Past* (New York: Harper and Row, 1976), 30.

3 Robert Somol, "Green Dots 101," *Hunch*, 11 (Winter 2007): 29.

The panel wishes to acknowledge the help of research assistant Lily C. Wong.

Architecture and Nature: A Recurring State of Mind

Emilio Ambasz

By the second quarter of the sixteenth century the rules of orderly certainty imposed by Renaissance architecture had wildly succeeded, with widespread roots anchored into Greco-Roman humus and branches reaching all over Europe. Nothing new could depart and prosper away from its firmly established set of canons. However, a few artists and architects liberated themselves from what had become a cage and, believing themselves free, roamed around like animals escaping from imprisonment without realizing that they had indeed chewed through their leash but they still had the Renaissance collar around their necks.

Such a process later became known as mannerism. It affected all the arts. However, mannerism is not a single historical episode, with a chronological beginning and end. It is a state of mind and a mode of revolt that manifests itself repeatedly throughout architectural history, returning with different forms each time, but with the same desperate longing to twist away from its shackles and reconcile itself with nature.

Pursuits of such revolt in the sixteenth century are found in examples such as Giulio Romano's Palazzo Te, where he upset the order of the Renaissance columnar grid to proclaim his departure from the old regime. Other instances can also be identified in the work of Bernardo Buontalenti, Romano's diametrically opposite counterpart in form and in spirit, who, a generation later, resorted to geomorphic naturalism in the magnificent gardens and anthropomorphic buildings he created in Pratolino for Francesco I de' Medici.

Centuries later, *rocaille*, or Rococo, upset the Baroque's pursuit of symmetry. Taking its clues from tree branches and conceiving, among many other things, of furniture with branch- or animal-like legs, it also found solace in the figment of a return to nature and domesticity in architecture. Centuries went by, and in a similar quest architecture and the decorative arts sought in Art Nouveau to escape from the elegant boundaries of the neoclassical period by conceiving many of their productions in the guise of nature, as evidence they longed for a return to it.

Modernism is today a golden cage from which many contemporary architects strive to escape. They fancy it as an already squeezed lemon but such perception notwithstanding, it still has enough juice in it to permeate all their creations. Imagine modernism today as a soft sponge, rectangular and prismatic in shape. They may twist it, bend it, squeeze it, compress it into spherical volumes, stretch it into a sharp, pointed geometric figure, elongate it into an Escher figure biting its own tail, deconstruct it into its planar components, cover it with a titanium handkerchief; however, it remains good old modernism. Maybe the quest for liberty started when one of the grand masters of modernism, Le Corbusier, feeling himself a prisoner of his own creations, deformed his pristine mental prisms into the Ronchamp Chapel.

Maybe we could conceive mannerism not as a mistakenly long-derided episode in art and architecture but, rather, as a *cri de coeur*, repeated over the ages in different forms by anguished artists and architects trying to free themselves from strictures. If we do, we may discern that many of our contemporaries are still wearing modernism's collar with a piece of the old chain rattling on the floor. In a seemingly deferential process, diverse only in its form, we might also recognize a similar quest today for new architectural models prompting the actions of a different group of architects who are now returning to the beginning and use the guises of land and nature as a way to grope for a new architecture.

If not used parsimoniously, parallelism, employed as an analytical device, may mislead to facile conclusions. So we should stop right here and reflect on our present situation. Modernism redressed as postmodernism, prevailing some years ago, saw its meagre achievements fall to the ground when the glue holding its pastiches aged. Then we got a reshaping of modernism declaimed in arcane concepts and rebaptized "deconstructivism." Sliced, swollen, twisted, and dispersed, modernism still breathed, albeit with some fatigue, under this new guise. Now we have it resurgent again, but under a green coat. Bedecking their old ideas with greenery, many have sought to legitimize it by resorting, for good measure, to proclamations of energy saving and sustainability. By themselves, these are most noble pursuits, but if the resulting constructions, with a few honorable exceptions, do not move us to lofty emotions, is it architecture or is it just building?

Let us examine the relation between an emerging green-sensitive culture of plant-covered buildings, and all the new—some very valid, but many quite superficial—technologies claiming to produce "green architecture."

Let us start from the beginning. The so-called Green Movement, in its many guises, of which sustainability is an honorable one, is a big umbrella where, at present, I would not dare to cast too much light because the shadows are still looking for their bodies. It is a state of awareness; it does not yet constitute a conceptual reality because it lacks a precise system of discourse and a theoretical structure that will allow it to transmit a body of knowledge, and to constantly reevaluate itself. It is an attitude so far; it is not yet a principle.

Green is at present a state of mind that may yet create its own cultural reality. To that end, technologies are being developed, but they have not yet created a reliable body of methods. I have no doubt that in time it will happen. The key point is not to confuse technological pyrotechnics with architecture. To make a green building you need technology; to create architecture you need art.

Building inevitably changes nature as found and turns it into a man-made nature. The goal should be to reduce and, if possible, compensate for our intrusion

138 Emilio Ambasz, ACROS Fukuoka Prefectural International Hall, Japan, 1990–95, facade.

in the Vegetal Kingdom. Building an individual energy-economical house is not always the best way to save or produce energy. Social investment in a communal method for producing solar, sea, or wind energy may prove to be far more productive and efficient. We must be careful to foresee the secondary and tertiary effects of our well-intentioned attempts at energy saving. In a parallel field of endeavor, we find recent studies intended to determine the amount of noxious emissions created when woodland or arable land are converted to the cultivation of biofuel crops.

We must build our house on this earth because we are not welcomed on the land. Every act of construction is a defiance of nature. We need to conceive of an architecture that stands as the embodiment of a pact of reconciliation between nature and building. We must create alternative models of the future proposing a better life to guide our actions if we do not wish to perpetuate present conditions. I believe that any architectural project not attempting to propose new or better modes of existence is unethical. This task may stagger the imagination and paralyze hope, but we cannot subtract ourselves from its pursuit.

Although I was not one of his students, Prof. Frampton's influence was pervasive throughout Princeton's School of Architecture. His precepts that an architectural design must take into account its built and social context inspired me also. However, sometimes I wondered if such respect for the context might not lead to a freezing respect for the present. Surely nothing is further away from Prof. Frampton's progressive optic. Years have gone by since then and my design concerns with

139 Emilio Ambasz, ACROS Fukuoka Prefectural International Hall, Japan, 1990–95, aerial view.

140 Emilio Ambasz, ACROS Fukuoka Prefectural International Hall, Japan, 1990–95, facade model.

context have grown to encompass the respectful contextual relation of the built environment with the natural environment.

I have been lucky to be able to demonstrate with the ACROS building in Fukuoka, Japan, that we can have in the midst of our cities "the green over the gray," and that it is not true that greenery is possible only in the suburbs (**138–140**). Moreover, given that heat and cold loads can also be greatly reduced using economic and ecological materials par excellence, such as earth and plants, we can have 100 percent of the land and at the same time 100 percent of the building. In other words, we can have "the house and the garden," 100 percent of both, instead of "the house in the garden," as modernism promised us in its beginnings. If an architectural work, regardless of how respectful of nature it may be, does not move the heart, is there a point in it? It is just one more building.

I have always believed that the supreme misfortune occurs when the Idea arrives before the Image. Ideas come wrapped in words, and words are part of our already established linguistic baggage. Words denote an established and culturally agreed-upon typology, when not a stereotype. As such, they inhibit the introduction of new meanings, i.e. of invention. Words operate in the domain of semantics, while images belong to the realm of visions.

My goal has always been to design without using words organized into ideas. Such a process requires that I remove from my design process any recourse to linguistic thoughts, or equivalent crutches, and that I try to enter a prelinguistic state of being. For me, linguistically formulated ideas give great comfort to those who are afraid of inventing, and allow for self-congratulatory exegesis. Therefore, I seek to let the images come to me, and only when they have assumed a form do I try to elicit the hidden ideas these images may contain.

Of course, here we encounter the risks inherent in any procedure of interpretation, but the idea(s) we may believe, rightly or wrongly, to be inherent in an image cannot change that image's already embodied substance. Let there be no misunderstanding. It is not a matter of Image versus Idea. An Image, once generated, if it is perceived to be prototypical, does contain an Idea, albeit in a way that is yet to be decoded. Suffice the above to justify my acknowledging being an imagemaker and not an intellectual.

The idea of sustainability only became clear to me after I designed La Casa de Retiro in 1975 (**141–142**). I did not deliberately intend it to be an energy-saving house. I just wanted to insulate it from the insufferable heat of the Andalusian summers. I was unaware that by this conceit I was designing a house that, when built with its roof and some walls shielded with earth, would have no need for heating or air-conditioning. Neither was I intending a house that would return almost all the earth occupied by its footprint. Only after I examined and tried to decipher the house's image did I realize that it contained the seed of some sensible ideas.

Notwithstanding this house's great glazed expanses toward the patio, when the outside temperature reaches 44 degrees Celsius, inside the temperature barely rises

141 Emilio Ambasz, Casa de Retiro Espiritual, Seville, Spain, 1975–2000, aerial view.

142 Emilio Ambasz, Casa de Retiro Espiritual, Seville, Spain, 1975–2000, facade.

to 23 degrees, reaching 27 degrees one summer day when there was a three-hour party, with closed windows, for over fifty people! In winter, when 5 degrees Celsius was registered outside, inside the temperature was 19 degrees. Did I consciously seek to build a sustainable house? No. To me it was just common sense to insulate the construction. Did I intend to become the "Messiah of Green Architecture," as James Wines has all too generously called me? No. Did I use sun collectors in the Mexican city computer project with the intention of turning the building into an energy factory? No (**143–144**). In this case, given the large number of sunny days in the region, I thought it made sense for the clients (who in those years were at the vanguard of digital technology and aimed to present themselves as pioneers) to adopt such technology even if we were all too aware that it was still unprofitable in terms of economic returns. The water basin was also a practical way of draining the area's swampy land while providing support to movable units floating on it.

This building was proposed as a public statement of the client's commitment to create a building in harmony not only with its climate but also with its *genius loci*. Like a Mayan temple, or a sixteenth-century colonial Catholic church, it was to be seen as the place where the new gods dwelt; in this project, the divinity was metamorphosed into a cold-water mist, which cast a rainbow whenever kissed by the sun.

In another instance, from the images I envisioned for the Casa de Retiro, upon later reflection, I derived my first set of ideas and principles. First, giving back the greatest possible amount of land covered by the building's footprint, in the form of gardens accessible to the building's users and, if possible, to the community. Second, designing a building so intricately related to its surrounding landscape that it is impossible to disengage one from the other. Third, creating seasonally changing types of ornaments, such as plants, to decorate the building. Fourth, putting earth and plants on the roof to create a garden, and extend it, wherever possible, to the building's walls. Fifth, and more importantly, to design buildings which sing with a loud voice but with a closed mouth.

143 Emilio Ambasz, Center for Applied Computer Research project, Mexico City, 1975, aerial view.

144 Emilio Ambasz, Center for Applied Computer Research project, Mexico City, 1975, facade.

Value and the Metaphor of Phenomenology in the "Visual Schemes" of Kenneth Frampton

Ashley Simone

> There are many kinds of architectural realities and interpretations of those realities, which include the major issue of representation or re-presentation. Whatever the medium used—be it a pencil sketch on paper, a small-scale model, the building itself, a sketch of the built building, a model of the built building, a film of the built building, or a photograph of the above realities—a process is taking place. Some sort of distortion is occurring, a distortion that has to do with the interpretation and reinterpretation of space and all the mysteries the word space encompasses, including its spirit.[1]
>
> John Hejduk, "The Flatness of Depth" (1980)

> And since you know you cannot see yourself, so well as by reflection, I, your glass will modestly discover to yourself, that of yourself which you yet know not of.[2]
>
> William Shakespeare, *Julius Caesar* (*c.* 1599)

My approach to the matter of Kenneth Frampton and the representation of built form commences here obliquely, proceeds sinuously, and unfolds episodically in an attempt to elucidate his position against the reductive representation of architecture in media. The desire is to acknowledge that representation can be calibrated to produce meaning, generate value, and approximate experience rather than enable a state of aesthetic detachment. And, beyond this, I want to show how Frampton operates as a theorist and a critic who is also a maker, constructing arguments through the confrontation of image and text and drawing attention to media that convey value—material, structural, cultural, social, political, and phenomenological—embedded in the built environment. In this way, he offers reflections that engender discovery. My understanding of Frampton's attitude in this regard deepened through the decade we worked together on *A Genealogy of Modern Architecture* (2015),[3] and later as I developed my own practice as an educator, editor, writer, and photographer at the intersection of art and architecture. My recent research on the issues of *Architectural Design* (*AD*) that were produced between 1962 and 1965, when Frampton was the journal's technical editor and also a practicing architect in London, has confirmed tendencies in his work that I had observed firsthand. This literature and related secondary sources fueled conversations with Frampton that have revealed details about his ideology with respect to the representation of architecture. My essay is a homage to Frampton, whose influence on my practice, and on my personal development, is

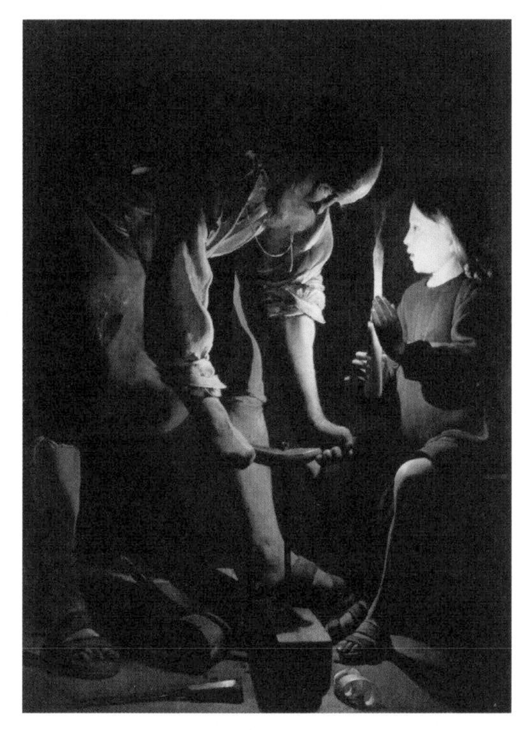

145 Georges de La Tour (1593–1662), *Saint Joseph in the Carpenter Shop*, oil on canvas, *c.* 1642.

indelible. He provided a scaffold that has cultivated an awareness in me of the value of looking critically. Along the way, he became my friend.

The presupposition of adequate intentions

Writing in the same year Frampton's seminal book *Modern Architecture: A Critical History* (1980) was first published, the English art critic and visual theorist John Berger qualified the French Baroque painter Georges de La Tour's *Saint Joseph in the Carpenter Shop* (*c.* 1642) as "modern" (**145**).[4] His qualification, which may seem dubious at the outset based on the artwork, is predicated on the circumstances surrounding the unearthing of La Tour's paintings, which had remained undiscovered until the early 1920s. In his book *About Looking* (1980), Berger further supports his postulation by revealing another motivation for it: the late paintings of La Tour, to which *Saint Joseph in the Carpenter Shop* belongs, are marked by invention.

> La Tour, I believe, saw the whole of life as a scheme over which nobody had any control, a scheme revealed in prophecy and the scriptures ... Yet the total faith of the middle ages has gone. Scientific observation has begun. The individuality of the thinker and the artist cannot be brushed aside or undone. Consequently[,] the painter cannot simply submit to a God-given iconography. He must invent. Yet if

146 View of the Athenian Acropolis from the top of Dimitris Pikionis's park paving on the Philopappus Hill, Athens, 1951–57, photograph by Aleksandros Papageorgíu, 1989.

> he accepts such a view of the world (the world as an unquestionable scheme) the only way he can invent is by imitating God, modestly and piously, within the small domain of his own art. Accepting the world as scheme, he makes his own harmonious visual schemes out of it. Before the world he is helpless except as a maker ...[5]

The scene depicted in La Tour's *Saint Joseph in the Carpenter Shop* cannot be reduced to the presentation of symbols; its elements do not operate exclusively as signs. Rather, the formal elements, their symbolic meanings, and the atmospheric qualities conveyed through rendering techniques evoke an ontological condition. In this way, the artist operates as an inventor and a maker; his work conveys a certain sense of reality contained within the chiaroscuro and material transparency of the allegorical scene, which transforms the information depicted and establishes ontic presence. For those sensitive to the representation and willing to suspend disbelief, a phenomenological experience awaits.[6] This conclusion recalls a Hans Sedlmayr phrase, often quoted by Frampton: "The appreciation of a work of art presupposes adequate intentions."[7] In other words, a reciprocal relationship exists between an observer's perceptive capacity and the maker's creative expression.

Photography and the Philopappus Hill, Athens

A similar ontological experience as that depicted in La Tour's scene of *Saint Joseph in the Carpenter Shop* derives from Hélène Binet's 1989 photograph of Dimitris

147 Dimitris Pikionis, park paving on the Philopappus Hill, Athens, 1951–57. Photograph by Hélène Binet, 1989.

Pikionis's park paving (1957) on the Philopappus Hill in Athens. When Binet's work was recently awarded the Ada Louise Huxtable Prize, Mark Pimlott featured a photograph of Pikionis's urban landscape (**147**) in an article he wrote for the *Architectural Review*, and suggested how observers experience its representation:

> In her photographs from 1989, for another [Architectural Association] commission on Dimitris Pikionis, the surfaces of his pathways around the Acropolis tilled their frames. The viewer's attention was drawn to the ways the pathways' stones received light and conformed to myriad nuanced patterns, assuming the character of an elaborate and archaic carpet. Binet both pictured Pikionis's work and created a palpable experience of it for the viewer mentally and physically: one could imagine walking on these paths and feeling them underfoot.[8]

Frampton was the first to bring the work of Binet to my attention. At the time, I was a graduate student in architecture at Columbia University and also working as his teaching assistant. Sensitive to my expressed interest in the photography of built form, he shared Binet's images with me, as well as a work by the photographer Aleksandros Papageorgíu (**146**). Through their images, I was introduced to Pikionis's paved landscape. The designer's project for Athens collages regional elements of folk architecture with local plants to create an intervention that humanizes architecture.[9] While I cannot recall the exact conversation we had about these photographs, which took place some fourteen years ago, I can imagine Frampton calling my attention to the hazy condition of the sky in Papageorgíu's photograph, through which the Parthenon is visible in the distance, atop the Athenian Acropolis. He also is likely to have made reference to the foliage (and to have known the plant species) that assumes nearly one-third of the frame. Perhaps he described this as compositionally unconventional but evincing Papageorgíu's sensitivity to the intentions of the designer or his ability to convey the haptic experience of being in and moving through the landscape. And maybe, finally, he would have pointed to how the captured light both reveals the tectonic value of the intervention and, as in the Baroque paintings of Caravaggio (known to have influenced La Tour), directs the observer's attention across the image, from foreground to background, to the edifice and symbol that embodies the legacy of ancient Greece that Pikionis's landscape was constructed to celebrate. Given the clarity of experience, it is far more obvious to me now than it was then why Frampton found this image so arresting. The photograph operates metaphorically like reflective glass, revealing latent dialectical oppositions embedded in the landscape by the architect: past and present, nature and artifice, tradition and innovation. Papageorgíu's image, like La Tour's late painting, transcends the reductive communication of information and serves as an adequate proxy for a phenomenological experience. Vision—that of the artist met with that of the observer—affords the apprehension of a tactile environment. While looking at the photograph one can easily imagine the balmy atmosphere, the musky smell of vegetation, and the awareness of depth as generated by the juxtaposition of distant light, diffused by smog, with the more sharply contrasting light and shadow in the foreground. In whichever words he may have said then, Frampton nevertheless described how both the values and concepts of a maker—whether an architect or, in this case, a photographer—and the quality of a given context can be articulated through considered representation and apprehended by way of attentive observation. The discussion shed light on a consistent standard or criteria by which Frampton evaluated built form and the representation of it.

In the summer of 2017, some time after our first conversation on the work of Binet and Papageorgíu, Frampton spoke about the Pikionis landscape in relation to his own practice. He recalled his experience, at age twenty-nine, of Dimitris's stone pathway in Athens as critical in developing his attitudes toward built form which would later coalesce in his theory of Critical Regionalism. Using Papageorgíu's photograph, in fact the same one we had discussed years earlier, he elaborated:

> This is, of course, the staging ground outside the Acropolis [in Athens] which I first experienced in 1959 on my way back [to England] from Israel. I came back to London rather overexcited about this work which is very much something to be experienced by the body as much [as] by the eyes because it was an extremely tactile landscape. Various Greek friends could not understand my enthusiasm in a way because they knew the work and it wasn't exactly modern.[10]

148 Ben Johnson, *Dock Reflections*, acrylic on canvas, 1974.

As Frampton continued charting his professional formation, from the 1950s through the early 1980s, Papageorgíu's image was replaced by the cover of his book *Modern Architecture and the Critical Present* (1982).[11] He characterized the book, released as a special edition of *AD*, as a record of critical reflections, both his own and those of his contemporaries who opined on his prior volume, *Modern Architecture: A Critical History* (first edition, 1980). My concern here, however, is the cover image selected by Frampton for the 1982 publication; an analysis of it further reveals his relation to the representation of built form. The cover features an image of the Fred Olsen Amenity Building at the Millwall Docks in London (*c.* 1970), designed by Norman Foster. Artist Ben Johnson produced the image in 1974 by transposing a photograph to canvas using acrylic paint (**148**).[12] In the resulting rendering, artifacts of maritime industry are reflected and curiously distorted in the flat, sunlit glass panels of Foster's High-Tech facade, which appear to fully obfuscate any view into the building. I posit that the distorted condition captured in the facade registers a reflection of a reflection of industrial artifacts in the adjacent, undulating surface of water. And, I imagine, the visually impenetrable volume could be read as carrying certain social, political, and economic meanings of the time. The possibilities are manifold, but the image certainly is not innocent. Johnson's rendering technique amplifies material sheen and erases the presence of any gritty quality expected around industrial docks, thus accentuating the expression of both the tectonic and material aspects of the building. As I read it, the image Frampton selected for the cover of *Modern Architecture and the Critical Present* renders the environmental phenomena of the context through abstraction and remarks, metaphorically, on the changing industrial landscape, acknowledging the tenuous relationship between old and new industry with the contorted forms of the outdated docklands in the glowing curtain-wall facade. Further, Johnson's image serves to capture the preoccupations symptomatic of the late-modern period of Structural Expressionism that crystallize in Foster's design.

Now I'll return to Athens, yet again. In 1983, one year after the special *Architectural Design* issue bearing Johnson's image was released, and more than two decades after walking on the stone paving designed by Pikionis, Frampton published the criteria outlining the attitudes he envisioned for the construction of modern form: first, under the title "Towards a Critical Regionalism: Six Points for an Architecture of Resistance" (1983),[13] and then again with the third edition of *Modern Architecture: A Critical History* (1992). In the latter, the summation of Critical Regionalism immediately follows a quotation of Alexander Tzonis and Liane Lefaivre that Frampton uses to describe Pikionis's project for Athens. The placement of this text seems to affirm the significance of his early impression of the landscape. Recall that the exuberance Frampton had for the Athenian project in 1959 was not initially shared by some of his colleagues, who could not see beyond the quotidian and vernacular elements and materials. But by the early 1980s, amid the postmodern era and an expanding desire to rehumanize architecture, others began to understand what Frampton had recognized two decades earlier. Writing in 1981, Tzonis and Lefaivre remarked:

> Pikionis proceeds to make a work of architecture free from technological exhibitionism and compositional conceit (so typical of the mainstream of architecture of the 1950s), a stark naked object almost dematerialized, an ordering of "places made for the occasion," unfolding around the hill for solitary contemplation, for intimate discussion, for small gathering, for a vast assembly ... To weave this extraordinary braid of niches and passages and situations, Pikionis identifies appropriate components from the lived-in spaces of folk architecture, but in this project the link with the regional is not made out of tender emotion. In a completely different attitude, these envelopes of concrete events are studied with a cold empirical method, as if documented by an archaeologist. Neither is their selection and their positioning carried out to stir easy superficial emotion. They are platforms to be used in an everyday sense but to supply that which, in the context of contemporary architecture, everyday life does not. The investigation of the local is the condition for reaching the concrete and the real, and for rehumanizing architecture.[14]

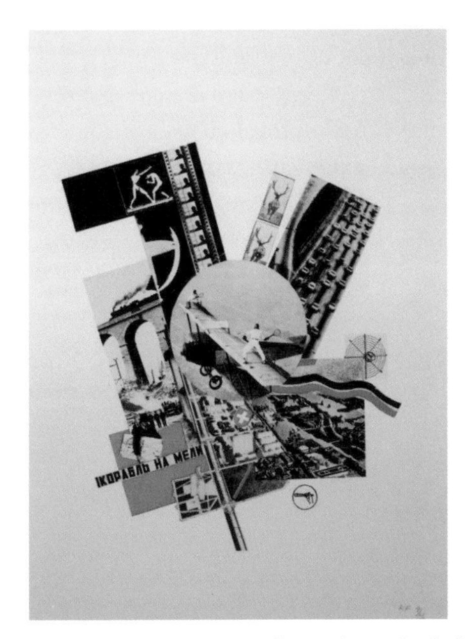

149 Kenneth Frampton, collage, *The Unfinished Modern Project in Homage to it and Habermas* (Christmas card for Atelier 5, 1991–92). Contents from left to right: André Kertész, Photograph Meudon, 1928; Eadweard Muybridge, Animal Locomotion, 1887; Man Ray, Rayograph, *c.* 1929; Ivan Unger and Gladys Roy playing tennis on the wings of a biplane in flight, *c.* 1925; Sonia Delaunay, "Etude de décor pour le ballet des Quatres Saisons," 1928–29; Stenberg Bros., poster for film *Ship Aground*, 1930; Le Corbusier, plans for Paris, 1937; Gustave Eiffel, Eiffel Tower, 1889 (oscillation graph).
150 Kenneth Frampton, "Eiffel Tower," cover of *Architectural Design* (November 1963).

Comparative method in *A Genealogy of Modern Architecture*

In 1959, after arriving back in London via Athens, Frampton began working for the architect Douglas Stephen. A few years later, in the summer of 1962, he succeeded Theo Crosby as technical editor of *Architectural Design*, working alongside Monica Pidgeon to produce the journal with "two editors working half-time, five days a week, assisted by a modest support team."[15] Frampton described the experience:

> I slipped into Theo's editorial chair with uncanny ease, from one day to the next found myself writing, editing and manipulating the yellow rolls of trace that we used to lay out the magazine, adopting Theo's primitive technique of tracing diagonals over the cropped photographs and drawings to control their proportion for the graphic mosaic which made up the copy ... I find it difficult to convey over a lapse of some 50 years how exciting it was to divide my time, on a daily basis, between mornings spent with Douglas Stephen & Partners in designing an eight-storey block of flats in Bayswater and afternoons devoted to editing the magazine in Bloomsbury.[16]

Reading this account for the first time conjured my experience with Frampton preparing to mock up the design for *A Genealogy of Modern Architecture*. The comparative method is used in the book to reveal "the diversely inflected modern traditions in architecture." It traces the cultural paradigms that defined the Modern Movement and examines their evolution beyond the unfinished modern project (**149**),[17] through postmodernism, and to the present. The means by which the detailed analyses were carried out—using photographic, orthographic, and other descriptive and referential material—are telling in regard to the point established at the outset of this essay; Frampton is a maker. Beyond words, his arguments are carefully constructed through the confrontation of images and drawings with text. The process at play in *A Genealogy* cannot be reduced to the presentation of information, rather his calibrated selections and carefully made associations serve to capture and reflect back the values embodied in architecture and approximate an experience of it. Frampton does not concede limits to the representation of built form, and on the consequences of using the aforementioned documents—sometimes in lieu of direct experience—to perform comparative analysis on the projects that comprise the book he has said:

> [T]he buildings are nonetheless envisaged as being directly experienced in tactile terms as the subject passes through space. In my view, architecture is consummated by the "body-being" at both a sensuous and a referential level, rather than as an aesthetic manifestation that is exclusively visual and abstract.[18]

During the early design-editorial phase of *A Genealogy*, we would often work side by side, me on a computer (the "machine" to him) and Frampton with a pen (usually black ink) and lined, letter-size paper (white, never yellow). In these moments, the fond (and sometimes contentious) memories he had of working alongside the graphic designer Massimo Vignelli to lay out issues of *Oppositions* were shared. The contention in one instance had to do with Vignelli's refusal to avoid cropping a spire that featured in the background context of Max Bill's Hochschule für Gestaltung (School of Design) in Ulm, Germany.[19] For Frampton, the exclusion of the contextual element, symbolic of culture, was unthinkable and tantamount to a reduction in the value of the representation and the communicative power of the photograph. As we laid out the book, I observed Frampton's adoption of Crosby's "primitive" technique because I can easily visualize him drawing squares and rectangles marked with diagonals and surrounded by lines standing in for text: the graphic argument reduced to an abstract field. The lines and shapes took on a certain compositional power due to their formal order and the genuine quality conveyed by the slightly wavering lines typical of drawings produced by hand.

At some point during the long duration of the *A Genealogy* project (2005–15), I arrived at Frampton's office to discover a syllabus on his desk titled "Values, Concepts and Methods." I recall it dated from the 1960s, when he taught in the

School of Architecture at Princeton University. The course was an early iteration of one he has given for many decades at Columbia University's Graduate School of Architecture, Planning and Preservation (GSAPP), which is titled "Comparative Critical Analysis of Built Form," and served as the impetus for *A Genealogy*. In this instant I came to understand the significance of the book as a record of a consistent pedagogy, which is best described in a brief excerpt from the course syllabus:

> The intention of the course is: (1) to sensitize the student to the multiple levels at which the built environment is able to convey cultural significance; (2) to forge or link between our understanding of the cultural past as embodied in built form and our potential for creativity in the process; and (3) to cultivate our capacity to interpret the built environment in the light of a particular mode of beholding; mainly, that built-form is to be seen not only as a representation of the human condition and of our capacity to constitute our being in terms of human institutions but also, at the same time, as being a literal embodiment of these implicit values.[20]

The course and the book are predicated on comprehensive analyses of the architectural projects under a consistent set of categories: type/context, private/public & goal/route, structure/membrane, and connotations & references. The origin of Frampton's preoccupation with these analyses and the production of *A Genealogy* actually goes back further than the 1960s. In 1951, Frampton encountered an issue of the *Architectural Review* dedicated entirely to the Royal Festival Hall in London.[21] While this issue had come up during our conversations about his editorial intentions for *AD*, Frampton has also made reference to it in writing: "It is difficult to recall the last time that an architectural editor had the courage to devote an entire issue to a particular significant building and hence to document it in its entirety."[22] At the same time, he celebrated a special issue of the Italian magazine *Quadrante* that was dedicated to the Casa del Fascio, Como. "In this case not only is the building exhaustingly documented, but a very precise complementary relationship is also established among the drawings, the photographer, the text, and the layout," which achieves "a graphics of commitment and of value rather than a value-free graphics of aesthetic detachment."[23]

Frampton's consistency in method can be traced with some ease across his pedagogical concerns, as in the aforementioned comparative analysis course which he gave over six decades. It is also evident through the work he chooses to validate, which may vary greatly in expression but coheres according to a core set of values that privilege the perceptual body and offer guidelines for design and negotiation of context that link to a larger social, political, and cultural agenda.[24]

The steadfast nature of Frampton again gave way to a conflict about representation while we were defining and collecting the connotations and references for the chapter of *A Genealogy* that compares the Centre Pompidou (Piano and Rogers, Paris, France, 1977) with the Médiathèque Carré d'Art (Foster, Nîmes,

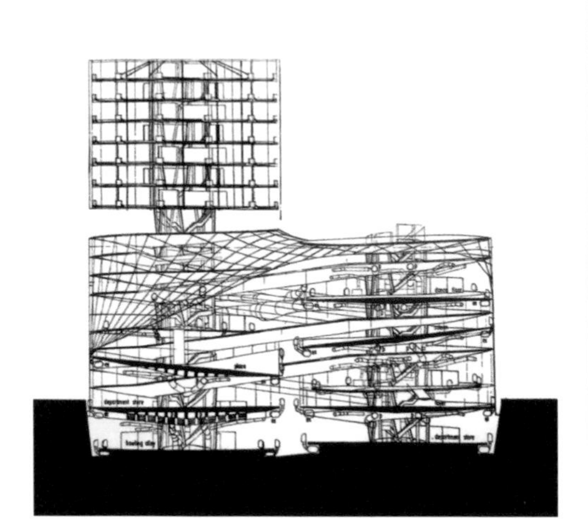

151, 152 Michael Webb, cross section of The Entertainments Palace, ink on tracing paper, 1961 (left); horizontal plan-section of Sin Palace, mixed-media drawing, 2015 (right).

France, 1993). Frampton requested the 1961 cross section of Sin Palace (originally known as The Entertainments Palace) from Michael Webb (**151**). He was the first to publish Webb's unbuilt project, in the November 1963 issue of *AD*, between Yona Friedman's Paris Spatial and the suspension structures of Frei Otto's International Garden Exhibition in Hamburg. The volume cover bore a worm's-eye detail of the Eiffel Tower and had been designed by Frampton (**150**). For his 2015 book, Frampton wanted the exact black-and-white, cross-sectional line drawing of Sin Palace that he had published more than fifty years earlier, which exposed roadways and mechanical systems contained by a "shrink-wrapped tension membrane roof."[25] It would be positioned in the connotation section in relation to the machine-like, High-Tech Centre Pompidou. Webb, on the other hand, saw an opportunity to metaphorically redact what he viewed as a flaw in the structure of the previously published Sin Palace. He wanted to overwrite the representation of the project in the public record and reveal the one that had been sequestered in his mind when the drawings were drafted in 1961. In Webb's words, "All too often in architectural design the idea leaps ahead of the means of expressing it. The idea is present, but one's ability to put form to it is mired in the past."[26] Webb assured he would complete the new version he had already begun for the book's deadline (**152**). At issue was the material specification of concrete indicated by the poché in the original sectional drawing. Driven by a different representational ideology than Frampton, Webb preferred to convey the aesthetic appearance of the ultrathin, aluminum roadways in the model of the project—a structural impossibility in reality—and the revised drawing he proposed, which took the form of a plan-section, expressed the appearance he had intended to

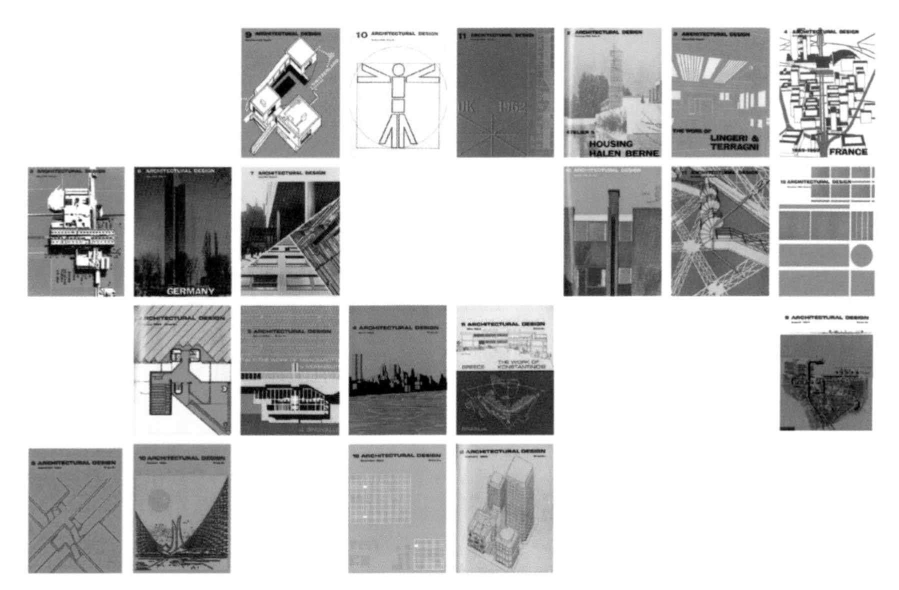

153 Select covers of *Architectural Design*, designed by Kenneth Frampton between August 1962 and February 1965, when he was the technical editor of the publication.

achieve. But Frampton would not accept the version with impossibly thin roadways that subverted tectonic integrity; the 1961 cross section of Sin Palace features in *A Genealogy*.

The authority of the critic: values and visual representation

The theme of consistency came up again during a recent conversation I had with the prominent architectural historian Robin Middleton who has long been Frampton's very close colleague at Columbia University and editor of Frampton's first edition of *Modern Architecture: A Critical History*. Over lunch, Middleton emphasized Frampton's "integrity and consistency" as the highest caliber in the criteria with which he evaluates architecture.[27] Middleton and I had met to discuss his experience at *AD*; he took over as technical editor of the magazine in early 1965 after Frampton decided to leave for the States.[28] Despite my interest in the cover designs Frampton executed during his *AD* tenure (**153**), Middleton insisted that any discussion of Frampton and representation must take caution not to dilute his authority as a critic. While acknowledging and affirming Middleton's point, I have nevertheless observed that Frampton's consistency and decisive authority permeate the representations that he chooses and, in some cases, constructs or directs. His approach to the visual means that interpret and reinterpret space are arguably Goethean in that they reflect a "higher reality." The images he reflects toward us, and the drawings and graphics he designs, convey respect for the underlying value and intention of that which is re-presented—whether that may be (echoing John Hejduk) "a pencil sketch on paper, a small-scale model, the building itself, a sketch of the built building, a model of the built building, a film of the built building, or a photograph of the above realities."[29] To Hejduk's list, I must add: a book on the built building, a zine on the built building, a journal on the built building, a journal cover on the built building, and, finally, a poster of the built building.

A part of a built building often appears on a poster released annually by GSAPP in anticipation of the Kenneth Frampton Endowed Lecture. Conceived and realized through a collaborative effort among Frampton, GSAPP, and the graphic designer Glen Cummings, the poster re-presents a fragment and participates in announcing the architect selected by Frampton to speak at the school.[30] On the communicative power of the detail in the context of representation, Frampton has said the following:

> The idea that constructional details may have poetic implications and that they may compensate for the inevitable misinformation that, by definition, arises from the extensive use of partial photographic images regardless of their size are both concepts that have been largely ignored by the editors of architectural journals over the past two decades.[31]

Cummings spoke to me about his experience producing the posters. While the process has evolved over the years, he explained that Frampton mines the materials sent by the selected architect in search of the "visualizations that capture the aspects of the work that resonate with him, the ones he wants to talk about."[32] Cummings has also come to recognize "a real specificity to what aspects of the architecture he [Frampton] wants to engage and how he reads the images; there is a very specific condition that he is looking for."[33] As our conversation continued, I remarked to Cummings on the poster for the 2015 lecture by Indian architect Bijoy Jain (**155**). It has been the only one to feature an image in lieu of a drawing. Like me, he had been surprised by Frampton's choice of medium in this case given that the line-drawn detail had been established as a standard. Responding to a question I casually posed about his decision to use an image over a drawing, Frampton, in a matter-of-fact manner, indicated that the poetics of Bijoy's work, its spirit, lay in the materials and that quality could only be captured in a photograph capable of communicating the tactile nature of the architect's designs.[34] Before my conversation with Cummings concluded, I learned that Frampton has not always been satisfied with the documents received from the architect selected to speak and has followed up to request additional information or pursued his own research. The design of the poster for the lecture given by Portuguese architect Eduardo Souto de Moura in 2012 (**154**) features an axonometric detail drawing of the highly articulated steel, granite, and glass structural facade of the Burgo Office Tower, Porto (2007), floating as a plastic object amid a field of gray. The drawn form was not supplied by the architect. Rather, the white lines that form the detail were projected from a plan

154, 155 Glen Cummings, MTWTF, Annual Kenneth Frampton Endowed Lecture poster, 2012 (left); Glen Cummings, MTWTF, Annual Kenneth Frampton Endowed Lecture poster, 2015 (right).

at Frampton's direction and serve to isolate the sculptural detail and highlight the poetic expression of Souto de Moura's design. And, it is this composition that leads me back to London in 1964, and toward concluding remarks.[35]

Graphic design as "surplus experience"

The abstract detail of the staircase system for the Craven Hill Gardens building, Bayswater, London (1964) that appears on the cover of the September 1964 issue of *AD* was the subject of a recent discussion I had with Frampton (**156**). Between 1961 and 1964, Frampton designed and managed the construction of the residential building while working as an architect for Douglas Stephen & Partners (**157**). As he examined the cover of this particular issue, Frampton remarked dismayingly about the regret he had for neither extending the lines of the detail to the edge of the page nor cropping it such that it could "float as a plastic object" within the field of red. The detail itself possesses a certain agency in its ability to render the plasticity of the volume's interior articulation, which regulates circulation and, therefore, the human occupation of space (**158**).

Flipping through the pages that Frampton laid out in 1964 to thoroughly document the project—even vehicular circulation in the basement is shown, as is the trajectory of the fresh-air intake—one apprehends the tactile qualities of steel, glass, and concrete that the photography by Michael Carapetian, Richard Einzig, and Sam

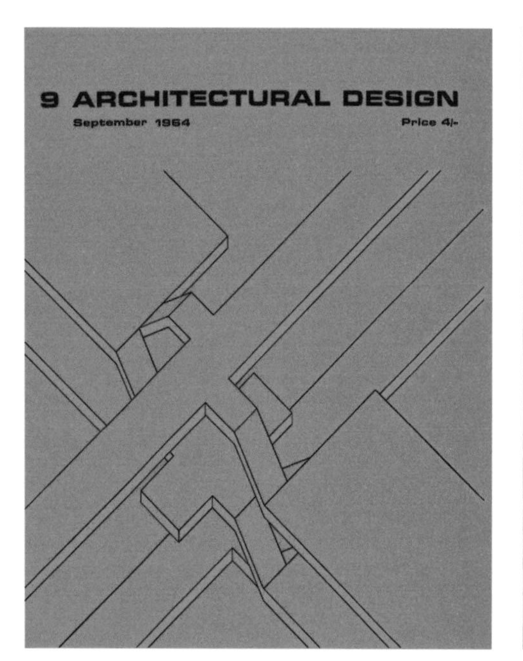

156, 157 Kenneth Frampton and Anthony Stockbridge, abstract detail of the stairs in the maisonettes at the Craven Hills Gardens building, cover of *Architectural Design* (September 1964) (left); Kenneth Frampton (project architect), Douglas Stephen and Partners, Corringham housing complex (13–15 Craven Hill Gardens), Bayswater, London, 1962–64, exterior view (right).

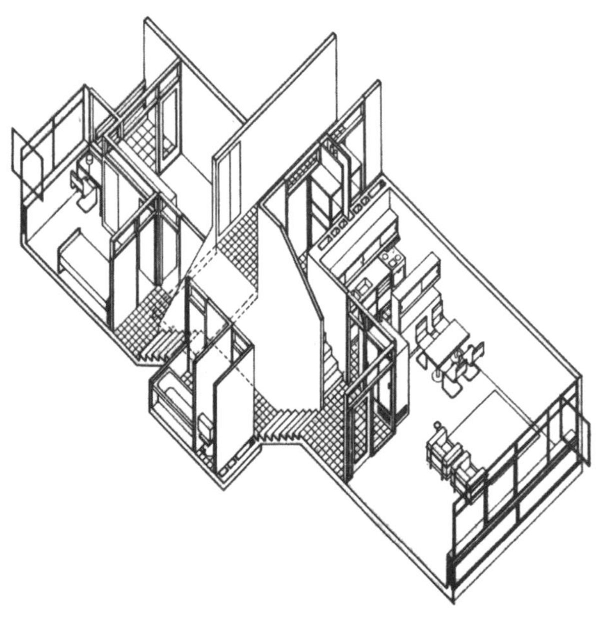

158 Kenneth Frampton, diagrammatic axonometric showing the stairs abstracted in detail form on the September 1964 cover of *AD* (above left) and the disposition of the spaces in a down-going unit.

Lambert convey. And one sees the carefully considered layouts for the flats comprising the eight-story residential block: "Each of the maisonettes is planned on three main levels, the maisonettes being served by either up-going or down-going staircases according to their situation."[36] Writing on both the building and the graphic design Frampton executed for the cover and spreads, Jorge Otero-Pailos notes the following:

> If Craven Hill Gardens did not succeed in presenting a unified experience between interior and exterior, then it is possible to read Frampton's publication of the building as an attempt to achieve that unity through another medium. Exploiting the analogy between the front cover of *AD* and the building's facade, he turned the interior into the exterior, prominently displaying a sectional axonometric drawing of the interior scissor section on the face of the issue. More precisely, the graphic choice to represent the interior with a diagonally oriented drawing visually brought forth the primary organizing experience of the interiors—the diagonal movement up and down the scissor stairs—while reviving the preferred drawing mode of Dutch constructivism. The emphasis on the diagonal structuring of the page served to set up a relationship of equivalency between the visual graphic design and the haptic experience of the stairs, both as a means of psychological orientation."[37]

This passage encapsulates what I set out to explore in this essay and the argument Otero-Pailos makes about Frampton's graphic design in *Architecture's Historical Turn: Phenomenology and the Rise of the Postmodern* (2010), that it affords a "surplus experience." This is embedded in a larger discussion of Frampton's attitude toward experience as the common denominator of aesthetic and intellectual approaches to architecture, and a conduit to a sociopolitical agenda aimed at bolstering the notion of Self in the postmodern era.[38]

Cultural objects and the embodiment of humanistic value

The collection of observations and accounts offered here, which are loosely structured about formative moments in Frampton's career and my experience with him, first as a student and then as a collaborator, are meant to elucidate an ideology regarding the representation of built form in media that can be read through the "visual schemes" Frampton reflects back to the world. These schemes—those he validates and the ones he constructs—reveal a commitment to communicate value embodied by architecture and, in the words of John Hejduk that introduce this essay, offer a "reinterpretation of space and all the mysteries the word space encompasses, including its spirit."[39] The common ground held by these constructs is the capture and articulation of intellectual (tectonic), somatic, and ontic characteristics that establish an operative capacity to serve as metaphor for phenomenological experience. While my focus has been to weave a narrative that presents graphics and circumstances surrounding their re-presentation as metaphor, it is important to acknowledge that the demands Frampton has for the design of conditions that engage the physical body in the haptic spatial domain are complex and foray into cultural, social, and political realms.

In this regard, it may be useful in closing to return to the paved Athenian landscape designed by Pikionis that Frampton first visited and celebrated in 1959, at the very beginning of his career (**146–147**). The intervention employs regional elements and components of folk architecture; the words of Tzonis and Lefaivre expand on the description of the project that appears in Frampton's *Modern Architecture: A Critical History*,

> Pikionis puts into action here the program of the epigones of the modern movement who, in reaction to the dehumanising effects of the modern escapades, embodied in the formalism of International Style, asked for the rehumanisation of architecture, for "a place made for an occasion" instead of one made as abstract space ... But the path is not only a facility ... it is a cultural object; it carries with it a commentary about contemporary architecture, life, society. It is a moral statement that this petrified stream of passages and places, these "vessels of life" carry; even when empty, they have a voice. It is a protest against the destruction of community, the splitting of human associations, the dissolution of human contact.[40]

The passage describes a process of invention and action that has taken place in this landscape and rendered the collective elements comprising it as more than the sum of its parts. Together, the elements obtain agency, and acknowledge the value of the social realm. The implication is that the social realm may be accessed through a "cultural object" and the experience it is programmed to afford. There is a related process at play in La Tour's *Saint Joseph in the Carpenter Shop* (**145**). Here the painter has collaged iconographic elements—an old, and presumably experienced, carpenter, fragments of wood that formally allude to a cross, a candle that operates to reveal the tactility of the scene—and rendered the phenomenological through the depiction of light and space. In so doing, he has implicated architecture as a participant in the translation of material, paint, and information into phenomena, a performance of invention, according to Berger.

An analogy can be drawn between the intervention Pikionis designed for Athens and the representation of built form that Frampton reflects towards us; both cohere as innovative form that is curated and constructed in pursuit of humanistic social and political ethics. Kenneth Frampton is a key participant in the translation of the material world for the field of architecture. Like La Tour, he acts to mine architecture and carefully render it with intention to convey the embodied experience and values that lie latent in the built environment.

Phenomenology and the ethics and method of architecture

"What would it mean to look at phenomenology through architecture rather than [at] architectural phenomenology?" The spatial and neuroaesthetics researcher Winifred Newman posed this question in a recent issue of *Log* titled "Disorienting Phenomenology" (2018).[41] She went on to write, "[t]he physical world we make is a kind of cognitive map reflecting back to us the agency of our sensual perceptions," and posits that the use of such "maps" in the process of designing architecture can be adopted as an "ethics and method" for conceiving architecture. While her argument bears relation to others pursued in built and written form by numerous contributors to this volume,[42] I appreciate that her neuroscientific perspective acknowledges the multimodal sensory aspects of vision. In other words, vision triggers psychological and physiological sense perceptions, which is a fact integral to this context, a discussion of media as metaphor for phenomenological experience.[43] It is my position that Newman's "maps" are Frampton's visual schemes. For decades, he has consistently examined phenomenology through architecture and reflected his findings back to the world as a means to convey his ethics, validate particular methods, engender discovery, and guide the discipline toward a humanistic approach.

1 John Hejduk, "The Flatness of Depth," *Judith Turner Photographs Five Architects* (New York: Rizzoli, 1980), 10.
2 William Shakespeare, *Julius Caesar*, Act 1, Scene 2, 4. Cassius speaking to Brutus.
3 Kenneth Frampton, *A Genealogy of Modern Architecture: Comparative Critical Analysis of Built Form*, ed. Ashley Simone, (Zurich: Lars Müller Publishers, 2015).
4 See John Berger, "La Tour and Humanism," *About Looking* (New York: Pantheon Books, 1980), 110–11. The common publication year of the first version of Frampton's *Modern Architecture: A Critical History* and *About Looking* gives additional context on aesthetic debate in that period. I use Berger here to draw a conclusion about representation in the form of an artistic likeness, image, or drawing.
5 Ibid., 115.
6 For more on the possibility of phenomenological representation, see Edmund Husserl, *The Crisis of European Sciences and Transcendental Philosophy: An Introduction to Phenomenological Philosophy* [1937] (Evanston, IL: Northwestern University Press, 1970).
7 Hans Sedlmayr, *Art in Crisis: The Lost Centre*, trans. Brian Battershaw (London: Hollis and Carter Ltd., 1957).
8 Mark Pimlott, "Hélène Binet," *Architectural Review*, 1459 (March 2019): 102–05. For the AA exhibition of Binet, see Savas Condaratos, "Dimitris Pikionis 1887–1986: A Sentimental Topography," *AA Files*, 20 (1990): 55–62.
9 Alexander Tzonis and Liane Lefaivre, "The Grid and the Pathway: An Introduction to the Work of Dimitris and Susana Antonakakis," *Architecture in Greece*, 15 (1981): 177–78.
10 Kenneth Frampton, lecture, New York City, July 13, 2017.
11 Kenneth Frampton, *Modern Architecture and the Critical Present*, *Architectural Design* Profile (London: Academy Editions, 1982).
12 Norman Foster Foundation Archive, https://archive.normanfosterfoundation.org/ben_johnson/en/micrositios/inicio.do (accessed November 9, 2019).
13 Kenneth Frampton, "Towards a Critical Regionalism: Six Points for an Architecture of Resistance," *The Anti-Aesthetic: Essays on Postmodern Culture*, ed. Hal Foster (Port Townsend, WA: Bay Press, 1983).
14 Tzonis and Lefaivre, "The Grid and the Pathway," 176, quoted in Kenneth Frampton, *Modern Architecture: A Critical History* (London: Thames & Hudson, 2004), 326–27.
15 Kenneth Frampton, "Homage à Monica Pidgeon: An *AD* Memoir," *AA Files*, 60 (2010): 23.

16 Ibid.
17 The inclusion of this image is an aside to the discussion at hand and offered as a means to show Frampton's facility for constructing graphic form.
18 Frampton, *A Genealogy of Modern Architecture*, 18.
19 My memory of this moment was rendered lucid by: Kenneth Frampton. "Notes on the Role of Photography and Graphic Design in the Phenomenological Representation of Architectural Forms" (unpublished). Produced for the conference "Still Architecture: Photography, Vision, Cultural Transmission" (University of Cambridge, May 3–5, 2012), organized by Marco Iuliano and François Penz. Thank you to M. Iuliano for the making the paper available to me.
20 Kenneth Frampton, syllabus for A4420 "Comparative Critical Analysis of Built Form," given at the Graduate School of Architecture, Planning and Preservation, Columbia University, New York (with frequency *c.* 1972–2017).
21 "Royal Festival Hall," *Architectural Review*, 654 (June 1951): 109, 341–44.
22 Kenneth Frampton, "A Note on Photography and its Influence on Architecture," *Perspecta*, 22, *Paradigms of Architecture* (1986): 41.
23 Ibid.
24 For a more detailed account, see Jorge Otero-Pailos, *Architecture's Historical Turn: Phenomenology and the Rise of the Postmodern* (Minneapolis, MN: University of Minnesota Press, 2010), 201–35.
25 Michael Webb and Ashley Simone, eds., *Two Journeys* (Zurich: Lars Müller Publishers, 2017), 38.
26 Michael Webb, correspondence with the author, October 27, 2019.
27 Robin Middleton, conversation with the author, October 30, 2019.
28 See also Beatriz Colomina, Craig Buckley, and Urtzi Grau, *Clip, Stamp, Fold: The Radical Architecture of Little Magazines, 196X to 197X* (Barcelona: Actar, 2010); and Frampton, "Homage á Monica Pidgeon," 2–29.
29 Hejduk, "The Flatness of Depth," 10.
30 Lecturers 2012–19: Eduardo Souto de Moura, Yvonne Farrell and Shelley McNamara (Grafton Architects), Angelo Bucci, Bijoy Jain, Lacaton & Vassal (cancelled), Rahul Mehrotra, Kongjian Yu, Marina Tabassum.
31 Frampton, "A Note on Photography and its Influence on Architecture," 40.
32 Glen Cummings, conversation with the author, November 8, 2019.
33 Ibid.
34 Kenneth Frampton, in conversation with the author, *c.* 2016.
35 Glen Cummings, conversation with the author, November 8, 2019.
36 "Maisonettes, Bayswater, London," *Architectural Design*, 34/9 (September 1964): 442–48.
37 Otero-Pailos, *Architecture's Historical Turn*, 209.
38 Otero-Pailos, *Architecture's Historical Turn*, 183–88. For more on phenomenology and politics: Joseph Bedford, "Toward Rethinking the Politics of Phenomenology in Architecture," *Log*, 42 (Spring 2018): 181–85.
39 Hejduk, "The Flatness of Depth," 10.
40 Tzonis and Lefaivre, "The Grid and the Pathway," 177.
41 Winifred E. Newman, "Counter Re-formations of Embodiment," *Log*, 42 (Spring 2018): 165–69.
42 See Sarah Robinson and Juhani Pallasmaa, eds., *Mind in Architecture: Neuroscience, Embodiment, and the Future of Design* (Cambridge, MA: MIT Press, 2015).
43 Winifred E. Newman, "Counter Re-formations of Embodiment," 169.

From the Archives of Kenneth Frampton

Brigitte Shim and Howard Sutcliffe

Exhibit #1 Between Aalto and Arendt

Our contribution to this publication began with a visit to examine the recently acquired Kenneth Frampton archive at the Canadian Centre for Architecture (CCA) in Montreal.[1] There, in the light-filled study center, as we contemplated a very large stack of archival boxes, we fully understood the breadth of Frampton's insatiable curiosity and prodigious interest in the world and its relationship to architecture and his life. Contained in these boxes are unpublished essays, annotated manuscripts, letters to and from architects around the world, sketches, leaflets, brochures, measured drawings, and all sorts of other stuff.

The Frampton archive was acquired by the CCA in 2016, and together with the archives of James Stirling, Cedric Price, John Hejduk, Álvaro Siza, and Peter Eisenman—to name a few—form an interesting constellation, and an important cornerstone of architectural history in the modern period.

159, 160 Detailed view of one of the boxes in the Frampton fonds at the Canadian Centre for Architecture (CCA, Montreal). View of Frampton fonds between Aalto and Arendt, 2019 (left); view in the CCA study center with a pile of acid-free boxes from the Frampton fonds with CCA study center team providing assistance, 2019 (right).

161 Cover of Hannah Arendt, *The Recovery of the Public World*, ed. Melvyn Hill (New York: St. Martin's Press, 1979). The last chapter includes transcripts from the 1972 conference on "The Work of Hannah Arendt."

This visual essay presents a portrait of Frampton using items selected from his archive that are of particular interest to us in our own teaching and architectural practice. The very first box we opened contained many well-organized manila file folders which were sandwiched between two labels: Aalto and Arendt (**159–160**).

Exhibit #2 The Work of Hannah Arendt

Frampton's long-standing interest in the writing of Hannah Arendt is well known. In November of 1972 he was invited to a conference on "The Work of Hannah Arendt" by the Toronto Society for the Study of Social and Political Thought (**161–163**). The conference organizer, Melvyn Hill, invited Frampton because he was delighted to have learned that the prominent architectural educator was so interested in her writings. At this conference Frampton presented a paper on "Architecture and Industrialization," with George Baird as the respondent. Arendt herself attended the conference, not as the guest of honor as per the invitation, but as a participant, at her request. Frampton and Baird are among a group of architect/educators who were profoundly influenced by Arendt, and her thinking

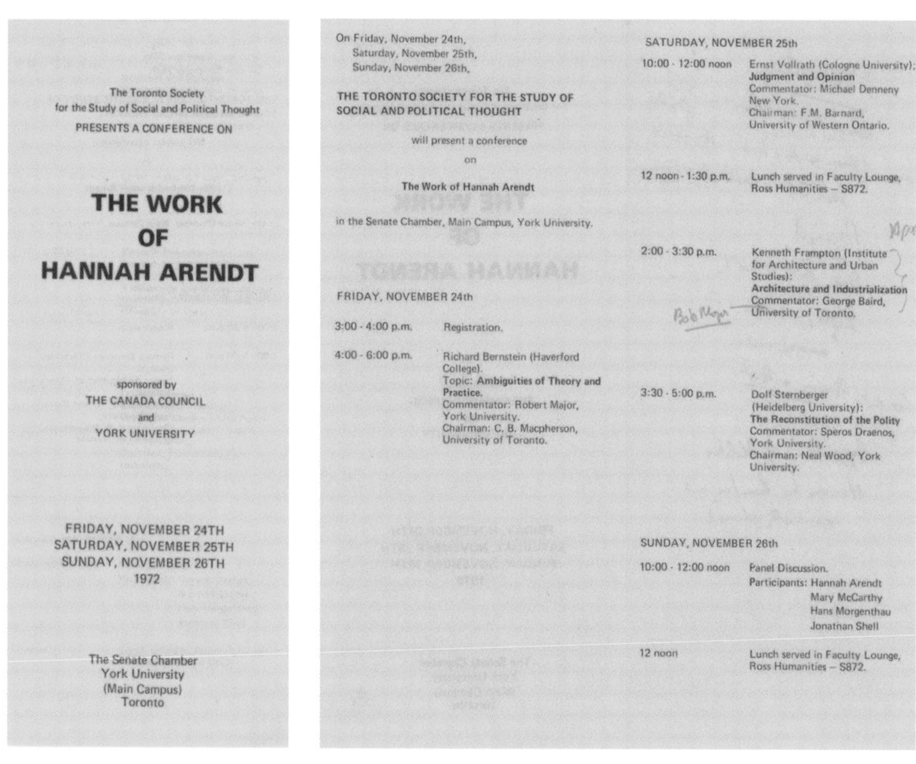

The Toronto Society
for the Study of Social and Political Thought
PRESENTS A CONFERENCE ON

THE WORK
OF
HANNAH ARENDT

sponsored by
THE CANADA COUNCIL
and
YORK UNIVERSITY

FRIDAY, NOVEMBER 24TH
SATURDAY, NOVEMBER 25TH
SUNDAY, NOVEMBER 26TH
1972

The Senate Chamber
York University
(Main Campus)
Toronto

On Friday, November 24th,
Saturday, November 25th,
Sunday, November 26th,

THE TORONTO SOCIETY FOR THE STUDY OF SOCIAL AND POLITICAL THOUGHT

will present a conference

on

The Work of Hannah Arendt

in the Senate Chamber, Main Campus, York University.

FRIDAY, NOVEMBER 24th

3:00 - 4:00 p.m.	Registration.
4:00 - 6:00 p.m.	Richard Bernstein (Haverford College). Topic: **Ambiguities of Theory and Practice.** Commentator: Robert Major, York University. Chairman: C. B. Macpherson, University of Toronto.

SATURDAY, NOVEMBER 25th

10:00 - 12:00 noon	Ernst Vollrath (Cologne University): **Judgment and Opinion** Commentator: Michael Denneny New York. Chairman: F.M. Barnard, University of Western Ontario.
12 noon - 1:30 p.m.	Lunch served in Faculty Lounge, Ross Humanities – S872.
2:00 - 3:30 p.m.	Kenneth Frampton (Institute for Architecture and Urban Studies): **Architecture and Industrialization** Commentator: George Baird, University of Toronto.
3:30 - 5:00 p.m.	Dolf Sternberger (Heidelberg University): **The Reconstitution of the Polity** Commentator: Speros Draenos, York University. Chairman: Neal Wood, York University.

SUNDAY, NOVEMBER 26th

10:00 - 12:00 noon	Panel Discussion. Participants: Hannah Arendt, Mary McCarthy, Hans Morgenthau, Jonatnan Shell
12 noon	Lunch served in Faculty Lounge, Ross Humanities – S872.

162, 163 Front cover of the program for the Toronto Society for the Study of Social and Political Thought conference, 1972 (left); inner pages outlining the three-day conference on "The Work of Hannah Arendt" (right).

reshaped their understanding of the potential of the public realm. As Frampton remarked,

> I think that when I moved to the United States in 1965, it "politicized" me, meaning that until I went to the United States, I was totally naïve about power for example, and the relationship between power and money ... And about the same time, I read Hannah Arendt's book *The Human Condition*, and there are some of the arguments of that book that I will never recover from.[2]

Exhibit #3 Alvar Aalto and the Future of the Modern Project

As practicing architects, we appreciate Frampton's long-standing recognition of Alvar Aalto and his ability to make modernist buildings accessible to the person on the street. Aalto's broad definition of design encompasses not only buildings but also includes landscapes, furniture, hardware, lighting, and fittings—all working in concert with one another to realize humane and meaningful spaces. From the beginning of our own architectural practice, this broad humanism of Aalto's work resonated deeply with us.

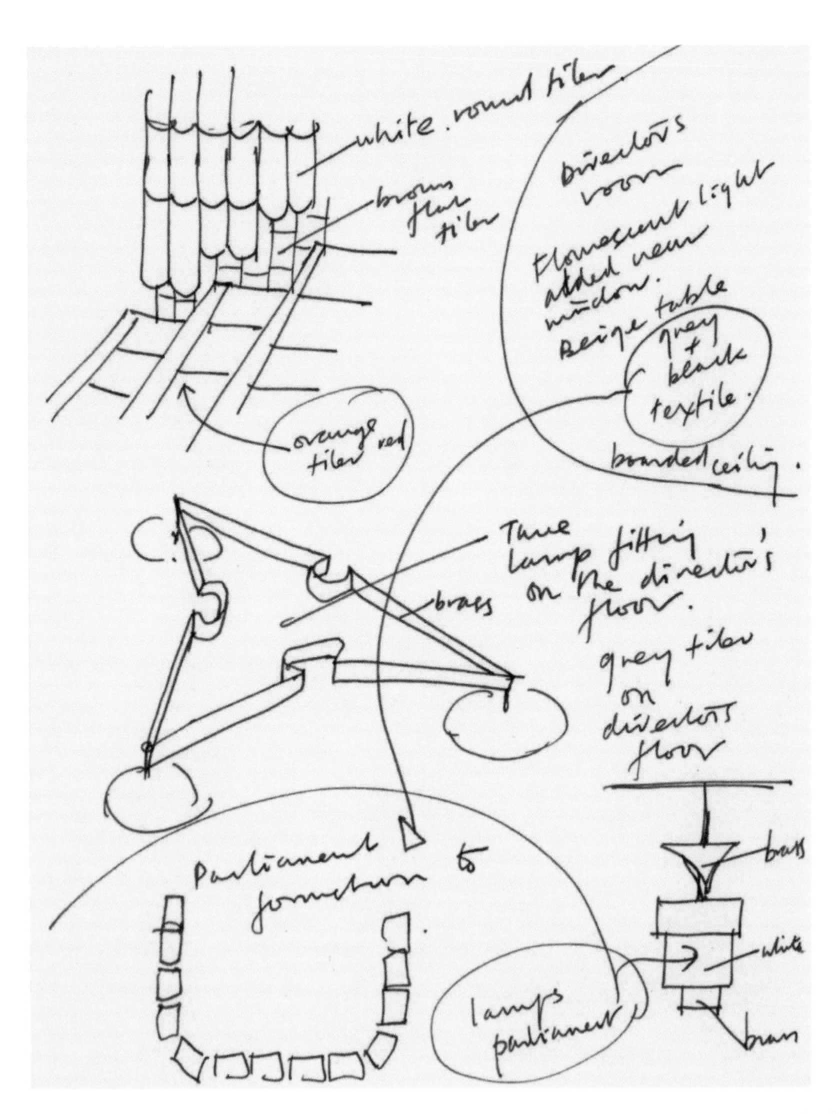

164 Sketches by Kenneth Frampton of Alvar Aalto's National Pensioners Institute, Helsinki, Finland, from the Frampton fonds, CCA, *c.* 1977.

In a 2015 Vitra Design Museum interview, Frampton stated that the second book of architecture he ever bought as a student was on the work of Alvar Aalto. He described the ability of Aalto's masterpiece, Villa Mairea, to "accommodate the vicissitudes of everyday life without losing its cultural depth and aesthetic coherence. One never feels that Aalto is either precious or unduly polemical."[3]

Frampton's initial education and training as an architect has influenced all of his academic work and writing. As a result of this training he resorts to the time-honored device of sketching to fully understand the underlying decision-making process of the building design. In the Frampton fonds, there is a series of sketches

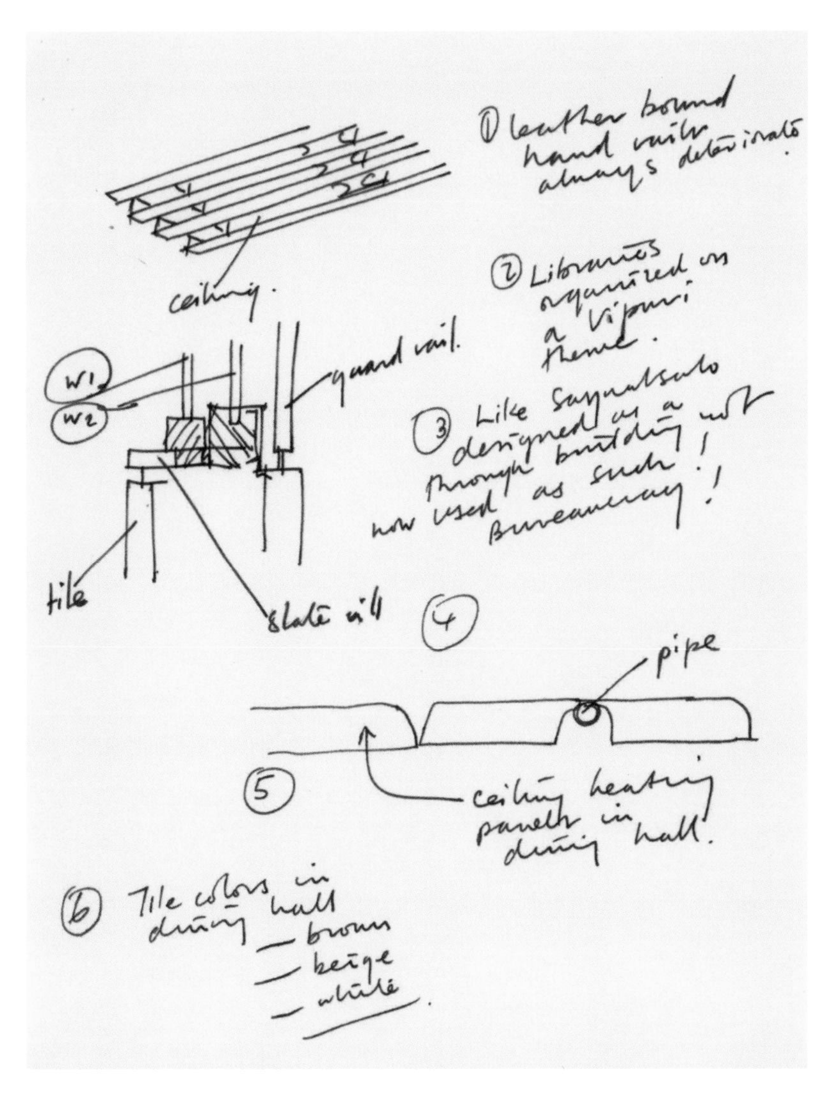

165 Sketches by Kenneth Frampton of Alvar Aalto's National Pensioners Institute, Helsinki, Finland, from the Frampton fonds, CCA, *c.* 1977.

of Aalto's National Pensioners Institute in Helsinki in which Frampton interrogates through his sketches Aalto's choice of building materials, examining carefully his construction details and building connections (**164–165**). The sketches reveal that Frampton fully understands the nature of the building as an architect and then he writes about the work as a theorist.

In February 2013, Frampton gave a lecture at the Daniels Faculty at the University of Toronto titled "Alvar Aalto and the Future of the Modern Project," where he shared his insights into the contribution of Aalto's forward-moving modernism through an ongoing conversation about the nature–culture dialectic.

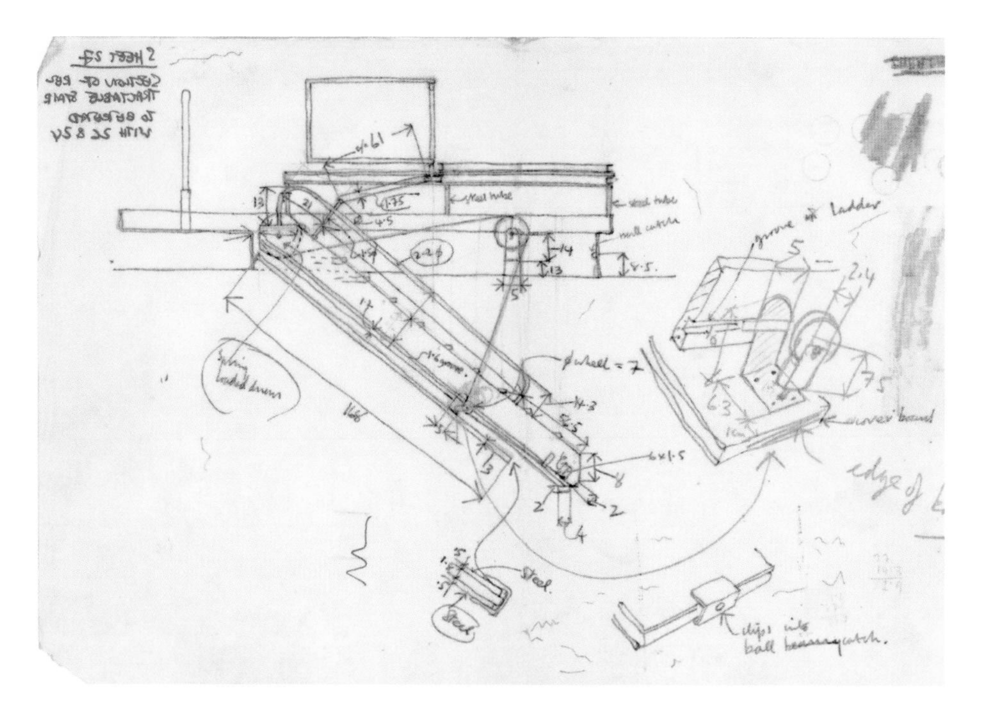

166 Kenneth Frampton, measured drawings of stairs in the Maison de Verre, Paris, from the Frampton fonds, CCA, *c.* 1965.

In a 2006 interview with the Norwegian editors of *Arkitektur N* on "Cultural Sustainability," Frampton stated:

> I think the most important architecture of the 20th century, in terms of the 21st century, is still Alvar Aalto. Because I think he is one of the very few architects who have been able to build a model world, in a way, but at the same time to provide a certain level of security for ordinary people, through his use of form and material.[4]

Exhibit #4 Maison de Verre—The Modern House

Frampton taught us that the modern house is inseparable from the modern project. As architecture students, we first encountered the Maison de Verre through his seminal article in Yale University's *Perspecta* 12.[5] This unique project left a deep impression on us as young architects. The extensive photographs combined with the meticulous line drawings in *Perspecta* 12 allowed one to inhabit this private and inaccessible residence. Frampton prepared measured drawings that enabled his ink on mylar drawings to be realized by others (**166–167**). Clearly, the drawings communicated the kinetic aspect of the house with its movable stairs and pivoting wardrobes.

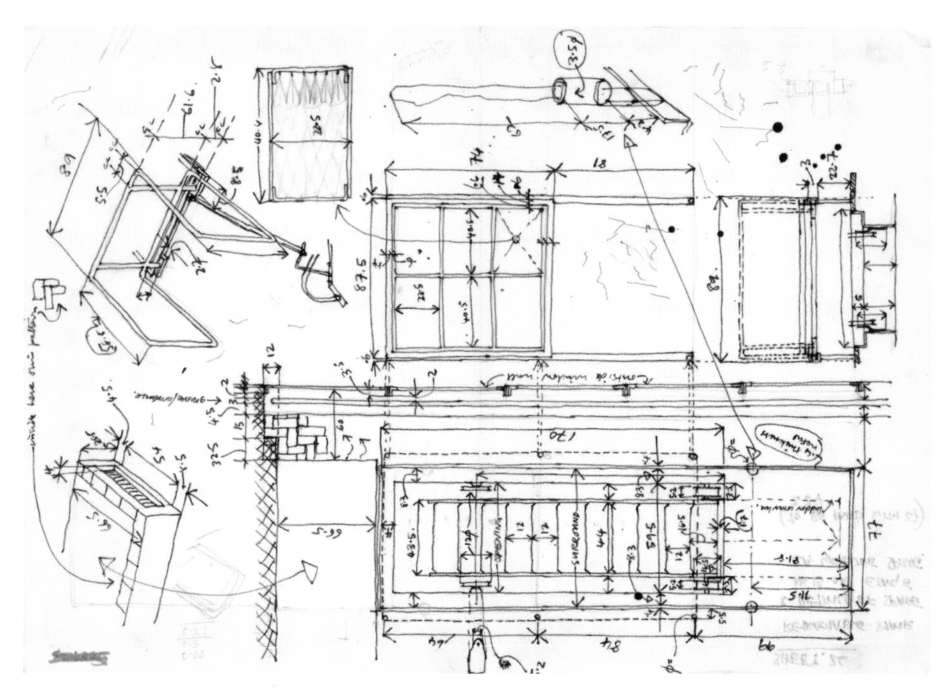

167 Ink on mylar drawing of the stairs in the Maison de Verre by others from measured drawings by Kenneth Frampton from the Frampton fonds, CCA, *c.* 1965.

Many years later, Frampton was appalled when he learned that we had never visited the Maison de Verre in person. He immediately contacted the owner of the house, who was a former student of his, and asked the owner if we could visit the house on an upcoming trip to Paris. Frampton felt that not visiting this important building was a major omission in our ongoing architectural education that had to be rectified immediately. In the Frampton archive we found this text:

> In the Maison de Verre, one is confronted with a work which defies any accepted form of clarification. It is not merely a question of an inability to place it from a stylistic or conceptual point of view. The genre of the work itself is problematic. Are we to regard it as a building in the accepted sense or should we rather think of it as a grossly enlarged piece of furniture interjected into an altogether larger realm?[6]

Exhibit #5 Comparative Critical Analysis of Built Form

As educators and practioners, we value Frampton's early recognition of the challenging gap in architectural education between studio instruction and academic courses in history and theory. He has stated that he is neither an architect nor strictly speaking a historian, and he prefers to think of himself as a teacher of

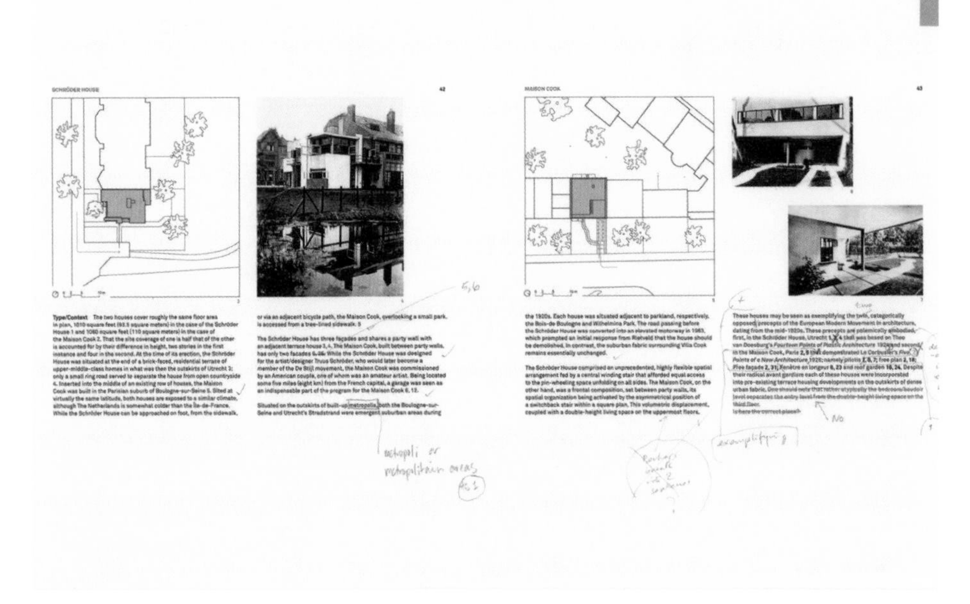

168 Draft of print layout with notes for *A Genealogy of Modern Architecture*, *c.* 2013–15. Site Plan and Photos. Houses. Maison Cook, Le Corbusier, 1926, Boulogne-sur-Seine, France, from the Frampton fonds, CCA.

architecture. In a university seminar initiated in the 1970s by Frampton titled "Comparative Critical Analysis of Built Form," he asked his students to analyze pairs of buildings in accordance with a clearly defined comparative methodology. Students compared projects with similar building programs—houses to houses, offices to offices, and pavilions to pavilions, etc. They studied the spatial hierarchy, tectonic expression, and critical details in each pair of buildings. This student assignment evolved and transformed into an initial book, and then to other subsequent books by Frampton, always linking two aspects within the discipline of architecture—design studio and history and theory—that have a tendency within the academic world to be separate. In the Frampton fonds at the CCA, there are many versions of each page of "Comparative Critical Analysis" with numerous edits, Post-it notes, and new insertions ensuring that the drawings and text are striving to articulate a strong and unified message about each pair of canonical buildings shown (**168–172**).

In this text, Frampton emphasizes the relationship between plan and section: "House is primarily activated in the terms of its plan, the Maison Cook is animated in section, as evidenced by the act that the top two public floors of the house are separated from the ground floor ... The promenade through the Maison Cook is

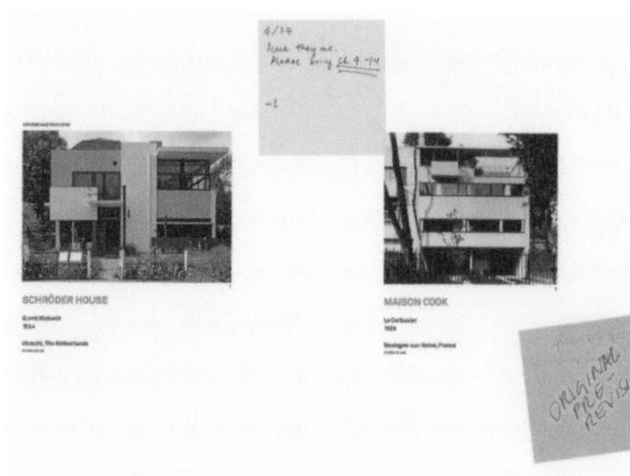

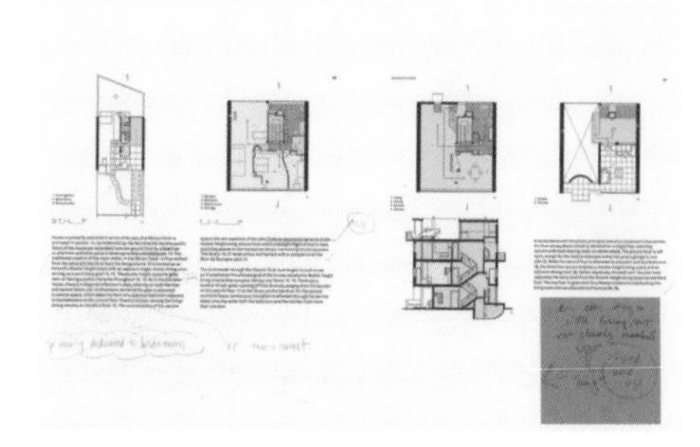

169 Cover of Kenneth Frampton, *A Genealogy of Modern Architecture: Comparative Critical Analysis of Built Form*, ed. Ashley Simone (Zurich: Lars Müller Publishers, 2015).
170–172 Draft of print layout with notes for *A Genealogy of Modern Architecture*, *c.* 2013–2015, from the Frampton fonds, CCA.[7]

arranged in such a way as to emphasize the ultimate goal of the house, namely the double-height living volume that occupies the top floors."[8]

Frampton, the educator/architect, presented architecture students with a way of analyzing and seeing architecture through its built form, deepening their understanding of its cultural role and simultaneously making an invaluable contribution to the training of architects and theorists of the next generation.

Exhibit #6 Regionalism in Architecture

In 1985, Frampton and Geoffrey Bawa both attended a conference on "Regionalism in Architecture"[9] organized by the Aga Khan Award for Architecture and held in Dhaka at the Bangladesh University of Engineering and Technology (**174**). At the time there were many cultural and political transformations taking place in the Indian subcontinent and during the seminar, contemporary ideas about how regionalism, the changing nature of architectural practice, and cultural identity were discussed and debated.

We associate Frampton with the term Critical Regionalism in North America. Frampton has been an integral part of a global conversation about how regionalism has been firmly linked to architecture and cultural identity for decades. Frampton

173 Courtyard of Geoffrey Bawa's Ena de Silva House, Columbo, Sri Lanka, 1960. Photograph by Hélène Binet.

has always been aware of—and a champion of—exemplary built work being realized in Latin America and Southeast Asia.

From 1999 to 2001, Frampton served on the Steering Committee for the Aga Khan Architecture Award (**175–176**). This Steering Committee gave the Chairman's Award to the distinguished Sri Lankan architect Geoffrey Bawa, citing that his work has always reflected in the most subtle way the tension between modernization and local culture (**173**). Bawa's aesthetic and visual sensibility, as well as his position on vernacular architecture, has shaped an entire generation of South Asian architects and his spirit has become part of the way architects in this region see themselves. In a 2018 interview in *Metropolis Magazine*, Frampton stated that:

> If one looks for examples of the Aga Khan Awards, one realizes there is a lot of talent all over the place producing very interesting modern work. The tendency is for places like New York to suffer from the illusion that they are at the center of the world.[10]

Exhibit #7 Landscape and Topos

Frampton has always been interested in the megaform, and particularly the integrated role of landscape, built form, and topography in shaping the public realm. In the Frampton fonds, we discovered a letter from Frampton to landscape architect

174 Cover of Robert Powell (ed.), *Regionalism in Architecture* (Singapore: Concept Media/Aga Kahn Award for Architecture, 1985).

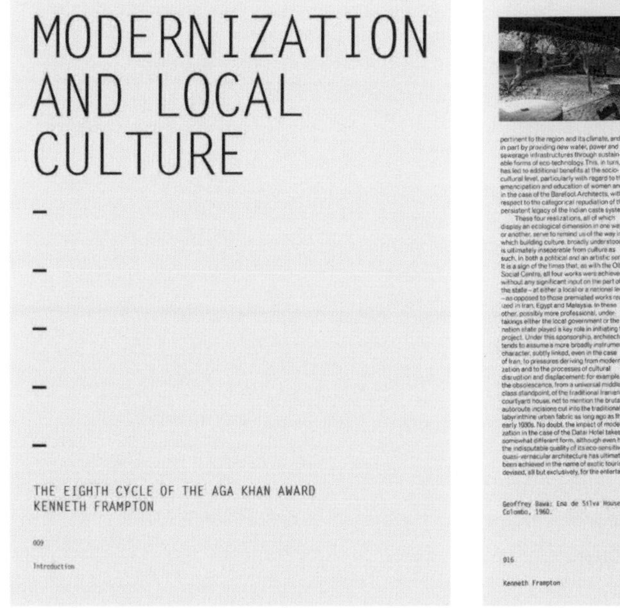

MODERNIZATION
AND LOCAL
CULTURE

THE EIGHTH CYCLE OF THE AGA KHAN AWARD
KENNETH FRAMPTON

009

Introduction

Geoffrey Bawa: Ena de Silva House, Colombo, 1960.

016

Kenneth Frampton

175, 176 Essay by Kenneth Frampton on "Modernization and Local Culture: The Eighth Cycle of the Aga Khan Award," in *Modernity and Community: Architecture in the Islamic World*, ed. Philippa Baker (London: Thames & Hudson, 2001).

Columbia University

IN THE CITY OF NEW YORK

THE GRADUATE SCHOOL OF ARCHITECTURE PLANNING AND PRESERVATION

400 AVERY HALL

March 19, 1999

Cornelia Oberlander
FAX: 604-224-7347

Dear Cornelia Oberlander,

I recently gave the Raoul Wallenberg Lecture at the Architectural School at the University of Michigan in Ann Arbor on the following theme (a copy of the text is enclosed). It is now to be published. I am looking for a very good photograph of Robson Square at a fairly high angle showing the whole development. I think this projects is possibly one of the most important urban set pieces carried out in North America since Rockefeller Center.

I recall with great pleasure the time that you lectured at Columbia University when I was acting chairman of the school of architecture. It is over 10 years ago and we have not been in touch since then unfortunately. However, there has not been a month when I do not think of you. Of your ginko leaf, of your mother in Weimar and of your superb work (when will someone publish a book on your work?). In the meantime I hope all is well with you .

Sincerely yours,

Kenneth Frampton/ah

Kenneth Frampton
Ware Professor of Architecture

NEW YORK, NEW YORK 10027
TEL: 212-854-3414
FAX: 212-864-0410
1172 AMSTERDAM AVENUE

177 Letter dated March 19, 1999, from Kenneth Frampton to Cornelia Oberlander, in the Frampton fonds, CCA.

178 Screenshot from YouTube, "Megaform as Urban Landscape," lecture by Kenneth Frampton, Senior Loeb Lecture at Graduate School of Design, Harvard University, October 25, 2017, showing a view of Robson Square, Vancouver, 1978–83, at a fairly high angle of the whole development.

Cornelia Oberlander dated March 19, 1999. Frampton was writing to Oberlander in search of a "very good photograph of Robson Square at a fairly high angle showing the whole development" (**177–178**).[11]

He was looking for a cover image for a book he was writing on megaforms, and he did not receive the photo from Cornelia Oberlander in time, so used another image instead. In his letter, he shared with Cornelia his belief that this project (Robson Square) was possibly one of the most important urban set pieces carried out in North America since Rockefeller Center.[12]

Robson Square is a three-block complex of buildings that include law courts and government offices, located in downtown Vancouver, Canada, and designed by distinguished architect Arthur Erickson. A linear urban park which is part of the Robson Square complex is a collaboration between Erickson and Oberlander. The park brings nature directly into the city, which results in a bold piece of landscape and urbanism simultaneously.

In October 2017, Frampton and Silvia Kolbowski were invited to Harvard's Graduate School of Design to give the Senior Loeb Scholar Lectures. Frampton's lecture, "Megaform as Urban Landscape," included a view of Robson Square at a fairly high angle showing the whole development, courtesy of Cornelia Oberlander.

When visiting one of our projects in the Canadian landscape, Frampton filled a sketchbook with a series of probing drawings that he used to identify the material palette, the found elements, and new interventions. Kenneth Frampton's Point William

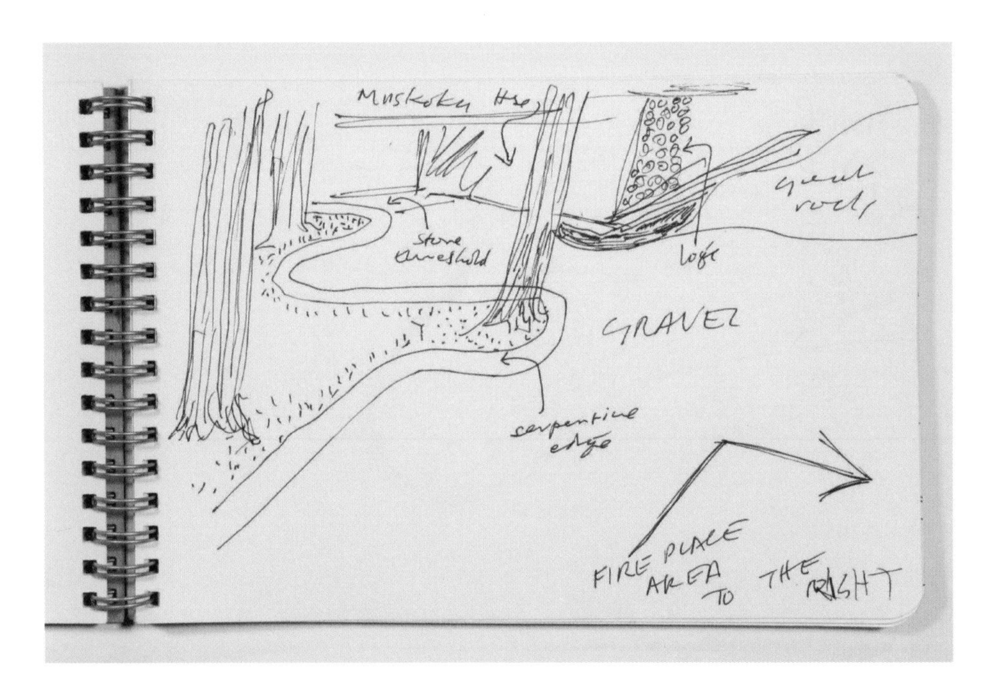

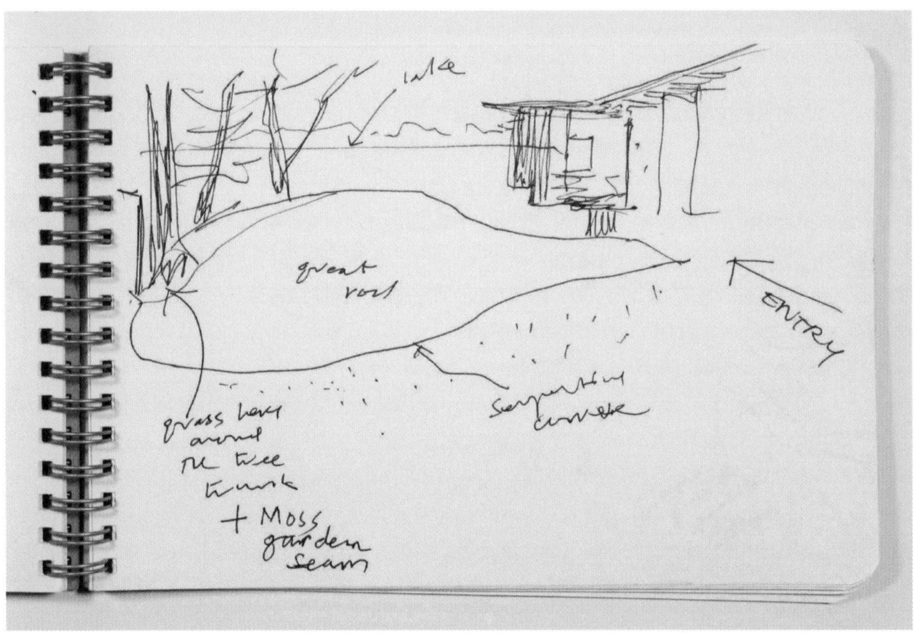

179–180 Sketches of landscape and rocks at Point William, Ontario, from Kenneth Frampton's personal sketchbook, 2017.

sketches of the lakeside and rocks reveal his long-standing interest in the crucial role of landscape and topography in the powerful act of placemaking (**179–180**).

1 The Kenneth Frampton fonds at the Canadian Centre for Architecture documents the professional career of Kenneth Frampton. Materials in this fonds span the years 1958 to 2016 and include more than 28 linear meters of textual materials and more than 7000 photographic materials. These materials demonstrate Frampton's activities as a teacher, researcher, and writer. The largest portion of the archive comprises drafts and final copies of Frampton's writings as well as extensive correspondence highlighting Frampton's relationships with universities, publishers, editors, architects, and students.

2 From "Cultural Sustainability," interview with Kenneth Frampton by Ingerid Helsing Almaas and Einmar Bjarki Malmquist for *Arkitektur N, The Norwegian Review of Architecture* (September 5, 2006), published by the National Association of Norwegian Architects, https://www.architecturenorway.no/stories/people-stories/frampton-06/ (accessed January 9, 2020).

3 Interview with Kenneth Frampton on Alvar Aalto, Vitra Design Museum (October 5, 2015), https://www.youtube.com/watch?v=SmBi_T-3ZAA (accessed December 18, 2019).

4 From "Cultural Sustainability," interview with Kenneth Frampton.

5 *Perspecta* is a non-profit journal edited, designed and published at intervals by the students in the Yale University School of Architecture, New Haven, CT. In *Perspecta* 12, published in 1969, there is a lengthy fifty-two-page article by Frampton on the Maison de Verre. Kenneth Frampton, Robert Vickery, and Michael Carapetian jointly measured and photographed the Maison de Verre in July 1965. Frampton's own measured drawings for one of the kinetic stairs was found in the Frampton fonds in the CCA. Frampton indicates that he is indebted to Michael Curtis, Harrison Fraker, John Harrell, William Johnson, Peter Mayer, Thomas Prichard, Salvatore Vasi, Augusto Villalon, and Jeremy Wood for their invaluable assistance in the preparation of drawings for publication.

6 Written text on the Maison de Verre from the Frampton fonds, CCA, Sub-Series Maison de Verre (1965–1969), Series: Works and Teaching.

7 Reprographic copy with annotations in graphite and Post-it notes with manuscript in ink and graphite in the Frampton fonds in the CCA.

8 Kenneth Frampton, *A Genealogy of Modern Architecture*, ed. Ashley Simone (Zurich: Lars Müller Publisher, 2015), M46.

9 Robert Powell, ed., *Regionalism in Architecture* (Singapore: Concept Media/Aga Khan Award for Architecture, 1985). Proceedings of the conference with list of all participants, including Geoffrey Bawa and Kenneth Frampton.

10 Zachary Edelson, "Kenneth Frampton Isn't Done Changing Architecture," *Metropolis Magazine* [New York] (March 2, 2018).

11 Letter dated March 19, 1999, from Kenneth Frampton to Cornelia Oberlander from 1999 Personal and Professional Correspondence in the Frampton fonds, CCA.

12 Ibid.

Picture Credits

Frontispiece courtesy Karla Cavarra Britton
1 Photograph by Jeff Bickert
2 Creative Commons, Wikimedia. Pierre Jeanneret / Public domain
3 Photograph by Jean-Pierre Dalbéra
4 Princeton School of Architecture
7 AKTC–Rajesh Vora
8 Modernist Estates
9 Douglas Stephen, Kenneth Frampton, and Michael Carapetian, *British Buildings 1955–1965* (London: Adam & Charles Black, 1965), p. 83
11–12 *Another Chance for Housing: Low Rise Alternatives*, catalogue, Museum of Modern Art, 1973, p. 20
14 Israel Museum, Jerusalem
15, 146, 149, 158, 179–180 Courtesy Kenneth Frampton
16–17 Photographs by Marc Treib
18 Photograph by Oscar Tenreiro
19–26 Courtesy Amateur Architecture Studio
27 Pikionis Archive, Neohellenic Architecture Archives, Benaki Museum, Athens, Greece
28–29 Photographs by Elias Constantopoulos
30 Sketch by Álvaro Siza Vieira
31 Plan by Álvaro Siza Vieira
32 Photograph by Giovanni Chiaramonte
33–34 Plans by TEd'A arquitectes
35–36 Photographs by TEd'A arquitectes
37 Creative Commons, Wikimedia. Photograph by Roger Culos
38 Creative Commons, Wikimedia. Photograph by Allan Gluck
39 Creative Commons, Wikimedia
40 Creative Commons, Wikimedia. Photograph by Michal Osmenda
41 Google Maps
42 Creative Commons, Wikimedia. Photograph by Cmglee
43 Creative Commons, Wikimedia. Photograph by Peter Milosevic
44, 49, 51 © Lu Guang / Contact Press Images
45–46 Courtesy Bruce Mau Design
47 bpk Bildagentur / Staatliche Museen Berlin / Wolfram Büttner
48 Public domain
50 Israel Museum, Jerusalem
59 © Editions Anthropos, Paris. Courtesy Jean-Louis Cohen
60 © Public domain. Courtesy Canadian Centre for Architecture
61–62 Public domain. Courtesy Jean-Louis Cohen
63 Public domain in Canada only; rights holder unknown. Courtesy Canadian Centre for Architecture
64 Getty Research Institute, Los Angeles (950076)
65 Courtesy Wittenborn Art Books, San Francisco, www.art-books.com
66 © NER Group Foundation Archive
67–69 Photographs by Soichi Sunami. Courtesy Photographic Archive. The Museum of Modern Art Archives, New York
70 Courtesy Photographic Archive. The Museum of Modern Art Archives, New York
76–77 Drawn by Lucy Navarro with Andrés Alvarez-Dávila
78 Robert Lawler, *Sacred Geometry* (London: Thames & Hudson, 1982)
79–85 Aulis Blomstedt Family
86 Eluveitie / CC BY-SA (https://creativecommons.org/licenses/by-sa/3.0)
87, 90 Photographs by Robert Maxwell
88 Photograph by Peter Inskip
89 Photograph by Sean Kernan
91–92 Photographs by Celia Scott
93–96 Photographs © Miguel Fernández-Galiano
97 Photograph by Lu Andrews. Courtesy Paul Rudolph Foundation
98 Photograph by Alan Weintraub
99 Courtesy Paul Rudolph Foundation
100 GSD History Collection. Courtesy the Frances Loeb Library, Harvard Graduate School of Design
101 Paul Rudolph Collection, Library of Congress, Prints & Photographs Division, LC-USZ62-134731
102 Photograph by Stanley Tigerman
103 Photograph by Elliott Erwitt © Magnum Photographs
104 Photograph by Robert C. Damora © Damora Archive
107–112 Courtesy Richard Barnes
113–116 Courtesy Wiel Arets
117 © Alan Paukman
118 © Architect: Mario Botta. Photograph by Alo Zanetta
119 © Fondo Aurelio Galfetti. Balerna, Archivio del Moderno. Photograph by Pino Brioschi
120–121 Photographs by Sally Schoolmaster
122 Photograph by Hélène Binet
123 Photograph by Brad Cloepfil
124 Photograph by Jeremy Bittermann
125 Courtesy La Biennale di Venezia
126 Ros Kavanagh
127 Kenneth Frampton, "The Anti-Aesthetic: Essays on Post-Modern Culture," *Towards a Critical Regionalism: Six Points for an Architecture of Resistance*, ed. Hal Foster (Port Townsend, Washington: Bay Press, 1983), p. 23
128–130 Courtesy Grafton Architects
131 © Dennis Gilbert
132 © Federico Brunetti
133, 135 © Iwan Baan
134 Pedregulho Social Housing; Photograph by Ana María León
136 L'Illa Diagonal, https://www.flickr.com/photos/lilladiagonal/3635554852/, CC-BY-NC-ND 2.0
137 Flickr user: wadester16, https://www.flickr.com/photos/36071029@N05/3537560291/, CC-BY-SA 2.0
138–144 Courtesy Emilio Ambasz
145 © RMN-Grand Palais / Art Resource, NY
147 Courtesy Hélène Binet
148 Courtesy Ben Johnson
151–152 Courtesy Archigram Archive and Michael Webb
154–155 Courtesy Glen Cummings, MTWTF
157 Photograph by Michael Carapetian
159–160 Courtesy Shim-Sutcliffe
162–168, 170–172, 177 Reproduced by permission from the Kenneth Frampton fonds, Canadian Centre for Architecture. Gift of Kenneth Frampton.
173 Reproduced by permission from the Aga Khan Trust for Culture / Aga Khan Award for Architecture. © Hélène Binet
174–176 Reproduced by permission from the Aga Khan Trust for Culture / Aga Khan Award for Architecture

Acknowledgments

We would like to begin by expressing our deepest appreciation for the exemplary intellectual leadership exhibited by Kenneth Frampton throughout his long career as a historian, critic, and teacher. For the two of us, his generous mentorship, personal support and deep friendship had their foundation in the three years, from 1988 to 1991, during which we shared with Frampton the office suite in the southeast corner of the second floor of Avery Hall at Columbia University. It is no exaggeration to say that those years, and our relationship with Frampton since that time, have changed both our lives for the better beyond measure.

This book can at best serve as a modest expression of the gratitude felt by so many for Frampton's seemingly inexhaustible collegial energy and his unfailingly constructive commitment to architecture. As editors, we have been acutely aware that there are numerous colleagues, former students, and fellow travelers who, due to limitations of space, we were regretfully not able to include. Many people feel that their relationship to Frampton is one of unique closeness, collegiality and warmth. Indeed, his ability to form deep and lasting friendships is perhaps his most endearing attribute. Our sincere hope is that this collection will inspire many other efforts to honor and explore Frampton's career and contributions.

In what is yet another indication of Frampton's degree of influence on the discipline of architecture, we are pleased to acknowledge the generous financial support provided by the donors who have made it possible for us to publish this book. The donors include:

Graham Foundation for Advanced Studies in the Fine Arts

Tianhua Architecture, Planning and Engineering Company
Architectural History Foundation / Victoria Newhouse
Legado Emilio Ambasz Fundacion / Emilio Ambasz
Yim Sen Kee, Architect
Gregg Pasquarelli, Coren Sharples, Christopher Sharples, William Sharples / SHoP Architects
Wang Shu and Lu Wenyu / Amateur Architecture Studio
James Stewart Polshek, Architect
Kengo Kuma, Architect
Zhu Tao, Architect
Wang Wei Jen, Architect
Karla Cavarra Britton, Professor
Robert McCarter, Architect and Professor
Richard Meier Foundation
Brad Cloepfil / Allied Works Architects

We would also like to recognize the Foundation of Washington University in St. Louis, as well as Dean Carmon Colangelo, John Foughty and Bobbe Winters of the Sam Fox School of Design and Visual Arts, for their essential assistance in this project.

Our debt to the authors in this volume should be obvious, but we would be remiss not to extend our profound gratitude formally—especially to those who contributed many powerful and provocative images at their own expense. Our appreciation goes as well to a number of others who considered our invitation to contribute an essay but for a variety of personal reasons were not able to do so. We similarly offer our thanks to the many photographers, archives and other sources for the illustrative materials that grace this book and for their generous help in making them available, especially the Canadian Centre for Architecture which holds Frampton's papers.

We extend our gratitude for the enormous efforts in realizing this project by the expert team at Thames & Hudson, publisher of Frampton's canonical *Modern Architecture: A Critical History*, now in its fifth edition. In particular, we gratefully acknowledge the support of commissioning editor Julian Honer, whose commitment to this project has never wavered since we first brought it to him several years ago; and to those who shepherded the book through to its final realization, including editors Susannah Lawson and Tamara Stanton, copy-editor Sarah Yates and designers Peter Dawson and Amy Shortis, among many others.

In closing, it is with great sadness that we note the passing in January 2020 of Robert Maxwell, whose essay is included in this volume. Our thanks go to Celia Scott for so graciously helping to finalize his text.

Biography of Kenneth Frampton

Kenneth Brian Frampton is a British architect, critic, historian, and teacher, born in 1930 in Woking, U.K. Since 1972, he has taught at the Graduate School of Architecture, Planning and Preservation at Columbia University in New York, where he now holds the position of Ware Professor of Architecture. Frampton studied architecture at the Architectural Association in London, graduating in 1956. He subsequently worked as an architect with Chamberlin, Powell and Bon in London, Dov Karmi in Israel, the Middlesex County Council, and Douglas Stephen and Partners in London from 1961 to 1965. While at Stephen's office, Frampton designed the Corringham Building, an 8-story block of flats in Bayswater, London. He also co-authored his first book (with Douglas Stephen and Michael Carapetian), *British Buildings 1955–65*, and served, from 1962 to 1965, as technical editor of the British journal *Architectural Design* (*AD*).

In 1966 Frampton came to the United States to take up a teaching position at Princeton University, later moving to Columbia. In 1972 he was also made a Fellow at the Institute for Architecture and Urban Studies (IAUS) in New York, where he was co-founding editor of the journal, *Oppositions*. He has also taught at the Royal College of Art, London; the University of Virginia; Rice University; all three Swiss schools of architecture (the Accademia di Architettura in Mendrisio, the ETH Zurich, and the EPFL Lausanne); and the Berlage Institute, Rotterdam, among other institutions.

The canonical writings by Frampton include *Modern Architecture: A Critical History* (1980, the fifth edition of which is to be published in 2020); *Modern Architecture and the Critical Present* (1982); the essay, "Towards a Critical Regionalism: Six Points for an Architecture of Resistance" (1983); *Pierre Chareau* (with Marc Vellay, 1984); *Studies in Tectonic Culture: The Poetics of Construction in Nineteenth and Twentieth Century Architecture* (1995); *American Masterworks: The Twentieth Century House* (1995); *Technology Place and Architecture* (1998); *Álvaro Siza: Complete Works* (2000); *Le Corbusier* (2001); *Steven Holl Architect* (2002); *Labour, Work and Architecture: Collected Essays on Architecture and Design* (2002); *The Evolution of 20th Century Architecture: A Synoptic Account* (2007); *Five North American Architects: An Anthology by Kenneth Frampton* (2010); *Kengo Kuma: Complete Works* (2012); *A Genealogy of Modern Architecture: Comparative Critical Analysis of Built Form* (2015); and *L'altro movimento Moderno* (2015, to be published in English as *The Other Modern Movement* in 2020). Frampton's teaching was the subject of the 2017 exhibition, *Educating Architects: Four Courses by Kenneth Frampton*, at the Canadian Centre for Architecture, which holds the archive of his teaching and scholarship. Frampton is the author of countless essays, chapters and introductions; he has lectured extensively at universities and conferences around the world; he has advised numerous doctoral students and formed generations of young architects; and he has consistently served on international juries both in schools of architecture and for awards and a wide variety of building commissions.

Abundant honors have been bestowed on Frampton, including the ACSA Topaz Medallion for lifetime contributions to architectural education; Fellow in the American Academy of Arts and Letters; the UIA Jean Tschumi Prize and the UIA Prize in Architectural Criticism; Medaille d'Or of the Académie d'Architecture, Paris; Fellow in the Society of Architectural Historians; Architecture League of New York's President's Medal; Columbia University's Presidential Teaching Award; Schelling Architecture Theory Prize; Lisbon Triennale Millennium BCP Lifetime Achievement Award; the Soane Medal; honorary doctorates from a half-dozen international universities; and the 2018 Golden Lion for Lifetime Achievement in Architecture at the 16th International Exhibition of Architecture, La Biennale, Venice.

Frampton lives in New York City with his partner, the artist and cultural critic Silvia Kolbowski.

Biographies of Contributors

Emilio Ambasz is an Argentinian architect and award-winning industrial designer. From 1969 to 1976 he was Curator of Design at the Museum of Modern Art in New York. He has taught at Princeton and the Hochschule für Gestaltung in Ulm, Germany.

Wiel Arets is a Dutch architect and architectural theorist, urbanist and industrial designer, and the former Dean of the Berlage Institute, Rotterdam, and the College of Architecture at the Illinois Institute of Technology in Chicago.

Barry Bergdoll is Meyer Schapiro Professor of Art History at Columbia University. From 2007 to 2014 he served as the Philip Johnson Chief Curator of Architecture and Design at the Museum of Modern Art, producing numerous exhibitions on historical and contemporary architectural topics.

Karla Cavarra Britton is an architectural historian whose work is shaped by the cultural specificities of place. She is Professor of Art at Diné College (Navajo Nation), directing a National Endowment for the Humanities grant documenting Navajo art. Receiving her PhD at Harvard's GSD, she co-directed Columbia's New York/Paris Program. She then taught at the Yale School of Architecture, focusing on modern sacred architecture, which led to *Constructing the Ineffable: Contemporary Sacred Architecture* (2011). In 2017 she was resident at the Center of Theological Inquiry, Princeton. She is author of *Auguste Perret* (2001), and edited (with Dean Sakamoto) *Hawaiian Modern: The Architecture of Vladimir Ossipoff* (2007).

Brad Cloepfil is an American architect and educator, and principal of Allied Works Architecture of Portland, Oregon, and New York City. Among his best-known works are the Contemporary Art Museum, St. Louis; the University of Michigan Museum of Art; the Clyfford Still Museum in Denver; and the National Music Centre of Canada in Calgary.

Jean-Louis Cohen is a French architect and architectural historian specializing in modern architecture and city planning. Since 1994 he has been the Sheldon H. Solow Professor in the History of Architecture at NYU's Institute of Fine Arts.

Yvonne Farrell and Shelley McNamara are the founding partners of Grafton Architects, Dublin, and Professors at the Accademia di Architettura in Mendrisio. They were the inaugural recipients of the RIBA International Prize, curators for the 16th International Exhibition of Architecture at the 2018 Venice Biennale, winners of the RIBA Gold Medal in 2020, and winners of the 2020 Pritzker Prize.

Kurt W. Forster is a Swiss and American art and architecture historian, author, educator, critic, and lecturer who has directed numerous research institutes. He is Visiting Professor Emeritus at the Yale School of Architecture, and has taught at Stanford University, MIT, ETH Zurich, and Bauhaus University in Weimar.

Steven Holl is a New York-based architect and watercolorist, and Professor of Architecture at Columbia University. Among his most recognized works are designs for the 1996 St. Ignatius Chapel in Seattle; the 2007 addition to the Nelson-Atkins Museum of Art in Kansas City; and the 2009 Linked Hybrid mixed-use complex in Beijing.

Harry Francis Mallgrave is Distinguished Professor Emeritus at the Illinois Institute of Technology, where he was also the Director of the International Center for Sustainable New Cities. He has worked as an architect, translator, editor, and award-winning scholar.

Michael A. Manfredi and Marion Weiss are co-founders of WEISS/MANFREDI. Weiss is the Graham Chair Professor of Architecture at the University of Pennsylvania's School of Design, and Manfredi is a Senior Design Critic at Harvard's GSD. They have received numerous awards for their design work, including the New York AIA Gold Medal.

Justin Fowler is Director of the Portland Architecture Program at the University of Oregon.

Robert M. Maxwell was an Anglo-Irish author, architect, and teacher. In London he taught at the Architectural Association and University College London. For eleven years he also taught at Princeton University, where he became Dean of Architecture in 1982. He died in January 2020.

Robert McCarter is a practicing architect, author, and Ruth and Norman Moore Professor of Architecture at Washington University in St. Louis. He taught at University of Florida, Columbia University, and four other schools. His architectural practice has constructed twenty-five works since 1982. He is the author of twenty-two books to date, including *Grafton Architects*; *Marcel Breuer*; *The Space Within*; *Steven Holl*; *Aldo van Eyck*; *Herman Hertzberger*; *Alvar Aalto*; *Carlo Scarpa*; *Understanding Architecture*; *Louis I. Kahn* and *Frank Lloyd Wright*. McCarter was an International Exhibitor in the 2018 Venice Biennale of Architecture, and he was named one of the "Ten Best Architecture Teachers in the US" in 2009.

Mary McLeod is Professor of Architecture at Columbia University, where she teaches architectural history and theory. Her research and publications have focused on the history of the Modern Movement and on contemporary architecture theory, examining issues concerning the connections between architecture and politics.

Rafael Moneo is a Spanish architect who has taught in the School of Architecture in both Barcelona and Madrid, and was Chair of the Architecture Department at Harvard's GSD in 1985. He received the 1996 Pritzker Prize and RIBA Royal Gold Medal in 2003.

Joan Ockman is an architectural educator, historian, writer, and editor. She is Senior Lecturer at the University of Pennsylvania's Stuart Weitzman School of Design, and previously taught at Columbia University where she was Director of the Buell Center for the Study of American Architecture.

Ken Tadashi Oshima is Professor in the Department of Architecture at the University of Washington, Seattle. He has taught at Harvard's GSD and Columbia University, and from 2003 to 2005 was a Fellow at the Sainsbury Institute for the Study of Japanese Arts and Cultures in London.

Juhani Pallasmaa is a Finnish architect, writer, and former professor of architecture and Dean of the School of Architecture at the Helsinki University of Technology. He was also Director of the Museum of Finnish Architecture (1978–83), and Rector of the Institute of Industrial Design Helsinki.

Alberto Pérez-Gómez is an eminent architectural historian, and the Saidye Rosner Bronfman Professor of the History of Architecture at McGill University. He is the author of numerous books, and is well known as a theorist with an orientation rooted in a phenomenological approach to architecture.

Richard Plunz is a Professor of Architecture at Columbia University, and is the founding Director of the Urban Design Lab, a research unit of the Earth Institute. He received the Andrew J. Thomas award from the AIA for his pioneering work in housing design and research.

Brigitte Shim and Howard Sutcliffe are Canadian architects and founding partners of Shim-Sutcliffe Architects, a Toronto-based practice established in 1994. Shim currently serves on the Aga Khan Architecture Award steering committee, and teaches at the University of Toronto and Yale School of Architecture. They have won many Canadian architecture awards, including 14 Governor General's Awards.

Ashley Simone is a designer, writer, photographer, and educator. She was editor of Kenneth Frampton's *A Genealogy of Modern Architecture*, and teaches at the School of Architecture at Pratt Institute, and for the College of Architecture, Planning, and Landscape Architecture at the University of Arizona.

Robert A.M. Stern is a New York-based architect, professor, and author. He is the founding partner of Robert A.M. Stern Architects. From 1998 to 2016 he was Dean of the Yale School of Architecture.

Anthony Vidler is an architectural critic and historian. He has taught at Brown University, The Cooper Union, UCLA, Cornell, Princeton, and Yale, and he is Dean Emeritus of The Cooper Union.

Leopoldo Villardi is Architectural Research Specialist at Robert A.M. Stern Architects.

Wang Shu is a Chinese architect based in Hangzhou, Zheijang Province. He is the Dean of the School of Architecture of the China Academy of Art. Wang Shu and his wife, Lu Wenyu, founded Amateur Architecture Studio in 1997. He won the Pritzker Prize in 2012.

Wilfried Wang is the O'Neil Ford Centennial Professor in Architecture at the University of Texas, Austin. He is a recognized author, editor, and competition juror, and is a registered architect in Berlin and, with Barbara Hoidn, founder of Hoidn Wang Partner, Berlin.

Index

Note: page numbers in italics refer to information contained in captions.

Aalto, Alvar 22, 66, 76, 150, 172, 181, 194, 220–21, 329–32
National Pensioners Institute 330–31, *330–31*
Säynätsalo Town Hall *36*, 285
Villa Mairea 330
Academy of Music, Vienna 178, 180
Acropolis, Athens *310*, 311–12
Adorno, Theodor 27, 31–32, 36, 154, 156
advocacy planning 165–66
aesthesis 100
aesthetics 86–88, 99–100, 258
affordance 75
afterlife 67, 71, 195–96
Aga Khan Architecture Award 335–36, *337*
Agamben, Giorgio 100–1
air flow 44–46, *45*
Akbar the Great 70–71
Alabama Polytechnic Institute 228, 230, *231*
Albers, Josef 124, 127, 128, 129–30
Alberti, Leon Battista 176, 179, 218
alchemy 172, 176
Alexander the Great 70
Alexander, Christopher 76, 164
Algiers 291, 292, 299
Allen, Stan 109, 111
"Alternative Suburbia" 162
Altona 128–29
Amateur Architecture Studio 18, 43, 48
New Village Houses *51*
Tiles Mountain *49*
Xiang Shan Campus 44, *45*, *49*
Ambasz, Emilio
ACROS building *302–3*, 304
Casa de Retiro Espiritual 304–6, *305*
Center for Applied Computer Research 306, *307*
ambiguity 187, 195, 215–17
ancient Egypt 173, *174*, 196
ancient Greeks 70, 171, 179, 181–83, 266
Andō, Tadao 15, 103, 138, 140, 148, *149*, 150, 268
1991 exhibition 103
Azuma House 268
Anthropocene 81, 83, 86–88
architectonic consciousness 252–53
Architect's Year Book 106, 153
Architectural Association (AA) 21, 24, 138, 140, 196, 250, 262, 279, 311
Architectural Association Journal 109, 139
architectural autonomy 266
Architectural Design (journal) 11, 12, 18, 22, 24–25, *24*, *28*, *31*, 32–34, 113, 138–39, 146, 150, 153, 158, 308, 314, 315, 317–19, *319*, 321, *322*, 323
architectural osmosis 278–86
Architectural Review (magazine) 109, 158, 311, 317
Architecture and Urbanism (A+U) (magazine) 140, 150
Arendt, Hannah 18, 24, 25, 29, 30–31, 34, 279, 296, 328–29
The Human Condition 9–10, 16, 24, 158–59, 329
The Recovery of the Public World *328*
Aristotle 70, 192
Arkitektur N (periodical) 332
Arnim, Achim von 200–1
Arnim, Bettine 200–1
arrière-garde 34–35, 52, 165
art
architecture as 38, 150, 171, 175, 177, 184–85, 192, 194
and mannerism 187
structure as domain for 272–74
works of 213
Art Nouveau 300
Art and Revolution (exhibition, 1971) 112–13
Ashurbanipal, Garden of, Nineveh *67*
Assyrian culture *67*, 68
Athens 310–12, *310–11*, 314–15, 324
atmosphere 99–101
Augustine 71, 72, 179
Aulenti, Gae 18, 22
Austria 125, 126
automobiles 163–65, 167, 260–61, 292
autonomization 19, 53–56, 62
avant-garde 11, 47–48, 103, 106–19, 120, 142, 207, 260, 266

Baburov, Andrey 116, *116*
Babylonians 68
Bacon, Francis 66, 194–95
Baird, George 328–29
Banham, Reyner 20–21, 24, 103, 108, 115, 138, 154, 155, 288–89
Baroque era 300, 309, 312
Barr, Alfred H., Jr. 120–24, 127, 128, 132, 134
Barragán, Luis 15, 17, 143
Barrata, Paulo 278, *278*
Bauhaus 11, 103, 107, 120–36, 208, 228, 242
Bauhaus 1919–1928 (exhibition) 124, *125*, 126, 130–34, *130–31*, *133*
Bauhaus: How it Worked, The (exhibition) 134
Bauhaus Staircase, The (1932) 124
Bauhaus Weimar Dessau (exhibition, 1930) 122
Bawa, Geoffrey 335, 336
Ena de Silva House *336*
Bayer, Herbert 122–23, 126–27, 129–311
Becherucci, Luisa 187
Beck, Ulrich 86
Beeby, Thomas 236, 243
Benjamin, Walter 18, 27–29, *30*, 31, 34, 35, 87, 91
Berger, John 309–10, 324
Berger, Otti 127
Berlin 121, 124, 126, 199, 204, 260
Berlin Wall 260
Bernard of Clairvaux 72
Beuth, Christian Peter Wilhelm Friedrich 88–89, 203
Bill, Max 126–27, 316
Binet, Hélène 249, 310–12, *311*, *336*
Black Mountain College 127–28, 130
Blackwood, Michael 148, *149*
Blomstedt, Aulis 173–74, *174*, 176, 180–83
Canon 60 *182*, 183
dimensional and proportional study of the great pyramids of Giza (1965) 173, *174*
Hans Kayser's Pythagorean harmonics applied to the human figure *178*
multiplication table of numbers ... *177*
special scale stick ... *182*
studies for the exhibition of Finnish architecture ... *184*
study of Pythagorean intervals applied to the human scale *181*
body 174, *178*, 179, 185, 261–62
Böhme, Gernot 175
Bond, Max 252
Boston–Washington corridor 15
Botta, Mario 16, 268–69
secondary school, Morbio Inferiore 268, *268*
Bötticher, Karl 270
Boulding, Kenneth 163–64, 167
Boullée, Étienne-Louis 109, 157
Bourdelle, Antoine, "La meditation d'Apollon et les Muses" *15*
Brandt, Marianne 127
Brasini, Armando, Orfanotrofio 218, 221
Brentano, Clemens 199–200
Breuer, Marcel 122, 125, 128, 133
Hagerty House 130, *130–31*
Whitney Museum of American Art 243–44
Brewer, Charles 232, 233–34
Brewster, Kingman 244, 245
"British Invasion" 239
Brooks, Cleanth 218

Brown, Capability 73
Buchanan, Colin 165
Buchanan, George 235
building 16, 76, 266–67, 276–77, 333–35
building regulations 56, 57, 62
Bunshaft, Gordon, Beinecke Rare Book and Manuscript Library 241–42
Buontalenti, Bernardo 300
Burns, Howard 188
Burtynsky, Edward 88

Cambridge University 72–75, *74*, 157
Can Lis, Majorca 281, *282*
Canada 20, 339–41, *340*
Canadian Centre for Architecture (CCA), Frampton archives 12, 249, 327–41, *327*
Candela, Félix 172
capitalism 32–34, 36, 58, 83–86, 90, 175, 196
Carapetian, Michael 321–23
Caravaggio 312
Casabella continuità (journal) 22
Cava, John 271
Chafee, Judith Bloom 238, *239*
Chamberlin, Powell and Bon 21
Chance Brothers Glassworks *89*, 91
Chang'an 69
Chareau, Pierre, Maison de Verre 29
Charlottenhof 205
Chermayeff, Serge 164, 241, 243
Chicago 127, 128, 129, 261, 263
China 11, 18, 20, 43–52, 69, 85–86, *90*, 91–92
Christopher Columbus 68, 79
Cité Radieuse 32
cities 85–86, 162–70
climate change 19, 53–64
Cloepfil, Brad
  Clyfford Still Museum 272–73, *275*
  Contemporary Art Museum, St. Louis 272, *273*
  National Veterans Memorial Museum 274, *275*
  "Sitings: Five Reflections on Architectural Domain" 271, 276
  The Maryhill Overlook 271–72, *272*
  Widen+Kennedy World Headquarters 272, *273*
Club of Rome 58, 163
cognitive science, enactive 19, 97, 98
Colombetti, Giovanna 77
Colquhoun, Alan 31, *31*
Columbia University, New York 12, 16, 22, 25–27, 31, 120, 162–63, 167, 228, 250, 252–55, 257, 264–65, 269–70, 311, 317, 319
  Graduate School of Architecture, Planning and Preservation (GSAPP) 11, 12, *22*, 104, 317, 321
commodification 32–33, 37
communication 19, 97, 99
comparative critical analysis of built form 25–27, 103, 163, 333–35
comparative method 315–19
complex architecture 220, 222–24, 226
composition 253–54
concrete 274
concrete-and-steel architecture 47, 49
Considerant, Victor 156
Constructivism 22, 24, 106–19
consumerism 163, 175, 258, 260, 264, 276
Cooke, Catherine 112
Cornford, John 158
Corringham housing complex 21–22, *23*
courtyard architecture 45–46, *46*, 72–73
"critical, the" 18, 20–42, 27
critical practice 43–52
Critical Regionalism 12–14, 22, *24*, 35, 59–60, 94, 138, 147–8, 265–77, 312, 314, 335
Critical Theory 27, 31, 154
Crosby, Theo 315, 316
Crutzen, Paul 83
Crystal Palace *89*, 90–91
culture 15, 19, 27, 34, 53, 59, 62–63, 66, 76, 95, 99–101, 104, 160, 258, 265–67, 276
Cummings, Glen 320
  Annual Kenneth Frampton Endowed Lecture posters 320, *321*
Cyrus the Great 68

Dadu 70
Darmstadt 125
De Carlo, Giancarlo 116
  Matteotti complex 104, 163–67
De Feo, Vittorio 107, 109
de Honnecourt, Villard, Villard's Diagram 176
De Masi, Domenico 165, 166
de-skilling 19, 56–59
Dearstyne, Howard 123, 126, 128
Deconstructivism 301
"Degenerate Art" 121, 125, 127
Demos, T.J. 87–88
Dessau 120–24, 126–28
Diderot, Denis 187, 188–89
digital technology 25, 56–57, 59, 185
Dorner, Alexander 127–28
Douglas Stephen & Partners 18, 21–22, 315, 321–23
  Corringham Housing complex *23*
Dudley, England 90, 91
Durand, Jean-Nicolas-Louis 101, 175
Düsseldorf 191, 194
"dwelling perspective" 76–77

Eckermann, Johann Peter 202
ecological architecture 47
ecology 91–92, 289
Eden, Garden of 68, 70, 71, 72, 82
Einstein, Albert 180
Einzig, Richard 321–23
Eisenman, Peter 140, 142, 145, 155, 250, 327
Eliot, T.S. 209–11, 212, 214, 216, 220, 226
embodied simulation 77
Empson, William 215–17, 219
energy-saving designs 44–45, *45*, 47, 302, 304–6
England 12, 18, 21–22, 89, 137–38, 188–91
Enlightenment 14, 28, 43, 52, 55, 57, 59, 157–58, 175
environmental issues 18–19, 82–84, 97–99
  degradation 15, 33, 35, 57, 104, 160
Erickson, Arthur, Robson Square 339, *339*
Eridu 67
ethics of architecture 324–25
Europe 21, 81, 230–32
Existenzminimum 33

factory tourism 90–91
Farrell, Yvonne 13, 20
  Ardscoil Mhuire, Secondary School 280, *281*
Fawcett, Chris 140–42, 142
Festschrift 8
Fibonacci series 180
Finland *36*, 137, 285, *330–31*
Finnish Association of Architects 180
First World War 228
Fletcher, Banister 138
Florida 230, 232
Focillon, Henri 155–56
folk architecture 324
form 290–94
Foster, Hal 33, 109, 111
Foster, Norman 236, 239–40
  Fred Olsen Amenity Building 313–14
Fourier, Charles 30, 155, 156
Frampton, Kenneth *10*, *20*, *38*, *211*, *216*, *221*, *226*, *259*, *260*, *263*, *278*
  archives 12, 249, 327–41, *327*
  awards 257, 278
  courses/lectures/seminars 25–27, 103, 106, 163, 270, 316–17, 331, 333–35, 339, *339*
  Craven Hill Gardens 321, *322*
  critical observer 262–64
  editorial role at *Architectural Design see Architectural Design* (journal)
  historian 106, 112
  the IAUS 24–25, 106, 113, 139, 140
  Japan: Three Generations of Avant-garde Japanese Architects (film 1989) 148, *149*
  Maison de Verre 332–33, *332–33*
  phenomenology in the "visual schemes" 308–26
sketches
  Alvar Aalto's National Pensioners Institute 330–31, *330–31*
  Point William landscape and rocks 339–41, *340*
teaching roles
  Harvard University 148, 339
    see also Columbia University; Princeton University

The Unfinished Modern Project in Homage to it and Habermas (Christmas card collage) *315*
training 21, 24, 138, 250, 279
work for *Oppositions* 25, 29, 32, 106, 113–14, 139, 145, 147, 150, 153, 228, 250, 316
written works
A Genealogy of Modern Architecture: ... (2015) 27, 29, 35, 103, 248, 279, 308, 315–19, *334–35*
"Apropos Ulm: Curriculum and Critical Theory" (1974) 32
"Architecture and Industrialization" 328
British Buildings 1955–65 22
"Constructivism: The Pursuit of an Elusive Sensibility" 109, 111
editor for *Modern Architecture and the Critical Present ...* (1982) *28*, 313–14
"Industrialization and the Crises in Architecture" 28–29
"Labour, Work and Architecture" 140, 150
Labour, Work and Architecture (2002) 38, 138, 279
L'altro Movimento Moderno 14
Megaform as Urban Landscape (1999) 288–94, 298–99
Modern Architecture: A Critical History 20, *21*, 27–28, 32–35, 106, 115, 137–38, 142, 148, 150, 153, 167, 279, 309, 313–14, 319, 324
Modern Architecture Vol.1 1851–1919 (GA Documents) 142, 148
Modern Architecture Vol.2 1919–1945 (GA Documents) 148
"Modernism's Diffusion, Japan Diary: Summer '81" 142–44, *143*, 147–48, 150
"Modernization and Local Culture ..." *337*
"Notes on a Lost Avant-Garde" 106, 109, 112
"Notes of Soviet Urbanism 1917–1932" 106, 109
"Rappel al'Oder: ..." 14
"Seven Points for the Millennium: An Untimely Manifesto" 150
Studies in Tectonic Culture: ... (1995) 14, 16–17, 148, 150, 271, 279
"Ten Points of an Architecture of Regionalism: ..." 59–60
"The City of Dialectic" (1969) *31*, 153, 155
The Evolution of 20th Century Architecture: ... 150
"The Evolution of Housing Concepts 1870–1970" 140
"The Humanist versus the Utilitarian Ideal" 22, 111
"The Status of Man and the Status of His Objects" 30–31
"The Volvo Case" (1976) 30
"The Work and Influence of El Lissitzky" 106, 109, 111
"Theses on the Philosophy of History" 28
"Towards a Critical Regionalism: ..." (1983) 12–14, 20, *20*, 25, 33–35, 43–45, 52, 94, 248, 265, 271, 274–76, 278–80, 283–86, 314
Francastel, Pierre 157
France 88, 110, 198
Frankfurt School 18, 27–28, 29–31, 33–34
Freespace 281
Friedrich Wilhelm III of Prussia 203
Fujii, Hiromi 140
Pharmacy House 145, *147*
Fuller Company 242
Functionalism 101, 192
Fuseli, Henry 187, 189
Futagawa, Yoshio 148
Futurism 111

Gadamer, Hans-Georg 78, 94
Galfetti, Aurelio, Bagno Pubblico 269, *269*
Gelassenheit (letting be) 16
Generalife Gardens 71, *71*
geometry 171, 172, 177, 183–85
German Democratic Republic 127, 260–61
Germany 121–22, 124–27, 132, 198
Gesamtwerk 87
Gibson, James 75
Giedion, Sigfried 18, 20, 24, 36, 108, 115, 212, 220
Gilgamesh 67–68
Gilly, Friedrich 199
Ginzburg, Moisei 107, 115
global warming 84, 196
globalization 35, 44, 53–56, 59
Gluck, Peter 243
Godard, Jean-Luc 260
Goethe, Johann Wolfgang von 176, 178, 200, 202
Goldberg, Bertrand 126, 129
Goldberger, Paul 9
Golden Lion Award 257, 278
Golden Section/Rule 178–80
Google headquarters, New York 298
Grafton Architects 20
Brick Wall *283*
Medical School, University of Limerick *284*, 285
Université Toulouse 1 Capitole *284*, 285
University Luigi Bocconi 285, *286*
UTEC University 285, *287*
Gramsci, Antonio 32, 36
graphic design 321–24
Gray, Camilla 24, 108, 109, 111, 112
Great Experiment (1962) 108
"Grays" 21
great pyramids of Giza 173–74, *174*
Green Movement 81, 85, 301, 306
Greenberg, Allan 234, 236
Griswold, A. Whitney 241, 242
Gropius, Walter 109, 120–22, 124–28, 130–34, 142, 144, 153, 228, 230, 233, 245
Chicago Tribune Tower (1922) *133*
Hagerty House 130, *130*, *131*
Gutnov, Aleksey 116, *116*

Habermas, Jürgen 8–9, 18, 31, 33–34, 36
Hanghzhou, China 18, 47, *51*
Hanging Gardens 68
Hara, Hiroshi 145–46, 148
Hardy, Thomas 279
harmonic systems 172, 175, 179–83, *182*, 185
Harrison, Wallace K. 126
Empire State Plaza 295, *296*
Hartoonian, Gevork 37
Harvard apostles 124
Harvard University 121–23, 130, 132, 235, 245
Busch-Reisinger Museum 125
Graduate School of Design (GSD) 230, *231*, 233, 268, 288, 339, *339*
Society for Contemporary Art 122
Hawksmoor, Nicholas 75, 187–89, 220
St. George-in-the-East 189, *189*
St. Mary Woolnoth 189, *189*
Hebei Province 19, *90*, 91
Heidegger, Martin 16, 34, 76, 280–81
Hejduk, John 308, 319–20, 323, 327
Hellenistic period 181–82, 220
Helsinki *330–31*, 331
hermeneutics 18, 34, 94–102
Herzog & De Meuron 263, 270
Hesse, Hermann 19
"The City" 80–81, 91
high-rise buildings 47, 297
Hill, Melvyn 328, *328*
historiography 103, 212–13
history 154, 158, 209, 210–11
Hitchcock, Henry-Russell 121, 123
Hitler, Adolf 121, 157
Hochschule für Gestaltung, Ulm 32
Hodgetts, Craig *26*, 268
Holl, Steven 180, 270, 294
Kennedy Center *251–57*
Horkheimer, Max 27, 31–32
Hübner, Johann 198
Humboldt, Wilhelm von 201–2
Husserl, Edmund 9
Huxley, Aldous 156
Huxtable, Ada Louise 142

Illinois Institute of Technology (IIT) 232
Illustrated London News *89*, 91
industrialization 88–92
infrastructure 47, 291–92, 298
evolutionary 288–89, 294
Ingold, Tim 76–77
Inner Mongolia 19, *90*, 91
Institute for Architecture and Urban Studies (IAUS) 24–25, *26*, 35, 106, 113–15, 139, 140, 250
Institute for Social Research 27
Institute without Boundaries, *Massive Change* (2004) 86–88, *86*
International Style 55–56, 137–38, 230, 242, 324

Ise Shrine, Japan 144
Isozaki, Arata 138–40, 142–44, 146–48
Tsukuba Centre Building 146
Israel 21, 138
Italy 11, 12, 107, 132
Itō, Toyo 138, 140, 142
Iyer, Pico 274

Jain, Bijoy 320
Jameson, Fredric 33, 84
Japan 11, 12, 70, 103, 137–52, 241, 258, *302–3*, 304
Japanese Metabolists 138, 139, 140, 142
Jarmusch, Jim 258
Jencks, Charles 21, 250, 266
Johnson, Ben, *Dock Reflections* (1974) 313–14, *313*
Johnson, Philip 122–24, 129, 217, 228, 230, *239*, 241–42
Jun, Tong 50–52

Kahn, Louis 14, 21, 145–46, 220–21, 243, 267–68, 274
National Assembly Building of Bangladesh *267*
Kandinsky, Wassily 122, 126
Kant, Immanuel 27
Katsura Imperial Villa 144–45
Kaufman, Emil 157
Kawamukai, Masato 150
Kayser, Hans 176, 178, *178*, 180, 181, 183
"Kenneth Frampton Architectural Book Collection," University of Hong Kong 12
Kepler, Johannes 175
Khan-Magomedov, Selim 106–9, 114–15
Khrushchev, Nikita 106, 115–16
Klee, Paul 122, 123
Angelus Novus (1920) 27–28, 29, *30*, *90*
Klein, Naomi 196
Kolbowski, Silvia 339
Koolhaas, Rem 87, 113, 114, 250, 262
Kopp, Anatole 109, 116, 117
Town and Revolution (1967) 107–8, *107*
Krier, Léon 167, 250
Kublai Khan 70
Kuma, Kengo 150
Kyoto 70, 258

La Tour, Georges de, *Saint Joseph in the Carpenter Shop* (*c.* 1642) 309–10, *309*, 312, 324
Lambert, Phyllis 234, 238
Seagram Building 238
Lambert, Sam 321–23
landforms 248–49
landmarks 290, 294, 296
landscape 336–41
language 19, 99, 100–1, 111, 115, 144
le Carré, John 194–95
Le Corbusier 14–16, 22–24, 103–4, 110–11, 114–15, 138–39, 144, 150, 153, 156, 172, 180, 220, 228, 243, 291–92, 299, 301
La Rochelle-Pallice 299
La Ville Radieuse 104, 153, 154–60
the Maison Cook house 334–35, *334*
the "Modulator" *15*, 180
the Paris Exposition (1937) 295
Ronchamp chapel 228
Unité d'Habitation 156, 299
Vers une Architecture (1923) 208
Villa Schwob 187, 188
Ville Contemporaine 156, 295
Ledoux, Claude-Nicolas 110, 146, 157, 220
Lefaivre, Diane 12, 314, 324
Lefebvre, Henri 35, 107–8
Leonardo da Vinci 176, 179
Leonidov, Ivan 109, 110, 112–15
project for a Lenin Institute *110*, 112
Lerner, Jaime 292
Lévi-Strauss, Claude 50
Lezhava, Ilya 116, *116*
Lissitzky, El 103, 106–7, 110–12, 114–15, 122
Russland: Die Rekonstruktion der Architektur in der Sowjetunion 108–9, *108*
Wolkenbügel 112, *113*
local, the 13, 44–50, 53, 59, 104, 160, 276
London 66, 75–76, 138, 157, 158, 250, 279, 308, 313, 321
Long, M.J. 238
Loos, Adolf 99, 261
Los Angeles 265, 267–68
low-rise, high-density housing 162, 164, 167
Lu, Guang 19, *84*, 91–92, *91*
Lu, Wenyu 18, 48–49
Lubetkin, Berthold 109, 112
Lutyens, Edwin 187, 190–91, 220
Homewood 190, *190*
Viceroy's Palace 190, *191*, 193

Mack, Ludwig Hirschfeld 127
Maekawa, Kunio 139, 148
Magaceen *211*, *216*, *221*
Maki, Fumihiko 140, 142
Maldonado, Tomás 32, 33, 159
Malm, Andreas 83
Malpas, Jeff 96–97
Mangiarotti, Angelo 22, *24*, 281
mannerism 187–96, 220, 300–1
Mannhein, Karl 157, 158
manufacturing 85–86, 88–92, *88*, *89–90*
Marcuse, Herbert 27, 34, 35, 154, 158, 159
Eros and Civilization 29–31, *31*, 33
Marx, Karl 27, 156, 157
Marxism 25, 27–28, 32–35, 37, 157
mass housing 56, 63, 299
masses 27, 56, 63, 258–61, 264, 276, 299
mathematical arts 176–78
mathematics 171–86
Mau, Bruce, *Massive Change* (2004) 86–88, *86*, *88*
McAndrew, John 123, 125–26, 128
McLeod, Mary 18, 155
McNamara, Shelley 13, 20
Ardscoil Mhuire, Secondary School 280, *281*
measures 173–75, 176, 180
MEDIKIT 154
megaforms 288–94, 296, 298–99, 336–39, *339*
megalopolis 288, 290, 293
megastructures 288–90, 299
Melnikov, Jonstantin, Makhorka pavilion (1923) 112
Merleau-Ponty, Maurice 25, 35, 99
Mesopotamia 68
metric system 173, 174, 180
Mexico City 306, *307*
Meyer, Hannes 22, 32, 103, 120, 122, 123, 128
Michelangelo 146, 188, 190, 220
Middleton, Robin 24, 138, 153, 319–20
Mies van der Rohe, Ludwig 14, 121, 123–24, 128–29, 139, 150, 153, 217, 228, 232, 234
Modern Architecture: International Exhibition (1930) 123–24
Modern Movement 9, 14, 33, 63, 103, 105, 153, 155–56, 208, 209, 226, 316, 329–32
modernism 11, 14, 114, 117, 191, 265, 300–1, 304
modernity 34, 46–47, 100, 185
Moffett, Noel 139, 142
Moholy-Nagy, László 121–22, 125, 127, 129, 132–33
Moholy-Nagy, Sibyl 228, 233, 244–45
Molnár, Farkas 126
Red Cube House (1923) *133*
Moneo, Rafael 11, *211*, *216*, *221*, *226*, 294
L'Illa Diagonal 292, 294, *295*
Monk, Tony 233
Morassutti, Bruno 22, *24*, 281
Morris, William 32, 157, 158
Moscow 107, 111, *113*
Moss, Eric Owen 267–68
Moura, Eduardo Souto de 320–21
Mozuna 140, 142
MTWTF *321*
Mughals 70–71
Mumford, Lewis 132, 133
Murano, Tōgo 146–47
Chapel for World Peace 147
Shima Kanko Hotel 147
Murcutt, Glenn 95
Melbourne mosque 95, *96–98*, *101*
Museum of Modern Art (MoMA), New York 103, 222, 256
Bauhaus 1938 120–36
Department of Architecture 123
Department of Industrial Design 124
Japanese Exhibition House 139
music 171, 176–83, *178*, *182*, 185
"Music of the Spheres" 172, 175, 179

musical harmony, Pythagorean 176–77, *178*

Narkomtyazhprom project 113–15
National Socialism (Nazism) 121, 123–24, 126, 132
nature 76, 82, 258, 259, 300–6
Navajo people 195–96
Nebuchadnezzar II 68
Nervi, Pier Luigi 288, 289
New Canaan Five 230
New Haven 239, *240*, 244
New Jerusalem 68–69, 71
New Towns 165
New Wave, Japanese 140–42, *141*, 145, 147, 148
New Wave of Japanese Architecture, (exhibition, catalogue and lecture tour, 1978) 140–42, *141*
New York 16, 82, 113, 120–26, 130–31, 138, 140, 142, 162, 165, 223, 243, 250, 258, 265, 298, 336
Newman, Winifred 325
Newton, Isaac 174–75, 188, 201
Nietzsche, Friedrich 80
Nimrud 68
Nineveh *67*, 68
Novy Element Rasselenia (NER) 116–17, *116*
number ratios *173*

Oberlander, Cornelia 336–39, *338*
Omnibus Housing Act 1960 165–66
Oorthuys, Gerrit 113, 114
operational criticism 248–49
Oppositions (IAUS journal) 25, 29, 32, 106, 113–14, 115, 139, 145, 147, *147*, 150, 153, 228, 250, 316
Orwell, George 156, 157
Otero-Pailos, Jorge 323
Other 14, 95, 264, 276
Oxford University 72–75
Oyama, Susan 76

Paccioli, Luca 179
Pakistan 70, 241
Palladio, Andrea 172, 176, 187–88, 220
Papageorgíu, Aleksandros *310*, 311–12, 313
paradise 19, 66–72, 76–79, 82
parallelism 301
Paris 123, 128, 131, 132
Parthenon 312
Pasargadae 68
Pataliputra 69
Paxton, Joseph 91
Perret, Auguste 14, *15*, 153
Persian empire 68, 69, 70
Perspecta (journal) 29, 230, 235, 332
perspective 183–84
Peru 11, 285, *287*
Peterhans, Walter 129
Pevsner, Nikolaus 242–43
Pfisterer, Henry 235, *239*
phenomenology 34–35, 66, 94–102, 167, 308–26
photography 91–92, 248–49, 310–14, *310–11*, *313*
Piano, Renzo 137, 166
Pidgeon, Monica 153, 315
Pikionis, Dimitris
Park Paving on the Philopappus Hill *55*, 310–12, *310–11*, 314, 324
St. Dimitris Loumbardiaris Church *55*
The Paved Path to the Acropolis (*c.* 1954–58) *54*
Pimlott, Mark 311
Pittsburgh 85–6
place 96–7, 99
planning regulations 56, 61
Plato 66, 70, 156–57, 179
Point William 339–41, *340*
Polanyi, Michael 25
pollution 82–83, 91–92, 160
Popper, Karl 156–57, 158
Port Authority of New York 289, 298
Portoghesi, Paolo 21, 33
positivism 27, 34, 83
postmodernism 14, 21, 33, 47–48, 77, 137, 226, 270, 301, 316, 323
poststructuralism 25, 77
Poteat, William 25
praxis 27, 32
pre-fabrication 57, 165
Price, Cedric 154–55, 158, 327
Princeton University 15, *20*, 22, 25, 32, 153, 180
School of Architecture 29, 159, 302
Pritzker Prize Laureates 11, 18, 43, 166–67, 240
privatization 290, 297
progress 80–93, 212
proportionality 173–76, *174*, 180, 253–54
public space 16, 261, 297, 336
Pyramids 173–74, *174*, 196
Pythagoras 171, *173*, 175–76, 179
Pythagoreans 175–76, *178*, 179–80, *181*, 185

Qian Xuan 70
Wang Xizhi (13th century) *69*
quadrangles 72–73
Quilici, Vieri 108, 115

rammed-earth buildings *49*
Ravenna *65*, 71
Ravnikar, Edvard 53, 61
Raymond, Antonin 138, 139
regionalism 19, 21, 34, 43, 60, 269, 285, 335–36
"Regionalism in Architecture" conference 1985 335–36, *337*
Reidy, Affonso Eduardo, Pedregulho Housing 291, *291*
Renaissance 176–77, 179, 300
répétition différente 150
representation 308, 310–13, 316–20, 323
resistance 33, 43–44, 105, 296
Rhode Island School of Design 127–28
Rice University 14, 270
Ricœur, Paul 13, 18, 34, 94
Rilke, Rainer Maria 265
Risselada, Max 113, *114*
Rockefeller Center 124, *125*, 126, 130–32
Rogers, Richard 239, 290
Romano, Giulio, Palazzo Te 300
Romans 68–69, 70
"romanticism" 265
Rome 70, 104
Rose, Hajo 126, 127
Rosenau, Helen 157
Rossi, Aldo 222
Rowe, Colin 157–58, 172, 187–88
royal cubits 173, *174*
Rudolph, Paul 105, 217, 228–47, *229*, *239*, *240*, 299
Art & Architecture (A&A) Building 148–50
Greek Temple (student project) *231*
Tastee-Freez Ice Cream Stand, Florida *233*
Weekend House for an Architect *231*
Russia 11, 106, 109–11, 114–15, 132
Russian avant-garde 11, 103, 106–19
Russian Constructivism 106
Russiesche Architectuur en Stedebouw 1917–1933 (exhibition) 113
Ruyer, Raymond 153

Saarinen, Eero 228, 242
Said, Edward 16
St. John's College 73, *74*
Saint-Simonian Architects 155–56
Sakakura, Junzō 148, 153
San Francisco 166, 250
Sartre, Jean-Paul 35
scenography 13, 14, 33, 84, 96, 266
Schawinsky, Xanti 125, 128, 132
Schelling, Friedrich von 178
Schindler, Rudolf M. 14, 183
Schinkel, Karl Friedrich 88–90, *89*, 91, 197, 199–205
Panorama of Palermo 200
Schleifer, Fritz 128–29
Schlemmer, Oskar 124, 127, 129, 132
Schnaidt, Claude 32–33
Schwartz Center for the Performing Arts, Cornell University 193
SCI-Arc 12
Scully, Vincent 21, 208–9, 226, 234–35, 241, 243
Second World War 137, 138, 180, 230, 238, 279
Semper, Gottfried 203, 253, 270–71
Sennacherib 68
sense experience 25, 184, 285–86
Seville, Spain 304, *305*
Shexian Tianjin Iron and Steel Plant *90*
Shikibu, Murasaki, *Tale of Genji* 258
Shinohara, Kazuo 138, 142
site-specificity 59–60, 62
Siza, Álvaro 11, 12, 103, 256, 263, 327
Schlesisches Tor *56*, *57*, *58*
Skyline (magazine) 142, *143*
Smithson, Alison 21, 139, 291

Smithson, Peter 21, 139, 154–55, 158, 291
social housing 11, 104, 162–70
Société des Nations Competition (1927) 103
Solà-Morales, Manuel de, L'Illa Diagonal 292, 294, *295*
SOM 265, 268
Somol, Robert 25, 294
soul 261–62
sound frequencies *173*
Southgate Corporation 167
Soviet Union 22, *23*, 106, 115–17, 159
Spain 12, 137, 304, *305*
standard measures 174–75, 180–81
Starr, Frederick S. 114, 115
Sterne, Laurence 187, 188–89
Steven Holl Architects 255, 257
Stimmung 99, 101, 200
Stimmungsbild 204
Stirling, James 18, 22, 139, 187, 190, 191–94, 234–35, 239, 327
  Clore Gallery, Tate Britain *192*, *193*
  Leicester Engineering Building 22, 234
  Museum of Art, Düsseldorf 191
  Neue Staatsgalerie *191*, 193
  Southgate complex 104, 163–67
Stockbridge, Anthony *322*
Sudjic, Deyan 240
Suger, Abbot, Abbey of St. Denis 72
Sumerian culture 67–68
Summerson, John 154–55, 193
sustainability 19, 44–45, 53, 58–60, 62, 65, 301, 304–6
Suzhou gardens *50*
Sweeny, James Johnson 132–33
symbols 94, 310

Tabassum, Marina, Bait Ur Rouf Mosque *22*
Tafuri, Manfredo 18, 21, 35, 36–37, 139, 248
Taj Mahal 71
Tange, Kenzō 140, 144, 148–50
  Kurashiki City Hall 146
  National Gymnasia for the Tokyo Olympics 146
  Tokyo Bay project 299
  Tokyo City Hall 137
Tanizaki, Jun'ichirō 144–45, 258
  Naomi 258
Tatlin, Vladimir, Monument to the 3rd International (1919) *108*, 109, 111–12, 114–15
Team 10 166
technocracy 85–86
technology 19, 35, 52, 56–59, 61, 63, 86, 88–89, 154, 158, 259, 264
tectonic culture 9, 14, 22, 77, 96, 99, 104, 148, 150, 160, 248–49, 262, 265–77, 292
Ted'A arquitectes, Can Gabriel *60*, *61*
Tegel 201–2
Temple of Jerusalem 68
Temple of Solomon 68
Thatcher, Margaret 15
Theodora, Empress Theodora and her entourage, Basilica of San Vitale *65*, 71, *78*
Thompson, Evan 66
Tigerman, Stanley 234, 236–39, 241, 243
  University of Illinois Chicago 237
topos 336–41
Toronto Society for the Study of Social and Political Thought conference (1972) 328, *329*
tradition 34, 45–50, *46*, *50*, 211
Trans-Manhattan Expressway 288, 294–95, 299
Trinity College 73, *74*
Twitchell, Ralph 230
Tzonis, Alexander 12, 314, 324

Udine 22
underdeveloped countries 61–62
United States 21–22, 25, 29–30, 58, 85, 137, 139, 155, 329
universal civilization 34, 60, 94–95
University College Dublin, School of Architecture 286
University of Oregon 267, 271
University of Pennsylvania 288
University of Toronto, Daniels Faculty 331
urban crises 18, 19
Urban Development Corporation (UDC) *26*
  Marcus Garvey Park Village 25, *26*, 162
"urban renewal" 208
urban resilience 85–86
urbanism 15, 85, 290, 292
urbanization 110, 163, 261–62
Uruk 67–68
U.S. Naval Reserve 230, 232, 236
utilitarianism 22, 32, 103, 110, 111
utopia 19, 66–67, 79, 81, 108, 153–61, 157, 289
Utzon, Jørn 14, 236, 281
  Bagsværd Church *37*, *282*, 283, 285
  Can Lis 281, *282*

Valle, Gino 22, *24*
van Eyck, Aldo 76, 211–12
Varela, Francisco 66
Venice Biennale
  1980 12, 33, 105
  2018 257, 278, 281
Venice School 25
Venturi, Robert 21, 191, 194, 243
  Complexity and Contradiction in Architecture 104, 190, 208–27
Vesely, Dalibor 19, 34, 78
Vesnin brothers 107, 109
  Leningradskaia Pravda 110, 112
Villard's Diagram 176
vision-centredness 184
Vitra Design Museum 2015 330
"Vitruvian Man" 176, 179
Vitruvius 171, 177, 179
von Kleist, Heinrich 198

Wagenfeld, Wilhelm 129
Waits, Tom 258
Waldheim, Charles 292–93
Wang, Shu 11, 13, 18, 18–19
Wang, Wilfred 19
Wanzel, J.G. 154
Warburg, Eddie 124
Warburg Institute 157
Warhol, Andy 262
Webb, Michael, Sin Palace 318–19, *318*
Webster, John 189
Weimar 120, 121, 127, 202
Weisman, Alan 81–83
Weiss/Manfredi Architects, Olympic Sculpture Park 293, *293*, 298
Wellesley College 121–22
Wencun Village *51*
Williams, Raymond 157
Wingler, Hans Maria 120
Wittkower, Rudolf 176–77, 179
world architecture 43–52
World Design Conference 1960 139, 150
World Economic Forum 2018, Davos 65–66
Wren, Christopher 73, 75, 76
Wright, Frank Lloyd 14, 139, 150, 208, 228, 243, 290
  Florida Southern College *229*, 230
  Guggenheim Museum 228
  Rosenbaum House 228–30, *229*

Yale Corporation, Buildings Committee 241
Yale University 29, 148, *149*, 228–47, 288
  School of Architecture 105, 228, 238
Yatsuka, Hajime 147
Yim, Rocco 20, 297
Young, Michael 157

zaibatsu approach 137
zaum (language) 111, 115
zeilenbau strip housing 164
zeitgeist 212, 228
Zenghelis, Elia 250
Zevi, Bruno 36, 212
Zhejiang Province *46*, 47
Zodiac (journal) 107
Zumthor, Peter 270
Zurich 126